the **cricinfo** guide to

international cricket 2008

edited by
**steven
lynch**

THE CRICINFO GUIDE TO INTERNATIONAL CRICKET 2008
Edited by **Steven Lynch**

Published by John Wisden & Co Ltd
© John Wisden & Co Ltd, 2007

"Cricinfo" is the registered trademark of Cricinfo Ltd
www.cricinfo.com

John Wisden & Co Ltd
13 Old Aylesfield, Golden Pot, Alton, Hampshire GU34 4BY

ISBN: 978-1-905625-09-3

1 3 5 7 9 10 8 6 4 2

Typeset in Mendoza Roman and Frutiger by Typematter, Basingstoke
Printed and bound in Great Britain by Clays Ltd, St Ives plc

Distributed by Macmillan Distribution Ltd

CONTENTS

ABOUT CRICINFO

Cricinfo is, by a distance, the world's No. 1 cricket website. It is also a triumph of passion and entrepreneurship. It began as a lark in 1993, when a group of cricket-besotted expatriates working in the United States created a software application that allowed similarly obsessed fellow fans to submit cricket scores from remote locations. Soon, what started as a form of social networking had turned into a serious business.

Ten years, a few million users, and a dotcom rollercoaster ride later – during which the site sponsored a women's World Cup and the English County Championship – Cricinfo merged with its main rival, Wisden.com, to produce a site of unmatched depth and breadth. Cricinfo not only covers every ball bowled in international cricket, but does so with a distinct and independent voice.

It is a voice now heard by more people around the world than ever before. Cricinfo is accessed by over seven million users every month. The site's worldwide reach, authority and brand recognition are unrivalled in online cricket – thanks in part to its editorial motto, which is not merely to report on what matters to cricket, but to make sense of it by bringing to bear a unique global perspective that is not the preserve of the traditional media.

The site's database is fully searchable and incorporates the full Wisden archive, dating right back to the first Almanack in 1864. There's a comprehensive records section, profiles for every current first-class player, and also **Statsguru**, an interactive query tool which allows users to set their own parameters while searching for statistics relating to every one of the 3000 international and 45,000 first-class cricketers to have played the game (*more details on page 6*).

Live scores and informed ball-by-ball text commentary continue to be the heart of the site, but they are supplemented by in-depth match reports, analysis and comments from a dedicated and talented editorial team across the world, and some of the most credible voices in world cricket, among them Ian Chappell, Geoffrey Boycott, Tony Greig, Michael Holding, Ravi Shastri, Sanjay Manjrekar and Kumar Sangakkara. These experts are the backbone of Cricinfo's audio service, which was launched last year and offers match analysis, panel discussions and interviews. And Cricinfo's roster of bloggers includes some of the finest cricket writers in the world.

Cricinfo is not just about text and audio. It has a games section, with Slogout!, a simulated cricket game, being the most popular one, and the site recently launched its own Fantasy League, which was a huge hit.

During 2007, Cricinfo was taken over by ESPN. The acquisition is expected to give the site access to better technology and more sophisticated multimedia content. From here, the Cricinfo story can only get bigger and better.

INTRODUCTION

Welcome to the second edition of the **Cricinfo Guide to International Cricket**, which brings you details – in words and pictures, facts and figures – of 200 players, taken from the well-stacked database of Cricinfo, the world's largest single-sport website. Some kind readers made suggestions about last year's book, and we have made some improvements, notably to the photographs, most of which have been changed and updated. We have also introduced sections on the leading non-Test countries – a category which, sadly, now includes Zimbabwe – and short profiles on the international umpires and referees.

The main pages feature a photo of each player, with a concise summary of his career, then mix some unusual facts – mostly taken from Cricinfo's searchable database, Statsguru – with statistics for Tests, one-day internationals and first-class matches. There is also a selection of records, both country-by-country and overall, and a handy guide to the coming year's international fixtures.

We have tried to include every player likely to appear in international cricket in 2008 – but, like all selectors, we will undoubtedly have left out someone who should have been included. Details of anyone who managed to escape our selectorial net can be found on Cricinfo.

Many of the profiles are edited and updated versions from Cricinfo's player pages, for which I must thank the site's current editorial staff, especially Sambit Bal (my successor as the site's global editor), Martin Williamson and Andrew Miller, and several former colleagues and contributors to the Cricinfo and Wisden websites, notably Kamran Abbasi, Tanya Aldred, Lawrence Booth, Simon Briggs, Don Cameron, Tim de Lisle, Rabeed Imam, Lynn McConnell, Neil Manthorp, S. Rajesh, Christian Ryan, Rob Smyth, Telford Vice and John Ward. Thanks are also due to Christopher Lane, Matthew Engel, Hugh Chevallier and Harriet Monkhouse of Wisden, the designer Ray Rich, the *Wisden Cricketer*'s art director Nigel Davies (who designed the cover), and Travis Basevi, the man who built Statsguru. The majority of the photographs are from Getty Images, apart from a few reproduced by kind permission of the Pakistan Cricket Board and the International Cricket Council, and some specially shot for Cricinfo.

The statistics have been updated to **September 10, 2007**, the end of the international season in England. The figures have been taken from Cricinfo and include the number of boundaries hit by each batsman in international cricket. The abbreviation "S/R" in the batting tables denotes runs per 100 balls; in the bowling it shows the balls required to take each wicket. A dash (–) in the records usually indicates that full statistics are not available (such as details of fours and sixes in all domestic matches). Individual figures for players who have appeared for more than one side in official internationals include the additional games, details of which are given in the player's "Facts" box. These matches are excluded in the national records sections, which explains any differences in the figures for the players concerned.

And finally, I couldn't have managed without the support of my wife Karina, who gave birth to our first baby, Daniel, just as this book was being finished off. Perhaps one day he'll claim a page of his own in here.

Steven Lynch
September 2007

ANY QUESTIONS? SEND FOR STATSGURU

by S. Rajesh, Cricinfo's statistics editor

More than 26,000 international runs, almost 80 hundreds, more than 200 scores of 50 and above, at least 1000 runs against eight different one-day opponents … all these staggering stats belong to one batsman, and the only database that can do justice to them is **Statsguru**, Cricinfo's one-stop shop for all kinds of numerical queries.

Sachin Tendulkar's numbers are awe-inspiring, but recently there have been reservations about his batting. Is he scoring enough in wins? What about his fourth-innings contributions in Tests? And how is he performing against the best teams in the world? All the debates about Tendulkar – or on most other topics to do with cricket – will probably need a healthy dose of numbers to help resolve them, and to get hold of the digits in detail you should log on to Cricinfo, then select "Statsguru" from the grey menu on the left of the home-page.

Cricket is such a numbers-driven game that there's plenty of scope for this sort of analysis, and Statsguru has the means to answer most of your queries. The database includes every single Test match and one-day international – Twenty20s too – and the easy-to-use query tool (a more powerful, and equally user-friendly, interface is on its way) enables you to find answers to questions which would otherwise require a complete set of *Wisden*.

Coming back to Tendulkar, his Test career summary page (which you get by typing "Tendulkar" in the Statsguru search page, and then selecting "career summary – batting") shows, in the list of annual averages, just how much his numbers have fallen in the last three years (91.50 in 2004, 44.40 in 2005, 24.27 in 2006). Scroll further down and you'll come across his not-so-flattering second-innings average of 42.21, which drops to 32.56 in the last innings of a match.

If you want to dig deeper into Tendulkar's numbers, then Statsguru allows that as well. Details of his second-innings stats (select "second innings" in his query page and then view by batting career summary) are quite revealing: he has been impressive against Sri Lanka, New Zealand, England and West Indies, but has struggled mightily against South Africa – in 16 efforts against them he has a highest score of 36. The table below, which is taken from Statsguru's career-summary page, offers more details:

Sachin Tendulkar in the second innings

Opponent	Tests	Inns	Runs	HS	Avge	100s	50s	0s
Australia	19	18	601	155*	37.56	1	4	2
Bangladesh	2	1	31	31	31.00	0	0	0
England	15	13	561	122	56.10	2	2	0
New Zealand	13	11	424	126*	60.57	2	1	0
Pakistan	12	9	341	136	37.88	1	2	0
South Africa	17	16	193	36	13.78	0	0	2
Sri Lanka	6	6	284	124*	71.00	2	0	0
West Indies	10	10	454	176	56.75	1	3	1
Zimbabwe	5	5	193	69	48.25	0	1	0

On the other hand, there are plenty of numbers to support the case for Tendulkar, the most compelling of which concerns his record against Australia, far and away the best team during his playing career. He averages 53.11 against them, and if you check Statsguru for other top batsmen against the Aussies since 1990, you'll find that only Kevin Pietersen has done better, and even then the difference is marginal:

The best Test batsmen against Australia since 1990 (min. 10 matches)

Batsman	Tests	Runs	Avge	100s/50s
Kevin Pietersen *England*	10	963	53.50	2/6
Sachin Tendulkar *India*	21	1859	53.11	7/7
VVS Laxman *India*	16	1457	52.03	4/6
Brian Lara *West Indies*	31	2856	51.00	9/11
Ijaz Ahmed *Pakistan*	11	913	50.72	5/1
Richie Richardson *West Indies*	14	1084	49.27	4/4
Rahul Dravid *India*	19	1503	48.48	2/8
Michael Vaughan *England*	10	959	47.95	4/1

Statsguru can do a lot more than just compare Tendulkar and Pietersen. The "basic filter" for any player (don't be fooled by the term – the information on offer is pretty meaty) gives series-by-series, ground-by-ground and cumulative averages. It also shows up the bowlers who had the wood on certain batsmen. Type in Daryll Cullinan, for example, and select "bowlers/fielders dismissed by" in batting formats for Tests, and you'll find that Muttiah Muralitharan and – quite surprisingly – Dinanath Ramnarine dismissed him most often, not Shane Warne. Where Warne had unmatched success, though, was in dismissing Cullinan as soon as he came in to bat: on the four occasions when Warne dismissed Cullinan, his average was 2.75. And in ODIs Cullinan fell eight times to Warne, which is more than he was dismissed by any other bowler.

The advanced filter can, as the name suggests, do even more. It can tell you, for instance, that in all the ODIs in which Shaun Pollock bowled at least eight overs, only eight times did he go for more than a run a ball; on the other hand, he conceded under two per over 17 times.

Statsguru can't quite tell you who's the best fast bowler of all time, but it can certainly provide some pointers: the table below looks at the numbers for three of the leading contenders from the 1970s and '80s. Dennis Lillee is often regarded the greatest, but he only played five of his 70 Tests outside Australia, England or New Zealand, and didn't do particularly well in those games. Malcolm Marshall and Richard Hadlee, on the other hand, have consistent numbers in all conditions:

	Malcolm Marshall			Richard Hadlee			Dennis Lillee		
In country	Tests	Wkts	Avge	Tests	Wkts	Avge	Tests	Wkts	Avge
Australia	10	45	23.15	12	77	17.83	44	231	23.73
England	18	94	18.70	14	70	24.94	16	96	20.56
India	9	36	24.61	6	31	22.22	0	0	–
New Zealand	3	9	32.11	43	201	22.96	5	22	22.50
Pakistan	10	35	21.45	3	10	44.70	3	3	101.00
Sri Lanka	0	0	–	4	27	12.29	1	3	35.66
West Indies	31	157	20.06	4	15	27.26	1	0	–

Cricket is more than just about batting and bowling, though, and Statsguru recognises that with a separate fielding filter as well. Check out Mark Taylor's fielding figures, for instance (in "fielding formats", select "batsmen/bowler summary") and you'll find that 51 of his 157 catches – that's 32.48% – came off the bowling of Shane Warne. Which fielder do you think has benefited the most by Muttiah Muralitharan's bowling?

If all this stats chat has whetted your appetite, then here's some more to keep you going. Which mode of dismissal has Lara fallen to most often? And how many times has he fallen to left-arm bowlers? And to spinners in general?

Happy hunting!

MARKING YOUR CARD

What to look out for in 2008, by Steven Lynch

TEN YOUNG PLAYERS TO WATCH IN 2008

Stuart Broad (England) Beanpole fast bowler whose Dad is in this book too *See p30 and 223*
Piyush Chawla (India) Impish young legspinner with a good googly *See p32*
Fawad Alam (Pakistan) Promising batsman who can bowl a bit too *See p49*
Ben Hilfenhaus (Australia) Burly bricklayer turned fast bowler *See p70*
Phil Jaques (Australia) May win the race to succeed Justin Langer as Test opener *See p82*
Morne Morkel (South Africa) Genuinely quick bowler, rated by Allan Donald *See p124*
Kieron Pollard (West Indies) Big-hitting Trinidadian allrounder *See p143*
Shakab Al Hasan (Bangladesh) Cool consistent batsman, tight tenacious spinner *See p167*
Chamara Silva (Sri Lanka) Wristy right-hander reminiscent of Aravinda de Silva *See p173*
Ross Taylor (New Zealand) Beefy hitter who just loves to play Otago *See p190*

TEN MILESTONES THAT SHOULD BE REACHED ...

Muttiah Muralitharan needs nine wickets to become Test cricket's leading bowler *See p228*
Mark Boucher needs four dismissals to become Test cricket's leading wicketkeeper *See p229*
The Melbourne Cricket Ground will stage its 100th Test match on Boxing Day
Sanath Jayasuriya needs to play two more ODIs to reach 400 matches *See p230*
West Indies' next Test win will be their 150th *See p265*
Adam Gilchrist is three short of becoming the first man to hit 100 sixes in Tests *See p229*
Inzamam-ul-Haq needs 21 runs to become Pakistan's highest Test runscorer *See p252*
Australia have 48 Test wins against West Indies, so could reach 50 in April *See page 272*
Herschelle Gibbs needs 57 runs for 6000 in Tests, and 111 for 7000 in ODIs *See p256 and 258*
Danish Kaneria and **Stuart MacGill** both need two wickets for 200 in Tests *See p40 and 103*

... AND TEN THAT MIGHT BE

Sachin Tendulkar needs 804 runs to become Test cricket's leading scorer *See p228*
Mahela Jayawardene needs 149 runs at Colombo's Sinhalese Sports Club to become
the leading Test runscorer on a single ground (Graham Gooch made 2015 at Lord's)
Rahul Dravid needs 508 runs for 10,000 in Tests *See p228*
Rudi Koertzen needs to stand in 23 ODIs to become the first to umpire 200 *See p225*
Ajit Agarkar needs 12 wickets for 300 in ODIs *See p246*
An ODI double-century – Saeed Anwar's highest score of 194 has lasted for ten years
now *See p230*
Matthew Hayden needs two Test hundreds to equal Don Bradman's tally *See p229*
Shaun Pollock needs 23 wickets for 400 in ODIs *See p230*
Sanath Jayasuriya needs eight sixes to become the first to hit 250 in ODIs *See p231*
Ricky Ponting needs 632 runs for 10,000 in Tests *See p228*

QUIZ
Wisden prizes to be won

First prize in our quiz is a searchable online ebook of the 2006, 2007 and 2008 *Wisden Cricketers' Almanack*, sport's most famous reference book, plus a year's subscription to *The Wisden Cricketer* magazine. You will find all the answers to the questions somewhere in this book – in the player profiles and elsewhere. It's simple to enter: just email your answers to the address shown below.

Which person who is featured in this book:

1 Offered to have a finger cut off if it would help him play in the World Cup?

2 Was the youngest man to appear in a Test match at Lord's?

3 Is colour-blind and sometimes struggles to see the ball?

4 Has also represented his country at water polo?

5 Has a father who is an umpire and has given him out in a one-day international?

6 Survived being shot in the hand at point-blank range to play again?

7 Once mistook a policeman for a mugger and shot him?

8 Owes his peculiar nickname to his love for Liverpool Football Club?

9 Played in a pop group called "Six and Out"?

10 Once withdrew from a tour claiming his grandmother had died when she hadn't?

11 Has a sister who captains their country's women's team?

12 Has taken more than 100 wickets in ODIs despite not playing for a Test nation?

13 Used to work as a prison warder?

14 Is named after a top tennis player from the 1980s?

15 Owes his nickname to a fictional pop group in an Eddie Murphy film?

16 Once stood behind the stumps to face a ball while batting against Shoaib Akhtar?

17 Hit 117 on first-class debut, with seven sixes, one of which got him off the mark?

18 Took four wickets on his ODI debut, on his 22nd birthday?

19 Scored 15,313 runs in first-class cricket before winning his first Test cap?

20 Had hit exactly 1,000 boundaries in Test cricket (by Sept 10, 2007)?

To enter, please email your answers, together with your name and email address, to quiz@johnwisden.co.uk by May 1, 2008. The first all-correct entry to be randomly drawn on that date will win ebook versions of the 2006, 2007 and 2008 editions of *Wisden Cricketers' Almanack*, and a year's subscription to *The Wisden Cricketer* magazine. Two runners-up will each receive an ebook version of *Wisden* 2008. The editor's decision is final; no correspondence will be entered into. The winners will be announced in the first "Ask Steven" column on www.cricinfo.com in May 2008.

PLAYER INDEX

PLAYER INDEX

ABDUL RAZZAQ

Full name	**Abdul Razzaq**
Born	**December 2, 1979, Lahore, Punjab**
Teams	**Lahore, Worcestershire**
Style	**Right-hand bat, right-arm fast-medium bowler**
Test debut	**Pakistan v Australia at Brisbane 1999-2000**
ODI debut	**Pakistan v Zimbabwe at Lahore 1996-97**

THE PROFILE Abdul Razzaq was once rapid enough to open the bowling, and remains composed enough to bat anywhere, although the lower order suits him nicely. His bowling, which first got him noticed, is characterised by a galloping approach, accuracy, and reverse-swing. But it is his batting that is more likely to win matches. He has all the shots, and is particularly strong driving through cover and mid-off off front or back foot. He has two gears: block or blast. Cut off the big shots and he can get bogged down, although he is very patient, as demonstrated by a match-saving 71 in almost six hours against India at Mohali in March 2005. Just before that he had batted bewilderingly slowly at Melbourne, scoring 4 in 110 minutes. But when the occasion demands he can still slog with the best of them: England were pillaged for 51 in 22 balls in December 2005. Razzaq suffered a slump, particularly in bowling, between 2002 and 2004, but has rediscovered some of his old guile, if not his nip. And if the pitch is helpful to seam – as Karachi's was for his only Test five-for in 2004, and also against India there in January 2006 – he can still be a danger. Razzaq's allround performance in that win over India was easily his most emphatic: he made 45 and 90 to add to seven wickets. An untimely knee injury kept him out of the 2007 World Cup, but Pakistan's disastrous form there meant he was hurried back when fit again, although his involvement with the breakaway Indian Cricket League put a question-mark over his international future.

THE FACTS Abdul Razzaq took a hat-trick against Sri Lanka at Galle in June 2000 ... He is one of only four players to have scored a hundred and taken a hat-trick in Tests: the others were England's Johnny Briggs, Wasim Akram of Pakistan and the New Zealander James Franklin ... Razzaq took 7 for 51 – still his best figures – on his first-class debut, for Lahore City v Karachi Whites in the Quaid-e-Azam Trophy final in November 1996 ... His highest score is 203 not out, for Middlesex v Glamorgan at Cardiff in 2003 ... His record includes four ODIs for the Asia XI ...

THE FIGURES

Batting and fielding   www.cricinfo.com

	M	Inns	NO	Runs	HS	Avge	S/R	100	50	4s	6s	Ct	St
Tests *to 10.9.07*	46	77	9	1946	134	28.61	41.04	3	7	230	23	15	0
ODIs *to 10.9.07*	231	198	49	4465	112	29.96	79.96	2	22	333	103	31	0
First-class *to 10.9.07*	108	168	26	4792	203*	33.74	–	8	23	–	–	28	0

Bowling

	M	Balls	Runs	Wkts	BB	Avge	RpO	S/R	5i	10m
Tests *to 10.9.07*	46	7008	3694	100	5–35	36.94	3.16	70.08	1	0
ODIs *to 10.9.07*	231	9797	7658	246	6–35	31.13	4.69	39.82	3	0
First-class *to 10.9.07*	108	17154	10071	307	7–51	32.80	3.52	55.87	10	2

ABDUR RAZZAK

Full name	**Khan Abdur Razzak**
Born	**June 15, 1982, Khulna**
Teams	**Khulna**
Style	**Left-hand bat, slow left-arm orthodox spinner**
Test debut	**Bangladesh v Australia at Chittagong 2005-06**
ODI debut	**Bangladesh v Hong Kong at Colombo 2004**

THE PROFILE The latest in Bangladesh's seemingly never-ending supply of left-arm spinners, Abdur Razzak (no relation to the similarly named Pakistan allrounder) made his mark when he helped unheralded Khulna to their first-ever National Cricket League title in 2001-02. Tall, with a high action, he was given his A-team debut during a five-match one-day series against Zimbabwe early in 2004, and took the opportunity well with 15 wickets, including a matchwinning 7 for 17 in the third encounter on the batting paradise of Dhaka's Bangabandhu National Stadium. He has an uncanny ability to pin batsmen down, although his action has been reported in the past. Bangladesh's coaching staff used video technology to help iron out anything suspicious. He took 3 for 17 on his one-day debut against Hong Kong in the Asia Cup in Colombo in 2004, but was reported for a suspect action after the next match, against Pakistan. Left out of the Champions Trophy in England later that year, "Raj" played just one ODI before he was recalled for the home series against Sri Lanka in February 2006. He made his Test debut two months later, called up for the second Test against Australia on a turning track at Chittagong (even the Aussies played three spinners), but failed to take a wicket, finally claiming an expensive scalp in Colombo in June 2007. But he has become an automatic one-day selection, playing in all Bangladesh's 30 matches in 2006-07 – including throughout the World Cup – taking 50 wickets and maintaining a mean economy rate.

THE FACTS Abdur Razzak's best bowling in ODIs is 5 for 33 against Zimbabwe at Bogra in December 2006 ... His best first-class figures of 7 for 11 (10 for 62 in the match) came for Khulna against Sylhet at Sylhet in 2003-04 ... Razzak's economy rate of 3.98 runs per over is the best by anyone for Bangladesh in ODIs, and is surpassed among current bowlers only by Shaun Pollock (3.71), Murali (3.84) and Prosper Utseya (3.97) ...

THE FIGURES

Batting and fielding

www.cricinfo.com

	M	Inns	NO	Runs	HS	Avge	S/R	100	50	4s	6s	Ct	St
Tests *to 10.9.07*	2	4	1	19	15	6.33	61.29	0	0	3	0	0	0
ODIs *to 10.9.07*	52	32	15	214	28	12.58	74.04	0	0	13	6	13	0
First-class *to 10.9.07*	38	60	8	997	83	19.17	56.42	0	5	–	–	13	0

Bowling

	M	Balls	Runs	Wkts	BB	Avge	RpO	S/R	5i	10m
Tests *to 10.9.07*	2	360	208	1	1–109	208.00	3.46	360.00	0	0
ODIs *to 10.9.07*	52	2749	1828	80	5–33	22.85	3.98	34.36	1	0
First-class *to 10.9.07*	38	8458	3665	127	7–11	28.85	2.59	66.59	5	1

ABDUR REHMAN

Full name	**Abdur Rehman**
Born	**March 1, 1980, Sialkot, Punjab**
Teams	**Sialkot, Habib Bank**
Style	**Left-hand bat, slow left-arm orthodox spinner**
Test debut	**No Tests yet**
ODI debut	**Pakistan v West Indies at Faisalabad 2006-07**

THE PROFILE Abdur Rehman made his international debut late in 2006 at the ripe old age of 26 (elderly considering the usual subcontinental trait of ruthlessly exposing youth to the world's best), and immediately impressed, with two wickets in each of his first three one-dayers against West Indies. He is not a huge turner of the ball, but he is accurate and consistent, and can exploit the rough well: so far this has paid off in first-class cricket, and also during his brief flirtation with the elite level. He first gave notice of his ability back in 1999, with five and six wickets in successive matches for Pakistan's Under-19s against South Africa, a home series for which he was chosen after only a couple of first-class matches. His senior opportunities have been limited by the side's several spinners, most of them better batsmen, but he kept himself in contention with good domestic performances: in 2006-07 he was the leading bowler as Habib Bank won the Pentangular Cup, with 11 in an important victory over Sind. He missed the World Cup – a blessing in disguise, perhaps – but was recalled for the one-day series against Sri Lanka in Abu Dhabi, although he played in only one of the three matches. Rehman probably lacks the artillery to cause major concern to batsmen in Tests, which may be why he missed out on a national contract for 2007-08. However, with Pakistan looking for variety and an ally for Danish Kaneria, he may get a chance.

THE FACTS Abdur Rehman took 26 wickets for Habib Bank in the 2006-07 Pentangular Cup in Pakistan, including 11 in the match against Sind ... He took 8 for 53 for Habib Bank against Sui Gas Pipelines in Karachi in December 2005, a week after claiming 5 for 120 and 6 for 28 against Khan Research Laboratories in the same competition ... Rehman made 96 for Habib Bank against National Bank at Multan in January 2006 ...

THE FIGURES

Batting and fielding   www.cricinfo.com

	M	Inns	NO	Runs	HS	Avge	S/R	100	50	4s	6s	Ct	St
Tests to 10.9.07	0	0	–	–	–	–	–	–	–	–	–	–	–
ODIs to 10.9.07	5	3	0	17	10	5.66	22.36	0	0	1	0	1	0
First-class to 10.9.07	69	93	10	1466	96	17.66	–	0	7	–	–	30	0

Bowling

	M	Balls	Runs	Wkts	BB	Avge	RpO	S/R	5i	10m
Tests to 10.9.07	0	0	–	–	–	–	–	–	–	–
ODIs to 10.9.07	5	252	163	7	2–20	23.28	3.88	36.00	0	0
First-class to 10.9.07	69	15343	5817	219	8–53	26.56	2.57	61.84	12	3

ANDRE **ADAMS**

NEW ZEALAND

Full name	**Andre Ryan Adams**
Born	**July 17, 1975, Auckland**
Teams	**Auckland, Nottinghamshire**
Style	**Right-hand bat, right-arm fast-medium bowler**
Test debut	**New Zealand v England at Auckland 2001-02**
ODI debut	**New Zealand v Sri Lanka at Sharjah 2000-01**

THE PROFILE A bowling allrounder, Andre Adams adds a touch of dash to New Zealand's batting armoury with his hard-hitting skills – he has scored his one-day runs at better than a run a ball. He started as a fast bowler before throttling back to a brisk medium with the occasional faster one. He did well against England in 2001-02, starting with 2 for 25 in the first one-dayer (and making 28 not out), then lifting the match award for 3 for 13 and 25 not out in the second game. But a stress fracture to the lower back hindered him, allowing Jacob Oram to move ahead in the pecking order. Adams returned for the 2003 World Cup, but made little impact beyond another award-winning performance, against West Indies, when he followed 35 from 24 balls with 4 for 44. He lost his place again, and seemed destined to remain on the outer until called up towards the end of the 2004 NatWest Series in England. He didn't actually play, but did sign up with Essex for the rest of the season: he returned there the following two years as well. Although he took six wickets on debut against England at Auckland early in 2002 – in a match New Zealand won to square the series – Adams is unlikely to add to his solitary Test cap. He had a turbulent 2006-07 season, with success on the field (32 wickets at 18.78 in the State Championship, and his first domestic century for Auckland) despite a one-month ban for tangling with an opposing batsman. In three one-day games against Sri Lanka he failed to reach double figures and took only one wicket, and was overlooked for the World Cup. Adams missed out on a central conract for 2007-08, and faces a battle to get back into the side.

THE FACTS Adams has made three centuries in first-class cricket – both of them for Essex ... He made a footnote in history in the last ODI against South Africa at Centurion in November 2005, when he was super-subbed out of the game before it had even started ... In ODIs against India Adams has taken 17 wickets at 13.82, more than twice as many as against any other country (eight v England) ...

THE FIGURES

Batting and fielding

www.cricinfo.com

	M	Inns	NO	Runs	HS	Avge	S/R	100	50	4s	6s	Ct	St
Tests *to 10.9.07*	1	2	0	18	11	9.00	90.00	0	0	3	0	1	0
ODIs *to 10.9.07*	42	34	10	419	45	17.45	100.47	0	0	31	18	8	0
First-class *to 10.9.07*	77	102	9	2363	124	25.40	–	3	10	–	–	48	0

Bowling

	M	Balls	Runs	Wkts	BB	Avge	RpO	S/R	5i	10m
Tests *to 10.9.07*	1	190	105	6	3-44	17.50	3.31	31.66	0	0
ODIs *to 10.9.07*	42	1885	1643	53	5-22	31.00	5.22	35.66	1	0
First-class *to 10.9.07*	77	15228	7401	290	6-25	25.52	2.91	52.51	10	1

AFTAB AHMED

Full name	**Aftab Ahmed Chowdhury**
Born	**November 10, 1985, Chittagong**
Teams	**Chittagong**
Style	**Right-hand bat, right-arm medium-pacer**
Test debut	**Bangladesh v New Zealand at Chittagong 2004-05**
ODI debut	**Bangladesh v South Africa at Birmingham 2004**

THE PROFILE Aftab Ahmed first came to notice by scoring 79 against South Africa in the Under-19 World Cup in 2002, and the following year he was pitched into the Test squad to face England, despite having failed to impress in two earlier warm-up matches. His selection was initially viewed with suspicion by the local media, who regarded Aftab as something of a one-day cowboy, and indeed his desire to belt the cover off the ball has resulted in some all-too-brief performances, and his Test career has stalled recently. He repaid the selectors at Chester-le-Street in 2005 with a defiant, carefree 82 not out, the highest score for Bangladesh in the Test series. He also finished off the historic one-day win over Australia at Cardiff, smashing Jason Gillespie for four and six to seal victory, and before that he had spirited Bangladesh to a 3-2 series triumph with an unbeaten 81 in the final match against Zimbabwe in January 2005. He has missed only one ODI since making his debut late in 2004, playing throughout Bangladesh's ups and downs in the 2007 World Cup, during which his form fell away after he made six half-centuries in 13 innings from midway in the Champions Trophy the previous October.

THE FACTS Aftab Ahmed's first five ODI wickets came in one spell, 5 for 31 against New Zealand at Dhaka in November 2004 ... His best bowling analysis in first-class cricket is 7 for 39, for a Bangladesh Cricket Board XI v Central Zone in India's Duleep Trophy in 2004-05 ... Aftab's solitary first-class century was 129 for Chittagong v Dhaka in Dhaka in 2002-03 ... He made 91 for Bangladesh Under-19s in a youth Test against England, captained by Alastair Cook, at Taunton in August 2004 ...

THE FIGURES

Batting and fielding   www.cricinfo.com

	M	Inns	NO	Runs	HS	Avge	S/R	100	50	4s	6s	Ct	St
Tests *to 10.9.07*	10	20	1	395	82*	20.78	58.08	0	1	60	3	4	0
ODIs *to 10.9.07*	69	69	6	1664	92	26.41	85.07	0	12	172	46	23	0
First-class *to 10.9.07*	26	49	3	1234	129*	26.82	63.24	1	5	–	–	18	0

Bowling

	M	Balls	Runs	Wkts	BB	Avge	RpO	S/R	5i	10m
Tests *to 10.9.07*	10	210	176	3	1–28	58.66	5.02	70.00	0	0
ODIs *to 10.9.07*	69	715	629	12	5–31	52.41	5.27	59.58	1	0
First-class *to 10.9.07*	26	1224	583	21	7–39	27.76	2.85	58.28	1	0

AJIT **AGARKAR**

INDIA

Full name	**Ajit Bhalchandra Agarkar**
Born	**December 4, 1977, Bombay**
Teams	**Mumbai**
Style	**Right-hand bat, right-arm fast-medium bowler**
Test debut	**India v Zimbabwe at Harare 1998-99**
ODI debut	**India v Australia at Kochi 1997-98**

THE PROFILE   Slight, fiery and gifted, Ajit Agarkar has never quite come to terms with being touted as Kapil Dev's replacement as India's matchwinner with bat and ball. The ingredients are there, and in the right proportions. But they have never quite formed the right long-lasting mix. Agarkar is a brisk, energetic fast-medium bowler from Mumbai, and his entry into international cricket in 1998 – with an avalanche of wickets that made him the fastest to 50 wickets in ODIs – was matched for speed only by an astonishing batting slump a couple of years later that saw him collect seven consecutive Test ducks against Australia. But all India knows he can bat, because tailenders simply do not score half-centuries in 21 balls, as Agarkar did in a one-dayer against Zimbabwe late in 2000, or score Test centuries at Lord's, as he did in some style in 2002, making a nonsense of a Test average of about 17. His aggression is an asset, but his body doesn't seem to be able to support it. India's succession of left-arm quicks have relegated Agarkar to Test afterthought now – he has played only four matches since the start of 2005 – but he's still a feature in the one-day side, grabbing nine wickets in five games in the West Indies in June 2006, and he was close to playing in the Tests there. He was dropped for a while after India crashed out of the World Cup, but was back for the one-dayers in Ireland and England later in 2007, where he looked to have lost a yard of pace – although he did take four wickets at Old Trafford.

THE FACTS   Agarkar took his 50th wicket in his 23rd ODI, a record for India ... He made seven successive ducks in Tests against Australia in 1999-2000 and 2000-01, and averages only 7.42 against them, compared with 42 against England and 30.66 against Sri Lanka ... Agarkar has taken 49 ODI wickets against Sri Lanka, and 45 v Zimbabwe ... Among recent Test century-makers, only Pakistan's Saqlain Mushtaq (14.48) has a lower batting average than Agarkar's 16.79 ...

THE FIGURES

Batting and fielding   www.cricinfo.com

	M	Inns	NO	Runs	HS	Avge	S/R	100	50	4s	6s	Ct	St
Tests *to 10.9.07*	26	39	5	571	109*	16.79	52.82	1	0	83	3	6	0
ODIs *to 10.9.07*	191	113	26	1269	95	14.58	80.62	0	3	103	22	52	0
First-class *to 10.9.07*	72	94	16	1945	109*	24.93	–	2	8	–	–	26	0

Bowling

	M	Balls	Runs	Wkts	BB	Avge	RpO	S/R	5i	10m
Tests *to 10.9.07*	26	4857	2745	58	6–41	47.32	3.39	83.74	1	0
ODIs *to 10.9.07*	191	9484	8021	288	6 42	27.85	5.07	32.93	?	0
First-class *to 10.9.07*	72	12401	6328	222	6–41	28.50	3.06	55.86	10	0

HASHIM **AMLA**

Full name	**Hashim Mahomed Amla**
Born	**March 31, 1983, Durban, Natal**
Teams	**Dolphins**
Style	**Right-hand bat, occasional right-arm medium-pacer**
Test debut	**South Africa v India at Kolkata 2004-05**
ODI debut	**No ODIs yet**

THE PROFILE An elegant, stroke-filled right-hander blessed with the temperament to make the most of his talent, Hashim Amla was the first South African of Indian descent to reach the national squad. His elevation was hardly a surprise after he reeled off four centuries in his first eight innings in 2004-05, after being appointed captain of the Dolphins (formerly Natal) at the tender age of 21. Ahmed, his older brother by four years, also plays for them, but there is little doubt that the younger Amla is the better player. He is also a devout Muslim, whose requests to have logos promoting alcohol removed from his playing gear have been successful so far. Amla toured New Zealand with the Under-19s in 2000-01, he captained South Africa at the 2002 Under-19 World Cup, and, after starring for the A team in 2004-05 – he made two hundreds against New Zealand A – made his Test debut against India. He was not an instant success, with serious questions emerging about his technique as he mustered only 36 runs in four innings against England later that season, struggling with an ungainly crouched stance and a bat coming down from somewhere in the region of gully. But when he was handed a second chance in April 2006 he made it count, with 149 against New Zealand at Cape Town, helping to ensure a draw. Amla remains a candidate to become South Africa's captain eventually, although currently he is not seen as a one-day player, and vies with Pakistan's Mohammad Yousuf for the most impressive beard in the game.

THE FACTS Amla's highest score is 249, made in nearly 11 hours, for the Dolphins against the Eagles at Bloemfontein in March 2005 ... He made his first-class debut for KwaZulu-Natal at 16, against Nasser Hussain's 1999-2000 England tourists (and scored 1) ... In his next match, in February 2002, Amla made his maiden first-class hundred – 103 against Easterns at Durban ...

THE FIGURES

Batting and fielding   www.cricinfo.com

	M	Inns	NO	Runs	HS	Avge	S/R	100	50	4s	6s	Ct	St
Tests to 10.9.07	13	25	1	616	149	25.66	42.98	1	4	82	0	15	0
ODIs to 10.9.07	0	0	–	–	–	–	–	–	–	–	–	–	–
First-class to 10.9.07	74	124	13	5017	249	45.19	–	15	25	–	–	55	0

Bowling

	M	Balls	Runs	Wkts	BB	Avge	RpO	S/R	5i	10m
Tests to 10.9.07	13	6	4	0	–	–	4.00	–	0	0
ODIs to 10.9.07	0	0	–	–	–	–	–	–	–	–
First-class to 10.9.07	74	150	101	1	1–10	101.00	4.04	150.00	0	0

JAMES **ANDERSON**

Full name **James Michael Anderson**
Born **July 30, 1982, Burnley, Lancashire**
Teams **Lancashire**
Style **Left-hand bat, right-arm fast-medium bowler**
Test debut **England v Zimbabwe at Lord's 2003**
ODI debut **England v Australia at Melbourne 2002-03**

ENGLAND

THE PROFILE A strapping fast bowler, and a superb fielder, James Anderson had played only three one-day games for Lancashire in 2002 – he'd played more for his club, Burnley – before being hurried into England's one-day squad in Australia that winter as cover for Andy Caddick, following an impressive stint at the Academy there. He didn't have a number – or even a name – on his shirt, but a remarkable ten-over stint, costing just 12 runs, in century heat at Adelaide earned him a World Cup spot. There, he produced a matchwinning spell against Pakistan before a sobering last-over disaster against Australia. Nonetheless his star was very much in the ascendant, and he took five wickets in the first innings of his debut Test, against Zimbabwe at home in 2003, almost to order. A one-day hat-trick followed against Pakistan ... but from then on, his fortunes waned for a while. South Africa's batsmen made his new go-faster hairstyle look a bit foolish, and although he toured Bangladesh and Sri Lanka in 2003-04 and South Africa the following winter, he was a peripheral net bowler – and a shadow of his former self when he did get on the field. Previously silent critics noted that his head pointed downwards at delivery, supposedly leading to a lack of control. Anderson sat on the sidelines until injuries led to a recall at Mumbai in 2005-06, and took six wickets in England's series-levelling triumph. A lower-back stress fracture kept him out for most of the 2006 home season, but he still made the Australian tour and the World Cup. Then, in the absence of the entire Ashes-winning attack in the second half of 2007, Anderson suddenly looked the part of pack-leader again, troubling Sachin Tendulkar in all three Tests against India, and finishing with 14 wickets.

THE FACTS Anderson was the first man to take an ODI hat-trick for England, against Pakistan at The Oval in 2003: Steve Harmison followed suit in 2004 ... His best figures of 6 for 23 came for Lancashire v Hampshire at Southampton in 2002, his first season ... Anderson was the Cricket Writers' Club's Young Cricketer of the Year in 2003, the first unanimous choice since the award began in 1950: all 175 members who voted went for him ...

THE FIGURES
Batting and fielding   www.cricinfo.com

	M	Inns	NO	Runs	HS	Avge	S/R	100	50	4s	6s	Ct	St
Tests to 10.9.07	19	28	17	123	21*	11.18	32.53	0	0	15	0	7	0
ODIs to 10.9.07	76	31	16	104	15	6.93	38.95	0	0	6	0	17	0
First-class to 10.9.07	66	76	36	362	37*	9.05	–	0	0	–	–	25	0

Bowling

	M	Balls	Runs	Wkts	BB	Avge	RpO	S/R	5i	10m
Tests to 10.9.07	19	3659	2264	60	5–42	37.73	3.71	60.98	3	0
ODIs to 10.9.07	76	3831	3077	113	4–23	27.23	4.81	33.90	0	0
First-class to 10.9.07	66	11499	6741	228	6–23	29.56	3.51	50.43	10	1

19

CULLEN **BAILEY**

AUSTRALIA

Full name	**Cullen Benjamin Bailey**
Born	**Feb 26, 1985, Bedford Park, Adelaide, South Australia**
Teams	**South Australia**
Style	**Right-hand bat, legspinner**
Test debut	**No Tests yet**
ODI debut	**No ODIs yet**

THE PROFILE Cullen Bailey forms half of South Australia's exciting slow-bowling partnership, with Daniel Cullen, that sounds more like a family accountancy firm. Cullen's offspin has already won him a Test cap, and now Bailey, a leggie, has been earmarked to follow in Shane Warne's footsteps, a task that will be harder than finding turn on a first-day pitch. Bailey flew out for his honeymoon in Malaysia in May 2007 on the day he was unveiled as one of Australia's new contracted players. With Warne in international retirement, the squad was heavy on spinners (old and new) with visions of replacing the irreplaceable. Warne's old mentor Terry Jenner also coaches Bailey, and has warned against early promotion for a bowler aged only 22: "It would be devastating for a young player to follow Warne straight in." Bailey's stats should also lead to caution, no matter how desperate the selectors are to find the next Warne, or even the next MacGill. His debut came in the final Pura Cup game of 2004-05 after a fine grade season for his club Sturt, and next summer he bowled the Redbacks to victory over Tasmania with 5 for 146, on his way to 18 wickets at 47.55 in six matches. Darren Lehmann, his captain then, would set attacking fields, ignoring the building runs for the increasing wickets, a contributing factor to that high average. In 2006-07 Bailey emerged as SA's first-choice spinner, playing eight Pura Cup games to Cullen's five, and collected 26 wickets at 41.15. He has started a media degree, and wrote columns about his time at the Centre of Excellence in 2006.

THE FACTS Bailey's best bowling figures are 5 for 146 for South Australia against Tasmania at Adelaide in January 2006 (he took 9 for 231 in the match) which included luring Michael Bevan, in the form of his life, down the pitch for a rare stumping ... His highest score is 54, to help South Australia (who were 163 for 6 when he came in) to 398 against Victoria in January 2007 ... Bailey dismissed Andrew Flintoff and Paul Collingwood (and James Anderson) when SA played the England tourists at Adelaide in 2006-07 ...

THE FIGURES

Batting and fielding

www.cricinfo.com

	M	Inns	NO	Runs	HS	Avge	S/R	100	50	4s	6s	Ct	St
Tests *to 10.9.07*	0	0	–	–	–	–	–	–	–	–	–	–	–
ODIs *to 10.9.07*	0	0	–	–	–	–	–	–	–	–	–	–	–
First-class *to 10.9.07*	17	26	6	310	54	15.50	30.75	0	1	–	–	6	0

Bowling

	M	Balls	Runs	Wkts	BB	Avge	RpO	S/R	5i	10m
Tests *to 10.9.07*	0	0	–	–	–	–	–	–	–	–
ODIs *to 10.9.07*	0	0	–	–	–	–	–	–	–	–
First-class *to 10.9.07*	17	3580	2242	54	5–146	41.51	3.75	66.29	1	0

MALINGA **BANDARA**

Full name	**Charitha Malinga Bandara**
Born	**December 31, 1979, Kalutara**
Teams	**Ragama**
Style	**Right-hand bat, legspinner**
Test debut	**Sri Lanka v New Zealand at Colombo 1997-98**
ODI debut	**Sri Lanka v New Zealand at Wellington 2005-06**

THE PROFILE   Malinga Bandara was earmarked early on as a legspinner of great potential. He doesn't turn it a long way, but varies his pace intelligently. His school performances won him selection for an Under-19 tour of India in 1997, the Youth World Cup in South Africa, and the Sri Lanka A tour of England in 1999. In between, he made his Test debut against New Zealand in May 1998, but looked at sea and was jettisoned. But he bowled consistently in domestic cricket, taking 45 wickets in 2000-01, and a match haul of 11 for 126 against England A in March 2005 confirmed his growing confidence. It also interested Gloucestershire, as they looked for a mid-season replacement for Upul Chandana: Bandara outbowled his more senior team-mate in county cricket in 2005, taking 45 wickets at 24.15 to Chandana's 16 at 42.25, although admittedly the pitches were drier and more suited to legspin when Bandara arrived. His performances helped him win a Test return against India at the end of 2005, and he finally took his first wicket more than six years after his debut. He chipped in with useful wickets and handy runs, and toured England in 2006 ahead of Chandana: he didn't play in the Tests, but deputised for Muttiah Muralitharan in the one-day series, which his side swept 5-0. Earlier his two four-wicket hauls had helped Sri Lanka reach the finals of the VB Series in Australia in February 2006. He didn't feature much in 2006-07, although he did enough to claim the final spot in the World Cup squad. He played only once in the Caribbean, though, in the qualifier against Australia when Murali and Chaminda Vaas were controversially rested. He bounced back after that with some handy performances against Pakistan in Abu Dhabi.

THE FACTS   Bandara took 8 for 49 as Sri Lanka A beat England A in Colombo in March 2005 ... His highest score came the following month, also for Sri Lanka A, v Pakistan A at Dambulla: he made 79, and put on 171 for the ninth wicket with Prasanna Jayawardene ... Bandara averages 12.11 with the ball in ODIs v South Africa – but 41.60 v Bangladesh ...

THE FIGURES

Batting and fielding

www.cricinfo.com

	M	Inns	NO	Runs	HS	Avge	S/R	100	50	4s	6s	Ct	St
Tests to 10.9.07	8	11	3	124	43	15.50	51.66	0	0	14	2	4	0
ODIs to 10.9.07	28	15	4	129	28*	11.72	73.29	0	0	7	5	8	0
First-class to 10.9.07	104	140	30	2003	79	18.20	–	0	8	–	–	69	0

Bowling

	M	Balls	Runs	Wkts	BB	Avge	RpO	S/R	5i	10m
Tests to 10.9.07	8	1152	633	16	3–84	39.56	3.29	72.00	0	0
ODIs to 10.9.07	28	1314	1105	34	4–31	32.50	5.04	38.64	0	0
First-class to 10.9.07	104	13561	7033	274	8–49	25.66	3.11	49.49	9	2

IAN **BELL**

Full name	**Ian Ronald Bell**
Born	**April 11, 1982, Walsgrave, Coventry**
Teams	**Warwickshire**
Style	**Right-hand bat, right-arm medium-pace bowler**
Test debut	**England v West Indies at The Oval 2004**
ODI debut	**England v Zimbabwe at Harare 2004-05**

THE PROFILE Ian Bell was earmarked for greatness long before he was drafted into the England squad in New Zealand in 2001-02, aged 19, as cover for the injured Mark Butcher. Tenacious and technically sound, Bell is in the mould of Michael Atherton, who was burdened with similar expectations on his England debut a generation earlier and was similarly adept at leaving the ball outside off. He had played only 13 first-class matches when called into that England squad, although he did score 836 runs at 64 for Warwickshire in 2001. Under the spotlight, his form slumped, but by 2004 he was on the up again. He finally made his Test debut against West Indies in August 2004, stroking 70 at The Oval, before returning the following summer to lift his average to an obscene 297 against Bangladesh. Such rich pickings soon ceased: found out by McGrath and Warne, like so many before him, Bell mustered just 171 runs in the 2005 Ashes series. But, like a true class act, he bounced back better for the experience, stroking 313 runs in three Tests in Pakistan, including a classy century at Faisalabad. And when Pakistan toured in 2006, Bell repeated the dose, with elegant hundreds in each of the first three Tests. He improved his record against the Aussies in 2006-07, without going on to the big score, a problem that placed – one he removed with some bravura performances, including a long-overdue century, against India late in 2007 in England.

THE FACTS After three Tests, and innings of 70, 65 not out and 162 not out, Bell's average was 297.00: he raised that to 303.00 before Australia started getting him out – only Lawrence Rowe (336), David Lloyd (308) and "Tip" Foster (306) have ever had better batting averages in Test history ... None of his six Test centuries has been the only one of the innings ... Bell averages 59.36 in the first innings, but only 23.95 in the second ... He made 262 not out for Warwickshire v Sussex at Horsham in May 2004, sharing a county-record seventh-wicket stand of 289 with Tony Frost ...

THE FIGURES

Batting and fielding   www.cricinfo.com

	M	Inns	NO	Runs	HS	Avge	S/R	100	50	4s	6s	Ct	St
Tests to 10.9.07	30	54	6	2035	162*	42.39	51.96	6	14	233	7	28	0
ODIs to 10.9.07	54	52	4	1890	126*	39.37	72.58	1	13	175	8	14	0
First-class to 10.9.07	115	197	18	7710	262*	43.07	–		19	43	–	–	72	0

Bowling

	M	Balls	Runs	Wkts	BB	Avge	RpO	S/R	5i	10m
Tests to 10.9.07	30	108	76	1	1–33	76.00	4.22	108.00	0	0
ODIs to 10.9.07	54	88	88	6	3–9	14.66	6.00	14.66	0	0
First-class to 10.9.07	115	2719	1490	47	4–4	31.70	3.28	57.85	0	0

SHANE **BOND**

Full name	**Shane Edward Bond**
Born	**June 7, 1975, Christchurch, Canterbury**
Teams	**Canterbury**
Style	**Right-hand bat, right-arm fast bowler**
Test debut	**New Zealand v Australia at Hobart 2001-02**
ODI debut	**New Zealand v Australia at Melbourne 2001-02**

THE PROFILE Shane Bond, for a while world cricket's most famous ex-policeman, is one of the fastest and most dangerous fast bowlers around ... when he's fit. Unfortunately for New Zealand, that hasn't been too often since his impressive introduction to international cricket in 2001-02, when his 21 wickets in the VB Series helped keep the Aussies out of the finals for once. Bond has suffered stress fractures in his back (something of an occupational hazard for fast bowlers) and also in his feet (rather less so). He zipped to 50 one-day wickets in only 27 matches, which included 6 for 23 as he unsettled Australia again in the 2003 World Cup. But those injuries have cost him numerous caps, and planned county stints with Warwickshire and Gloucestershire. Bond's speciality is the fast, inswinging yorker, which he used to great effect against the callow Zimbabweans in 2005, when most of his ten wickets in the Bulawayo Test were lbw or caught in the cordon. He reached 50 wickets in that match, only his 12th Test, and shook up the West Indians with 5 for 86 as they narrowly failed to chase 291 at Auckland in March 2006. But a knee injury sidelined him on the South African tour that followed. He had a productive season in 2006-07, his 5 for 23 setting up the first of three straight wins over Australia in the Chappell-Hadlee one-day series at home, and followed that with some incisive displays in the World Cup – until the semi-final, when he proved expensive as New Zealand lost to Sri Lanka. Fingers, and much else, are crossed in New Zealand that he can maintain full fitness.

THE FACTS Bond was the first super-sub to win a Man of the Match award in an ODI, after coming off the bench to take 6 for 19 v India at Bulawayo in 2005-06 ... Those are New Zealand's best figures in ODIs, beating his own 6 for 23 v Australia in the 2003 World Cup ... In ODIs Bond has taken 34 wickets against Australia at 13.88, including a hat-trick at Hobart in January 2007 – but in Tests against them he has only three wickets at 96.33 ... He made 100 for Canterbury v Northern Districts in Christchurch in 2004-05 ...

THE FIGURES

Batting and fielding

www.cricinfo.com

	M	Inns	NO	Runs	HS	Avge	S/R	100	50	4s	6s	Ct	St
Tests *to 10.9.07*	16	17	7	138	41*	13.80	41.81	0	0	18	3	6	0
ODIs *to 10.9.07*	67	28	14	200	31*	14.28	72.20	0	0	13	7	15	0
First-class *to 10.9.07*	51	57	20	694	100	18.75	–	1	2	–	–	22	0

Bowling

	M	Balls	Runs	Wkts	BB	Avge	RpO	S/R	5i	10m
Tests *to 10.9.07*	16	2881	1636	74	6–51	22.10	3.40	38.93	4	1
ODIs *to 10.9.07*	67	3446	2416	125	6–19	19.32	4.20	27.56	4	0
First-class *to 10.9.07*	51	8619	4486	181	6–51	24.78	3.12	47.61	9	1

RAVI **BOPARA**

Full name	**Ravinder Singh Bopara**
Born	**May 4, 1985, Forest Gate, London**
Teams	**Essex**
Style	**Right-hand bat, right-arm medium-pace bowler**
Test debut	**No Tests yet**
ODI debut	**England v Australia at Sydney 2006-07**

THE PROFILE Ravi Bopara has rarely looked back since he signed for Essex at 17 in 2002. He played a few Championship matches that year, then represented England at the Youth World Cup. He's a busy allrounder – a batsman with a double-century under his belt, and a handy medium-pacer. Kevin Mitchell observed in the *Wisden Cricketer*: "He bats with combativeness around No. 6, bowls skiddy cutters and fields loudly. He is impossible to ignore." Bopara joined England A in the West Indies early in 2006 after injuries in the senior side left spaces to fill. He did little then, but a good county season got him into England's preliminary 30 for the Champions Trophy, and the Academy squad based in Perth during the Ashes series. When Kevin Pietersen broke a rib in the first match of the one-day triangular, Bopara was summoned: not worried about having such big boots to fill, he made his debut in front of the Sydney Hill, and bowled Australia's "finisher", Michael Hussey, as England began the amazing turnaround that eventually won them that series. Bopara didn't appear again, but he had done enough to make the World Cup squad, and he showed impressive resolve in making 52, which almost conjured an unlikely victory against Sri Lanka, the eventual finalists. A thigh injury prevented him from building on this during the early-season ODIs which followed at home, but he was back in September for the series against India, combining with Stuart Broad in the amazing rearguard which stole the Old Trafford match, before a broken thumb in the next game forced him to miss the inaugural World Twenty20 championships.

THE FACTS Bopara made 229, his first double-century, for Essex v Northamptonshire at Chelmsford in June 2007, putting on 320 for the third wicket with Grant Flower ... He made 52 for England v Sri Lanka in the World Cup in April 2007, being bowled by the last ball of the match with three runs needed to win; England were 133 for 6, chasing 236, before he faced a ball ... Bopara took 5 for 75 for Essex v Surrey at Colchester in August 2006 ...

THE FIGURES

Batting and fielding   www.cricinfo.com

	M	Inns	NO	Runs	HS	Avge	S/R	100	50	4s	6s	Ct	St
Tests *to 10.9.07*	0	0	–	–	–	–	–	–	–	–	–	–	–
ODIs *to 10.9.07*	14	12	4	253	52	31.62	72.91	0	1	25	0	3	0
First-class *to 10.9.07*	60	97	15	3206	229	39.09	48.53	6	12	–	–	40	0

Bowling

	M	Balls	Runs	Wkts	BB	Avge	RpO	S/R	5i	10m
Tests *to 10.9.07*	0	0	–	–	–	–	–	–	–	–
ODIs *to 10.9.07*	14	139	121	3	2–43	40.33	5.22	46.33	0	0
First-class *to 10.9.07*	60	4100	2831	58	5–75	48.81	4.14	70.68	1	0

RANADEB **BOSE**

Full name	**Ranadeb Ranjit Bose**
Born	**February 27, 1979, Calcutta (now Kolkata)**
Teams	**Bengal**
Style	**Right-hand bat, right-arm fast-medium bowler**
Test debut	**No Tests yet**
ODI debut	**No ODIs yet**

THE PROFILE Ranadeb Bose was called up to the conditioning camp held by the new Indian coach Greg Chappell in Bangalore in 2005 ... and promptly forgotten, which could easily have persuaded him to give up on his hopes of an international career. The 30 players at that camp were supposed to be the best in India, and it was due recognition for a bowler with a flowing action and a nice leap in the delivery stride that makes optimum use of his height, who had earned his wickets cheaply over a longish career. But Bose disappeared from view after that, and it was widely assumed his chance had gone. He refused to give up, though. He cut down his pace a little, focused more on accuracy and movement, and had a second coming on the back of an exceptional 2006-07 domestic season, which brought him 57 wickets in eight matches in the Ranji Trophy, one of the competition's largest-ever hauls. Remarkably, he has never overstepped for a front-foot no-ball throughout his career. Injuries to other fast bowlers meant he was included for the 2007 tour of England, although once there he couldn't force his way into the successful Test side, which remained unchanged throughout the series. He did well enough when he did get onto the field, taking 5 for 51 against Sri Lanka A at Leicester, and Bose, a genuine rabbit with the bat, will be hoping for more opportunities – and maybe for the odd not-too-serious injury to his rivals – during 2007-08.

THE FACTS Bose has sent down more than 11,000 deliveries in first-class cricket – and another 2500 in one-day games – without incurring a front-foot no-ball ... He took 7 for 24 in only his second first-class match, as Bengal bowled Tripura out for 59 at Kolkata in January 1999: he also took 7 for 25 for Bengal v Hyderabad at Uppal in January 2007 ... Bose has reached double figures only eight times in 61 first-class innings ...

THE FIGURES
Batting and fielding

www.cricinfo.com

	M	Inns	NO	Runs	HS	Avge	S/R	100	50	4s	6s	Ct	St
Tests to 10.9.07	0	0	–	–	–	–	–	–	–	–	–	–	–
ODIs to 10.9.07	0	0	–	–	–	–	–	–	–	–	–	–	–
First-class to 10.9.07	56	61	3	204	21	4.25	–	0	0	–	–	11	0

Bowling

	M	Balls	Runs	Wkts	BB	Avge	RpO	S/R	5i	10m
Tests to 10.9.07	0	0	–	–	–	–	–	–	–	–
ODIs to 10.9.07	0	0	–	–	–	–	–	–	–	–
First-class to 10.9.07	56	11002	4898	202	7–24	24.24	2.67	54.46	17	4

JOHAN **BOTHA**

Full name	**Johan Botha**
Born	**May 2, 1982, Johannesburg**
Teams	**Warriors**
Style	**Right-hand bat, offspinner**
Test debut	**South Africa v Australia at Sydney 2005-06**
ODI debut	**South Africa v India at Hyderabad 2005-06**

THE PROFILE A determined, fiercely competitive individual, Johan Botha started life as a rather ordinary medium-pacer, but one day Mickey Arthur – now South Africa's coach – spotted something else, and Botha dropped his ambitions for speed. Botha became an offspinner, and started studying the doosra – the ball that turns away from the right-hander – in the hope of emulating the likes of Muttiah Muralitharan and Harbhajan Singh. A year later he was touring Sri Lanka with South Africa A, scoring a few runs as well as taking key wickets, which put him under consideration as a potential future Test spinner who could bat – and, when Nicky Boje skipped a one-day series in India late in 2005, Botha got the call. He made a promising debut, gating Irfan Pathan during six tidy overs at Hyderabad, and when the selectors later suspected that the Sydney Test pitch would turn, Botha was sent for (he was already due to go to Australia for the one-dayers) and actually played ahead of Boje. He managed a couple of wickets, but joy turned to dismay when his jerky action was reported, and he was banned by the ICC on suspicion of throwing. Tests in August 2006 showed the right elbow was still flexing more than the permitted 15 degrees, but after further remedial action he was given the green light later that year. Botha made a low-key international return in the Afro-Asia Cup in India in June 2007, but remains in the frame as South Africa continue their long search for a matchwinning spinner.

THE FACTS Botha's bowling action was declared illegal by the ICC in February 2006, and again that August: he was finally cleared in November 2006 ... His best bowling is 6 for 42, for Eastern Province v Northerns at Port Elizabeth in March 2004, when still a medium-pacer ... He scored 98 for Warriors v Dolphins at Durban late in 2006 ... Botha made 101 for South Africa in an Under-19 Test v New Zealand (for whom Brendon McCullum made 186) in February 2001 ... His record includes two ODIs for the Africa XI ...

THE FIGURES

Batting and fielding   www.cricinfo.com

	M	Inns	NO	Runs	HS	Avge	S/R	100	50	4s	6s	Ct	St
Tests *to 10.9.07*	1	1	1	20	20*	–	43.47	0	0	2	0	0	0
ODIs *to 10.9.07*	13	8	4	129	46	32.25	87.16	0	0	12	1	8	0
First-class *to 10.9.07*	44	76	11	1978	98	30.43	–	0	13	–	–	29	0

Bowling

	M	Balls	Runs	Wkts	BB	Avge	RpO	S/R	5i	10m
Tests *to 10.9.07*	1	117	103	2	1–26	51.50	5.28	58.50	0	1
ODIs *to 10.9.07*	13	558	461	7	2–49	65.85	4.95	79.71	0	0
First-class *to 10.9.07*	44	6140	3046	102	6–42	29.86	2.97	60.19	4	1

SOUTH AFRICA

MARK **BOUCHER**

Full name **Mark Verdon Boucher**
Born **December 3, 1976, East London, Cape Province**
Teams **Warriors**
Style **Right-hand bat, wicketkeeper**
Test debut **South Africa v Pakistan at Sheikhupura 1997-98**
ODI debut **South Africa v New Zealand at Perth 1997-98**

THE PROFILE It is a measure of the rapidity of Mark Boucher's rise that no-one is quite sure exactly how many records he holds. Fastest to 100 dismissals, highest score by a night-watchman, most innings without a bye ... they tumbled out so quickly that it has been difficult to keep up. Probably his most significant achievement, however, came in only his second Test, against Pakistan at Johannesburg in February 1998, when he and Pat Symcox added 195, a new Test record for the ninth wicket, from a desperate 166 for 8. Boucher had made his debut a few months previously when still not 21, rushing to Sheikhupura to replace the injured Dave Richardson, who retired after the Australian tour that followed. Boucher was not everyone's first choice to succeed him – Nic Pothas had also been waiting patiently – but once Boucher got his hands into the gloves, he refused to let them go. He found conditions in England difficult, in the 1998 Tests and the 1999 World Cup, but demonstrated courage and determination in what became a run of 75 consecutive Tests. Those qualities brought him three hundreds in his first 25 matches, and he was also named vice-captain when Shaun Pollock took over from Hansie Cronje, recognition of his willingness to get down and scrap when needed. And Boucher scrapped successfully to regain his spot when a form dip eventually did cost him his place – to Thami Tsolekile, and then AB de Villiers – late in 2004. He's now one of the first names on any South African teamsheet.

THE FACTS Only Ian Healy (395) has made more dismissals than Boucher in Tests, and only Adam Gilchrist (439) heads him in ODIs ... His 125 v Zimbabwe at Harare in 1999-2000 was a Test record for a nightwatchman until Jason Gillespie surpassed it in 2006 ... He reached his century against Zimbabwe at Potchefstroom in September 2006 in only 44 balls, the second-fastest in all ODIs ... Boucher's run of 75 consecutive Tests between 1997-98 and 2004-05 is a South African record ... His figures include one Test for the World XI and five ODIs for the Africa XI ...

THE FIGURES
Batting and fielding   www.cricinfo.com

	M	Inns	NO	Runs	HS	Avge	S/R	100	50	4s	6s	Ct	St
Tests to 10.9.07	102	145	18	3844	125	30.26	50.98	4	25	481	14	376	16
ODIs to 10.9.07	250	183	44	3980	147*	28.63	84.78	1	25	304	72	351	18
First-class to 10.9.07	159	235	34	6836	134	34.00	–	8	42	–	–	543	29

Bowling

	M	Balls	Runs	Wkts	BB	Avge	RpO	S/R	5i	10m
Tests to 10.9.07	102	8	6	1	1–6	6.00	4.50	8.00	0	0
ODIs to 10.9.07	250	0	–	–	–	–	–	–	–	–
First-class to 10.9.07	159	26	26	1	1–6	26.00	6.00	26.00	0	0

27

NATHAN **BRACKEN**

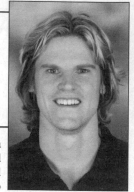

AUSTRALIA

Full name	**Nathan Wade Bracken**
Born	**September 12, 1977, Penrith, New South Wales**
Teams	**New South Wales**
Style	**Right-hand bat, left-arm fast-medium bowler**
Test debut	**Australia v India at Brisbane 2003-04**
ODI debut	**Australia v West Indies at Melbourne 2000-01**

THE PROFILE The search for a Test-class left-armer, a universal pursuit, first led Australia to Nathan Bracken. Tall and slim like Bruce Reid, Bracken bowls a full length, moves the ball both ways in the air and off the seam, and fitted easily into Australia's rampant one-day squad in 2000-01. He has also been instrumental in resuscitating New South Wales's fortunes, including 6 for 27 in their 2004-05 final win over Queensland and an amazing 7 for 4 earlier that season when South Australia fell for just 29 at the SCG. A shoulder injury cut short his maiden Ashes tour in 2001 after only two matches, but after a spell on the sidelines he returned to the side during the 2003 World Cup, when Jason Gillespie dropped out with a heel injury. Bracken's Test debut finally came in 2003-04, but in three outings against the powerful Indian batting line-up he failed to make real inroads. In the spring of 2004 he was omitted from Cricket Australia's list of centrally contracted players, but returned to the ODI scene for the Super Series late the following year and became a regular in green and gold, prompting him to withdraw from a planned county stint with Worcestershire. He elbowed his way past Mitchell Johnson to cement a one-day place in 2006-07, and contributed several telling performances in the defence of the World Cup, finishing with 16 wickets at 16.12.

THE FACTS Bracken's figures of 7-5-4-7 for New South Wales against South Australia at Sydney in December 2004 were described as "more like a PIN number than a bowling analysis" in the *Sydney Morning Herald*, which also called his yorker-heavy bowling to the South Africans "foot theory" ... He is 6ft 5ins (195cm) tall ... Seven of his 12 Test wickets have come at Brisbane ... Bracken has played 14 ODIs against New Zealand, but has never played against Pakistan ... He averages 14.40 with the ball in ODIs against Sri Lanka – but 94 against Zimbabwe ...

THE FIGURES

Batting and fielding

www.cricinfo.com

	M	Inns	NO	Runs	HS	Avge	S/R	100	50	4s	6s	Ct	St
Tests *to 10.9.07*	5	6	2	70	37	17.50	62.50	0	0	7	0	2	0
ODIs *to 10.9.07*	67	19	10	144	21*	16.00	85.20	0	0	7	5	14	0
First-class *to 10.9.07*	57	77	28	845	38*	17.24	–	0	0	–	–	15	0

Bowling

	M	Balls	Runs	Wkts	BB	Avge	RpO	S/R	5i	10m
Tests *to 10.9.07*	5	1110	505	12	4–48	42.08	2.72	92.50	0	0
ODIs *to 10.9.07*	67	3303	2393	112	5–67	21.36	4.34	29.49	1	0
First-class *to 10.9.07*	57	11346	4835	181	7–4	26.71	2.55	62.68	8	0

DWAYNE **BRAVO**

Full name	**Dwayne John Bravo**
Born	**October 7, 1983, Santa Cruz, Trinidad**
Teams	**Trinidad & Tobago**
Style	**Right-hand bat, right-arm fast-medium bowler**
Test debut	**West Indies v England at Lord's 2004**
ODI debut	**West Indies v England at Georgetown 2003-04**

THE PROFILE Dwayne Bravo is that creature long needed by West Indies, an allrounder. Born in Santa Cruz, like Brian Lara, Bravo made his one-day debut in April 2004, on the tenth anniversary of Lara's 375. He made his Test debut at Lord's three months later, and took three wickets in the first innings with his medium-paced swingers. He also showed a cool enough temperament to forge a confident start at the crease, displaying a straight bat even though his team was facing a big England total of 568. His follow-ups were even better. By the end of the series, West Indies were down and out, but at least they knew they had unearthed a special talent in Bravo. He scored plenty of runs and claimed a bunch of wickets in the four Tests, but nowhere was his ability more evident than at Manchester, where he top-scored and then restricted England with a six-wicket haul. He hit 107 against South Africa in Antigua in April 2005 as his maiden century, and played an even better innings the following November, a magnificent 113 at Hobart which forced the rampant Australians to wait till the fifth day to complete victory. He continued to chip in with handy runs, while a selection of slower balls makes him a handful in one-dayers, if less so in Tests. He's also assured in the field, and was one of the few plusses of the miserable 2007 tour of England, although even he was not immune to throwing his wicket away when well set.

THE FACTS Bravo's second Test century – 113 at Hobart late in 2005 – came during a stand of 182 with his fellow-Trinidadian Denesh Ramdin, the day after Trinidad & Tobago qualified for the soccer World Cup for the first time ... He was West Indies' leading wicket-taker (with 16) in his first Test series, in England in 2004 ... Bravo has now played 23 Tests without finishing on the winning side – a number exceeded over a whole career only by Bert Sutcliffe of New Zealand (42) and Zimbabwe's Bryan Strang (26) ...

THE FIGURES

Batting and fielding

www.cricinfo.com

	M	Inns	NO	Runs	HS	Avge	S/R	100	50	4s	6s	Ct	St
Tests *to 10.9.07*	23	42	1	1404	113	34.24	48.29	2	8	186	3	23	0
ODIs *to 10.9.07*	71	55	14	992	112*	24.19	79.10	1	2	85	8	30	0
First-class *to 10.9.07*	76	139	6	4121	197	30.98	–	7	22	–		62	0

Bowling

	M	Balls	Runs	Wkts	BB	Avge	RpO	S/R	5i	10m
Tests *to 10.9.07*	23	3558	1952	45	6–55	43.37	3.29	79.06	2	0
ODIs *to 10.9.07*	71	2726	2406	78	4–39	30.84	5.29	34.94	0	0
First-class *to 10.9.07*	76	7319	4057	120	6–11	33.80	3.32	60.99	6	0

ENGLAND

STUART **BROAD**

Full name **Stuart Christopher John Broad**
Born **June 24, 1986, Nottingham**
Teams **Leicestershire (Nottinghamshire in 2008)**
Style **Left-hand bat, right-arm fast-medium bowler**
Test debut **No Tests yet**
ODI debut **England v Pakistan at Cardiff 2006**

THE PROFILE   Stuart Broad was shaping up to be an opening bat just like his dad, Chris, until he suddenly shot up. Already well over six feet, he grew three inches over the winter of 2005. He had already transformed himself into a fast-medium bowler good enough to play for England Under-19s. And by the end of the 2006 season he was called into the full England one-day side. Talk about a meteoric rise: "I thought I may as well try bowling because I can't just stand around in the field all day," he said of the change that, in 2005, brought him nine cheap wickets in three U-19 ODIs against Sri Lanka, and 30 first-class wickets at 27.69 for Leicestershire too. And it got even better in 2006, as he collected four five-fors before that increasingly inevitable one-day summons. But his game could yet change again: Broad junior has aspirations to be an allrounder, and got close to a maiden century (and a maiden Test cap) in 2007. At just 19 he replaced James Anderson in the West Indies with England A, then made an impressive start to his full international career, keeping a cool head in the mayhem of a Twenty20 international, then claiming the early wicket of Shoaib Malik on his ODI debut, at Cardiff at the end of August 2006. He just missed selection for the World Cup, but stepped in when Jon Lewis returned home, and nervelessly hit the winning runs in England's last game, against West Indies. Nerves were also notably absent later in 2007 when Broad and Ravi Bopara took England to an unlikely one-day win over India at Old Trafford, and he even kept his cool shortly afterwards when being swatted for six sixes in an over by India's Yuvraj Singh in a Twenty20 international. He's got a smooth action, and as long as his not-so-broad back stands up to all that bowling – and all that growing – he has a glittering future.

THE FACTS   Broad took nine wickets for 72 in three Under-19 ODIs v Sri Lanka in England in 2005 ... He scored 91 not out for Leicestershire against Derbyshire in 2007 ... Broad's father, Chris, played 25 Tests for England in the 1980s, scoring 1661 runs with six centuries – he's now a match referee (see page 223) ...

THE FIGURES

Batting and fielding   www.cricinfo.com

	M	Inns	NO	Runs	HS	Avge	S/R	100	50	4s	6s	Ct	St
Tests *to 10.9.07*	0	0	–	–	–	–	–	–	–	–	–	–	–
ODIs *to 10.9.07*	16	11	7	126	45*	31.50	75.00	0	0	8	2	4	0
First-class *to 10.9.07*	33	40	11	643	91*	22.17	46.15	0	4	–	–	8	0

Bowling

	M	Balls	Runs	Wkts	BB	Avge	RpO	S/R	5i	10m
Tests *to 10.9.07*	0	0	–	–	–	–	–	–	–	–
ODIs *to 10.9.07*	16	812	697	19	4–51	36.68	5.15	42.73	0	0
First-class *to 10.9.07*	33	5253	3181	112	5–67	28.40	3.63	46.90	6	0

SHIVNARINE **CHANDERPAUL**

Full name	**Shivnarine Chanderpaul**
Born	**August 16, 1974, Unity Village, Demerara, Guyana**
Teams	**Guyana, Durham**
Style	**Left-hand bat, occasional legspinner**
Test debut	**West Indies v England at Georgetown 1993-94**
ODI debut	**West Indies v India at Faridabad 1994-95**

THE PROFILE Crouched and crabby at the crease, Shivnarine Chanderpaul proves there is life beyond the coaching handbook. He never seems to play in the V, or off the front foot, but uses soft hands, canny deflections and a whiplash pull to maintain an average in the mid-forties over more than 100 Tests. Early on he had a problem converting fifties into hundreds, and also missed a lot of matches, to the point that some thought him a hypochondriac. That was rectified when a large piece of floating bone was removed from his foot late in 2000, and, suitably liberated, he set about rectifying his hundreds problem too, collecting three in four Tests against India early in 2002, and two more against Australia the following year, including 104 in the successful chase for a world-record 418 in Antigua. A good run in South Africa in 2003-04 preceded a tough one at home against England – only his second lean trot in a decade – but he rediscovered his form in England, narrowly missing twin tons in the 2004 Lord's Test. The following year he was appointed captain during an acrimonious contracts dispute, and celebrated with 203 at home in Guyana, although he was too passive in the field to prevent South Africa taking the series. In April 2006 he stood down, after a tour of Australia where he struggled at the crease and in front of the microphone. In England in 2007 he was back to his limpet best, top-scoring in each of his five innings, and going more than 1000 minutes without being dismissed for the second time in his career. He can blast with the best in ODIs, and collected three unbeaten hundreds in the first half of 2007.

THE FACTS Chanderpaul averages 71.86 in Tests against India, but only 28.77 against Zimbabwe ... He scored 303 not out for Guyana against Jamaica at Kingston in January 1996 ... At Georgetown in April 2003 Chanderpaul reached his century against Australia in only 69 balls – the third-fastest in Test history by balls faced ... He once managed to shoot a policeman in the hand in his native Guyana, mistaking him for a mugger ...

THE FIGURES

Batting and fielding

www.cricinfo.com

	M	Inns	NO	Runs	HS	Avge	S/R	100	50	4s	6s	Ct	St
Tests to 10.9.07	104	178	24	7182	203*	46.63	43.31	16	43	837	17	44	0
ODIs to 10.9.07	222	208	29	6975	150	38.96	70.36	7	47	608	69	61	0
First-class to 10.9.07	207	339	56	14753	303*	52.13	–	41	73	–	–	125	0

Bowling

	M	Balls	Runs	Wkts	BB	Avge	RpO	S/R	5i	10m
Tests to 10.9.07	104	1680	845	8	1–2	105.62	3.01	210.00	0	0
ODIs to 10.9.07	222	716	617	14	3–18	44.07	5.17	51.14	0	0
First-class to 10.9.07	207	4610	2434	56	4–48	43.46	3.16	82.32	0	0

PIYUSH **CHAWLA**

Full name	**Piyush Pramod Chawla**
Born	**December 24, 1988, Aligarh, Uttar Pradesh**
Teams	**Uttar Pradesh**
Style	**Left-hand bat, legspinner**
Test debut	**India v England at Mohali 2005-06**
ODI debut	**India v Bangladesh at Dhaka 2006-07**

INDIA

THE PROFILE Less than a month after he was one of the stars of the Youth World Cup early in 2006, 17-year-old Piyush Chawla was making his Test debut against England, dismissing Andrew Flintoff for 51 as India glided to a nine-wicket win at Mohali. He had always been a young achiever: Chawla first hit the headlines for Uttar Pradesh's Under-14s, scoring 121 then taking 15 wickets for 69 in the demolition of Rajasthan's juniors. In October 2005 he bamboozled Sachin Tendulkar with a googly in the final of the Challenger Trophy (a trial tournament for India's one-day team), and dismissed Mahendra Singh Dhoni and Yuvraj Singh as well: then he led the wicket-takers at the Youth World Cup in Sri Lanka. He took 4 for 8 as the holders Pakistan were shot out for 109 in the final, then surveyed the wreckage with 25 not out as India were demolished for 79 themselves. Although he is no slouch with the bat, it is as a legspinner that Chawla has made his mark – he already has wonderful control of his variations, with a well-disguised googly and a flipper, and is not afraid to give the ball air. In 2007, he was given an extended run in the one-day team, replacing Anil Kumble who retired from ODIs after the World Cup, and impressing with his cool bowling against England. He also did well with India's A team in Zimbabwe and Kenya, and is very much a star in the making – he could well develop into a formidable allrounder.

THE FACTS Piyush Chawla was 17 years and 75 days old when he made his Test debut in March 2006: the only younger Indian debutant was Sachin Tendulkar ... He took 4 for 12 and 6 for 46 as India A hammered a Zimbabwe Select XI at Bulawayo in July 2007... Chawla scored 146 while captaining India in an Under-19 Test v Pakistan at Peshawar in September 2006: he added 119 (and then took 5 for 19) v New Zealand U19s at Lincoln in January 2007 ... For Uttar Pradesh Under-14s v Rajasthan at Kanpur in December 2001 Chawla made 121 and then took 7 for 32 and 8 for 37 ...

THE FIGURES

Batting and fielding
www.cricinfo.com

	M	Inns	NO	Runs	HS	Avge	S/R	100	50	4s	6s	Ct	St
Tests to 10.9.07	1	1	0	1	1	1.00	11.11	0	0	0	0	0	0
ODIs to 10.9.07	13	7	3	20	13*	5.00	58.82	0	0	1	0	5	0
First-class to 10.9.07	24	34	2	818	75	25.56	–	0	7	–	–	11	0

Bowling

	M	Balls	Runs	Wkts	BB	Avge	RpO	S/R	5i	10m
Tests to 10.9.07	1	85	53	1	1–8	53.00	3.74	85.00	0	0
ODIs to 10.9.07	13	666	538	17	3–29	31.64	4.84	39.17	0	0
First-class to 10.9.07	24	5190	2501	110	6–46	22.73	2.89	47.18	8	1

AUSTRALIA

STUART **CLARK**

Full name	**Stuart Rupert Clark**
Born	**September 28, 1975, Sutherland, Sydney, NSW**
Teams	**New South Wales, Hampshire**
Style	**Right-hand bat, right-arm fast-medium bowler**
Test debut	**Australia v South Africa at Cape Town 2005-06**
ODI debut	**Australia v World XI at Melbourne 2005-06**

THE PROFILE Stuart Clark is a tall and lanky opening bowler often described as "in the Glenn McGrath mould". Appropriately, in his opening Test series in South Africa early in 2006, 30-year-old Clark replaced McGrath, who was caring for his sick wife, and experienced a dream entry: 20 wickets at 15.75 made him Player of the Series. A borderline selection for the first Test, he earned victory with 5 for 55 and 4 for 34, the third-best match figures by an Australian debutant after Bob Massie and Clarrie Grimmett. A former real-estate agent in Sydney who crams in study for a commerce and law degree, Clark was a late cricket developer, finally emerging at 27 after a battle with body as much as talent. Not to be confused with NSW team-mate Michael Clarke, or Michael Clark, the WA left-armer, this Clark earned a central contract with 45 wickets in 2001-02, but lost it the following summer after ankle and rib injuries. Hernia surgery was next, quickly followed by a leg problem, but he took 40 wickets in NSW's 2004-05 Pura Cup triumph. Clark, who troubles batsmen with his height (197cm) and seam movement, showed there was room for him and McGrath in the same side by topping the averages (26 wickets at 17.03) in the 2006-07 Ashes whitewash, although after that he was a back number in the World Cup. The child of Indian-born parents who met in England, he wants to be the chief executive of New South Wales Cricket when he grows up. After his dramatic entry into Test cricket's playground, that may not be for some time.

THE FACTS During the memorable 2005 Ashes tour, Clark was twice called into the Australian squad from county cricket with Middlesex as cover for injured bowlers, but did not play in a Test ... His nickname is "Sarfraz", after a vague resemblance – in appearance and run-up – to the former Pakistan fast bowler Sarfraz Nawaz ... Clark's international debut was against the World XI in October 2005, and his first wicket was Kevin Pietersen ... He took 8 for 58 for NSW v Western Australia – a hat-trick reducing them to 2 for 4 – at Perth in Feb 2007 ...

THE FIGURES

Batting and fielding   www.cricinfo.com

	M	Inns	NO	Runs	HS	Avge	S/R	100	50	4s	6s	Ct	St
Tests *to 10.9.07*	9	10	2	116	39	14.50	69.46	0	0	8	2	2	0
ODIs *to 10.9.07*	25	8	5	59	16*	19.66	86.76	0	0	6	1	7	0
First-class *to 10.9.07*	79	106	29	1092	62	14.18	–	0	1	–	–	24	0

Bowling

	M	Balls	Runs	Wkts	BB	Avge	RpO	S/R	5i	10m
Tests *to 10.9.07*	9	2048	837	47	5-55	17.80	2.45	43.57	1	0
ODIs *to 10.9.07*	25	1266	1133	36	4-54	31.47	5.36	35.16	0	0
First-class *to 10.9.07*	79	16290	7926	294	8-58	26.95	2.91	55.40	12	1

MICHAEL **CLARKE**

AUSTRALIA

Full name **Michael John Clarke**
Born **April 2, 1981, Liverpool, New South Wales**
Teams **New South Wales**
Style **Right-hand bat, slow left-arm orthodox spinner**
Test debut **Australia v India at Bangalore 2003-04**
ODI debut **Australia v England at Adelaide 2002-03**

THE PROFILE   Michael Clarke was being touted as Australia's next captain before he'd even played a Test. And when he marked his eventual debut with 151 against India in October 2004, his future looked even brighter than the yellow motorbike he received as Man of the Match. Another thrilling century followed on his home debut, and his first Test season ended with the Allan Border Medal. Then came the fall. Barely a year later came the fateful phone-call: dropped after 15 century-less Tests. He was told to tighten his technique, especially early on against swing. Clarke remained a one-day fixture, but had to wait until the low-key Bangladesh series early in 2006 to reclaim that Test place. He cemented his place with two tons in the 2006-07 Ashes whitewash, and did well in the World Cup, averaging 87.20. Until his sacking he was a ravishing shot-maker who did not so much take guard as take off: he radiated a pointy-elbowed elegance reminiscent of the young Greg Chappell or Mark Waugh – who both also waited uncomplainingly for a Test opening then started with a ton. Unlike them, Clarke cut his teeth in Australia's one-day side. His impact in pyjamas was startling: 208 runs before being dismissed. His bouncy fielding and searing run-outs, usually from square on, add to his value, while his left-arm tweakers can surprise (they shocked six Indians in a Test at Mumbai). A cricket nut since he was in nappies, "Pup" honed his technique against the bowling machine at his dad's indoor centre.

THE FACTS   Clarke scored a century on his Test debut, 151 v India at Bangalore in 2004-05, and the following month added another in his first home Test, 141 v New Zealand at Brisbane: only two other batsmen have done this for Australia – Harry Graham and Kepler Wessels ... Clarke played county cricket for Hampshire, under the captaincy of Shane Warne ... He averages 57.14 in Tests in India, but only 30.28 in ten other overseas Tests ... A skin-cancer scare late in 2005 persuaded Clarke to swap a traditional cap for a wide-brimmed sunhat ...

THE FIGURES
Batting and fielding
www.cricinfo.com

	M	Inns	NO	Runs	HS	Avge	S/R	100	50	4s	6s	Ct	St
Tests *to 10.9.07*	27	41	5	1512	151	42.00	56.48	4	5	178	13	20	0
ODIs *to 10.9.07*	112	98	25	3329	105*	45.60	82.85	2	25	294	23	42	0
First-class *to 10.9.07*	80	135	12	5111	201*	41.55	–	17	18	–	–	74	0

Bowling

	M	Balls	Runs	Wkts	BB	Avge	RpO	S/R	5i	10m
Tests *to 10.9.07*	27	260	128	8	6–9	16.00	2.95	32.50	1	0
ODIs *to 10.9.07*	112	1376	1198	32	5–35	37.43	5.22	43.00	1	0
First-class *to 10.9.07*	80	1209	684	15	6–9	45.60	3.39	80.60	1	0

PAUL **COLLINGWOOD**

Full name	**Paul David Collingwood**
Born	**May 26, 1976, Shotley Bridge, Co. Durham**
Teams	**Durham**
Style	**Right-hand bat, right-arm medium-pace bowler**
Test debut	**England v Sri Lanka at Galle 2003-04**
ODI debut	**England v Pakistan at Birmingham 2001**

THE PROFILE While Paul Collingwood was flitting around the fringes of the England team, it seemed that he was perhaps the first specialist fielder to earn regular selection in a Test squad. He made the one-day side in 2001, but four years and numerous tours later had won only three Test caps. The third of those, however, was the single biggest match of his generation: the Ashes decider against Australia at The Oval in 2005. He still seemed destined to be the uncomplaining stand-in – but that winter struck 96 and 80 at Lahore, and added a brilliant century against India, as England struggled with injuries. Then at home in 2006 he cracked a coruscating 186 against Pakistan at Lord's, to make a middle-order place his own at last, and joined rarefied company the following winter with an Ashes double-century at Adelaide. He had already become probably the finest fielder around, capable of breathtaking moments at backward point or in the slips. With the bat he stands still, plays straight, and has all the shots. In Australia in 2002-03 he started the one-dayers as 12th man, but was soon spanking a memorable maiden century against Sri Lanka at Perth – a round 100 that cemented his spot for the 2003 World Cup: after England's travails in the 2007 tournament, he took over as one-day captain. His bowling, which verges towards the dibbly-dobbly, is negligible in Tests, but given the right conditions he can be irresistible in one-dayers – as at Trent Bridge in 2005, when he followed a rapid century against Bangladesh with 6 for 31.

THE FACTS Collingwood's century and six wickets in the same match – against Bangladesh at Nottingham in 2005 – is unmatched in ODI history: his 6 for 31 that day are also England's best one-day bowling figures ... He made 206 at Adelaide in December 2006, England's first double-century in a Test in Australia since Wally Hammond in 1936-37 ... In September 2006 Collingwood became the 11th man to play 100 ODIs for England ...

THE FIGURES

Batting and fielding

www.cricinfo.com

	M	Inns	NO	Runs	HS	Avge	S/R	100	50	4s	6s	Ct	St
Tests *to 10.9.07*	27	51	5	2016	206	43.82	45.14	5	6	224	12	37	0
ODIs *to 11.9.06*	131	119	27	3290	120*	35.76	75.44	4	17	244	35	79	0
First-class *to 11.9.06*	146	257	19	8573	206	36.02	–	10	40		–	157	0

Bowling

	M	Balls	Runs	Wkts	BB	Avge	RpO	S/R	5i	10m
Tests *to 11.9.06*	27	773	425	6	2–24	70.83	3.29	128.83	0	0
ODIs *to 11.9.06*	131	3266	2750	67	6–31	41.04	5.05	48.74	1	0
First-class *to 11.9.06*	146	8425	4241	105	5–52	40.39	3.02	80.23	1	0

PEDRO **COLLINS**

Full name	**Pedro Tyrone Collins**
Born	**August 12, 1976, Boscobelle, St Peter, Barbados**
Teams	**Barbados**
Style	**Right-hand bat, left-arm fast-medium bowler**
Test debut	**West Indies v Australia at Port-of-Spain 1998-99**
ODI debut	**West Indies v Pakistan at Sharjah 1999-2000**

THE PROFILE A fast-medium left-armer, Pedro Collins has bowled alongside genuine pacemen like Curtly Ambrose, Courtney Walsh and Ian Bishop, but initially failed to display the kind of stamina required to sustain long spells. Collins's bowling follows the lineage of Bernard Julien and Garry Sobers: like them he finds enough swing into the right-hander to cause the best of them difficulty. In November 1998 he took three wickets in 11 balls for West Indies A against India, which led to his Test debut against Australia the following March. For a long time after that he was best remembered for an injury of the cruellest kind, when a Jason Gillespie delivery trapped a testicle outside his box. After getting his breath back he worked on his fitness, and returned to the side in 2001-02, with a higher arm action and an extra yard of pace. He took just nine wickets in West Indies' series victory over India, but that included Sachin Tendulkar three times. He struggled on India's flat pitches, though, before terrorising Bangladesh in 2002-03. Then, after struggling against the Aussies, Collins didn't play for close to a year. But he returned to take on England in March 2004 and immediately removed Michael Vaughan, before taking three more wickets. He found himself overtaken by a clutch of other pace bowlers – including his half-brother Fidel Edwards – and couldn't force his way back into the international side in 2006-07, despite claiming a career-best 6 for 24 for Barbados against the Windward Islands in Dominica.

THE FACTS Uniquely, Collins has three times taken a wicket with the first ball of a Test – and the victim each time was Bangladesh's Hannan Sarkar ... He averages 21.00 with the ball in Tests v New Zealand, but 102.33 v Pakistan ... Collins opened the bowling against England at Bridgetown in April 2004 (and several times subsequently) with his half-brother, Fidel Edwards ... In two home Tests against Australia in 2003 Collins took 1 for 263 – he recovered with 25 in five matches against England and Bangladesh the following year ...

THE FIGURES

Batting and fielding   www.cricinfo.com

	M	Inns	NO	Runs	HS	Avge	S/R	100	50	4s	6s	Ct	St
Tests to 10.9.07	32	47	7	235	24	5.87	33.52	0	0	30	0	7	0
ODIs to 10.9.07	30	12	5	30	10*	4.28	60.00	0	0	1	0	8	0
First-class to 10.9.07	100	126	30	621	25	6.46	–	0	0	–	–	26	0

Bowling

	M	Balls	Runs	Wkts	BB	Avge	RpO	S/R	5i	10m
Tests to 10.9.07	32	6964	3671	106	6–53	34.63	3.63	65.69	3	0
ODIs to 10.9.07	30	1577	1212	39	5–43	31.07	4.61	40.43	1	0
First-class to 10.9.07	100	17513	8805	341	6–24	25.82	3.01	51.35	7	0

COREY **COLLYMORE**

Full name	**Corey Dalanelo Collymore**
Born	**December 21, 1977, Boscobelle, St Peter, Barbados**
Teams	**Barbados**
Style	**Right-hand bat, right-arm fast-medium bowler**
Test debut	**West Indies v Australia at St John's 1998-99**
ODI debut	**West Indies v India at Toronto 1999-2000**

THE PROFILE   Corey Collymore isn't genuinely fast, but he is accurate and aggressive at a shade above fast-medium. His sprint to the crease is reminiscent of Malcolm Marshall's, but there the similarities largely end: Collymore's open-chested delivery seems to limit his ability to move the ball away from right-handers. He has suffered from the bane of modern fast bowlers – stress fractures. But he is a determined man, who recovered from injuries when critics had written him off at the end of the 2000 England tour, and fulfilled his promise to get back into the game. He took four wickets on his return to the one-day side in Zimbabwe in 2001, as West Indies beat India in the final of the Coca-Cola Cup, and after a moderately successful 2003 World Cup he was recalled to the Test team for the home series against Sri Lanka. He responded with five wickets in the drawn first Test, and 7 for 57 in the second as West Indies sealed a seven-wicket victory. Despite that, Collymore remained a fringe member of the side, frequently left out then included mid-series to add experience. In England in 2004 he often opened the bowling, but although he put the ball in the right place his inability to put the wind up batsmen meant he was largely ineffective. But still he hung in there, taking another seven-wicket haul against Pakistan at Sabina Park in June 2005, and 15 wickets in the four matches against India the following year. Back in England in 2007 he again looked innocuous at times, before occasionally producing some late swing and finishing with 11 rather expensive wickets in the four Tests.

THE FACTS   Collymore's 11 for 134 against Pakistan in June 2005 are the best match figures in any Test at Kingston, Jamaica – and his 7 for 57 against Sri Lanka at Sabina Park two years previously are West Indies' best figures in an innings there ... Collymore averages 11.35 with the ball in Tests against Sri Lanka – and 57.00 against South Africa ... He has taken 48 wickets at 22.79 in home Tests, and 45 at 42.44 away ...

THE FIGURES

Batting and fielding

www.cricinfo.com

	M	Inns	NO	Runs	HS	Avge	S/R	100	50	4s	6s	Ct	St
Tests *to 10.9.07*	30	52	27	197	16*	7.88	30.68	0	0	19	0	6	0
ODIs *to 10.9.07*	84	35	17	104	13*	5.77	39.84	0	0	5	2	12	0
First-class *to 10.9.07*	85	125	61	502	20	7.84	–	0	0	–	–	28	0

Bowling

	M	Balls	Runs	Wkts	BB	Avge	RpO	S/R	5i	10m
Tests *to 10.9.07*	30	6337	3004	93	7–57	32.30	2.84	68.13	4	1
ODIs *to 10.9.07*	84	4074	2924	83	5–51	35.22	4.30	49.08	1	0
First-class *to 10.9.07*	85	14877	7054	266	7–57	26.51	2.84	55.92	10	2

ALASTAIR **COOK**

Full name	**Alastair Nathan Cook**
Born	**December 25, 1984, Gloucester**
Teams	**Essex**
Style	**Left-hand bat, occasional offspinner**
Test debut	**England v India at Nagpur 2005-06**
ODI debut	**England v Sri Lanka at Manchester 2006**

THE PROFILE   Those in the know were saying that the tall, dark and handsome Alastair Cook was destined for great things very early on. A stylish left-hander with a simple approach to batting, Cook was thrown straight in at the deep end by Essex only a year after he left Bedford School, where he broke all sorts of records. He captained England in the Under-19 World Cup early in 2004, making two centuries in leading them to the semi-final, then scored his maiden first-class hundred later that year, impressing his seasoned Essex team-mates Andy Flower and Darren Gough. After a fine 2005 season, which included a double-century against the touring Australians, he was called up by England when injuries struck the following spring. He had been touring the Caribbean with England A when the SOS came but, unfazed, he racked up 60 in his first Test innings, against India at Nagpur, then added a magnificent 104 to become the 16th England batsman to make a century on debut. He succumbed to illness himself before that tour was done, but bounced back with 89 against Sri Lanka at Lord's in May 2006, then made sure his name was on MCC's honours board by adding 105 against Pakistan two months later. He made another upright century in the next Test, at Manchester, and survived a tough Ashes baptism, making 276 runs (with 116 at Perth) in the 2006-07 whitewash. Bowlers began to notice a tendency to play around the front pad, but Cook still had a good home summer in 2007, failing to reach double figures only once in 13 Test innings, and collecting two more hundreds, both against West Indies.

THE FACTS   Cook was the 16th England batsman to make a century on Test debut: the previous two (Andrew Strauss and Graham Thorpe) were also left-handers ... Cook's stand of 127 with Marcus Trescothick v Sri Lanka at Lord's in 2005 was the second-highest in Tests by unrelated players who share a birthday (they were both born on Christmas Day), behind the 163 of Vic Stollmeyer and Kenneth Weekes (both born Jan 24) for West Indies at The Oval in 1939 ... Cook won the Cricket Writers' Club's Young Cricketer of the Year award in 2005 ...

THE FIGURES

Batting and fielding   www.cricinfo.com

	M	Inns	NO	Runs	HS	Avge	S/R	100	50	4s	6s	Ct	St
Tests to 10.9.07	21	39	2	1658	127	44.81	47.10	6	6	190	0	19	0
ODIs to 10.9.07	11	11	0	328	102	29.81	76.10	1	0	42	0	3	0
First-class to 10.9.07	69	123	11	5297	195	47.29	54.85	17	25	–	–	71	0

Bowling

	M	Balls	Runs	Wkts	BB	Avge	RpO	S/R	5i	10m
Tests to 10.9.07	21	0	–	–	–	–	–	–	–	–
ODIs to 10.9.07	11	0	–	–	–	–	–	–	–	–
First-class to 10.9.07	69	156	117	3	3–13	39.00	4.50	52.00	0	0

DAN **CULLEN**

Full name **Daniel James Cullen**
Born **April 10, 1984, Woodville, Adelaide, South Australia**
Teams **South Australia**
Style **Right-hand bat, offspinner**
Test debut **Australia v Bangladesh at Chittagong 2005-06**
ODI debut **Australia v Bangladesh at Chittagong 2005-06**

THE PROFILE South Australia's impressive list of slow bowlers has a new addition: after Clarrie Grimmett, Ashley Mallett, Terry Jenner and Tim May, meet offspinner Dan Cullen. An exciting dyed-blond deceiver, Cullen was originally tipped to replace Shane Warne as Australia's top spinner, and has developed similar characteristics to the hero he chased for an autograph as a ten-year-old. A crafty heavy-turner who can send down the occasional mysterious doosra, Cullen has shown that he is unafraid to upset batsmen with flight, dip, spin ... or verbal banter. At 20 in 2004-05, he burst into the Pura Cup with 43 wickets at 30.37, and while his second summer was harder – there was a broken finger to go with 27 victims at 47.88 – he was named the Bradman Young Cricketer of the Year. "He has all the toys, he is young and he has got a bit of fire about him," said Warne. "He will definitely play for Australia." That prediction was fulfilled in Bangladesh early in 2006, when – after being given the baggy green by his hero Warne – Cullen formed part of a three-pronged spin attack for the second Test, taking one wicket in his 14 overs. He stayed on for the one-day series, and was economical, securing a central contract ahead of the Victoria legspinner Cameron White. But Cullen went backwards in 2006, making little impression at Somerset, where he averaged 54.42 with the ball, and struggling further back home, losing his state place after an indifferent start to the season. He has much ground to make up in the race to replace his hero.

THE FACTS When Cullen made his Test debut at Chittagong in April 2006 alongside Shane Warne and Stuart MacGill, it was the first time since January 1999 that Australia had fielded three specialist spinners in the same side (Warne, MacGill and Colin Miller against England at Sydney) ... Two of Cullen's four five-wicket hauls have come against Western Australia, including his career-best 5 for 38 in March 2005 ...

THE FIGURES

Batting and fielding

www.cricinfo.com

	M	Inns	NO	Runs	HS	Avge	S/R	100	50	4s	6s	Ct	St
Tests *to 10.9.07*	1	0	–	–	–	–	–	–	–	–	–	0	0
ODIs *to 10.9.07*	5	1	1	2	2*	–	66.66	0	0	0	0	2	0
First-class *to 10.9.07*	32	42	18	376	42	15.66	–	0	0	–	–	9	0

Bowling

	M	Balls	Runs	Wkts	BB	Avge	RpO	S/R	5i	10m
Tests *to 10.9.07*	1	84	54	1	1–25	54.00	3.85	84.00	0	0
ODIs *to 10.9.07*	5	213	147	2	2–25	73.50	4.14	106.50	0	0
First-class *to 10.9.07*	32	7400	3999	97	5–38	41.22	3.24	76.28	4	0

DANISH KANERIA

Full name	**Danish Parabha Shanker Kaneria**
Born	**December 16, 1980, Karachi, Sind**
Teams	**Karachi, Habib Bank, Essex**
Style	**Right-hand bat, legspinner**
Test debut	**Pakistan v England at Faisalabad 2000-01**
ODI debut	**Pakistan v Zimbabwe at Sharjah 2001-02**

THE PROFILE A tall, wiry legspinner, and only the second Hindu to play Test cricket for Pakistan, Danish Kaneria mastered the dark arts of wrist-spin at an early age. His stock ball drifts in to the right-hander, and he has a googly as cloaked as any in recent history. His whirling approach is reminiscent of Abdul Qadir's, and he has now picked up the baton from Mushtaq Ahmed as Pakistan's premier legspinner. Kaneria was hyped as a secret weapon when England toured Pakistan in 2000-01, and although his impact in that Test series was minimal, he has since made his mark. Initially he did so against Bangladesh, but then turned it on against South Africa too, in October 2003, when his five-for decided the Lahore Test. Since then, Kaneria has confirmed himself as a matchwinner, and has quietly moved to the verge of 200 Test wickets. Two tours in 2004–05 – to Australia and the graveyard of legspin, India – were arduous but satisfying stepping stones to the big league. In each series he outscalped the opposition's leading legspinner – Shane Warne, then Anil Kumble – and although Pakistan still lost to Australia, Kaneria's 19 wickets were crucial in securing a morale-boosting draw in India. He ended 2005 with two more matchwinning last-day turns against England at home, but proved expensive when the teams reconvened the following summer in England, where he has had a lot of success with Essex. A back number in one-dayers, he had played only one of Pakistan's previous 27 ODIs before being a surprise inclusion for the 2007 World Cup. He did well enough, but lost his place in the shake-up after that disastrous campaign.

THE FACTS Danish Kaneria was only the second Hindu to play for Pakistan – the first, 1980s wicketkeeper Anil Dalpat, is his cousin ... He took 12 for 92 in his third Test, against Bangladesh in August 2001 ... Kaneria averages 16.41 v Bangladesh – but 45.14 v England ... He has conceded more than 100 runs in an innings 28 times in 46 Tests ... He took 0 for 208 for Essex v Lancashire at Manchester in 2005, equalling the most expensive wicketless spell in the County Championship, set by Peter Smith, another Essex legspinner, in 1934 ...

THE FIGURES

Batting and fielding   www.cricinfo.com

	M	Inns	NO	Runs	HS	Avge	S/R	100	50	4s	6s	Ct	St
Tests *to 10.9.07*	46	62	29	230	29	6.96	48.01	0	0	30	2	15	0
ODIs *to 10.9.07*	18	10	8	12	6*	6.00	54.54	0	0	1	0	2	0
First-class *to 10.9.07*	121	149	65	819	65	9.75	–	0	1	–	–	39	0

Bowling

	M	Balls	Runs	Wkts	BB	Avge	RpO	S/R	5i	10m
Tests *to 10.9.07*	46	13034	6408	198	7-77	32.36	2.94	65.82	12	2
ODIs *to 10.9.07*	18	854	683	15	3-31	45.53	4.79	56.93	0	0
First-class *to 10.9.07*	121	32336	15410	582	7-39	26.47	2.85	55.56	42	6

AB de VILLIERS

Full name	**Abraham Benjamin de Villiers**
Born	**February 17, 1984, Pretoria**
Teams	**Titans**
Style	**Right-hand bat, occ. medium-pacer, wicketkeeper**
Test debut	**South Africa v England at Port Elizabeth 2004-05**
ODI debut	**South Africa v England at Bloemfontein 2004-05**

THE PROFILE Few Test newcomers can have been asked to play so many roles so quickly as AB de Villiers, and fewer still can have risen to the challenge with such alacrity that, at just 21, he was already being regarded as the future of South African cricket.

de Villiers is a natural sportsman: tennis, golf, cricket or rugby could have been his calling. Cricket won out, however, and after starring in the national Under-19 team he made his debut for Titans in 2003-04, racking up five half-centuries in his 438 runs. He won his first Test cap the following season against England, and after a composed debut as an opener, he was handed the wicketkeeping gloves for the second Test at Durban, which he helped save with a maiden half-century down at No. 7. By the end of the series, however, he was going in first again, and after falling eight short of a deserved century in the first innings at Centurion, he made instant amends second time around. His development continued apace in the Caribbean, where he helped seal the series with a wonderful 178 at Bridgetown. Then came the almost inevitable dip in fortunes. In Australia in 2005-06 de Villiers managed just 152 runs at 25.33 – despite playing Shane Warne well – and missed the one-day VB Series. But he re-established himself in 2006-07, especially impressive in ODIs. He had a curious World Cup, collecting four ducks as well as a rousing 92 against Australia and a stroke-filled 146 – despite suffering with terrible cramp – against West Indies.

THE FACTS AB de Villiers averages 55.42 in four Tests at Centurion – but only 8.50 from four at Johannesburg ... He scored 151, his maiden first-class century, for Titans v Western Province Boland at Benoni in October 2004, sharing a stand of 317 with Martin van Jaarsveld ... de Villiers has not yet been dismissed for 0 in Tests, but collected four ducks during the 2007 World Cup ... His record includes five ODIs for the Africa XI ...

THE FIGURES

Batting and fielding

	M	Inns	NO	Runs	HS	Avge	S/R	100	50	4s	6s	Ct	St
Tests to 10.9.07	28	52	2	1757	178	35.14	52.52	3	10	239	4	41	1
ODIs to 10.9.07	51	50	4	1626	146	35.34	87.13	2	10	188	34	28	0
First-class to 10.9.07	47	88	5	3265	178	39.33	58.03	5	22	–	–	83	2

Bowling

	M	Balls	Runs	Wkts	BB	Avge	RpO	S/R	5i	10m
Tests to 10.9.07	28	198	99	2	2-49	49.50	3.00	99.00	0	0
ODIs to 10.9.07	51	12	22	0	–	–	11.00	–	0	0
First-class to 10.9.07	47	204	99	2	2-49	49.50	3.00	102.00	0	0

MAHENDRA SINGH **DHONI**

Full name	**Mahendra Singh Dhoni**
Born	**July 7, 1981, Ranchi, Bihar**
Teams	**Jharkhand**
Style	**Right-hand bat, wicketkeeper**
Test debut	**India v Sri Lanka at Chennai 2005-06**
ODI debut	**India v Bangladesh at Chittagong 2004-05**

THE PROFILE   The spectacular arrival of Virender Sehwag was bound to inspire others to bat with the same approach. But the odds of a clone emerging from the backwaters of Jharkhand (formerly Bihar), whose state side has consistently floundered, were highly remote. That was until Mahendra Singh Dhoni arrived (a one-time railway ticket collector, his first love was football). He can be muscularly swashbuckling with the bat, and secure with the wicketkeeping gloves. His long hair adds to his dash. He started in first-class cricket in 1999-2000, but it wasn't until 2004 that he became a serious contender for national selection, after some stirring performances when the occasion demanded – a rapid hundred as East Zone clinched the Deodhar Trophy, and an audacious 60 in the Duleep Trophy final. But it was his two centuries against Pakistan A, in a triangular tournament in Kenya, that established him as a clinical destroyer of bowling attacks and earned him a senior chance. In just his fifth ODI – against Pakistan at Visakhapatnam in April 2005 – Dhoni cracked a dazzling 148, putting even Sehwag in the shade, and followed that with a colossal 183 not out against Sri Lanka in November, breaking Adam Gilchrist's record for the highest score by a wicketkeeper in ODIs. He made an instant impact at Test level, too, pounding 148 at Faisalabad in only his fifth match, when India were struggling to avoid the follow-on. His keeping has improved – he was impressive in the Caribbean in 2006 – and he has quickly established himself as a key member of a revitalised side. He stepped up to captain India in the World Twenty20 championship in September 2007.

THE FACTS   Dhoni's unbeaten 183 against Sri Lanka at Jaipur in November 2005 is the highest score in ODIs by a wicketkeeper, and included 120 in boundaries – 10 sixes and 15 fours – a record at the time but later beaten by Herschelle Gibbs ... The only other Indian to score a century in an ODI in which he kept wicket is Rahul Dravid ... Dhoni's record includes three ODIs for the Asia XI ...

THE FIGURES

Batting and fielding   www.cricinfo.com

	M	Inns	NO	Runs	HS	Avge	S/R	100	50	4s	6s	Ct	St
Tests to 10.9.07	20	32	4	1019	148	36.39	72.94	1	6	130	23	53	10
ODIs to 11.9.06	84	75	19	2477	183*	44.23	96.26	3	14	206	71	82	21
First-class to 11.9.06	58	95	7	3082	148	35.02	–	4	19	–	–	157	26

Bowling

	M	Balls	Runs	Wkts	BB	Avge	RpO	S/R	5i	10m
Tests to 11.9.06	20	6	13	0	–	–	13.00	–	0	0
ODIs to 11.9.06	84	0	–	–	–	–	–	–	–	–
First-class to 11.9.06	58	36	33	0	–	–	5.50	–	0	0

TILLAKARATNE **DILSHAN**

Full name	**Tillakaratne Mudiyanselage Dilshan**
Born	**October 14, 1976, Kalutara**
Teams	**Bloomfield**
Style	**Right-hand bat, offspinner**
Test debut	**Sri Lanka v Zimbabwe at Bulawayo 1999-2000**
ODI debut	**Sri Lanka v Zimbabwe at Bulawayo 1999-2000**

THE PROFILE Tillakaratne Mudiyanselage Dilshan, who started life as Tuwan Mohamad Dilshan before converting to Buddhism, is a light-footed right-hander who burst onto the international scene with an unbeaten 163 against a strong Zimbabwe side in only his second Test in November 1999. Technically sound, comfortable against fast bowling, possessed of quick feet, strong wrists and natural timing, Dilshan has talent in abundance. But the bright start to his career was followed by a frustrating 15 months when he was shovelled up and down the order, and in and out of the side. After a lean series against England in 2001 – 51 runs in four innings – he didn't play another Test until England toured again at the end of 2003. He came back mentally stronger, and determined to play his own natural aggressive game. This approach was immediately successful, with several good scores against England and Australia, and then – rather more surprisingly for someone who started as a wicketkeeper – came some matchwinning bowling performances with his offspin. He has continued to be a steady influence in the middle order, although his Test average is still below 40. He put a lean trot in ODIs in 2006-07 behind him just in time for the World Cup, where he made some useful runs, without going on to a big score, in Sri Lanka's march to the final. He brings an added dimension to the team, especially in one-day cricket, with his brilliant fielding – he effected four run-outs in the first final of the VB Series at Adelaide in February 2006.

THE FACTS Dilshan's 21 first-class centuries include a score of 200 not out while captaining North Central Province against Central in Colombo in February 2005 ... His highest Test score of 168 came against Bangladesh in Colombo in September 2005: he put on 280 with Thilan Samaraweera, a Sri Lankan fifth-wicket record in Tests ... Dilshan made his first ODI century in the record total of 443 for 9 against the Netherlands at Amstelveen in July 2006 ... He started as a wicketkeeper and has 23 first-class stumpings to his name ...

THE FIGURES

Batting and fielding   www.cricinfo.com

	M	Inns	NO	Runs	HS	Avge	S/R	100	50	4s	6s	Ct	St
Tests to 10.9.07	42	66	8	2152	168	37.10	56.76	4	10	276	5	45	0
ODIs to 10.9.07	126	106	23	2444	117*	29.44	79.06	1	9	201	12	58	1
First-class to 10.9.07	167	270	19	9363	200*	37.30	–	21	41	–	–	297	23

Bowling

	M	Balls	Runs	Wkts	BB	Avge	RpO	S/R	5i	10m
Tests to 10.9.07	42	630	298	7	2–4	42.57	2.83	90.00	0	0
ODIs to 10.9.07	126	2307	1814	41	4–29	44.24	4.71	56.26	0	0
First-class to 10.9.07	167	2896	1373	45	5–49	30.51	2.84	64.35	1	0

BOETA **DIPPENAAR**

Full name	**Hendrik Human Dippenaar**
Born	**June 14, 1977, Kimberley, Cape Province**
Teams	**Eagles**
Style	**Right-hand bat, occasional offspinner**
Test debut	**South Africa v Zimbabwe at Bloemfontein 1999-2000**
ODI debut	**South Africa v India at Nairobi 1999-2000**

THE PROFILE A year after making his Test debut in 1999, Boeta Dippenaar scored his maiden century against New Zealand at Johannesburg, before unluckily losing his place at the top of the order to the recalled Herschelle Gibbs. He grabbed his chance of returning to the Test team, after South Africa's disastrous 2003 World Cup, with an unbeaten 178 against lowly Bangladesh. But he remains on the fringe of the Test side, playing only once in each of the last two seasons. Prolific first-class run-scorers occasionally have their weaknesses exposed by top-class opposition, and so it was with Dippenaar, who quickly found that his tendency to play across and around his back-foot defensive strokes was costly against better bowlers. He worked hard to rectify the problem. He is not a tall man, yet he bats like one, seemingly able to reach the pitch of every ball bowled on or outside off stump and drive it through the covers. Reach and sweetness of timing are the foundations of his game; his ability as a cover fielder is a bonus. He has had success opening the batting in one-dayers, enjoying a fantastic series against West Indies in May 2005, when he averaged more than 100 and stroked a superb 123 at Bridgetown. Two years later, though, he could not make the World Cup squad. Dippenaar revels in the outdoor pursuits which kept him busy as a boy growing up in Free State, and touring is almost as much an opportunity to fish new waters as it is to play cricket.

THE FACTS Dippenaar's highest Test score is 177 not out, v Bangladesh at Chittagong in April 2003: he and Jacques Rudolph put on 429 for the third wicket, a South African Test record ... Dippenaar made 250 not out for Eagles v Warriors at Kimberley in February 2007 ... He averages 66 in Tests against West Indies, but only 16 v Zimbabwe ... Dippenaar made 133 in an Under-19 Test at Leeds in 1995, against an England side captained by Marcus Trescothick and a new-ball attack of Andrew Flintoff and Alex Tudor ... His record includes six ODIs for the Africa XI ...

THE FIGURES

Batting and fielding www.cricinfo.com

	M	Inns	NO	Runs	HS	Avge	S/R	100	50	4s	6s	Ct	St
Tests *to 10.9.07*	38	62	5	1718	177*	30.14	41.61	3	7	237	5	27	0
ODIs *to 10.9.07*	107	95	14	3421	125*	42.23	67.78	4	26	334	16	36	0
First-class *to 10.9.07*	123	204	18	8047	250*	43.26	–	25	32	–	–	98	0

Bowling

	M	Balls	Runs	Wkts	BB	Avge	RpO	S/R	5i	10m
Tests *to 10.9.07*	38	12	1	0	–	–	0.50	–	0	0
ODIs *to 10.9.07*	107	0	–	–	–	–	–	–	–	–
First-class *to 10.9.07*	123	19	13	0	–	–	4.10	–	0	0

RAHUL **DRAVID**

Full name	**Rahul Sharad Dravid**
Born	**January 11, 1973, Indore, Madhya Pradesh**
Teams	**Karnataka**
Style	**Right-hand bat, occasional wicketkeeper**
Test debut	**India v England at Lord's 1996**
ODI debut	**India v Sri Lanka at Singapore 1995-96**

THE PROFILE Rahul Dravid, who seamlessly blends old-world classicism with new-age professionalism, is the best No. 3 batsman to play for India. He averages around 60 from there – but impressive as his stats are, they don't show his importance, or the beauty of his batting. When he started, he was pigeonholed as a blocker: his early nickname was "The Wall". But as the years passed, Dravid – who brings humility and intelligence to his study of the game – grew in stature, finally reaching maturity under Sourav Ganguly's captaincy. As a New India emerged, so did a new Dravid: first, he transformed himself into an astute middle-order one-day finisher, then strung together a series of awe-inspiring performances in Tests. His golden phase really began with a supporting act, at Kolkata early in 2001, when his 180 helped VVS Laxman create history against Australia. But from then on, Dravid became India's most valuable player, saving Tests at Port Elizabeth, Georgetown and Nottingham, and winning them at Leeds, Adelaide, Kandy and Rawalpindi. At one point he hit four double-centuries in 15 Tests. As India finished off their 2004 Pakistan tour with a win, thanks to Dravid's epic 270, his average crept past Tendulkar's – and he has stayed ahead. In October 2005 he was appointed captain of the one-day side, began with a 6-1 hammering of Sri Lanka at home, and soon succeeded Ganguly as Test skipper too. He continued to score well, and bounced back from the crushing disappointment of an early exit from the 2007 World Cup by leading India to a rare series victory in England, although his own batting lacked sparkle.

THE FACTS Dravid hit centuries in four successive Test innings in 2002, three in England and one against West Indies ... He kept wicket in 73 ODIs ... Unusually, Dravid averages more in away Tests (60.32) than at home in India (51.52) ... He averages more than 50 in Tests against everyone except Australia (48.48) and South Africa (35.33) ... Dravid's record includes one Test and three ODIs for the World XI, and one ODI for the Asia XI ...

THE FIGURES

Batting and fielding   www.cricinfo.com

	M	Inns	NO	Runs	HS	Avge	S/R	100	50	4s	6s	Ct	St
Tests *to 10.9.07*	112	191	23	9492	270	56.50	42.40	24	48	1182	14	153	0
ODIs *to 10.9.07*	327	303	40	10534	153	40.05	71.26	12	81	925	39	188	14
First-class *to 10.9.07*	228	374	54	18240	270	57.00	–		49	95	–	–	268	1

Bowling

	M	Balls	Runs	Wkts	BB	Avge	RpO	S/R	5i	10m
Tests *to 10.9.07*	112	120	39	1	1–18	39.00	1.95	120.00	0	0
ODIs *to 10.9.07*	327	186	170	4	2–43	42.50	5.48	46.50	0	0
First-class *to 10.9.07*	228	617	273	5	2–16	54.40	2.65	123.40	0	0

FIDEL **EDWARDS**

WEST INDIES

Full name	**Fidel Henderson Edwards**
Born	**February 6, 1982, Gays, St Peter, Barbados**
Teams	**Barbados**
Style	**Right-hand bat, right-arm fast bowler**
Test debut	**West Indies v Sri Lanka at Kingston 2002-03**
ODI debut	**West Indies v Zimbabwe at Harare 2003-04**

THE PROFILE   Fidel Edwards had an extraordinary start in international cricket, the kind that can either haunt or add lustre to a career. He was spotted in the nets by Brian Lara ("I just bowled about four balls at him," said Edwards) and called up for his Test debut after only one match for Barbados: he promptly took five wickets against Sri Lanka at Kingston in June 2003. He added five in his first overseas Test, and six in his first ODI. Edwards has a slingy round-arm action not unlike Jeff Thomson's – or Lasith Malinga's – which leaves him vulnerable to back strains. It doesn't often seem to result in him straying down leg, though, which seems likely when you first see him, and his unusual action has caught out several distinguished batsmen. He is more of a protégé of his neighbour Corey Collymore than of his half-brother Pedro Collins, a left-armer – who replaced him when another injury (a hamstring this time) forced him out of the series against India in mid-2006. Edwards bowls fast, can swing the ball and reverse it too, but insists that he doesn't go for out-and-out pace – which is just as well, because he is learning that pace without control leads straight to the boundary at international level. He showed his increased maturity with a testing spell in Antigua in June 2006 that had India's Virender Sehwag in all kinds of trouble before that hamstring twanged. And he hurried England's batsmen up in 2007, taking nine wickets in his two Tests and ten – including 5 for 45 at Lord's – as West Indies won the one-day series 2-1.

THE FACTS   Edwards had played only one first-class match – taking one wicket – before his Test debut against Sri Lanka at Kingston in June 2003, when he took 5 for 36 ... He also took 6 for 22 on his ODI debut, against Zimbabwe at Harare in November 2003 ... Edwards opened the bowling against England at Bridgetown in April 2004 (and several times subsequently) with his half-brother, Pedro Collins ... Edwards averages 29.96 with the ball in home Tests, but 51.31 overseas ... Unoriginally, his nickname is "Castro" ...

THE FIGURES

Batting and fielding

www.cricinfo.com

	M	Inns	NO	Runs	HS	Avge	S/R	100	50	4s	6s	Ct	St
Tests *to 10.9.07*	27	45	12	136	20	4.12	22.70	0	0	17	1	4	0
ODIs *to 10.9.07*	29	9	5	20	4*	5.00	30.76	0	0	0	0	3	0
First-class *to 10.9.07*	43	66	22	190	20	4.31	–	0	0	–	–	7	0

Bowling

	M	Balls	Runs	Wkts	BB	Avge	RpO	S/R	5i	10m
Tests *to 10.9.07*	27	4587	3097	72	5–36	43.01	4.05	63.70	5	0
ODIs *to 10.9.07*	29	1343	997	40	6–22	24.92	4.45	33.57	2	0
First-class *to 10.9.07*	43	6681	4526	125	5–22	36.20	4.06	53.44	7	1

FAISAL IQBAL

Full name	**Faisal Iqbal**
Born	**December 30, 1981, Karachi, Sind**
Teams	**Karachi, Sind, Pakistan International Airlines**
Style	**Right-hand bat, occasional right-arm medium-pacer**
Test debut	**Pakistan v New Zealand at Auckland 2000-01**
ODI debut	**Pakistan v Sri Lanka at Lahore 1999-2000**

THE PROFILE   A gutsy strokeplayer with a sound defence and attitude to boot, Faisal Iqbal is an exciting middle-order prospect. He was a prolific junior performer, but his elevation to Pakistan's Test squad was criticised as nepotism – he's the nephew of the great Javed Miandad, the coach when Iqbal made his debut in New Zealand in 2000-01. But he demonstrated that he was worth his place with three pleasing knocks then, and a counter-attacking 83 off 85 balls against Australia in Colombo in October 2002. He was particularly impressive against Shane Warne, using his feet superbly to seize the momentum for Pakistan, and did it all with a swagger reminiscent of his uncle. However, he couldn't repeat his performance in the rest of that series, or in two Tests in South Africa shortly afterwards. He lost his place, but continued to score heavily in domestic cricket, and that finally paid off three years later when he was recalled to replace the injured Inzamam-ul-Haq against India at home in Karachi in January 2006. Failure in the first innings meant the pressure was on in the second, but it didn't seem to affect Iqbal, who made an attractive 139, his first Test hundred, with some assured back-foot play and composed defence, helping Pakistan to a comfortable series-clinching win. A battling 60 followed against Murali in Colombo, then he got stuck in against England at Lord's in July to ensure a draw. The 2006-07 season was a disappointing one, though; he failed in his only Test, in South Africa, and played only one ODI. At least that meant he missed the World Cup, which may do him no harm in the long term.

THE FACTS   Faisal Iqbal's maiden Test century, 139 at Karachi in January 2006, helped Pakistan defeat India by a record margin of 341 runs, even though they were 0 for 3 after the first over of the match, and later 39 for 6 ... His highest score is 200, for Karachi Blues v Sargodha in January 2001 ... Iqbal's best in ODIs is 100 not out, v Zimbabwe at Harare in November 2002: in 17 other matches his highest score is 32 ... His uncle Javed Miandad is Pakistan's leading scorer in Tests, with 8832 runs from 124 matches ...

THE FIGURES
Batting and fielding
www.cricinfo.com

	M	Inns	NO	Runs	HS	Avge	S/R	100	50	4s	6s	Ct	St
Tests to 10.9.07	18	32	2	773	139	25.76	44.04	1	5	96	4	12	0
ODIs to 10.9.07	18	16	2	314	100*	22.42	60.50	1	0	24	4	3	0
First-class to 10.9.07	111	175	18	6402	200	40.77	–	13	35	–	–	90	0

Bowling

	M	Balls	Runs	Wkts	BB	Avge	RpO	S/R	5i	10m
Tests to 10.9.07	18	6	7	0	–	–	7.00	–	0	0
ODIs to 10.9.07	18	18	33	0	–	–	11.00	–	0	0
First-class to 10.9.07	111	138	98	1	1–6	98.00	4.26	138.00	0	0

BANGLADESH

FARHAD REZA

Full name	**Farhad Reza**
Born	**June 16, 1986, Rajshahi**
Teams	**Rajshahi**
Style	**Right-hand bat, right-arm medium-pacer**
Test debut	**No Tests yet**
ODI debut	**Bangladesh v Zimbabwe at Harare 2006**

THE PROFILE Farhad Reza is a busy player: a middle-order batsman who loves to pull, a skiddy medium-pacer, and a fine fielder. He was called up to the national squad for the tour of Zimbabwe in July 2006 after scoring the most runs in the previous season's domestic club league. He had made an even more eye-catching start in first-class cricket the year before, when he was only 18, starting with 99 on debut and finishing up with 769 runs at 42 for Rajshahi in 2004-05. Reza made his international debut in the second one-dayer at Harare, and made 50 – off 57 balls – to become the first Bangladeshi to score a half-century in his first match. He continued this good start when the team moved on to Kenya, with unbeaten knocks of 34 and 41 steering his side home in two of the games. He also opened the bowling in a couple of those Kenyan matches, but proved a little expensive: batting is definitely his stronger suit. Almost inevitably, tougher times followed against stronger opposition, and he lost his place for a while after the Champions Trophy in India in 2006-07, when he made only 41 runs and failed to take a wicket in three games. He missed out on initial selection for the 2007 World Cup, although Habibul Bashar, the captain at the time, hinted that he might have been useful. He was called up to the squad when Tapash Baisya was injured, but didn't actually get a game in the Caribbean.

THE FACTS Farhad Reza made 50 in his first ODI, the first man to make a half-century on debut for Bangladesh ... His highest score (and only first-class century) is 177 for Rajshahi against Khulna at Rajshahi in April 2005 ... On his first-class debut, earlier in that 2004-05 season, Reza was out for 99 for Rajshahi against Chittagong at Bogra ... He took 6 for 54 for Rajshahi against Sylhet at Rajshahi in February 2007, and a week later took 5 for 70 (his only other five-for) against Dhaka at Fatullah ...

THE FIGURES

Batting and fielding   www.cricinfo.com

	M	Inns	NO	Runs	HS	Avge	S/R	100	50	4s	6s	Ct	St
Tests *to 10.9.07*	0	0	–	–	–	–	–	–	–	–	–	–	–
ODIs *to 10.9.07*	15	13	2	268	50	24.36	77.90	0	1	26	7	5	0
First-class *to 10.9.07*	24	43	5	1240	177	32.63	57.64	1	8	–	–	13	0

Bowling

	M	Balls	Runs	Wkts	BB	Avge	RpO	S/R	5i	10m
Tests *to 10.9.07*	0	0	–	–	–	–	–	–	–	–
ODIs *to 10.9.07*	15	480	402	4	1–19	100.50	5.02	120.00	0	0
First-class *to 10.9.07*	24	2110	1049	36	6–54	29.13	2.98	58.61	2	0

FAWAD ALAM

Full name	**Fawad Alam**
Born	**October 8, 1985, Karachi, Sind**
Teams	**Karachi, Sind, National Bank**
Style	**Left-hand bat, slow left-arm orthodox spinner**
Test debut	**No Tests yet**
ODI debut	**Pakistan v Sri Lanka at Abu Dhabi 2006-07**

THE PROFILE Fawad Alam is one of Pakistan's young achievers: he made his first-class debut at 17, and was part of the side that won the Under-19 World Cup in Dhaka in 2003-04. He didn't sparkle in the final, but his unbeaten 43 against India in the semi had done much to get Pakistan there in the first place. A talented left-hander, Fawad was among the Quaid-e-Azam Trophy's leading batsmen in 2006-07, and overall made 884 runs at 49, to show that his performance the previous season (1072 at 53.60) was no fluke. He has another string to his bow as a handy slow left-armer. In December 2006 he guided Karachi Dolphins to the final of the Twenty20 Cup, where they lost to the defending champions Sialkot Stallions despite Fawad's valiant 54, which followed five wickets ... he left without a winner's medal but with a clutch of other awards – Man of the Final, Man of the Series, Best Batsman and Best Bowler. Shortly afterwards he led Pakistan's Academy on their tour of Bangladesh. All this led to a call to the full national team in the wake of the disastrous 2007 World Cup campaign. He made a low-key start, falling to the only ball he faced on his ODI debut, against Sri Lanka in the heat of Abu Dhabi: surprisingly, he wasn't given a bowl. The selectors kept faith, however, retaining him for the brief tour of Scotland that followed in mid-2007 – sadly, both the scheduled ODIs there were rained off.

THE FACTS Fawad Alam took 5 for 27 and then hit 54 for Karachi against Sialkot in the final of the ABN-AMRO Cup, Pakistan's domestic Twenty20 Cup competition, in December 2006: they still lost ... Fawad was part of the Pakistan side that won the Under-19 World Cup in Bangladesh in March 2004 ... His father, Tariq Alam, had a long first-class career in Pakistan ...

THE FIGURES

Batting and fielding www.cricinfo.com

	M	Inns	NO	Runs	HS	Avge	S/R	100	50	4s	6s	Ct	St
Tests *to 10.9.07*	0	0	–	–	–	–	–	–	–	–	–	–	–
ODIs *to 10.9.07*	1	1	0	0	0	0.00	0.00	0	0	0	0	0	0
First-class *to 10.9.07*	28	51	8	2047	128*	47.60	–	3	14	–	–	14	0

Bowling

	M	Balls	Runs	Wkts	BB	Avge	RpO	S/R	5i	10m
Tests *to 10.9.07*	0	0	–	–	–	–	–	–	–	–
ODIs *to 10.9.07*	1	0	–	–	–	–	–	–	–	–
First-class *to 10.9.07*	28	1000	458	12	4–27	38.16	2.74	83.33	0	0

SRI LANKA

DILHARA **FERNANDO**

Full name	**Congenige Randhi Dilhara Fernando**
Born	**July 19, 1979, Colombo**
Teams	**Sinhalese Sports Club**
Style	**Right-hand bat, right-arm fast-medium bowler**
Test debut	**Sri Lanka v Pakistan at Colombo 2000**
ODI debut	**Sri Lanka v South Africa at Paarl 2000-01**

THE PROFILE When Dilhara Fernando burst onto the international scene, young and raw, he soon inspired hope that he would be the long-term replacement for Chaminda Vaas as the cutting edge of Sri Lanka's attack. He has natural pace – six months after his debut he was clocked at 91.9mph in Durban – hits the pitch hard, and moves the ball off the seam. He rattled India at Galle in 2001, taking five wickets and sending Javagal Srinath to hospital. At first he paid for an inconsistent line and length, but worked hard with the former Test opening bowler Rumesh Ratnayake and became more reliable. He also learnt the art of reverse swing, and developed a well-disguised slower one. But injuries intervened. Fernando was quick during the 2003 World Cup, but bowled a lot of no-balls – a problem he later blamed on a spinal stress fracture. He returned after six months, only for another one to be detected in January 2004. He reclaimed his place in the national squad later that year, and has been thereabouts ever since, often going for a few in ODIs but always threatening wickets. Between injuries, he has been a Test regular too, although the no-ball problem resurfaced, and he was omitted after the first Test against Pakistan in March 2006 before returning later that year for the one-day series in England, which Sri Lanka swept 5-0, with Fernando grabbing three quick wickets in the first match at Lord's. He beat off the challenge of Nuwan Zoysa for a place in the 2007 World Cup, where he did well against England but managed only two other wickets – one in the final, when he brought down the curtain on Adam Gilchrist's epic 149.

THE FACTS Fernando averages 17.69 with the ball in Tests against Bangladesh – but 43.63 v India, even though his best figures of 5 for 42 came against them ... He averages 23.25 against England in ODIs, but 70.42 in 14 matches v South Africa ... 41 (28%) of his ODI wickets have been left-handers ... His record includes one ODI for the Asia XI ...

THE FIGURES
Batting and fielding
www.cricinfo.com

	M	Inns	NO	Runs	HS	Avge	S/R	100	50	4s	6s	Ct	St
Tests to 10.9.07	26	31	10	124	16	5.90	25.99	0	0	14	1	8	0
ODIs to 10.9.07	118	43	27	143	13*	8.93	55.85	0	0	11	1	21	0
First-class to 10.9.07	83	86	25	420	42	6.88	–	0	0	–	–	33	0

Bowling

	M	Balls	Runs	Wkts	BB	Avge	RpO	S/R	5i	10m
Tests to 10.9.07	26	3890	2338	77	5–42	30.36	3.60	50.51	3	0
ODIs to 10.9.07	118	5034	4408	146	4–24	30.19	5.25	34.47	0	0
First-class to 10.9.07	83	11137	6598	245	6–29	26.93	3.55	45.45	6	0

STEPHEN **FLEMING**

Full name **Stephen Paul Fleming**
Born **April 1, 1973, Christchurch, Canterbury**
Teams **Wellington, Nottinghamshire**
Style **Left-hand bat**
Test debut **New Zealand v India at Hamilton 1993-94**
ODI debut **New Zealand v India at Napier 1993-94**

THE PROFILE Maturity as a player and as a captain finally brought reward for Stephen Fleming, New Zealand's longest-serving Test skipper. A season with Middlesex in 2001 laid the foundations of a successful re-evaluation of his batting methods: before, an inability to convert half-centuries into hundreds did little justice to his quality as a languid left-hander often reminiscent of another born on April Fools' Day – David Gower. But shortly after a breakout innings of 134 to steer New Zealand to a classy World Cup victory over South Africa, Fleming confirmed his greater batting consistency with an unbeaten 274 against Sri Lanka in Colombo in April 2003. He added an equally impressive 192 against Pakistan at Hamilton later that year. He's also a slip catcher up there with the very best. In 2005 he captained newly promoted Nottinghamshire to their first County Championship title since Richard Hadlee's last season there in 1987. Then, five months after having a benign tumour removed from his face, in April 2006 Fleming became the first New Zealander to win 100 Test caps, reaching the mark, appropriately enough, at Centurion Park: another double-century followed in the next match. He continued to sparkle with the bat, reeling off scores of 60, 66, 45 and 102 not out as New Zealand started the 2007 World Cup well. But he fell away after that, and stepped down as one-day skipper (after a record 218 matches) following defeat in the semi-final.

THE FACTS Fleming made 92 on his Test debut, against India at Hamilton in 1993-94 – and uniquely added 90 on his ODI debut, against India at Napier two days later ... He averages 58.30 in Tests against Sri Lanka, but only 25.18 v Australia ... Fleming holds the New Zealand records for Test appearances, matches captained (and won), runs, and catches ... Fleming was lbw to Chaminda Vaas for 0 four times running against Sri Lanka in 2006 and 2007 (in their next match, the World Cup semi-final, he was lbw to Lasith Malinga for 1) ... His record includes one ODI for the World XI ...

THE FIGURES
Batting and fielding

www.cricinfo.com

	M	Inns	NO	Runs	HS	Avge	S/R	100	50	4s	6s	Ct	St
Tests *to 10.9.07*	104	177	10	6620	274*	39.64	44.93	9	41	838	21	159	0
ODIs *to 10.9.07*	280	269	19	8037	134*	32.40	71.49	8	49	823	63	133	0
First-class *to 10.9.07*	238	390	32	15793	274*	44.11	–	–	35	88	–	–	326	0

Bowling

	M	Balls	Runs	Wkts	BB	Avge	RpO	S/R	5i	10m
Tests *to 10.9.07*	104	0	–	–	–	–	–	–	–	–
ODIs *to 10.9.07*	280	29	28	1	1–8	28.00	5.79	29.00	1	0
First-class *to 10.9.07*	238	102	129	0	–	–	7.58	–	0	0

ANDREW **FLINTOFF**

Full name **Andrew Flintoff**
Born **December 6, 1977, Preston, Lancashire**
Teams **Lancashire**
Style **Right-hand bat, right-arm fast bowler**
Test debut **England v South Africa at Nottingham 1998**
ODI debut **England v Pakistan at Sharjah 1998-99**

THE PROFILE In 2005, "Freddie" Flintoff established himself as England's best allrounder since Ian Botham, reaping 402 runs and 24 wickets in an unforgettable Ashes series. It propelled him to the superstar status his admirers had long believed was within his grasp. Big, northern and proud of it, he hammers the ball, then uses his colossal frame to reach 90mph – which, with his accuracy and burgeoning mastery of reverse-swing, make him among the most intimidating bowlers around. Flintoff's precocious skills led to a Test debut at 20, but then he struggled with weight, motivation and back trouble. By 2001-02 he was a reformed character, and tonked a maiden Test ton in New Zealand, then did well at home. But when England flew to Australia in October 2002, Flintoff could hardly walk after a hernia operation. He returned as the most economical bowler at the 2003 World Cup, then starred against South Africa in England, thumping a therapeutic 95 in the remarkable Oval comeback after a defiant Lord's century. In the Caribbean early in 2004 he finally learned to slip the handbrake and become a genuine attacking option with the ball, something he continued in that amazing Ashes series. Then, when Michael Vaughan was injured, he stepped into the breach as captain in India, setting him up for the fall; Australia's revenge. Flintoff occasionally looked powerless during the Ashes whitewash, struggling for runs and wickets, and things got worse during the World Cup, when he lost the vice-captaincy after being found drunk in charge of a pedalo at 3am. A third ankle operation ruined his 2007 summer and, not for the first time, England followers went into the winter worrying about their talisman.

THE FACTS Flintoff won 47 Test caps before he played against Australia ... In 2005 he was the fourth cricketer to be voted BBC Sports Personality of the Year, following Jim Laker (1956), David Steele (1975) and Ian Botham (1981) ... He took 68 Test wickets in 2005, a record for an England bowler ... Flintoff averages 51.25 with the bat and 24.69 with the ball in Tests v West Indies ... His record includes one Test and three ODIs for the World XI ...

THE FIGURES
Batting and fielding   www.cricinfo.com

	M	Inns	NO	Runs	HS	Avge	S/R	100	50	4s	6s	Ct	St
Tests *to 10.9.07*	67	110	6	3381	167	32.50	64.17	5	24	457	77	44	0
ODIs *to 10.9.07*	127	112	14	3090	123	31.53	87.46	3	16	275	87	41	0
First-class *to 10.9.07*	163	257	18	8343	167	34.90	–	15	49	–	–	168	0

Bowling

	M	Balls	Runs	Wkts	BB	Avge	RpO	S/R	5i	10m
Tests *to 10.9.07*	67	12562	6308	197	5–58	32.02	3.01	63.76	2	0
ODIs *to 10.9.07*	127	5026	3665	146	5–56	25.10	4.37	34.42	1	0
First-class *to 10.9.07*	163	19182	9452	297	5–24	31.82	2.95	64.58	3	0

JAMES **FRANKLIN**

Full name	**James Edward Charles Franklin**
Born	**November 7, 1980, Wellington**
Teams	**Wellington**
Style	**Left-hand bat, left-arm fast-medium bowler**
Test debut	**New Zealand v Pakistan at Auckland 2000-01**
ODI debut	**New Zealand v Zimbabwe at Taupo 2000-01**

THE PROFILE A left-armer who can swing the ball, James Franklin was introduced to international cricket when barely out of his teens after New Zealand suffered a run of injuries. He made his one-day debut in 2000-01, and played two home Tests against Pakistan the same season, but struggled to make an impact and lost his place after the Sharjah Cup in April 2002. Back in domestic cricket he worked on his batting, which he had neglected, and filled out generally. He returned to the side in England in 2004. He was playing league cricket in Lancashire, but was called up when Shane Bond went home with a back injury. Franklin was included for the third Test at Trent Bridge, and although New Zealand lost he did his cause no harm with six wickets, five of them Test century-makers. He stayed on for the one-dayers that followed, and picked up the match award at Chester-le-Street for his 5 for 42 as England were skittled for 101. He was retained for the tour of Bangladesh, and took a hat-trick at Dhaka. Back home he took 6 for 119 against Australia in March 2005, and bowled superbly – getting the ball to reverse-swing – against Sri Lanka a month later, although his figures didn't reflect his excellence. More wickets followed against West Indies, then in April 2006 Franklin did his allrounder claims no harm with an unbeaten 122 – and a stand of 256 with Stephen Fleming – against South Africa at Cape Town. He bowled capably during the 2007 World Cup, although he was occasionally expensive – as when he took 3 for 74 in eight overs as Australia cut loose in Grenada.

THE FACTS Franklin is only the fourth man to have taken a hat-trick and scored a century in Tests – the others are Johnny Briggs of England and Pakistan's Abdul Razzaq and Wasim Akram ... The only other New Zealander to take a Test hat-trick was Peter Petherick in 1976-77 ... Franklin's highest first-class score is 208, for Wellington against Auckland in 2005-06: in the previous match, against Central Districts also at Wellington, he had taken his career-best figures of 7 for 30 ...

THE FIGURES

Batting and fielding

www.cricinfo.com

	M	Inns	NO	Runs	HS	Avge	S/R	100	50	4s	6s	Ct	St
Tests to 10.9.07	21	28	5	505	122*	21.95	40.46	1	1	50	4	9	0
ODIs to 10.9.07	65	44	15	508	45*	17.51	74.81	0	0	35	6	19	0
First-class to 10.9.07	89	131	19	3106	208	27.73	–	3	14	–	–	31	0

Bowling

	M	Balls	Runs	Wkts	BB	Avge	RpO	S/R	5i	10m
Tests to 10.9.07	21	3577	2143	76	6–119	28.19	3.59	47.06	3	0
ODIs to 10.9.07	65	2804	2392	64	5–42	37.37	5.11	43.81	1	0
First-class to 10.9.07	89	14655	7689	310	7–30	24.80	3.14	47.27	11	1

PETER **FULTON**

Full name **Peter Gordon Fulton**
Born **February 1, 1979, Christchurch, Canterbury**
Teams **Canterbury**
Style **Right-hand bat, occasional right-arm medium-pacer**
Test debut **New Zealand v West Indies at Auckland 2005-06**
ODI debut **New Zealand v Bangladesh at Chittagong 2004-05**

THE PROFILE Peter Fulton, a tall middle-order batsman nicknamed "Two-Metre Peter", initially made his mark on first-class cricket by extending his maiden century to 301 not out for Canterbury against Auckland in March 2003, in only his second full season. His 9½-hour innings, against an attack containing the Test bowlers Heath Davis and Brooke Walker, contained 45 fours and three sixes. Fulton is a product of Canterbury Country, an area rich in cricket history but which had never previously produced an international player. His 301 also broke the monopoly of Otago, where the five previous New Zealand triple-centurions came from. The following season he made 728 runs at 42.82, including two more centuries, and – after a consistent tour of South Africa with New Zealand A – was called up to the one-day squad for the tour of Bangladesh in November 2004. He played one match there, but it was another 12 months before he featured again. This time he made the most of his chance, with 70 not out, 32, 50 and 112 against Sri Lanka, which led to a Test baptism: he added 75 in his second match, as New Zealand took an unbeatable lead over West Indies. *Wisden* called him "one for the future, provided he could retain his simple, uncomplicated batting style": John Bracewell, NZ's coach, believes he has the tools to open, although he had problems there against South Africa early in 2006. Fulton played in 26 of New Zealand's 30 ODIs in 2006-07 without setting the world alight – 730 runs at 31.73 – and the 2007-08 season will be a crucial one for him.

THE FACTS Fulton's 301 not out was the fifth-highest maiden century in all first-class cricket: the highest is 337 not out by Pervez Akhtar for Pakistan Railways in 1964-65 ... Fulton also scored 221 not out for Canterbury v Otago in Dunedin in 2004-05, when he shared an unbroken national sixth-wicket record stand of 293 with Neil Broom ... Half of Fulton's 50-plus scores in ODIs have come against Australia ... His uncle, Roddy Fulton, played for Canterbury and Northern Districts in the 1970s ...

THE FIGURES

Batting and fielding www.cricinfo.com

	M	Inns	NO	Runs	HS	Avge	S/R	100	50	4s	6s	Ct	St
Tests to 10.9.07	5	7	0	185	75	26.42	46.25	0	1	27	3	3	0
ODIs to 10.9.07	36	35	4	1112	112	35.87	74.28	1	7	93	16	10	0
First-class to 10.9.07	53	87	9	3659	301*	46.91	–	6	20	–	–	38	0

Bowling

	M	Balls	Runs	Wkts	BB	Avge	RpO	S/R	5i	10m
Tests to 10.9.07	5	0	–	–	–	–	–	–	–	–
ODIs to 10.9.07	36	0	–	–	–	–	–	–	–	–
First-class to 10.9.07	53	673	399	11	4-49	36.27	3.55	61.18	0	0

GAUTAM **GAMBHIR**

Full name **Gautam Gambhir**
Born **October 14, 1981, Delhi**
Teams **Delhi**
Style **Left-hand bat, occasional legspinner**
Test debut **India v Australia at Mumbai 2004-05**
ODI debut **India v Bangladesh at Dhaka 2002-03**

THE PROFILE As a 17-year-old stripling opener in 2000, left-hander Gautam Gambhir's attacking strokeplay for Delhi set tongues wagging. Compact footwork and high bat-speed befuddled the bowlers, who paid the price for mistaking his slight build and shy demeanour for signs of meekness, as cautious defence was replaced by the aerial route over point. His success took him close to the Test side when Zimbabwe toured early in 2002. He pasted successive double-centuries, for Delhi and for the Board President's XI against the tourists, and seemed to be a certainty as Shiv Sunder Das's opening partner – but the selectors persisted with the band-aid solution of Deep Dasgupta. Gambhir soldiered on, pressing his case in the Caribbean with India A early in 2003, and joined the one-day squad when several senior players asked to be rested following that year's World Cup. He made the Test side late the following year, hitting 96 against South Africa in his second match and 139 v Bangladesh in his fifth. Leaner times followed, punctuated by cheap runs in Zimbabwe, and although he celebrated his one-day return after 30 months on the sidelines with 103 against Sri Lanka at Ahmedabad in April 2005, he struggled for big scores and found himself on the outer again, missing the following year's tour of West Indies. After the disasters of the 2007 World Cup Gambhir was tried again, collecting another one-day hundred against Bangladesh, which earned him a trip to England. He sat out the Tests, but made a mark in the one-dayers with 51 at Headingley.

THE FACTS Gambhir has scored three first-class double-centuries, the highest 233 not out for Delhi against Railways at Delhi in November 2002 ... He averages 87.00 in Tests against Bangladesh – and 2.00 v Australia ... In January 2001 Gambhir scored 212 in an Under-19 Test against England (captained by Ian Bell) at Chennai, sharing an opening stand of 391 with Vinayak Mane ...

THE FIGURES

Batting and fielding

www.cricinfo.com

	M	Inns	NO	Runs	HS	Avge	S/R	100	50	4s	6s	Ct	St
Tests to 10.9.07	13	21	2	684	139	36.00	60.21	1	3	97	1	12	0
ODIs to 10.9.07	29	29	2	885	103	32.77	76.42	2	5	112	4	11	0
First-class to 10.9.07	88	144	15	6766	233*	52.44	–	20	26	–	–	58	0

Bowling

	M	Balls	Runs	Wkts	BB	Avge	RpO	S/R	5i	10m
Tests to 10.9.07	13	0	–	–	–	–	–	–	–	–
ODIs to 10.9.07	29	6	13	0	–	–	13.00	–	0	0
First-class to 10.9.07	88	385	277	7	3–12	39.57	4.31	55.00	0	0

DAREN **GANGA**

Full name **Daren Ganga**
Born **January 14, 1979, Barrackpore, Trinidad**
Teams **Trinidad & Tobago**
Style **Right-hand bat, occasional offspinner**
Test debut **West Indies v South Africa at Durban 1998-99**
ODI debut **West Indies v South Africa at Cape Town 1998-99**

THE PROFILE Daren Ganga is a survivor at international level, bouncing back after seemingly flunking his last chance more than once. His 2000-01 tour of Australia was rather like Mark Ramprakash's debut Test series for England in 1991, featuring several characterful twenties and thirties – but, a studious opener whose runs came mostly in the V, he could be becalmed all too easily. Like the unfortunate Ramprakash, he yo-yoed in and out of the Test side, and it wasn't until his fourth coming that he really made his mark, with back-to-back centuries against the mighty Australians in April 2003. Suddenly his phlegmatic approach seemed to be the ideal counterpoint for the rejuvenated Brian Lara, his fellow Trinidadian. But Ganga's form fell away again, and he was dropped after the first Test against South Africa in April 2005. Still it wasn't over: after missing ten Tests he was recalled for the tour of New Zealand early in 2006, and secured his place with 95 at Auckland, then led Trinidad & Tobago to the domestic title. He did well in the home series that followed against India, playing a calming role as a runner as West Indies hung on to save the first Test in Antigua, then making 135 and 66 not out in St Kitts' maiden Test. In England in 2007 he impressed in the first Test, but then struggled after Ramnaresh Sarwan's injury at Headingley handed him the captaincy. Ganga failed to reach double figures in six innings while in charge, including four successive lbws, and presided over three heavy defeats before, no longer wanted in the one-day side, he returned home to an uncertain future.

THE FACTS Ganga made 265 for Trinidad & Tobago v Leeward Islands in Montserrat in March 2005, sharing a stand of 307 with Gregory Mahabir ... He has also passed 150 twice, both times v Windward Islands at Pointe-à-Pierre ... Ganga averages 49.14 in Tests against India, but only 13.13 v South Africa ... His brother Sherwin also played for T&T ...

THE FIGURES

Batting and fielding

www.cricinfo.com

	M	Inns	NO	Runs	HS	Avge	S/R	100	50	4s	6s	Ct	St
Tests to 10.9.07	45	80	2	2043	135	26.19	39.50	3	9	271	2	28	0
ODIs to 10.9.07	35	34	1	843	71	25.54	59.61	0	9	69	7	11	0
First-class to 10.9.07	137	238	20	7955	265	36.49	–		19	37	–	–	82	0

Bowling

	M	Balls	Runs	Wkts	BB	Avge	RpO	S/R	5i	10m
Tests to 10.9.07	45	186	106	1	1–20	106.00	3.41	186.00	0	0
ODIs to 10.9.07	35	1	4	0	–	–	24.00	–	0	0
First-class to 10.9.07	137	610	328	4	1–7	82.00	3.22	152.50	0	0

SOURAV **GANGULY**

Full name **Sourav Chandidas Ganguly**
Born **July 8, 1972, Calcutta, Bengal**
Teams **Bengal**
Style **Left-hand bat, right-arm medium-pace bowler**
Test debut **India v England at Lord's 1996**
ODI debut **India v West Indies at Brisbane 1991-92**

THE PROFILE Some felt he couldn't play the bouncer, others swore he was divine on the off side; some laughed at his lack of athleticism, others admired his ability to galvanise a side. Sourav Ganguly's ability to polarise opinion has been an ongoing Indian soap opera. Nobody can dispute that he was India's most successful captain, forging a winning unit from a bunch of talented individuals, and nobody denies that he was among the best one-day batsmen, combining grace with surgical precision in his strokeplay. After he toured Australia at 19 his career stalled before a scintillating debut century at Lord's in 1996: soon he was forming a destructive opening partnership in one-dayers with Sachin Tendulkar. He took over the captaincy in 2000, and quickly proved to be tough and intuitive. India started winning overseas, and began a streak that took them all the way to the 2003 World Cup final. Later that year, Ganguly's unexpected, incandescent hundred at Brisbane set the tone for an epic series in which India fought the Aussies to a standstill. Victory in Pakistan turned him into a cult figure, but that turned out to be a watershed: things went pear-shaped when his loss of form coincided with India's insipid one-day performances. Breaking point came when his differences with new coach Greg Chappell were leaked. Ganguly looked to be finished – but fought back for another World Cup in 2007, and another tour of England, where his forthright 57 at The Oval steadied India's nerves as the series was won.

THE FACTS Ganguly made 131 on his Test debut, at Lord's in 1996, and scored 136 in his next innings, at Nottingham ... He is one of only seven batsmen to score 10,000 runs in ODIs ... Ganguly averages 59.50 in ODIs against South Africa, but only 22.31 v Australia ... He averages 57.82 in Tests against England, but 28.30 v Pakistan ... Ganguly captained in 49 Tests, winning 21, both Indian records ... Ganguly's record includes three ODIs for the Asia XI ...

THE FIGURES
Batting and fielding

www.cricinfo.com

	M	Inns	NO	Runs	HS	Avge	S/R	100	50	4s	6s	Ct	St
Tests to 10.9.07	96	155	14	5812	173	41.21	49.66	13	29	744	47	64	0
ODIs to 10.9.07	302	292	23	11147	183	41.43	73.69	22	71	1097	186	100	0
First-class to 10.9.07	222	346	40	13385	200*	43.74	–		28	77	–	–	158	0

Bowling

	M	Balls	Runs	Wkts	BB	Avge	RpO	S/R	5i	10m
Tests to 10.9.07	96	2708	1506	28	3–28	53.78	3.33	96.71	0	0
ODIs to 10.9.07	302	4459	3734	99	5–16	37.71	5.02	45.04	2	0
First-class to 10.9.07	222	10499	5829	160	6–46	36.43	3.33	65.61	4	0

CHRIS **GAYLE**

WEST INDIES

Full name	**Christopher Henry Gayle**
Born	**September 21, 1979, Kingston, Jamaica**
Teams	**Jamaica**
Style	**Right-hand bat, offspinner**
Test debut	**West Indies v Zimbabwe at Port-of-Spain 1999-2000**
ODI debut	**West Indies v India at Toronto 1999-2000**

THE PROFILE   A thrusting left-hander, Chris Gayle earned himself a black mark on his first senior tour – to England in 2000 – when the new boys were felt to be insufficiently respectful of their elders. But a lack of respect, for opposition bowlers at least, has served him well since then. Tall and imposing at the crease, he loves to carve through the covers off either foot, and has the ability to decimate the figures of even the thriftiest of opening bowlers. In a lean era for West Indian cricket in general – and fast bowling in particular – Gayle's pugnacious approach has become an attacking weapon in its own right, in Tests as well as one-dayers. His 79-ball century at Cape Town in January 2004, after South Africa had made 532, was typical of his no-holds-barred approach. Gayle's good run ended when England came calling early in 2004, and he averaged only 26 against a potent pace attack which exposed a lack of positive footwork. But men with little footwork often baffle experts, and after returning to form with an uncharacteristic century against Bangladesh, he exacted his revenge on England's bowlers with a battering not seen since Lara's 400, before coming within a whisker of emulating Lara himself with 317 against South Africa in Antigua. Gayle also bowls brisk non-turning offspin, with which he has turned himself into a genuine one-day allrounder. In England in 2007 he took over the one-day captaincy after a miserable Test series, and electrified the side with unexpected flair: they took the one-dayers 2-1, leaving Gayle – whose initial appointment was vetoed by an out-of-touch board – suddenly a realistic option as Test captain.

THE FACTS   Gayle's 317 v New Zealand in Antigua in May 2005 has been exceeded for West Indies only by Brian Lara (twice) and Garry Sobers ... Only Lara (19) and Desmond Haynes (17) have scored more ODI centuries for West Indies than Gayle's 15 ... Gayle made 208 for Jamaica v West Indies B in February 2001, sharing an unbroken opening stand of 425 with Leon Garrick ... His record includes three ODIs for the World XI ...

THE FIGURES

Batting and fielding   www.cricinfo.com

	M	Inns	NO	Runs	HS	Avge	S/R	100	50	4s	6s	Ct	St
Tests to 10.9.07	68	121	4	4479	317	38.28	56.21	7	27	706	32	69	0
ODIs to 10.9.07	174	170	11	6184	153*	38.89	80.39	15	33	751	96	81	0
First-class to 10.9.07	139	248	17	10046	317	43.48	–	22	52	–	–	126	0

Bowling

	M	Balls	Runs	Wkts	BB	Avge	RpO	S/R	5i	10m
Tests to 10.9.07	68	5267	2336	59	5–34	39.59	2.66	89.27	2	0
ODIs to 10.9.07	174	5909	4583	140	5–46	32.73	4.65	42.20	1	0
First-class to 10.9.07	139	10141	4197	107	5–34	39.22	2.48	94.77	2	0

HERSCHELLE **GIBBS**

Full name **Herschelle Herman Gibbs**
Born **February 23, 1974, Green Point, Cape Town**
Teams **Cape Cobras**
Style **Right-hand bat, occasional legspinner**
Test debut **South Africa v India at Calcutta 1996-97**
ODI debut **South Africa v Kenya at Nairobi 1996-97**

THE PROFILE Herschelle Gibbs was summoned from the classroom at 16 to make his first-class debut in 1990: his feet moved beautifully at the crease, but struggled to find the ground in real life. Admitting that a Test debut in front of 70,000 at Eden Gardens wasn't as nerve-wracking as sitting his final exams, as well as the fact that he reads little other than magazines and comics, contributed to a reputation for simplicity. In fact, Gibbs can be a warm and generous person. His passion for one-liners and verbal jousting continues to hamper his advancement, and his brush with career death in the match-fixing scandal added to the impression of one who had failed to grasp the magnitude of his impact on the nation's youth. At the crease, however, Gibbs can be invincible. No shot is beyond him, while opening has not tempered his desire for explosive entertainment. The speed of his hands is hypnotic, frequently allowing him to hook off the front foot and keep out surprise lifters. His trademark is the lofted extra-cover drive, hit inside-out with the certainty of a square cut. At backward point he is almost the equal of Jonty Rhodes. Gibbs has two double-centuries (and two more 190s) among his 14 Test tons, and 17 one-day hundreds too – the best of them in March 2006, when his 111-ball 175 powered South Africa to an amazing triumph at Jo'burg, overhauling Australia's 434 with a ball to spare in arguably the greatest one-day cracker of them all. He had a subdued 2006-07, not managing an international century and being briefly banned after an injudicious remark about spectators was picked up by the stump mikes. He started and finished the World Cup well, though, ending with scores of 56, 61, 60 and 39 after blasting six sixes in an over in the first game, against Holland.

THE FACTS Gibbs and Graeme Smith are the only opening pair to share three stands of 300 or more in Tests ... He hit six sixes in an over from Holland's Daan van Bunge during the 2007 World Cup, winning a million dollars for charity ... He averages 63.09 in Tests v New Zealand, but only 23.30 v Sri Lanka ... He has been bowled in 33 (23%) of his Test innings ...

THE FIGURES
Batting and fielding

www.cricinfo.com

	M	Inns	NO	Runs	HS	Avge	S/R	100	50	4s	6s	Ct	St
Tests *to 10.9.07*	84	144	7	5943	228	43.37	50.14	14	24	852	46	85	0
ODIs *to 10.9.07*	213	206	16	6889	175	36.25	82.64	17	32	778	107	90	0
First-class *to 10.9.07*	179	309	13	12852	228	43.41	–	31	56	–	–	155	0

Bowling

	M	Balls	Runs	Wkts	BB	Avge	RpO	S/R	5i	10m
Tests *to 10.9.07*	84	6	4	0	–	–	4.00	–	0	0
ODIs *to 10.9.07*	213	0		–	–	–	–	–	–	–
First-class *to 10.9.07*	179	138	78	3	2–14	26.00	3.39	46.00	0	0

AUSTRALIA

ADAM **GILCHRIST**

Full name	**Adam Craig Gilchrist**
Born	**November 14, 1971, Bellingen, New South Wales**
Teams	**Western Australia**
Style	**Left-hand bat, wicketkeeper**
Test debut	**Australia v Pakistan at Brisbane 1999-2000**
ODI debut	**Australia v South Africa at Faridabad 1995-96**

THE PROFILE Going in first or seventh, wearing whites or coloureds, Adam Gilchrist has been the symbolic heart of Australia's steamrolling agenda and the most exhilarating cricketer of the modern age. It was arguably Gilchrist's belated Test arrival that turned the Australian XI from powerful to overpowering. He is a throwback to more innocent times, a flap-eared country boy who walked in a World Cup semi-final, and swatted his second ball for six while on a pair in a Test. "Just hit the ball," is how he described his batting philosophy. Employing a high-on-the-handle grip, he pokes good balls into gaps and throttles most others. Only at the death does he jettison the textbook, whirling his bat like a hammer-thrower. He bludgeoned 81 on debut, pouched five catches and a stumping, and has barely paused for breath since. Only recently has his appetite slowed: he was troubled by Andrew Flintoff's around-the-wicket barrage in 2005, and found the flaw difficult to overcome. But two of his Test innings rank among Australia's greatest: his unbeaten 149 against Pakistan at Hobart in November 1999 when all seemed lost, and a savage 204 at Johannesburg in February 2002, while his coruscating century lit up the 2007 World Cup final. As a wicketkeeper he lacks Rod Marsh's acrobatics and Ian Healy's finesse, and he probably peaked at 30. But if he clutches few screamers he drops even fewer sitters. He is closing on Healy's record 396 Test dismissals, and already has the most centuries of any keeper-batsman.

THE FACTS Gilchrist was on the winning side in each of his first 15 Tests, the best start of any player ... He averages 68.44 in Tests against Pakistan, but only 29.95 against India ... Gilchrist averaged 171.50 in the series in New Zealand in 2004-05, with innings of 121, 162 and 60 not out: in all he averages 76.91 from 11 Tests against NZ ... As Ricky Ponting's stand-in he led Australia to their first series win in India for 35 years in 2004-05 ... Only Ian Healy (395) and Mark Boucher (392) have made more wicketkeeping dismissals in Tests, and Gilchrist leads the way in ODIs ... His record includes one ODI for the World XI ...

THE FIGURES
Batting and fielding   www.cricinfo.com

	M	Inns	NO	Runs	HS	Avge	S/R	100	50	4s	6s	Ct	St
Tests to 10.9.07	90	129	19	5353	204*	48.66	82.29	17	24	652	97	344	37
ODIs to 10.9.07	268	261	10	9038	172	36.00	96.65	15	50	1099	136	388	51
First-class to 10.9.07	182	269	45	10002	204*	44.65	–	30	40	–	–	714	55

Bowling

	M	Balls	Runs	Wkts	BB	Avge	RpO	S/R	5i	10m
Tests to 10.9.07	90	0	–	–	–	–	–	–	–	–
ODIs to 10.9.07	268	0	–	–	–	–	–	–	–	–
First-class to 10.9.07	182	0	–	–	–	–	–	–	–	–

JASON **GILLESPIE**

Full name	**Jason Neil Gillespie**
Born	**April 19, 1975, Darlinghurst, Sydney, New South Wales**
Teams	**South Australia, Yorkshire**
Style	**Right-hand bat, right-arm fast-medium bowler**
Test debut	**Australia v West Indies at Sydney 1996-97**
ODI debut	**Australia v Sri Lanka at Colombo 1996-97**

THE PROFILE   Jason Gillespie's bouncing mullet, hooked nose and Spofforth-like glare were a feature of Australia's pace attack in the first five years of the 2000s. Gillespie had played only 52 of a possible 92 Tests after his 1996-97 debut thanks to various ailments, including stress fractures in the back and a broken leg. Each time he recovered and, until dropped during the 2005 Ashes, had missed only two Tests since November 2002. He blossomed into half of Australia's statistically most-successful opening pair. But if Glenn McGrath's strength was his ability to make the ball do just enough, then Gillespie's flaw is his tendency for it to do too much. No other contemporary fast man elicits so many plays-and-misses. Operating from a shorter, reconfigured run-up, he is not so consistently quick. However, few Australian fast men can have owned such deep wells of tenacity. Gillespie bowls long spells in the hottest conditions – always uncomplainingly, always with seam upright and ball jagging both ways – and he had another long spell when he returned to the Test side against Bangladesh early in 2006 ... with the bat, as his maiden century turned into a magnificent 201. It was appropriate recognition for a hardy and valuable batting approach that also produced two unbeaten half-centuries. Oddly, it may prove to be Gillespie's last act in Tests: he hasn't played since, and was surprised to earn another contract for 2007-08. "I had to look at the calendar," he said of the offer, "I thought it was April 1." The great-grandson of a Kamilaroi warrior, Gillespie occupies a significant niche in Australian history as the first acknowledged Aboriginal Test cricketer.

THE FACTS   Gillespie's 201 not out against Bangladesh at Chittagong in April 2006 was easily the highest score by a nightwatchman in a Test, beating Mark Boucher's 125 for South Africa v Zimbabwe at Harare in 1999-2000 ... Gillespie has taken 50 wickets at 21.12 against West Indies, but only 10 at 37.50 against Pakistan ... He averages 2.80 with the bat against South Africa – and 247.00 against Bangladesh ...

THE FIGURES

Batting and fielding   www.cricinfo.com

	M	Inns	NO	Runs	HS	Avge	S/R	100	50	4s	6s	Ct	St
Tests *to 10.9.07*	71	93	28	1218	201*	18.73	31.96	1	2	146	8	27	0
ODIs *to 10.9.07*	97	39	16	289	44*	12.56	78.53	0	0	16	6	10	0
First-class *to 10.9.07*	166	219	54	3101	201*	18.24	–		2	7	–	–	62	0

Bowling

	M	Balls	Runs	Wkts	BB	Avge	RpO	S/R	5i	10m
Tests *to 10.9.07*	71	14234	6770	259	7–37	26.13	2.85	54.95	8	0
ODIs *to 10.9.07*	97	5144	3611	142	5–22	25.42	4.21	36.22	3	0
First-class *to 10.9.07*	166	31156	14630	563	8–50	25.98	2.81	55.33	21	2

NEW ZEALAND

MARK **GILLESPIE**

Full name	**Mark Raymond Gillespie**
Born	**October 17, 1979, Wanganui**
Teams	**Wellington**
Style	**Right-hand bat, right-arm fast-medium bowler**
Test debut	**No Tests yet**
ODI debut	**New Zealand v Sri Lanka at Napier 2006-07**

THE PROFILE With a run-up reminiscent of Bob Willis or even Dennis Lillee – although he lacks the pace of either – Mark Gillespie came to prominence as a specialist one-day "death" bowler for Wellington. He backed that up in first-class cricket with 43 wickets at 23.16 in 2005-06, although that season ended badly when he was struck below the eye, suffering multiple fractures and a smashed eye socket, while batting against Canterbury. Three months later he was back, taking three quick wickets (Phil Jaques, Brad Haddin and Mark Cosgrove) as New Zealand A beat their Australian counterparts at Darwin: he followed that up with 5 for 35 against India A at Cairns. Gillespie was rewarded with a place in the full Champions Trophy squad in October 2006, although he did not actually get a game. When he was finally given an opportunity, at home against Sri Lanka, he showed signs that his domestic form could translate to the international arena, his 3 for 39 in a heavy defeat at Auckland being particularly impressive. He followed that up with a decent showing in the tri-series in Australia, where he deceived some with his pace but also leaked too many runs on occasions. His best moment was probably a stunning tumbling outfield catch to dismiss top-scorer Ed Joyce as England slid to a heavy defeat at Adelaide. Overall Gillespie did enough to be named in New Zealand's World Cup squad, although he was restricted by a shoulder problem there, and failed to take a wicket in his two appearances.

THE FACTS Gillespie took 5 for 58 on his first-class debut, for Wellington against Otago at Alexandra in March 2000 ... The following season he made 81 not out, still his highest score, against the same opponents ... Over half Gillespie's international wickets (11 out of 18) have come against Australia ... He has made a century for Tawa, his Wellington club, and is nicknamed the "Tawa Terror" ...

THE FIGURES

Batting and fielding   www.cricinfo.com

	M	Inns	NO	Runs	HS	Avge	S/R	100	50	4s	6s	Ct	St
Tests to 10.9.07	0	0	–	–	–	–	–	–	–	–	–	–	–
ODIs to 10.9.07	17	9	4	63	28	12.60	79.74	0	0	5	0	2	0
First-class to 10.9.07	43	55	10	838	81*	18.62	–	0	3	–	–	8	0

Bowling

	M	Balls	Runs	Wkts	BB	Avge	RpO	S/R	5i	10m
Tests to 10.9.07	0	0	–	–	–	–	–	–	–	–
ODIs to 10.9.07	17	813	759	18	3–39	42.16	5.60	45.16	0	0
First-class to 10.9.07	43	8016	4166	167	6–81	24.94	3.11	48.00	7	0

HABIBUL BASHAR

Full name	**Qazi Habibul Bashar**
Born	**August 17, 1972, Nagakanda, Kushtia**
Teams	**Khulna**
Style	**Right-hand bat, occasional offspinner**
Test debut	**Bangladesh v India at Dhaka 2000-01**
ODI debut	**Bangladesh v Sri Lanka at Sharjah 1994-95**

THE PROFILE Impish and impulsive, Habibul Bashar has the style and strokes of a genuine Test player. Most of his runs come from cultured drives through midwicket, and most of his dismissals from a Hilditch-style addiction to the hook. Before Bangladesh's inaugural Test, "Sumon" promised he would kick the habit, but although he made 71 and 30 he was still out hooking ... twice. After that he carried Bangladesh's flimsy middle-order hopes, and inherited the captaincy from Khaled Mahmud in January 2004. After a shaky start in Zimbabwe, he came into his own with a century in St Lucia, as Bangladesh took a first-innings lead in their first Test in the Caribbean. He missed the 2004 Champions Trophy in England with an injured thumb – overall he has underperformed in ODIs for such an attacking player – but returned to captain in England in 2005 when, lo and behold, the hook habit cut him down twice at Lord's. But he restored pride with a hard-hitting 61 to conclude a disappointing series. Habibul's greatest moment as captain came a few weeks later at Cardiff, with a convincing five-wicket win over Australia in the NatWest Series. The strain of leading a side which kept collapsing started to show, and he hasn't managed a Test century since that one in St Lucia in May 2004. He resigned the one-day captaincy after the 2007 World Cup, and was relieved of the Test job too, leaving his future in doubt – rising 35, he's positively ancient in the current Bangladesh set-up (in the first ODI of the post-Habibul era, their oldest player was only 25).

THE FACTS Habibul Bashar passed 2000 Test runs for Bangladesh before anyone else had reached 1000 ... He scored 94 and 55 in captaining Bangladesh to their first Test victory, v Zimbabwe at Chittagong in January 2005 ... Habibul only missed two of Bangladesh's first 49 Tests, at home against New Zealand in 2004-05 when he had a broken thumb ... He averages 50.36 against Pakistan in Tests, but 20.60 against India ... Habibul made 224 for Biman Bangladesh v Khulna at Jessore in 2000-01 ....

THE FIGURES

Batting and fielding

www.cricinfo.com

	M	Inns	NO	Runs	HS	Avge	S/R	100	50	4s	6s	Ct	St
Tests *to 10.9.07*	47	93	1	2953	113	32.09	60.38	3	24	393	2	21	0
ODIs *to 10.9.07*	111	105	5	2168	78	21.68	60.45	0	14	–	10	26	0
First-class *to 10.9.07*	77	145	4	4731	224	33.55	–	6	34	–	–	32	0

Bowling

	M	Balls	Runs	Wkts	BB	Avge	RpO	S/R	5i	10m
Tests *to 10.9.07*	47	282	217	0	–	–	4.61	–	0	0
ODIs *to 10.9.07*	111	175	142	1	1–31	142.00	4.86	175.00	0	0
First-class *to 10.9.07*	77	802	513	8	2–28	64.12	3.83	100.25	0	0

BRAD **HADDIN**

AUSTRALIA

Full name	**Bradley James Haddin**
Born	**October 23, 1977, Cowra, New South Wales**
Teams	**New South Wales**
Style	**Right-hand bat, wicketkeeper**
Test debut	**No Tests yet**
ODI debut	**Australia v Zimbabwe at Hobart 2000-01**

THE PROFILE Brad Haddin holds the most nerve-fraying position in Australian cricket. He is the wicketkeeper-in-waiting, entrusted with warming the seat whenever Adam Gilchrist needs a rest. Slip up and be forgotten; perform well, as he has over the past couple of seasons, and suffer a speedy demotion when the incumbent returns. He's already seen off Darren Berry, Wade Seccombe and Ryan Campbell, but now has to look out for up-and-comers like Chris Hartley, Luke Ronchi and Adam Crosthwaite. At 30 Haddin has time – and talent – on his side for a decent international career, but the scheduling of Gilchrist's eventual departure will be crucial. The pressure of being No. 2 has not hindered Haddin's batting, and his keeping to a New South Wales attack swinging from Brett Lee to Stuart MacGill has remained sharp. In 2004-05 he scored 916 first-class runs at 57.25, leading the Blues to a one-wicket Pura Cup victory over Queensland, and he also posted an impressive limited-overs century for Australia A against Pakistan. Haddin passed 600 runs in each of the following seasons, and played a few ODIs when Gilchrist was rested. He also shadowed Gilchrist on the 2005 Ashes tour, and in the 2007 World Cup. A former Australia Under-19 captain who grew up in Gundagai, Haddin began his senior domestic career in 1997-98 with the Australian Capital Territory in their debut Mercantile Mutual Cup season: two years later he was playing for NSW.

THE FACTS Haddin took up a novel batting position *behind* the stumps when facing a Shoaib Akhtar "free ball" (after a no-ball) in a Twenty20 game for Australia A against Pakistan early in 2005: he reasoned that he had more time to sight the ball, and if it hit the stumps it would confuse the fielders. It did hit the stumps, and he managed a bye ... Haddin was also the unwitting "villain" of the 2005 Ashes Test at Edgbaston: he was the man who threw a ball to Glenn McGrath, who badly sprained his ankle in catching it and missed the match, which England eventually won by just two runs ...

THE FIGURES

Batting and fielding

www.cricinfo.com

	M	Inns	NO	Runs	HS	Avge	S/R	100	50	4s	6s	Ct	St
Tests *to 10.9.07*	0	0	–	–	–	–	–	–	–	–	–	–	–
ODIs *to 10.9.07*	21	19	1	467	70	25.94	80.93	0	1	38	14	28	4
First-class *to 10.9.07*	82	138	16	4933	154	40.43	–	7	30	–	–	229	21

Bowling

	M	Balls	Runs	Wkts	BB	Avge	RpO	S/R	5i	10m
Tests *to 10.9.07*	0	0	–	–	–	–	–	–	–	–
ODIs *to 10.9.07*	21	0	–	–	–	–	–	–	–	–
First-class *to 10.9.07*	82	0	–	–	–	–	–	–	–	–

ANDREW **HALL**

Full name	**Andrew James Hall**
Born	**July 31, 1975, Johannesburg, Transvaal**
Teams	**Dolphins, Kent**
Style	**Right-hand bat, right-arm fast-medium bowler**
Test debut	**South Africa v Australia at Cape Town 2001-02**
ODI debut	**South Africa v West Indies at Durban 1998-99**

THE PROFILE Probably the only cricketer to have been shot at point-blank range and live to tell the tale, Andrew Hall has seized the opportunity to play international cricket with both hands. Which is remarkable really, considering that Hall fielded a bullet in his left hand when a mugger fired six shots at him at a cash machine late one night in 1998. Miraculously, the slug caused no serious damage, and Hall recovered to win a place in South Africa's one-day side against West Indies in January 1999. He appeared to have slipped out of the selectors' minds until Australia arrived the following April for another one-day series. With Herschelle Gibbs struggling for form, Hall was tried at the top of the order. And he looked the part against Brett Lee, scoring a composed 46 – enough to win a place on the ensuing tour of Sri Lanka, where he made an equally impressive 81 against Murali at Galle. An allrounder who played indoor cricket for South Africa before breaking into the first-class game, Hall was initially seen as a bowler who batted a bit, then got pigeonholed as a one-day specialist. But as a late call-up in England in 2003 he took 16 wickets in the Tests, and ensured victory at Leeds with a buccaneering 99 not out. Then he defied the Indians for 588 minutes in the heat of Kanpur to make 163 as an emergency opener. Test opportunities have been few since, but he remains in the one-day frame. Initially out of favour in 2006-07, he forced his way back, and finished the World Cup as South Africa's joint-highest wicket-taker. After that, though, miffed at missing the World Twenty20 championships, he threatened retirement.

THE FACTS At Leeds in 2003 Hall was only the fifth man to be marooned on 99 not out in a Test, after Geoff Boycott, Steve Waugh, Alex Tudor and Shaun Pollock ... In the four innings either side of his 99 he made just one run, with three ducks ... Hall's 5 for 18 against England at Bridgetown were the best bowling figures of the 2007 World Cup ... Hall averages 17.33 with the ball in Tests against Pakistan – and 193.00 v West Indies ...

THE FIGURES

Batting and fielding

	M	Inns	NO	Runs	HS	Avge	S/R	100	50	4s	6s	Ct	St
Tests to 10.9.07	21	33	4	760	163	26.20	46.06	1	3	96	4	16	0
ODIs to 10.9.07	88	56	13	905	81	21.04	75.04	0	3	90	10	29	0
First-class to 10.9.07	126	184	25	5553	163	33.66	–	5	36	–	–	91	0

Bowling

	M	Balls	Runs	Wkts	BB	Avge	RpO	S/R	5i	10m
Tests to 10.9.07	21	3001	1617	45	3–1	35.93	3.23	66.68	0	0
ODIs to 10.9.07	88	3341	2515	95	5–18	26.47	4.51	35.16	1	0
First-class to 10.9.07	126	21210	9993	382	6–77	26.15	2.82	55.52	13	1

HARBHAJAN SINGH

Full name **Harbhajan Singh**
Born **July 3, 1980, Jullundur, Punjab**
Teams **Punjab, Surrey**
Style **Right-hand bat, offspinner**
Test debut **India v Australia at Bangalore 1997-98**
ODI debut **India v New Zealand at Sharjah 1997-98**

THE PROFILE Harbhajan Singh represents the spirit of the new Indian cricketer. His arrogance and cockiness – traits that earned him a rebuke from the establishment and suspension from India's National Cricket Academy – translate into self-belief and passion on the field, and Harbhajan has the talent to match. An offspinner with a windmilling, whiplash action, remodelled after he was reported for throwing, he exercises great command over the ball, has the ability to vary his length and pace, and can turn it the other way too. His main wicket-taking ball, however, is the one that climbs wickedly on the unsuspecting batsman from a good length, forcing him to alter his stroke at the last second. In March 2001, it proved too much for the all-conquering Australians, as Harbhajan collected 32 wickets in three Tests, while none of his team-mates managed more than three. Purists might mutter about a lack of loop and flight, but this was one of the greatest performances ever by a finger-spinner – at a time when orthodox offspin was supposed to be history. He has since been bothered by injury, while in Pakistan early in 2006 he finished with 0 for 355 in two Tests before bouncing back with five-fors against West Indies in St Kitts and Jamaica (5 for 13 in only 4.3 overs) in June. He had 50 Test caps and more than 200 wickets – and nearly 1000 runs with his occasionally explosive batting – before he turned 26, and although a slump in 2006-07 cost him his place (and a tour of England) it would be a surprise if he was out of favour for too long.

THE FACTS Harbhajan's match figures of 15 for 217 against Australia at Chennai in 2000-01 have been bettered for India only by Narendra Hirwani (16 for 136 in 1987-88, also at Chennai) ... Harbhajan took 32 wickets at 17.03 in that three-match series: his haul at Kolkata included India's first-ever Test hat-trick, when he dismissed Ricky Ponting, Adam Gilchrist and Shane Warne ... He has taken 56 wickets at 24.17 in Tests against Australia, but only 15 at 57.33 against Pakistan ... His record includes two ODIs for the Asia XI ...

THE FIGURES
Batting and fielding   www.cricinfo.com

	M	Inns	NO	Runs	HS	Avge	S/R	100	50	4s	6s	Ct	St
Tests to 10.9.07	57	79	18	986	66	16.16	67.95	0	2	142	16	30	0
ODIs to 10.9.07	151	79	22	728	46	12.77	79.47	0	0	63	18	41	0
First-class to 10.9.07	120	158	34	2368	84	19.09	–	0	6	–	–	63	0

Bowling

	M	Balls	Runs	Wkts	BB	Avge	RpO	S/R	5i	10m
Tests to 10.9.07	57	15162	7108	238	8–84	29.86	2.81	63.70	19	4
ODIs to 10.9.07	151	8131	5619	174	5–31	32.29	4.14	46.72	2	0
First-class to 10.9.07	120	28934	13566	509	8–84	26.65	2.81	56.84	33	6

STEVE **HARMISON**

Full name	**Stephen James Harmison**
Born	**October 23, 1978, Ashington, Northumberland**
Teams	**Durham**
Style	**Right-hand bat, right-arm fast bowler**
Test debut	**England v India at Nottingham 2002**
ODI debut	**England v Sri Lanka at Brisbane 2002-03**

THE PROFILE With his lofty, loose-limbed action and his painful knack of jamming fingers against bat-handles, Steve Harmison had long been likened, tongue-in-cheek, to the great Curtly Ambrose, when suddenly he loped in and produced a spell that Ambrose himself could hardly have bettered. West Indies were humbled for 47 at Kingston in March 2004, with Harmison taking a remarkable 7 for 12. It was a stunning riposte from a man who, only months earlier, had flown home crocked from Bangladesh. He was initially held back by niggling injuries (including somehow dislocating his shoulder after catching his hand in his trouser pocket while bowling) and a tendency to homesickness on overseas tours, and he mixed magical spells with moments when the radar went on the blink. But in the Caribbean he seemed finally to come of age. There were more wickets at home in 2004, as England won all seven Tests against West Indies and New Zealand. A dip followed in South Africa, but after a cathartic five-wicket haul against Bangladesh at home in Durham, he tore into Australia's top order at Lord's on the first morning of the 2005 Ashes series. He couldn't secure victory then, but popped up to seal the thrilling two-run win at Birmingham. A year later he demolished Pakistan with 6 for 19 at Birmingham, but the much-hyped 2006-07 Ashes rematch was the pits, kicked off by Harrison's mega-wide with the first ball of the series. He often looked fed up, retired from one-day cricket after being left out of the side for the Australian triangular series ... then picked up a hernia during a hit-and-miss series against West Indies. He'll be back – unless the selectors have finally lost patience with his moods.

THE FACTS Harmison's 7 for 12 at Kingston in March 2004, as West Indies were shot out for 47, are the best Test bowling figures at Sabina Park ... Harmison took 67 Test wickets in 2004, a record for an England bowler at the time (Andrew Flintoff beat it by one in 2005) ... His brother Ben also plays for Durham: they were born in Ashington, the same Northumberland village as football's Charlton brothers ... His record includes one Test for the World XI ...

THE FIGURES

Batting and fielding

www.cricinfo.com

	M	Inns	NO	Runs	HS	Avge	S/R	100	50	4s	6s	Ct	St
Tests *to 10.9.07*	54	73	18	632	42	11.49	58.19	0	0	81	9	7	0
ODIs *to 10.9.07*	46	22	13	67	13*	7.44	57.75	0	0	2	0	8	0
First-class *to 10.9.07*	147	204	55	1493	42	10.02	–	0	0	–	–	24	0

Bowling

	M	Balls	Runs	Wkts	BB	Avge	RpO	S/R	5i	10m
Tests *to 10.9.07*	54	11788	6319	205	7–12	30.82	3.21	57.50	8	1
ODIs *to 10.9.07*	46	2443	2057	67	5–33	30.70	5.05	36.46	1	0
First-class *to 10.9.07*	147	28644	14960	516	7–12	28.99	3.13	55.51	18	1

PAUL **HARRIS**

Full name **Paul Lee Harris**
Born **Nov 2, 1978, Salisbury (now Harare), Zimbabwe**
Teams **Titans, Warwickshire**
Style **Right-hand bat, slow left-arm orthodox spinner**
Test debut **South Africa v India at Cape Town 2006-07**
ODI debut **No ODIs yet**

THE PROFILE Slow left-armer Paul Harris is the latest man to be tasked with curing South African cricket's chief ailment – their continued failure to develop matchwinning spinners for the national team. Tall and not unlike the former England star Phil Tufnell in appearance and style, Harris eventually made it into the squad for the 2006-07 series against India, making his debut in the New Year Test at Cape Town, taking four wickets in the first innings, including Sachin Tendulkar and Virender Sehwag, and adding the scalp of Rahul Dravid in the second: his nagging, over-the-wicket line kept the Indians quiet, and helped his side reclaim the initiative. Until then the selectors had ignored Harris, even though he led the wicket-takers with 49 in the 2005-06 SuperSport Series, and it seemed possible that he might be lost to South African cricket altogether after a successful stint for Warwickshire in 2006 as a Kolpak player. But then Nicky Boje stormed into retirement, finally disenchanted with his country's treatment of spinners, and the call went out to Harris – a departure from South Africa's usual policy of choosing slow bowlers who can also contribute with the bat and in the field. Harris, who was born in Zimbabwe but grew up in Cape Town – where his rise was originally blocked by Paul Adams and Claude Henderson – combines accuracy, turn and bounce, from an unprepossessing approach described by one local journalist as "shuffling up like a right-hand bowler trying to bowl left-arm for a laugh".

THE FACTS Harris took 8 for 58 for Western Province B against Northerns B in the final of the UCB Bowl at Cape Town in December 2002 ... For Warwickshire against Durham at Chester-le-Street in July 2007 Harris reached his maiden fifty in 34 balls, scoring 45 of his first 51 runs off the bowling of Mark Davies, including five sixes ... He took 6 for 54 for Titans against Cape Cobras at Benoni in March 2006 ...

THE FIGURES

Batting and fielding   www.cricinfo.com

	M	Inns	NO	Runs	HS	Avge	S/R	100	50	4s	6s	Ct	St
Tests *to 10.9.07*	4	7	1	26	11*	4.33	29.54	0	0	3	0	2	0
ODIs *to 10.9.07*	0	0	–	–	–	–	–	–	–	–	–	–	–
First-class *to 10.9.07*	57	69	10	834	55	14.13	–	0	1	–	–	21	0

Bowling

	M	Balls	Runs	Wkts	BB	Avge	RpO	S/R	5i	10m
Tests *to 10.9.07*	4	703	314	11	4–46	28.54	2.67	63.90	0	0
ODIs *to 10.9.07*	0	0	–	–	–	–	–	–	–	–
First-class *to 10.9.07*	57	12538	5701	198	6–54	28.79	2.72	63.32	11	0

MATTHEW **HAYDEN**

AUSTRALIA

Full name **Matthew Lawrence Hayden**
Born **October 29, 1971, Kingaroy, Queensland**
Teams **Queensland**
Style **Left-hand bat, occasional right-arm medium-pacer**
Test debut **Australia v South Africa at Johannesburg 1993-94**
ODI debut **Australia v England at Manchester 1993**

THE PROFILE Strength is Matthew Hayden's strength – both mental and physical. It enabled him to shrug off carping that he was too limited for Test cricket because of the way he plays around his front pad. Before his maiden first-class innings, he asked if anyone had made 200 on debut, then went out and smacked 149. The runs have rarely abated since. Tall and powerful, he batters the ball at and through the off side. He has also made himself a fine catcher in the cordon. Hayden's earliest Tests were all against South Africa and West Indies: he didn't impress, but patience and willpower won through. In 2001-01 he slog-swept his way to 549 runs in India, an Australian record for a three-Test series, and by the end of 2001 he had formed a prolific opening partnership with Justin Langer. Hayden belatedly came good in ODIs, and was ranked among the top three batsmen in both forms of the game by the 2003 World Cup. Later that year he hammered 380 against Zimbabwe, briefly borrowing the Test record from Brian Lara. He experienced a rare extended slump during 2004-05, and lost his one-day place. That lack of form and footwork continued in 2005, but a disastrous Ashes series was salvaged with 138 at The Oval. It was the awkward beginning of a resurgence that saved his career. Usually playing more patiently, he collected hundreds in the next three Tests, and passed 1000 runs in a calendar year for the fifth time. He remained determined to win back his one-day place, too: after 18 months out of favour he roared back in 2006-07, and finished the World Cup as the leading runscorer, with 659 at more than a run a ball.

THE FACTS Hayden held the record for the highest Test innings for six months, hitting 380 v Zimbabwe at Perth in October 2003: Brian Lara reclaimed the record with 400 not out, but Hayden's remains the highest in a Test in Australia ... He has scored 18 of his 27 Test centuries in Australia, where his overall average is 62.43 ... Hayden's 181 not out v New Zealand at Hamilton in 2006-07 is Australia's highest score in ODIs (they still lost) ... His record includes one ODI for the World XI ...

THE FIGURES

Batting and fielding   www.cricinfo.com

	M	Inns	NO	Runs	HS	Avge	S/R	100	50	4s	6s	Ct	St
Tests to 10.9.07	89	159	13	7739	380	53.00	60.08	27	27	942	79	118	0
ODIs to 10.9.07	145	140	15	5499	181*	43.99	78.53	10	30	561	79	61	0
First-class to 10.9.07	279	486	46	23484	380	53.37	–	75	98	–	–	286	0

Bowling

	M	Balls	Runs	Wkts	BB	Avge	RpO	S/R	5i	10m
Tests to 10.9.07	89	54	40	0	–	–	4.44	–	0	0
ODIs to 10.9.07	145	6	18	0	–	–	18.00	–	0	0
First-class to 10.9.07	279	1097	671	17	3–10	39.47	3.67	64.52	0	0

BEN **HILFENHAUS**

AUSTRALIA

Full name	Benjamin William Hilfenhaus
Born	March 15, 1983, Ulverstone, Tasmania
Teams	Tasmania
Style	Right-hand bat, right-arm fast-medium bowler
Test debut	No Tests yet
ODI debut	Australia v New Zealand at Hobart 2006-07

THE PROFILE A couple of years ago Ben Hilfenhaus was working on a building site, but now he can safely lay down his trowel after a series of dramatic performances in his first two seasons catapulted him to a national contract. "It has been a fast ride," he admitted after picking up the Bradman Young Cricketer of the Year prize in February 2007. A month earlier he played a Twenty20 international and then his first ODI, on his home ground at Hobart, needing only 12 balls before trapping Brendon McCullum in front. Now he waits for a second chance in the wake of Glenn McGrath's retirement. Strong and fit, Hilfenhaus is only the second fast bowler from Tasmania to play for Australia after Ricky Ponting's uncle Greg Campbell. Shaping the ball away is his speciality, but he can also angle it in: his repertoire was crucial to the Tigers' maiden Pura Cup victory in 2006-07. Hilfenhaus took 60 wickets at 25.38, the third-most in the competition's history, but he and the selectors will have to watch a back-breaking workload – in 2006-07 he delivered 509.1 first-class overs, nearly 200 more than any of his domestic fast-bowling counterparts. He had established himself quickly the previous summer – Man of the Match against Victoria in only his second game, ten wickets against NSW, then called up for Australia A after 39 wickets at 30.82 in his first season. He also returned to the Academy, having been there in 2002 when it was based in Adelaide (it's now in Queensland).

THE FACTS Hilfenhaus made his debut for Australia in a Twenty20 international against England at Sydney in January 2007, taking 2 for 16 in his four overs: he had "Hilfy" on his back, as the Aussies had their nicknames on their shirts ... He took 7 for 58 (and 10 for 87 in the match) for Tasmania against New South Wales at Hobart in March 2006 ... Hilfenhaus was named Australia's Bradman Young Cricketer of the Year for 2006-07 by a landslide, polling 97 votes to 11 for the next man (Cullen Bailey) ...

THE FIGURES

Batting and fielding   www.cricinfo.com

	M	Inns	NO	Runs	HS	Avge	S/R	100	50	4s	6s	Ct	St
Tests to 10.9.07	0	0	–	–	–	–	–	–	–	–	–	–	–
ODIs to 10.9.07	1	0	–	–	–	–	–	–	–	–	–	1	0
First-class to 10.9.07	21	27	11	150	34	9.37	–	0	0	–	–	6	0

Bowling

	M	Balls	Runs	Wkts	BB	Avge	RpO	S/R	5i	10m
Tests to 10.9.07	0	0	–	–	–	–	–	–	–	–
ODIs to 10.9.07	1	42	26	1	1–26	26.00	3.71	42.00	0	0
First-class to 10.9.07	21	5128	2725	99	7–58	27.52	3.18	51.79	4	1

BRAD **HODGE**

Full name	**Bradley John Hodge**
Born	**December 29, 1974, Sandringham, Victoria**
Teams	**Victoria, Lancashire**
Style	**Right-hand bat, occasional offspinner**
Test debut	**Australia v West Indies at Hobart 2005-06**
ODI debut	**Australia v New Zealand at Auckland 2005-06**

THE PROFILE Brad Hodge has been the nearly man of Australia's batting in the last couple of years. Picked for his first Test in November 2005 after being the reserve on three tours, he started with a fluent 60, and soon had 409 runs at the envious average of 58.42. That included a sumptuous 203 against South Africa at Perth. But two Tests later Hodge, a small right-hander who is more quiet and laid-back than his boyhood hero Dean Jones, was dropped amid whispers of a technical flaw against fast bowling, not helped by a brief drought in the Pura Cup. Hodge picked himself up with a century in the Pura final loss to Queensland, and signed for Lancashire, his third English county. It was a similar story in ODIs: picked as the spare batsman in the 2007 World Cup squad, he spanked an 82-ball century against Holland ... but didn't bat in the next three games and was then dropped when Andrew Symonds regained full fitness. A regular and consistent domestic performer, he first played for Victoria in 1993-94 at 18, and threatened 1000 runs as he settled quickly at No. 4. The following years were more difficult, but he returned from dips in form a more complete player, with a classical technique and the ability to direct shots to all parts. Rewarded with his first central contract in 2004, Hodge toured India that year. He was considered for the opening Test, but missed the place grabbed spectacularly by Michael Clarke. And now Hodge is again behind Clarke in the pecking order, although he remains in sight of resuming his short – and stunning – Test career.

THE FACTS Hodge was the fifth Australian to turn his maiden Test century into a double, following Bob Simpson, Sid Barnes, Syd Gregory and Hodge's boyhood idol Dean Jones: Jason Gillespie later joined their ranks ... In 2003 Hodge made 302 not out v Nottinghamshire, the highest score in Leicestershire's history at the time; the following year he was the Man of the Match as Leicestershire won the Twenty20 Cup final ...

THE FIGURES

Batting and fielding

www.cricinfo.com

	M	Inns	NO	Runs	HS	Avge	S/R	100	50	4s	6s	Ct	St
Tests to 10.9.07	5	9	2	409	203*	58.42	51.77	1	1	47	0	9	0
ODIs to 10.9.07	18	15	2	516	123	39.69	93.98	1	3	44	12	12	0
First-class to 10.9.07	198	348	35	15089	302*	48.20	–	46	55	–	–	113	0

Bowling

	M	Balls	Runs	Wkts	BB	Avge	RpO	S/R	5i	10m
Tests to 10.9.07	5	12	8	0	–	–	4.00	–	0	0
ODIs to 10.9.07	18	54	33	1	1–17	33.00	3.66	54.00	0	0
First-class to 10.9.07	198	4881	2751	68	4–17	40.45	3.38	71.77	0	0

AUSTRALIA

BRAD **HOGG**

Full name	**George Bradley Hogg**
Born	**February 6, 1971, Narrogin, Western Australia**
Teams	**Western Australia**
Style	**Left-hand bat, slow left-arm unorthodox spinner**
Test debut	**Australia v India at Delhi 1996-97**
ODI debut	**Australia v Zimbabwe at Colombo 1996-97**

THE PROFILE With his zooming flipper and hard-to-pick wrong'un, Brad Hogg is Australia's best chinaman bowler since Chuck Fleetwood-Smith in the 1930s. He announced himself with a stupendous flipper in the 2003 World Cup: Andy Flower leapt back, waited for the away-spin and then slumped, bamboozled, as the ball fizzed straight through onto his stumps. Until then, Hogg's progress had been anything but straightforward. Like Stuart MacGill, he spent years in Shane Warne's shadow. He went to that World Cup hoping to pick Warne's brains, and unexpectedly ended up filling his boots after Warne's drugs ban. Hogg's initial Test opportunity, at Delhi way back in October 1996, also came as Warne's stand-in. He took only one wicket – the story goes that he had long waited to hear Ian Healy growl "Bowled, Hoggy" from behind the stumps, but performed so badly that the call never came. Seven years in the wilderness followed. Hogg began as a solid left-hand batsman, before flirting with chinamen in the nets. His batting has fallen away a little, but his jack-in-a-box fielding makes up for it. Hogg used to be a postman – "I do my round like a Formula One driver," he once bragged – and has the ever-present smile of a postie who's never known yappy dogs or rainy days. He roared past 100 one-day wickets in Bangladesh early in 2006, and played a telling role as the World Cup was retained in 2007, with 21 wickets at 15.80. He is a youthful 36, but his days as an international are shortening – and sometimes recently he has been WA's second spin option.

THE FACTS There were seven years – and 78 matches – between Hogg's first and second Tests, an Australian record: Alan Hurst (30 matches) had the previous-longest wait for a second cap ... Hogg averages 15.50 with the ball in ODIs against Bangladesh, but 58.00 v India ... He has taken more wickets in ODIs than any other Australian left-arm bowler, with a best of 5 for 32 v West Indies at Melbourne in January 2005 ... Hogg played county cricket for Warwickshire in 2004, making his highest score of 158 for them against Surrey at Edgbaston ...

THE FIGURES

Batting and fielding   www.cricinfo.com

	M	Inns	NO	Runs	HS	Avge	S/R	100	50	4s	6s	Ct	St
Tests *to 10.9.07*	4	5	1	38	17*	9.50	27.94	0	0	2	0	0	0
ODIs *to 10.9.07*	106	58	25	705	71*	21.36	81.22	0	2	39	5	33	0
First-class *to 10.9.07*	92	136	29	3679	158	34.38	–	4	24	–	–	53	0

Bowling

	M	Balls	Runs	Wkts	BB	Avge	RpO	S/R	5i	10m
Tests *to 10.9.07*	4	774	452	9	2–40	50.22	3.50	86.00	0	0
ODIs *to 10.9.07*	106	4814	3605	133	5–32	27.10	4.49	36.19	2	0
First-class *to 10.9.07*	92	11918	6453	160	6–44	40.33	3.24	74.48	7	0

MATTHEW **HOGGARD**

ENGLAND

Full name	**Matthew James Hoggard**
Born	**December 31, 1976, Leeds, Yorkshire**
Teams	**Yorkshire**
Style	**Right-hand bat, right-arm fast-medium bowler**
Test debut	**England v West Indies at Lord's 2000**
ODI debut	**England v Zimbabwe at Harare 2001-02**

THE PROFILE Big and bustling, with the sort of energy coaches kill for, Matthew Hoggard shapes the ball away at pace and is surprisingly slippery off the pitch, although he can look innocuous when the ball refuses to move. He's also a reliable blocker with the bat. Hoggard was one of Yorkshire's bright young things in the late '90s, but it was under Duncan Fletcher and Nasser Hussain that he grew into a senior bowler in the England quartet that swept all before them in 2004. He had done well at home in 2002, after taking 7 for 63 at Christchurch the previous winter, but suffered later Down Under, where his arcing inswing was meat and drink to Australia's left-handers, especially Matthew Hayden. To his credit, Hoggard retreated to the Adelaide Academy, and returned with a snappier run-up to contribute to the fifth-Test win at Sydney. Flashier colleagues still stole the limelight, but Hoggard's moments in the sun were worth waiting for: a fine hat-trick in Barbados in April 2004, then a phenomenal 12-wicket haul at Johannesburg the following winter, setting up a series-clinching 2–1 lead. Next summer, he did well after a quiet start as the Ashes were recaptured: satisfyingly, he nailed his old nemesis Hayden three times, including a first-baller at Edgbaston. Unlike some, he never flagged when the Aussies hit back, hard, in 2006-07. A perspiring Hoggard claimed 7 for 109 at Adelaide, before the body finally protested and he missed the Sydney finale after playing in all England's previous 40 Tests. Back trouble restricted him to two home Tests in 2007, but no-one is writing him off just yet.

THE FACTS Hoggard became the third Englishman to take a Test hat-trick against West Indies, following Peter Loader (1957) and Dominic Cork (1995), at Bridgetown in March 2004 ... Rather surprisingly for a swing bowler he has a better bowling average overseas (29.30) than in England (30.73) ... Hoggard took 7 for 61 v South Africa at Jo'burg in 2003-04, and 12 for 205 in the match ... 86 (36%) of his Test wickets have been left-handers ... Hoggard rarely plays in ODIs now, but he did take 5 for 49 v Zimbabwe at Harare in October 2001 ...

THE FIGURES
Batting and fielding   www.cricinfo.com

	M	Inns	NO	Runs	HS	Avge	S/R	100	50	4s	6s	Ct	St
Tests to 10.9.07	64	87	27	444	38	7.40	22.13	0	0	38	0	23	0
ODIs to 10.9.07	26	6	2	17	7	4.75	56.66	0	0	0	0	5	0
First-class to 10.9.07	159	202	61	1266	89*	8.97	–	0	3	–	–	45	0

Bowling

	M	Balls	Runs	Wkts	BB	Avge	RpO	S/R	5i	10m
Tests to 10.9.07	64	13297	7208	240	7–61	30.03	3.25	55.40	7	1
ODIs to 10.9.07	26	1306	1152	32	5–49	36.00	5.29	40.81	1	0
First-class to 10.9.07	159	29471	15141	558	7–49	27.13	3.08	52.81	18	1

JAMES **HOPES**

Full name	**James Redfern Hopes**
Born	**October 24, 1978, Townsville, Queensland**
Teams	**Queensland**
Style	**Right-hand bat, right-arm medium-pacer**
Test debut	**No Tests yet**
ODI debut	**Australia v New Zealand at Wellington 2004-05**

THE PROFILE James Hopes was earmarked for higher honours in Australia's youth teams, but took a few years to settle once he made it to the first-class scene. A brisk medium-pacer whose aggressive, exciting batting has been shuffled around the Queensland order, Hopes has scored three Pura Cup centuries, and in 2004-05 his average was in the mid-forties. Bowling was his main weapon in 2005-06 – he had 16 wickets in the Pura Cup and 15 more in the one-day competition – but he was unable to transfer his regular success into the international arena. In nine ODI appearances, he did not manage more than one wicket in a match, although his batting showed some promise, with a top score of 43 against Sri Lanka. He was dropped from the squad at the end of the VB Series, but when Shane Watson suffered a calf problem in Bangladesh he was replaced by his Queensland team-mate. Despite that, Hopes was cut from the national-contract list and returned to the domestic fray: he has remained there ever since, although he was put on standby when Watson suffered an injury scare during the 2007 World Cup. A regular sweater in the gym, Hopes would love to be a professional golfer, but instead drives powerfully through the covers. Evenly balanced as an allrounder – both disciplines still need polish if he is to survive in the international game – his bowling has variety, and tight final overs have regularly picked up wickets and saved runs.

THE FACTS Hopes made his highest score of 146 when opening (with Michael Hussey) for Australia A v Pakistan A in an unofficial Test at Rawalpindi in September 2005 ... He scored 105 (against West Indies), 51 (v India) and 71 (v Pakistan) in successive innings during the 1997-98 Youth World Cup in South Africa ... Hopes took 6 for 70 (his only first-class five-for) for Queensland v Tasmania at Hobart in March 2006 ... Only Michael Kasprowicz (112) has taken more one-day wickets for Queensland than Hopes, who has 101 since his debut in January 2001 ...

THE FIGURES

Batting and fielding   www.cricinfo.com

	M	Inns	NO	Runs	HS	Avge	S/R	100	50	4s	6s	Ct	St
Tests *to 10.9.07*	0	0	–	–	–	–	–	–	–	–	–	–	–
ODIs *to 10.9.07*	9	3	0	84	43	28.00	87.50	0	0	4	0	3	0
First-class *to 10.9.07*	44	74	1	2226	146	30.49	–	4	10	–	–	19	0

Bowling

	M	Balls	Runs	Wkts	BB	Avge	RpO	S/R	5i	10m
Tests *to 10.9.07*	0	0	–	–	–	–	–	–	–	–
ODIs *to 10.9.07*	9	336	269	4	1–8	67.25	4.80	84.00	0	0
First-class *to 10.9.07*	44	5946	2886	78	6–70	37.00	2.91	76.23	1	1

NEW ZEALAND

GARETH **HOPKINS**

Full name	**Gareth James Hopkins**
Born	**November 24, 1976, Lower Hutt, Wellington**
Teams	**Auckland**
Style	**Right-hand bat, wicketkeeper**
Test debut	**No Tests yet**
ODI debut	**New Zealand v England at Chester-le-Street 2004**

THE PROFILE Gareth Hopkins started as a specialist wicketkeeper, but over time his uncompromising batting improved to the point where he was called up for the one-day NatWest Series in England in 2004, after Brendon McCullum
went home to be with his wife, who was expecting their first child. Hopkins didn't get much chance with the bat – in fact he was run out without facing the only time he made it out to the middle – but performed well enough behind the stumps. McCullum's continued excellence with bat and gloves has meant no chances since then, but Hopkins hung in there, and scored 514 runs at 85 for Otago during 2006-07, with three hundreds, which earned him a central contract for 2007-08. "I've been working quite hard towards this," said Hopkins, "and it's good to get a little bit of recognition." McCullum has loomed like an unwanted wedding guest almost throughout Hopkins's career: he was playing for Canterbury when McCullum moved to Christchurch from Otago, which persuaded Hopkins to make the reverse move. Now McCullum has decided to return to Otago, so Hopkins is upping sticks again and moving to Auckland, where his wife works, even though the Otago think-tank promised that he would still be their preferred keeper. A much-travelled cricketer, Hopkins spent the northern summer of 2007 playing in Holland, and represented Northern Districts and Canterbury before moving to Otago at the end of 2003.

THE FACTS Hopkins has batted only once in his five ODIs, against West Indies in the NatWest Series final at Lord's in 2004 – and was run out without facing a ball ... He scored 113 and 175 not out (still his highest score) for Canterbury against Auckland in February 2003 ... Hopkins has twice made ten dismissals in a match, equalling the New Zealand record – in an unofficial Test against Sri Lanka A at Kandy in October 2005 (including seven in an innings, which also equalled the NZ record), and for Otago v Canterbury at Dunedin in January 2005.

THE FIGURES
Batting and fielding   www.cricinfo.com

	M	Inns	NO	Runs	HS	Avge	S/R	100	50	4s	6s	Ct	St
Tests to 10.9.07	0	0	–	–	–	–	–	–	–	–	–	–	–
ODIs to 10.9.07	5	1	0	0	0	0.00	0.00	0	0	0	0	8	0
First-class to 10.9.07	94	150	24	3866	175*	30.68	–	7	14	–	–	250	18

Bowling

	M	Balls	Runs	Wkts	BB	Avge	RpO	S/R	5i	10m
Tests to 10.9.07	0	0	–	–	–	–	–	–	–	–
ODIs to 10.9.07	5	0	–	–	–	–	–	–	–	–
First-class to 10.9.07	94	6	13	0	–	–	–	13.00	0	0

JAMIE **HOW**

Full name **Jamie Michael How**
Born **May 19, 1981, New Plymouth, Taranaki**
Teams **Central Districts**
Style **Right-hand bat, right-arm medium-pacer/offspinner**
Test debut **New Zealand v West Indies at Auckland 2005-06**
ODI debut **New Zealand v Sri Lanka at Queenstown 2005-06**

THE PROFILE Jamie How stepped up to the full New Zealand side in 2004-05 after some solid performances for Central Districts – 704, 682 and 592 runs in the three seasons from 2002-03. A well-organised opener, more of an accumulator than a dasher, How has a penchant for big scores: after taking a while to find his first-class feet, he scored 163 not out and 158 in consecutive innings in March 2003, against Northern Districts and Canterbury, and started the following season with 169 against Otago. Picked for his one-day debut against Sri Lanka at Queenstown on New Year's Eve, 2005, How ensured his celebrations would go well with a sparky 58, including eight fours and a six, as New Zealand won easily. His first encounter with West Indies resulted in 66 in an opening stand of 136 with Nathan Astle, but his other four one-day innings brought him only 17 runs. He played all three Tests against West Indies, and one in South Africa in May 2006 as a late replacement for the injured Peter Fulton. The rampant Dale Steyn removed him cheaply in both innings in that Test at Johannesburg, and 37 in his first match, against the Windies at Auckland, remains How's best in six Tests so far. He had a moderate domestic season in 2006-07, managing only 419 runs at 29.92. He played in both Tests against Sri Lanka, but fell off the one-day radar and missed the World Cup. He is keen to develop his bowling, and although a knee injury held him back for a while, he wants to pick national coach John Bracewell's brains about offspin.

THE FACTS How's 58 against Sri Lanka at Queenstown in December 2005 was the highest score by a New Zealand opener on ODI debut ... He played in the 1999-2000 Under-19 World Cup in Sri Lanka, when his captain was James Franklin and the wicketkeeper was Brendon McCullum ... How also played soccer for New Zealand's youth sides, but eventually chose cricket ...

THE FIGURES

Batting and fielding   www.cricinfo.com

	M	Inns	NO	Runs	HS	Avge	S/R	100	50	4s	6s	Ct	St
Tests *to 10.9.07*	6	10	1	131	37	14.55	55.04	0	0	16	1	8	0
ODIs *to 10.9.07*	6	5	0	141	66	28.20	65.58	0	2	20	1	2	0
First-class *to 10.9.07*	59	100	8	3018	169	32.80	–	8	14	–	–	66	0

Bowling

	M	Balls	Runs	Wkts	BB	Avge	RpO	S/R	5i	10m
Tests *to 10.9.07*	6	0	–	–	–	–	–	–	–	–
ODIs *to 10.9.07*	6	0	–	–	–	–	–	–	–	–
First-class *to 10.9.07*	59	1788	1012	19	3–55	53.26	3.39	94.10	0	0

MICHAEL **HUSSEY**

AUSTRALIA

Full name	**Michael Edward Killeen Hussey**
Born	**May 27, 1975, Morley, Western Australia**
Teams	**Western Australia**
Style	**Left-hand bat, occasional right-arm medium-pacer**
Test debut	**Australia v West Indies at Brisbane 2005-06**
ODI debut	**Australia v India at Perth 2003-04**

THE PROFILE English fans couldn't understand why Australia took so long to recognise Michael Hussey's claims. Bradmanesque in county cricket, he was less prolific in Australia, and seemed destined to remain unfulfilled unless the Langer-Hayden-Ponting top-order triumvirate cracked. Finally, late in 2005 Langer's fractured rib gave Hussey his break after 15,313 first-class runs, a record for an Australian before wearing baggy green. His first Test was a disappointment, but he relaxed for his second and made an attractive century. Three more hundreds followed, including a memorable 122 against South Africa at the MCG, when he and Glenn McGrath added 107 for the last wicket. The fairy tale continued in the 2006-07 Ashes series, when he topped the batting averages with 91.60, although his one-day form did finally drop off a little. Like Langer and Graeme Wood, predecessors as left-hand Western Australian openers, Hussey has a tidy, compact style. Skilled off front foot and back, he is attractive to watch once set, which he was regularly at Northamptonshire, Gloucestershire and Durham. Reinventing himself in one-day cricket as an agile fielder and innovative batsman with cool head and loose wrists, once he made the national side Hussey underlined his credentials with some more Bradmanesque figures, and supplanted Michael Bevan as the Aussies' one-day "finisher", although he was hardly needed as Australia steamrollered to victory in the 2007 World Cup.

THE FACTS Hussey scored 229 runs in ODIs before he was dismissed, and had an average of 100.22 after 32 matches ... He took only 166 days to reach 1000 runs in Tests, beating the 228-day record established by England's Andrew Strauss in 2005 ... Hussey's 331 not out against Somerset at Taunton in 2003 is the highest individual score for Northamptonshire, and he was only the third man to make three triple-centuries in the County Championship ... He has captained Australia in four ODIs, and lost the lot ...

THE FIGURES
Batting and fielding

www.cricinfo.com

	M	Inns	NO	Runs	HS	Avge	S/R	100	50	4s	6s	Ct	St
Tests to 10.9.07	16	26	6	1597	182	79.85	52.72	5	8	181	11	8	0
ODIs to 10.9.07	72	54	23	1826	109*	58.90	90.39	2	10	152	37	43	0
First-class to 10.9.07	193	345	33	16956	331*	54.34	–		44	75	–	–	209	0

Bowling

	M	Balls	Runs	Wkts	BB	Avge	RpO	S/R	5i	10m
Tests to 10.9.07	16	30	23	0	–	–	4.60	–	0	0
ODIs to 10.9.07	72	192	167	2	1-22	83.50	5.21	96.00	0	0
First-class to 10.9.07	193	1440	762	20	3-10	38.10	3.17	72.00	0	0

RAO **IFTIKHAR ANJUM**

PAKISTAN

Full name	**Rao Iftikhar Anjum**
Born	**December 1, 1980, Khanewal, Punjab**
Teams	**Islamabad, Zarai Taraqiati Bank**
Style	**Right-hand bat, right-arm fast-medium bowler**
Test debut	**Pakistan v Sri Lanka at Kandy 2005-06**
ODI debut	**Pakistan v Zimbabwe at Multan 2004-05**

THE PROFILE With a high-arm action modelled on Glenn McGrath's, Iftikhar Anjum is another addition to Pakistan's seemingly endless production line of pace bowlers. Iftikhar, however, is more Aqib Javed than Waqar Younis, and his outswinger is considered by many to be just as lethal as Aqib's. He can bowl reverse-swing – when the ball gets a bit rougher, and has good control over his yorkers. Iftikhar has performed consistently well on the domestic circuit, taking almost 300 wickets on Pakistan's generally lifeless pitches, including 73 in 2000-01, his first full season. Two years later, some stellar performances propelled him towards the national side: Iftikhar captained the Zarai Taraqiati Bank to victory in the Patron's Trophy final over WAPDA at Karachi, taking 7 for 85 in the first innings and ending with ten in the match. Not surprisingly, he was included in Pakistan's one-day squad for the series against India early in 2004, before making his debut in the Paktel Cup that September. He has since been a handy back-up bowler in one-dayers, although he rarely plays when everyone is fit. A long injury list meant he won his first Test cap in Sri Lanka in April 2006: he was expensive at Kandy, and didn't take a wicket as Pakistan won inside three days. That probably led to his initial exclusion from the England tour in 2006, although he was called up later as injuries struck the squad again, only to go home himself after his father died. He was one of the few to emerge with much credit from the 2007 World Cup, taking five wickets in the first two games. He wasn't needed with the ball in the final match, against Zimbabwe, but earlier made 32 – from just 16 balls – to boost the total to a massive 349.

THE FACTS Iftikhar Anjum's best bowling figures are 7 for 59, for Zarai Taraqiati Bank against WAPDA at Hyderabad in February 2005 ... Two years previously he took 7 for 85 (10 for 116 in the match) against the same opposition in the Patron's Trophy final at Karachi ... Iftikhar took 7 for 94 – after a career-best innings of 78 – for Zarai Taraqiati Bank against Karachi Port Trust at Peshawar in December 2003 ...

THE FIGURES
Batting and fielding

	M	Inns	NO	Runs	HS	Avge	S/R	100	50	4s	6s	Ct	St
Tests *to 10.9.07*	1	1	1	9	9*	–	23.07	0	0	2	0	0	0
ODIs *to 10.9.07*	30	19	14	158	32	31.60	58.73	0	0	7	2	8	0
First-class *to 10.9.07*	81	125	27	1638	78	16.71	–	0	5	–	–	49	0

Bowling

	M	Balls	Runs	Wkts	BB	Avge	RpO	S/R	5i	10m
Tests *to 10.9.07*	1	84	62	0	–	–	4.42	–	0	0
ODIs *to 10.9.07*	30	1385	1051	27	3–44	38.92	4.55	51.29	0	0
First-class *to 10.9.07*	81	14845	7904	338	7–59	23.38	3.19	43.92	21	3

IMRAN NAZIR

Full name	**Imran Nazir**
Born	**December 16, 1981, Gujranwala, Punjab**
Teams	**Sialkot, National Bank**
Style	**Right-hand bat, occasional legspinner**
Test debut	**Pakistan v Sri Lanka at Lahore 1998-99**
ODI debut	**Pakistan v Sri Lanka at Visakhapatnam 1998-99**

THE PROFILE Imran Nazir has long been thought of as another of Pakistan's prodigiously gifted players, and the suspicion always was that he offered even more genuine promise than most. An opener who is particularly strong off the back foot, he loves forcing through the covers. At first his aggressive approach got him labelled as a one-day player, but he didn't fare badly in Tests to start with. He made 65 in his first, then 131 in his second, against West Indies at Bridgetown in May 2000. Another hundred followed against New Zealand at Lahore in May 2002, when he put on 204 with Inzamam-ul-Haq, who was en route to 329. But then reality set in, in the shape of Glenn McGrath and Shane Warne: Imran's technique, especially his lack of footwork, was found out rather cruelly in two Tests against the Aussies late in 2002, which included an embarrassing two-day rout in Sharjah. He was then upstaged by the likes of Mohammad Hafeez, Yasir Hameed, Imran Farhat and Taufeeq Umar, and hasn't played a Test since – but consistent domestic form eventually won him a one-day recall in 2006-07. A typically explosive 39-ball 57 against South Africa earned Imran a World Cup place, and he blazed a cathartic 160 – with eight sixes – in the consolation victory over Zimbabwe after all the heartache of elimination and Bob Woolmer's death. He is one of the side's best fielders, and is thought to be the first Pakistani to achieve an onfield cartwheel (while intercepting a square cut).

THE FACTS Imran Nazir's 160 against Zimbabwe at Kingston in the 2007 World Cup has been surpassed in ODIs for Pakistan only by Saeed Anwar's 194 against India in 1996-97 ... His innings included eight sixes, equalling the record for a World Cup innings, held by Ricky Ponting and Adam Gilchrist ... Nazir was only 18 years 121 days old when he made 105 not out against Zimbabwe in Grenada in April 2000: only Shahid Afridi (16 years 217 days old in 1996-97) has made an ODI century at a younger age ...

THE FIGURES
Batting and fielding   www.cricinfo.com

	M	Inns	NO	Runs	HS	Avge	S/R	100	50	4s	6s	Ct	St
Tests *to 10.9.07*	8	13	0	427	131	32.84	58.49	2	1	63	4	4	0
ODIs *to 10.9.07*	70	70	2	1729	160	25.42	80.53	2	9	204	32	21	0
First-class *to 10.9.07*	94	153	9	4722	164	32.79	–	7	24	–	–	73	0

Bowling

	M	Balls	Runs	Wkts	BB	Avge	RpO	S/R	5i	10m
Tests *to 10.9.07*	8	0	–	–	–	–	–	–	–	–
ODIs *to 10.9.07*	70	49	48	1	1–3	48.00	5.87	49.00	0	0
First-class *to 10.9.07*	94	311	269	5	3–61	53.80	5.18	62.20	0	0

INZAMAM-UL-HAQ

Full name	**Inzamam-ul-Haq**
Born	**March 3, 1970, Multan, Punjab**
Teams	**Multan, WAPDA, Yorkshire**
Style	**Right-hand bat, occasional slow left-armer**
Test debut	**Pakistan v England at Birmingham 1992**
ODI debut	**Pakistan v West Indies at Lahore 1991-92**

THE PROFILE Inzamam-ul-Haq is a symbiosis of strength and subtlety. Power is no surprise, but sublime touch is remarkable for one of his bulk. He loathes exercise, and often looks a passenger in the field, but with bat in hand he is suddenly alive – strong off his legs, and unleashing ferocious pulls and drives. He sometimes plays across his front pad early on, but uses his feet well to spin. His hapless running is legendary, and most dangerous for his partners. Inzamam belted 329 against New Zealand at a boiling Lahore in May 2002, but struggled afterwards, making only 16 runs in the 2003 World Cup. He was briefly dropped, but roared back with a magnificent century to clinch a one-wicket victory over Bangladesh at Multan, his home town. He was rewarded with the captaincy, but faced criticism after losing at home to India. But he took a team thin on bowling to India early in 2005, and levelled the series with a rousing 184 in the final Test, his 100th. After that, he went from strength to strength as captain – and premier batsman – until it all ended in tears (literally) at the 2007 World Cup, following which Inzamam retired from one-day cricket, and lost the Test captaincy too: he also joined the breakaway Indian Cricket League, leaving a question-mark over his future. The home series against England at the end of 2005 was arguably his finest hour: he never failed to reach 50. He slipped a little in England in 2006, losing the series then becoming embroiled in the ball-tampering row at The Oval, writing an unwanted note in history as the first captain to forfeit a Test match.

THE FACTS Inzamam-ul-Haq made 329 against New Zealand at Lahore in May 2002: the only higher score for Pakistan in Tests is Hanif Mohammad's 337 v West Indies at Bridgetown in 1957-58 ... He was the fifth man to score a century in his 100th Test, following Colin Cowdrey, Javed Miandad, Gordon Greenidge and Alec Stewart (Ricky Ponting later did it too) ... Inzamam averages 66.18 in Tests against New Zealand, but only 31.40 v Australia ... His record includes one Test for the World XI, and three ODIs for the Asia XI ...

THE FIGURES

Batting and fielding

www.cricinfo.com

	M	Inns	NO	Runs	HS	Avge	S/R	100	50	4s	6s	Ct	St
Tests to 10.9.07	119	198	22	8813	329	50.07	54.03	25	46	1104	48	81	0
ODIs to 10.9.07	378	350	53	11739	137*	39.52	74.24	10	83	–	–	113	0
First-class to 10.9.07	243	390	58	16717	329	50.35	–		45	86	–	–	171	0

Bowling

	M	Balls	Runs	Wkts	BB	Avge	RpO	S/R	5i	10m
Tests to 10.9.07	119	9	8	0	–	–	5.33	–	0	0
ODIs to 10.9.07	378	58	64	3	1–0	21.33	6.62	19.33	0	0
First-class to 10.9.07	243	2704	1295	38	5–80	34.07	2.87	71.15	2	0

WASIM **JAFFER**

INDIA

Full name	**Wasim Jaffer**
Born	**Feb 16, 1978, Bombay (now Mumbai), Maharashtra**
Teams	**Mumbai**
Style	**Right-hand batsman, occasional offspinner**
Test debut	**India v South Africa at Mumbai 1999-2000**
ODI debut	**India v South Africa at Durban 2006-07**

THE PROFILE A triple-century in only his second first-class game meant Wasim Jaffer was anointed as the great new hope of Mumbai cricket. He is a tall, slim opener with the style and panache of the young Mohammad Azharuddin, and much was expected of him on his Test debut in February 2000. But Allan Donald and Shaun Pollock proved too hot to handle – even though he showed glimpses of a steely and unflappable temperament – and his international career was put on hold. He continued to pile up the runs in domestic cricket, and a string of big scores in 2001-02 won him a place on the tour of the West Indies. Once there, he stroked two elegant half-centuries, though a worrying tendency to give it away when well set resulted in him losing his place at the top of the order. He reminded the selectors of his quality with some superb batting for the A team in England in 2003, but spent three years in the domestic wilderness before being recalled to the national squad. He made most of his first chance on return, against England at Nagpur in March 2006, following up a forthright 81 with his maiden Test hundred. He added 212 against West Indies in Antigua in June, and continued to score well as Virender Sehwag's opening partner in the Tests in the Caribbean, doing enough to keep Gautam Gambhir on the sidelines – and when Sehwag was dropped for the 2007 England tour Jaffer formed a surprisingly successful alliance with Dinesh Karthik.

THE FACTS Jaffer scored 314 not out in only his second first-class match, for Mumbai v Saurashtra at Rajkot in November 1996: he shared an opening stand of 459 with Sulakshan Kulkarni ... Jaffer made two more double-centuries, including 218 for India A v Warwickshire at Edgbaston in 2003, before making 212 in the first Test against West Indies at St John's in June 2006 ... He was the first man to bag a pair in a Test against Bangladesh, at Chittagong in May 2007: in the next match he made 138 not out ...

THE FIGURES

Batting and fielding

	M	Inns	NO	Runs	HS	Avge	S/R	100	50	4s	6s	Ct	St
Tests to 10.9.07	22	41	1	1391	212	34.77	46.47	4	8	189	2	17	0
ODIs to 10.9.07	2	2	0	10	10	5.00	43.47	0	0	2	0	0	0
First-class to 10.9.07	142	238	25	10596	314*	49.74	–	30	50	–	–	155	0

Bowling

	M	Balls	Runs	Wkts	BB	Avge	RpO	S/R	5i	10m
Tests to 10.9.07	22	66	18	2	2–18	9.00	1.63	33.00	0	0
ODIs to 10.9.07	2	0	–	–	–	–	–	–	–	–
First-class to 10.9.07	142	138	74	2	2–18	37.00	3.21	69.00	0	0

PHIL **JAQUES**

Full name	**Philip Anthony Jaques**
Born	**May 3, 1979, Wollongong, New South Wales**
Teams	**New South Wales, Worcestershire**
Style	**Left-hand bat, occasional left-arm spinner**
Test debut	**Australia v South Africa at Melbourne 2005-06**
ODI debut	**Australia v South Africa at Melbourne 2005-06**

THE PROFILE   Phil Jaques was on holiday when the Test call finally came. It meant an early-career gamble had paid off: a British passport-holder, Jaques had been the subject of a national tug-of-war in 2003. He had scored 1409 runs for Northamptonshire, but refused to commit to England as "My heart says Australia". After that Jaques maintained such a consistent standard with New South Wales and Yorkshire that when Justin Langer was ruled out of the Boxing Day Test against South Africa in December 2005 Trevor Hohns admitted that he "virtually demanded selection". His Test debut was quiet – he walked after squirting Shaun Pollock to short leg for 2, and added 28 in the second innings – but he had been earmarked as a long-term prospect. Another opportunity came in Bangladesh, and he produced a capable 66. Jaques, who has shown the ability to score big runs on English greentops and hard-baked tracks in Australia and Pakistan, is the front-runner to succeed the retired Justin Langer in the Test side. Another injury – to Simon Katich this time – led to a one-day call-up during the 2005-06 VB Series. He made a stunning impact with 94, but when Katich returned he was harshly dropped, amid suggestions that his fielding was substandard. Jaques had to introduce himself to Ricky Ponting before his debut, but his reputation had already excited the previous captain: "Australia is lucky to have a player like him coming through," said Steve Waugh. "He is the prototype for young players."

THE FACTS   Jaques's 94 against South Africa in Melbourne in January 2006 was the highest by any player making his ODI debut for Australia (beating Kepler Wessels's 79 in 1982-83), and the fifth-highest for all countries, behind four century-makers ... His second ODI was less memorable: out fourth ball for 0 as South Africa bowled Australia out for 93 ... Jaques was the first batsman to score double-centuries for and against Yorkshire, following 222 for Northamptonshire in 2003 with 243 for Yorkshire against Hampshire the following year ... He made 244 and 202 in successive matches for Worcestershire in 2006 ...

THE FIGURES

Batting and fielding   www.cricinfo.com

	M	Inns	NO	Runs	HS	Avge	S/R	100	50	4s	6s	Ct	St
Tests *to 10.9.07*	2	3	0	96	66	32.00	62.33	0	1	11	1	1	0
ODIs *to 10.9.07*	6	6	0	125	94	20.83	71.02	0	1	16	1	3	0
First-class *to 10.9.07*	107	189	8	9885	244	54.61	–		29	46	–	–	86	0

Bowling

	M	Balls	Runs	Wkts	BB	Avge	RpO	S/R	5i	10m
Tests *to 10.9.07*	2	0	–	–	–	–	–	–	–	–
ODIs *to 10.9.07*	6	0	–	–	–	–	–	–	–	–
First-class *to 10.9.07*	107	68	87	0	–	–	7.67	–	0	0

JAVED OMAR

Full name	**Mohammad Javed Omar Belim**
Born	**November 25, 1976, Dhaka**
Teams	**Dhaka**
Style	**Right-hand batsman, occasional legspinner**
Test debut	**Bangladesh v Zimbabwe at Bulawayo 2000-01**
ODI debut	**Bangladesh v India at Sharjah 1994-95**

THE PROFILE With a priceless ability to occupy the crease, Javed Omar Belim has developed into the closest thing to a Test-class opener that Bangladesh have produced in their torrid early years of senior international cricket. A glut of one-day internationals early in his career did not help his development, but grumbles that he scored his runs too slowly were silenced by a historic Test debut in April 2001, when he carried his bat for 85 not out, only the third player in history to achieve this in his first match. "Gulla" underlined his limpet-like qualities later the same year with a painstaking 80, in more than 100 overs, in his sixth Test, against Zimbabwe at Chittagong. His maiden international hundred, against Pakistan at Peshawar in August 2003, gave Bangladesh a first-innings lead for the first time and showed the first glimpse of a new steelier attitude from his side. He has chalked up a half-century of one-day caps, with a highest score of 85 not out against Sri Lanka back in the pre-Test days of 2000, but it is in the five-day arena that his obduracy is best received, and Omar was the only man to come to terms with England's early-season conditions on a traumatic tour in 2005. He reached double figures in all four innings in the Tests, including a brave 71 at the final attempt at Chester-le-Street. He remained in the Test frame, although big scores were elusive, and earned a surprise call-up for the 2007 World Cup despite missing the previous 21 ODIs. He showed he was still a one-day force with 80 against India at Mirpur in May 2007.

THE FACTS Javed Omar carried his bat for 85 on his Test debut, against Zimbabwe at Bulawayo in 2000-01: he was the first man to do this in his first Test since 1898-99, when Pelham Warner managed it for England (Dr John Barrett also did it for Australia in 1890) ... He averages 40.18 in Tests against Zimbabwe, but 11.85 v India ... Omar's highest first-class score is 173, for Bangladesh A v Zimbabwe A at Fatullah in December 2006 ... He made 106 and 151 for Dhaka v Barisal in Dhaka in 2005-06 ...

THE FIGURES
Batting and fielding

www.cricinfo.com

	M	Inns	NO	Runs	HS	Avge	S/R	100	50	4s	6s	Ct	St
Tests *to 10.9.07*	40	80	2	1720	119	22.05	38.14	1	8	240	1	10	0
ODIs *to 10.9.07*	59	59	4	1312	85*	23.85	51.89	0	10	139	5	12	0
First-class *to 10.9.07*	82	156	2	4357	173	28.29	–	8	20	–	–	28	0

Bowling

	M	Balls	Runs	Wkts	BB	Avge	RpO	S/R	5i	10m
Tests *to 10.9.07*	40	6	12	0	–	–	12.00	–	0	0
ODIs *to 10.9.07*	59	0	–	–	–	–	–	–	–	
First-class *to 10.9.07*	82	240	153	2	2–75	76.50	3.82	120.00	0	0

SANATH **JAYASURIYA**

SRI LANKA

Full name	**Sanath Teran Jayasuriya**
Born	**June 30, 1969, Matara**
Teams	**Bloomfield, Lancashire**
Style	**Left-hand bat, slow left-arm orthodox spinner**
Test debut	**Sri Lanka v New Zealand at Hamilton 1990-91**
ODI debut	**Sri Lanka v Australia at Melbourne 1989-90**

THE PROFILE One of the most uncompromising strikers in world cricket, Sanath Jayasuriya found fame as a pinch-hitter at the 1996 World Cup, then showed he was also capable of massive scoring in Tests, collecting 340 in one innings against India and eventually becoming the first Sri Lankan to win 100 caps. He remains dizzily dangerous, especially on the subcontinent's slower surfaces. Short but powerfully built, he cuts and pulls with great power; his brutal bat-wielding is at odds with his shy, gentle nature. Streetwise opponents set traps in the gully and third man, but on song Jayasuriya can be virtually unstoppable, capable of scoring freely on both sides of the wicket. He is also a canny left-arm spinner, mixing his leg-stump darts with clever variations of pace. He had a successful stint as captain after Arjuna Ranatunga was dumped in 1999, but the responsibility took its toll. He stepped down after the 2003 World Cup, and a one-day slump immediately prompted calls for his retirement. But Jayasuriya was far from finished: he bounced back in 2004 with a blazing hundred against Australia, and a marathon double-century against Pakistan. He added twin centuries in the Asia Cup, and sailed past 10,000 one-day runs the following year. He looked rusty at first in England in 2006 when summoned from Test retirement, but soon showed his old form in pyjamas, with 122 at The Oval then 152 and 157 in successive innings against England and Holland. Although he now struggles in Tests, he remains a one-day force, collecting two more tons during the 2007 World Cup before briefly giving Sri Lanka hope in the final with 63. He is about to play his 400th ODI, and has more than 300 wickets too.

THE FACTS Jayasuriya made 340 against India in Colombo in August 1997, as Sri Lanka made the highest Test total of 952 for 6: he shared a world-record second-wicket partnership of 576 with Roshan Mahanama ... In the next Test Jayasuriya scored 199 ... He made his first-class debut for Sri Lanka B in Pakistan in 1988-89, and hit 203 and 207, both not out, in successive "Tests" there ... His record includes four ODIs for the Asia XI ...

THE FIGURES
Batting and fielding   www.cricinfo.com

	M	Inns	NO	Runs	HS	Avge	S/R	100	50	4s	6s	Ct	St
Tests *to 10.9.07*	107	182	14	6791	340	40.42	–	14	30	885	57	78	0
ODIs *to 10.9.07*	398	387	18	12116	189	32.83	90.50	25	64	–	242	114	0
First-class *to 10.9.07*	252	397	33	14295	340	39.27	–	29	67	–	–	158	0

Bowling

	M	Balls	Runs	Wkts	BB	Avge	RpO	S/R	5i	10m
Tests *to 10.9.07*	107	8002	3281	96	5–34	34.17	2.46	83.35	2	0
ODIs *to 10.9.07*	398	13963	11092	304	6–29	36.48	4.76	45.93	4	0
First-class *to 10.9.07*	252	14450	6352	192	5–34	33.08	2.63	75.26	2	0

MAHELA **JAYAWARDENE**

Full name	**Denagamage Proboth Mahela de Silva Jayawardene**
Born	**May 27, 1977, Colombo**
Teams	**Sinhalese Sports Club**
Style	**Right-hand bat, occ. right-arm medium-pacer**
Test debut	**Sri Lanka v India at Colombo 1997-98**
ODI debut	**Sri Lanka v Zimbabwe at Colombo 1997-98**

THE PROFILE A fine technician with an excellent temperament, Mahela Jayawardene's exciting arrival in 1997 heralded the start of a new era for Sri Lanka's middle order. He was the best batsman they had produced since Sanath Jayasuriya, and his rich talent fuelled towering expectations. Perhaps mindful of his first Test, when he went in against India with the score at 790 for 4, he soon developed an appetite for big scores. His 66 then, in the world-record 952 for 6, was followed by a masterful 167 on a Galle minefield against New Zealand in only his fourth Test, and a marathon 242 against India in his seventh. However, after a purple patch from 2000, Jayawardene's form became more patchy in 2002. His declining one-day productivity was particularly alarming, although that was partly explained by his being shuffled up and down the order. He hardly scored a run in the 2003 World Cup, and was dropped afterwards. However, he soon regained his confidence, and benefited from a settled spot at No. 4 after Aravinda de Silva retired. A good Test series against England was followed by more runs in 2004. He deputised as captain for the injured Marvan Atapattu in England in 2006, producing a stunning double of 61 and 119 to lead the amazing rearguard which saved the Lord's Test. Later he put South Africa to the sword in Colombo, hitting a colossal 374, and sharing a world-record stand of 624 with Kumar Sangakkara. He cemented his position as captain during 2006-07, inspiring his side to the World Cup final with 548 runs at 60, including a century in the semi-final victory over New Zealand.

THE FACTS Jayawardene made 374 against South Africa in Colombo in July 2006, sharing a world-record stand of 624 with Kumar Sangakkara (287) ... He has taken 63 catches off Muttiah Muralitharan in Tests, a record for a fielder-bowler combination, beating c Mark Taylor b Shane Warne (51) ... Jayawardene averages 67.84 in Tests against India, but only 27.33 against Pakistan ... His record includes five ODIs for the Asia XI ...

THE FIGURES

Batting and fielding

www.cricinfo.com

	M	Inns	NO	Runs	HS	Avge	S/R	100	50	4s	6s	Ct	St
Tests to 10.9.07	88	143	10	6630	374	49.84	52.69	18	29	817	36	123	0
ODIs to 10.9.07	256	239	26	7141	128	33.52	76.93	10	41	605	42	128	0
First-class to 10.9.07	166	260	19	12214	374	50.68	–	35	56	–	–	207	0

Bowling

	M	Balls	Runs	Wkts	BB	Avge	RpO	S/R	5i	10m
Tests to 10.9.07	88	458	228	4	2–32	57.00	2.98	114.50	0	0
ODIs to 10.9.07	256	582	558	7	2–56	79.71	5.75	83.14	0	0
First-class to 10.9.07	166	2858	1531	50	5–72	30.62	3.21	57.16	1	0

PRASANNA **JAYAWARDENE**

Full name	**Hewasandatchige Asiri Prasanna Wishvanath Jayawardene**
Born	**October 9, 1979, Colombo**
Teams	**Sebastianites**
Style	**Right-hand bat, wicketkeeper**
Test debut	**Sri Lanka v Pakistan at Kandy 2000**
ODI debut	**Sri Lanka v Pakistan at Sharjah 2002-03**

THE PROFILE A neat, unflashy wicketkeeper, Prasanna Jayawardene looked set for a long international career after touring England in 1998 at 19, but he became a bit of a back number after the rocket-fuelled arrival of Kumar Sangakkara in 2000. Waiting on the sidelines had already been a feature of Jayawardene's career: he made his Test debut against Pakistan in June 2000, but was confined to the dressing-room throughout, as Sri Lanka batted over the first three days before rain washed out play on the last two. The return of Romesh Kaluwitharana briefly pushed him even further down the pecking order, but with the Sri Lankan selectors voicing their concerns about overburdening Sangakkara, Jayawardene was recalled to the Test squad for the tour of Zimbabwe in April 2004. Sangakkara soon got the gloves back that time, but there was something of a sea-change after the 2006 England tour, during which Jayawardene showed that his batting had improved. He was recalled for South Africa's visit in July 2006, and this time the decision to lighten Sangakkara's load paid off spectacularly – he hammered 287, and shared a world-record stand of 642 with Mahela Jayawardene in the first Test in Colombo. Prasanna Jayawardene (no relation to Mahela) contented himself with a couple of catches and a stumping as the South Africans went down by an innings, but finally seemed to have booked in for a long run behind the stumps – at least in Tests – and he cemented his place in June 2007 with a Test ton of his own, against Bangladesh.

THE FACTS Prasanna Jayawardene made 120 not out, his first Test century, against Bangladesh in Colombo in June 2007, sharing a record seventh-wicket stand of 223 with Chaminda Vaas ... He has scored four other first-class centuries, the highest 166 not out for Sebastianites against Panadura at Moratuwa in February 2007 ... All Jayawardene's ODIs have come in the United Arab Emirates (Sharjah and Abu Dhabi) ...

THE FIGURES
Batting and fielding   www.cricinfo.com

	M	Inns	NO	Runs	HS	Avge	S/R	100	50	4s	6s	Ct	St
Tests *to 10.9.07*	12	11	1	295	120*	29.50	49.16	1	0	31	2	26	6
ODIs *to 10.9.07*	6	5	0	27	20	5.40	61.36	0	0	3	0	4	1
First-class *to 10.9.07*	133	203	24	4542	166*	25.37	–	5	17	–	–	318	58

Bowling

	M	Balls	Runs	Wkts	BB	Avge	RpO	S/R	5i	10m
Tests *to 10.9.07*	12	0	–	–	–	–	–	–	–	–
ODIs *to 10.9.07*	6	0	–	–	–	–	–	–	–	–
First-class *to 10.9.07*	133	0	–	–	–	–	–	–	–	–

MITCHELL **JOHNSON**

Full name	**Mitchell Guy Johnson**
Born	**November 2, 1981, Townsville, Queensland**
Teams	**Queensland**
Style	**Left-hand bat, left-hand fast-medium bowler**
Test debut	**No Tests yet**
ODI debut	**Australia v New Zealand at Christchurch 2005-06**

THE PROFILE Mitchell Johnson is Australia's most exciting fast-bowling prospect since Brett Lee first dyed his roots. He's quick, he's tall, he's talented – but most of all, he's a left-armer. Only digging up a blond legspinner could create more excitement in Australia, which has seen only two of this style of diamond – Alan Davidson and Bruce Reid – reach 100 Test wickets. Johnson was picked in the one-day side after just 12 first-class games, and his future depends on whether he can stay fit. Dennis Lillee spotted him as a 17-year-old, calling him "a once-in-a-generation bowler". Injuries kept intruding, but he played a full season in 2004-05 and was a fixture with Queensland a year later, after being picked for the Australia A tour of Pakistan. Another representative catapult arrived in December 2005, when he was supersubbed into the final match of the one-day series in New Zealand. The following May he was given a central contract, only two years after driving a delivery truck and considering walking away from the game because of his fourth back stress injury. However, the 2006-07 season was a sobering one. Johnson started by reducing India to 35 for 5 in a one-dayer in Kuala Lumpur, but narrowly missed out to the steadier Stuart Clark in the Ashes series, then had to sit on the sidelines throughout the World Cup as Shaun Tait and Nathan Bracken (another left-armer) bowled consistently well. At 6ft 2ins (189cm), Johnson has the height to worry batsmen and is intent on scaring them as well. Shane Watson, his Queensland team-mate, is impressed: "He has just about the most talent I've ever seen in an allround athlete ... If he can keep improving the sky's the limit."

THE FACTS Johnson was the bowling star of the 2005-06 Pura Cup final, taking 6 for 51 – and ten wickets in the match – as Queensland followed up their mammoth total of 900 for 6 by routing a demoralised Victoria: "What a performance on a flat wicket," said his captain Jimmy Maher ...

THE FIGURES

Batting and fielding   www.cricinfo.com

	M	Inns	NO	Runs	HS	Avge	S/R	100	50	4s	6s	Ct	St
Tests *to 10.9.07*	0	0	–	–	–	–	–	–	–	–	–	–	–
ODIs *to 10.9.07*	18	6	2	29	15	7.25	76.31	0	0	7	1	3	0
First-class *to 10.9.07*	20	27	9	435	54	24.16	–	0	3	–	–	2	0

Bowling

	M	Balls	Runs	Wkts	BB	Avge	RpO	S/R	5i	10m
Tests *to 10.9.07*	0	0	–	–	–	–	–	–	–	–
ODIs *to 10.9.07*	18	816	725	26	4–11	27.88	5.33	31.38	0	0
First-class *to 10.9.07*	20	3397	1859	67	6–51	27.74	3.28	50.70	2	1

MOHAMMAD **KAIF**

Full name	**Mohammad Kaif**
Born	**December 1, 1980, Allahabad, Uttar Pradesh**
Teams	**Uttar Pradesh**
Style	**Right-hand bat, occasional offspinner**
Test debut	**India v South Africa at Bangalore 1999-2000**
ODI debut	**India v England at Kanpur 2001-02**

THE PROFILE An elegant batsman who evokes memories of the young Azharuddin, Mohammad Kaif comes from the cricket backwater of Uttar Pradesh. He first came to prominence with India's Under-19s: he captained the side, which also included Yuvraj Singh, Ajay Ratra and Reetinder Sodhi, that won the 2000 Youth World Cup. Kaif's assured strokeplay, and composure that belied his age, earned him a Test cap against South Africa soon after his 19th birthday. The selectors subsequently discarded him, but stints at the Australian Cricket Academy and its Indian equivalent in Bangalore helped iron out some of the kinks in his technique. Recalled to the one-day side during 2001-02, he made an impact with some steady and purposeful batting. But it was during the 2002 NatWest Series in England that he truly hit the high notes, culminating in a magnificent unbeaten 87 as India shocked England by successfully chasing 326 for victory in the final at Lord's. A superb century followed against Zimbabwe, but he struggled to kick on after that and had a quiet World Cup in 2003. Kaif's exceptional fielding, usually at cover, often compensated for his poor scores – but it wasn't enough to win him a permanent place in the Test team, although it usually ensured a one-day spot. Things seemed to have changed after a good start to 2006: after a poor run he recovered with 91 against England at Nagpur in March, and followed that with a maiden Test century in St Lucia in June. But after another indifferent run he was out again, missing the World Cup, and this time it looked permanent – although he was offered the consolation prize of the captaincy of India's A team.

THE FACTS Kaif scored 100 in his second first-class match, for Uttar Pradesh against Haryana at Kanpur in April 1998, when he was 17 ... He averages 45.11 in ODIs against New Zealand, but only 11.83 against Australia ... Kaif averages 26.25 in home ODIs, and 26.55 in away ones – but in 33 ODIs on "neutral" territory he averages 53.11 ... Kaif's brother, Mohammad Saif, and his father, Mohammad Tarif, also played for Uttar Pradesh ...

THE FIGURES

Batting and fielding   www.cricinfo.com

	M	Inns	NO	Runs	HS	Avge	S/R	100	50	4s	6s	Ct	St
Tests *to 10.9.07*	13	22	3	624	148*	32.84	40.31	1	3	64	2	14	0
ODIs *to 10.9.07*	125	110	24	2753	111*	32.01	72.03	2	17	228	9	55	0
First-class *to 10.9.07*	86	138	15	4764	148*	38.73	–	7	30	–	–	62	0

Bowling

	M	Balls	Runs	Wkts	BB	Avge	RpO	S/R	5i	10m
Tests *to 10.9.07*	13	18	4	0	–	–	1.33	–	0	0
ODIs *to 10.9.07*	125	0	–	–	–	–	–	–	–	–
First-class *to 10.9.07*	86	1292	612	19	3–4	32.21	2.84	68.00	0	0

JACQUES **KALLIS**

Full name	**Jacques Henry Kallis**
Born	**October 16, 1975, Pinelands, Cape Town**
Teams	**Cape Cobras**
Style	**Right-hand bat, right-arm fast-medium bowler**
Test debut	**South Africa v England at Durban 1995-96**
ODI debut	**South Africa v England at Cape Town 1995-96**

THE PROFILE In an era of fast scoring and high-octane entertainment, Jacques Kallis is a throwback – an astonishingly effective one – to a more sedate age, when your wicket was to be guarded with your life, and runs were an accidental by-product of crease-occupation. He blossomed after a quiet start into arguably the world's leading batsman, with the adhesive qualities of a Cape Point limpet. He nailed down the No. 3 position after several others had been tried, and his stock rose from then on. In 2005, he was the ICC's first Test Player of the Year, after a run of performances against West Indies and England that marked him out as the modern game's biggest scalp. His batting is not for the romantic: a Kallis century tends to be a soulless affair, with ruthless efficiency taking precedence over derring-do, and he has never quite dispelled the notion that he is a selfish batsman, something the Aussies played on during the 2007 World Cup. But he has sailed to the top of South Africa's batting charts, and until Andrew Flintoff's emergence he was comfortably the world's leading allrounder, capable of swinging the ball sharply at a surprising pace off a relaxed run-up. Strong, with powerful shoulders and a deep chest, Kallis has the capacity to play a wide array of attacking strokes, if not always the inclination. He played his 100th Test in April 2006, not long after his 30th birthday, and has a batting average in the mid-fifties and 200 wickets in both Tests and ODIs. He's a fine slip fielder too.

THE FACTS Kallis and Shaun Pollock were the first South Africans to play 100 Tests, reaching the mark at Centurion in April 2006 ... Kallis averages 169.75 in Tests against Zimbabwe, and scored 388 runs against them in two Tests in 2001-02 without being dismissed ... Including his next innings he batted for a record 1241 minutes in Tests without getting out ... Kallis scored hundreds in five successive Tests in 2003-04 (only Don Bradman, with six, has done better) ... His record includes one Test and three ODIs for the World XI, and two ODIs for the Africa XI ...

THE FIGURES

Batting and fielding

www.cricinfo.com

	M	Inns	NO	Runs	HS	Avge	S/R	100	50	4s	6s	Ct	St
Tests to 10.9.07	107	182	29	8433	189*	55.09	42.75	24	44	945	55	105	0
ODIs to 10.9.07	261	247	46	9144	139	45.49	71.42	15	63	708	112	100	0
First-class to 10.9.07	193	316	43	14466	200	52.98	–	40	80	–	–	164	0

Bowling

	M	Balls	Runs	Wkts	BB	Avge	RpO	S/R	5i	10m
Tests to 10.9.07	107	14297	6756	213	6–54	31.71	2.83	67.12	4	0
ODIs to 10.9.07	261	9160	7335	233	5–30	31.48	4.80	39.31	2	0
First-class to 10.9.07	193	22876	10650	347	6–54	30.69	2.79	65.92	7	0

KAMRAN AKMAL

Full name	**Kamran Akmal**
Born	**January 13, 1982, Lahore, Punjab**
Teams	**Lahore, National Bank**
Style	**Right-hand bat, wicketkeeper**
Test debut	**Pakistan v Zimbabwe at Harare 2002-03**
ODI debut	**Pakistan v Zimbabwe at Bulawayo 2002-03**

THE PROFILE   Kamran Akmal made his first-class debut at the age of 15 as a useful wicketkeeper and a hard-hitting batsman. Several good performances earned him an A-team spot in 2002, and after doing well he was called up for the Zimbabwe tour ahead of the veteran Moin Khan. He was not expected to play in the Tests, but made his debut – and chipped in with a handy 38 – when Rashid Latif suffered a recurrence of an old back injury. Initially most of his matches came when Latif and Moin were unavailable: he stood in when Latif was suspended against Bangladesh, and then played against India when Moin was injured. However, from October 2004, with Latif out of favour and Moin no longer at his peak, Akmal became Pakistan's first-choice keeper. He responded with a magnificent showing with the gloves in Australia, despite repeated calls from home for a return to the old guard. In 2005, Akmal silenced those critics: as well as maintaining a high standard behind the stumps, he scored five international centuries. Three of them came while opening in one-dayers, and two in Tests, the first saving the match against India at Mohali, while the second, a blistering knock, came in the emphatic series-sealing win over England at Lahore. It seemed to have confirmed him as Pakistan's No. 1 – but a nightmare series in England in 2006 set him back again. He retained his place throughout 2006-07, without quite regaining his best touch with bat or gloves.

THE FACTS   Four of Kamran Akmal's eight first-class centuries have come in Tests: he scored five international hundreds in December 2005 and January 2006, including 154 in the Lahore Test against England, when he shared a sixth-wicket stand of 269 with Mohammad Yousuf (223) ... Moin Khan is the only other Pakistan wicketkeeper to score four Test hundreds ... Akmal scored 102 and 109 in successive ODIs against England in December 2005 ... His brother Adnan has also played first-class cricket in Pakistan ...

THE FIGURES
Batting and fielding   www.cricinfo.com

	M	Inns	NO	Runs	HS	Avge	S/R	100	50	4s	6s	Ct	St
Tests to 10.9.07	33	55	4	1521	154	29.82	62.23	4	5	227	2	108	18
ODIs to 10.9.07	68	59	9	1253	124	25.06	82.48	3	2	147	8	60	11
First-class to 10.9.07	120	185	24	5071	174	31.49	–	8	23	–	–	378	37

Bowling

	M	Balls	Runs	Wkts	BB	Avge	RpO	S/R	5i	10m
Tests to 10.9.07	33	0	–	–	–	–	–	–	–	–
ODIs to 10.9.07	68	0	–	–	–	–	–	–	–	–
First-class to 10.9.07	120	0	–	–	–	–	–	–	–	–

CHAMARA **KAPUGEDERA**

Full name **Chamara Kantha Kapugedera**
Born **February 24, 1987, Kandy**
Teams **Colombo Cricket Club**
Style **Right-hand bat, occasional right-arm medium-pacer**
Test debut **Sri Lanka v England at Lord's 2006**
ODI debut **Sri Lanka v Australia at Perth 2005-06**

THE PROFILE A naturally aggressive right-hander, Chamara Kapugedera is one of the few genuinely exciting batsmen the Sri Lankan selectors have unearthed from the Under-19 team in recent times. From his first appearances for Dharmaraja College in Kandy when he was 11, "Kapu" has rarely wasted an opportunity. After a prolific 2003-04 season, when he scored over 1000 runs at schoolboy level, he was picked for the following year's Under-19 tour of Pakistan. He made 112 in the first "Test", and bettered that with a stunning 131 in the third ODI against youth cricket's world champions at Karachi. He still rates that as his best innings, although he batted equally well for 70 on his first-class debut, for Sri Lanka A against the strong New Zealand A tourists in October 2005. The selectors eventually gambled, and fast-tracked him into the national squad after glowing reports from his youth coaches. Kapugedera was picked to tour India in November 2005, but injured his knee. However, he made his ODI debut, still only 18, against Australia at Perth early in 2006. A maiden fifty followed against Pakistan in March. He won his first Test cap at Lord's in May 2006, but was unlucky enough to receive the perfect inswinging yorker first ball from Sajid Mahmood. But he put that disappointment behind him with a composed 50 in the third Test, which Sri Lanka won to level the series. He had a quiet time in 2006-07, missing the World Cup after going 12 ODIs without reaching 50. However, Kapugedera, who is also an excellent fielder, is very much one for the future.

THE FACTS Kapugedera scored 70 on his first-class debut, for Sri Lanka A v New Zealand A in Colombo in October 2005 ... He was selected for the 2006 tour of England after playing only three first-class matches, and made his maiden century – 134 not out v Sussex at Hove – the game after collecting a first-ball duck on his Test debut at Lord's ... Kapugedera played three Under-19 ODIs and finished them with a batting average of 154 ...

THE FIGURES

Batting and fielding   www.cricinfo.com

	M	Inns	NO	Runs	HS	Avge	S/R	100	50	4s	6s	Ct	St
Tests to 10.9.07	6	11	1	221	63	22.10	44.20	0	2	31	2	3	0
ODIs to 10.9.07	22	18	1	273	50	16.05	77.11	0	1	29	5	5	0
First-class to 10.9.07	20	35	5	983	134*	32.76	56.01	1	7	–	–	13	0

Bowling

	M	Balls	Runs	Wkts	BB	Avge	RpO	S/R	5i	10m
Tests to 10.9.07	6	0	–	–	–	–	–	–	–	–
ODIs to 10.9.07	22	0	–	–	–	–	–	–	–	–
First-class to 10.9.07	20	114	72	0	–	–	3.78	–	0	0

DINESH **KARTHIK**

Full name **Krishnakumar Dinesh Karthik**
Born **June 1, 1985, Madras (now Chennai)**
Teams **Tamil Nadu**
Style **Right-hand bat, wicketkeeper**
Test debut **India v Australia at Mumbai 2004-05**
ODI debut **India v England at Lord's 2004**

INDIA

THE PROFILE It took just one season for Dinesh Karthik to be transformed from obscure second-choice wicketkeeper for Tamil Nadu to serious contender for an Indian spot. Karthik may be cherub-faced and shy off the field, but he has shown his ability to attack under pressure and improvise on it. As a 17-year-old in 2002, he gave glimpses of batting talent, but his keeping wasn't up to scratch and he was dropped for the later stages of the Ranji Trophy. However, in 2004 an impressive display in the Under-19 World Cup in Dhaka (including a whirlwind 70 in a must-win game against Sri Lanka), two vital hundreds in the Ranji Trophy knockout games, and an improved showing behind the stumps inevitably resulted in interest from the national selectors. He replaced Parthiv Patel in the one-day squad for the NatWest Challenge in England in September 2004, and made his debut at Lord's, pulling off a superb stumping to dispose of Michael Vaughan. Then he made his Test debut against Australia, but after managing just one fifty in ten matches, he was dropped in favour of the flamboyant Mahendra Singh Dhoni, whose instant success meant Karthik had to rethink. He reinvented himself as a specialist batsman. After India's forgettable World Cup (for which he was selected but didn't play), Karthik made his first Test century in Bangladesh, forging a successful opening partnership with Wasim Jaffer which continued in England, where he was India's leading scorer in the Tests with 263.

THE FACTS Karthik's highest score of 134 helped rescue Tamil Nadu from 91 for 6 in a Ranji Trophy match against Mumbai in December 2005 ... He averages 49.33 in Tests against South Africa, but only 7.00 v Australia (and 1.00 in two Tests against Zimbabwe) ... Karthik scored two double-centuries for Tamil Nadu Under-19s in September 2002 ... He prefers his surname to be spelt with two As ("Kaarthik") as it is more astrologically propitious ...

THE FIGURES

Batting and fielding   www.cricinfo.com

	M	Inns	NO	Runs	HS	Avge	S/R	100	50	4s	6s	Ct	St
Tests *to 10.9.07*	16	24	1	816	129	35.47	49.21	1	6	108	1	39	2
ODIs *to 10.9.07*	25	19	5	330	63	23.57	70.66	0	2	30	2	22	2
First-class *to 10.9.07*	52	82	5	2514	134	32.64	–	4	16	–	–	143	14

Bowling

	M	Balls	Runs	Wkts	BB	Avge	RpO	S/R	5i	10m
Tests *to 10.9.07*	16	0	–	–	–	–	–	–	–	–
ODIs *to 10.9.07*	25	0	–	–	–	–	–	–	–	–
First-class *to 10.9.07*	52	30	28	0	–	–	5.60	–	0	0

JUSTIN **KEMP**

Full name	**Justin Miles Kemp**
Born	**October 2, 1977, Queenstown, Cape Province**
Teams	**Cape Cobras**
Style	**Right-hand bat, right-arm fast-medium bowler**
Test debut	**South Africa v Sri Lanka at Centurion 2000-01**
ODI debut	**South Africa v Sri Lanka at Bloemfontein 2000-01**

THE PROFILE Justin Kemp is tall and powerful, and the smiter of the biggest sixes in the world today. But Kemp, who also bowls at a handy fast-medium, has had a stop-start international career. He was tipped for great things when he broke into the South African side in 2000-01, taking five wickets in his first Test, against Sri Lanka at Centurion, and winning two more caps in the West Indies soon afterwards. Shortly after his Test debut, on his way to 188 in a domestic match, he smacked five sixes off one over, and the final ball fell two yards short of the man on the deep square-leg boundary. However, in the Caribbean he disappointed on the field and got into hot water off it, after admitting to smoking marijuana. After some undistinguished one-day outings the following season he disappeared until England toured in 2004-05. Filling the Lance Klusener one-day role to perfection, he clumped 80 from 50 balls in the series clincher at East London, and by the time New Zealand toured late in 2005 Kemp was looking like the genuine article. A crucial 73 off 64 balls in the first match, and a 19-ball 30 to clinch the series in the third, established him as one of the most dangerous hitters around. Although he is a back number in Tests – he has won only one more cap since his first season – he is a regular in the one-day side, with almost a quarter of his runs coming in sixes. He had a quiet World Cup in 2007, missing some of the Super Eight games after his bowling proved toothless, but made a gritty 49 to spare South Africa's blushes in the semi-final against Australia, and then – as Africa's captain – enlivened the final match of the Afro-Asia Cup in Chennai in June by smiting seven sixes in his rapid 86.

THE FACTS Kemp hit 31 off an over (666661) from offspinner Morne Strydom during his career-best 188 for Eastern Province v North West at Port Elizabeth in February 2001 ... Kemp's father and grandfather also played first-class cricket, and his cousin Dave Callaghan played 29 ODIs for SA in the 1990s ... His record includes six ODIs for the Africa XI ...

THE FIGURES
Batting and fielding

www.cricinfo.com

	M	Inns	NO	Runs	HS	Avge	S/R	100	50	4s	6s	Ct	St
Tests *to 10.9.07*	4	6	0	80	55	13.33	32.00	0	1	11	0	3	0
ODIs *to 10.9.07*	82	63	18	1461	100*	32.46	84.89	1	10	98	58	31	0
First-class *to 10.9.07*	91	147	18	4796	188	37.17	–		11	23	–	–	105	0

Bowling

	M	Balls	Runs	Wkts	BB	Avge	RpO	S/R	5i	10m
Tests *to 10.9.07*	4	479	222	9	3–33	24.66	2.78	53.22	0	0
ODIs *to 10.9.07*	82	1303	1015	32	3–20	31.71	4.67	40.71	0	0
First-class *to 10.9.07*	91	10059	4747	176	6–56	26.97	2.83	57.15	5	0

KHALED MASHUD

Full name **Khaled Mashud**
Born **February 8, 1976, Rajshahi**
Teams **Rajshahi**
Style **Right-hand bat, wicketkeeper**
Test debut **Bangladesh v India at Dhaka 2000-01**
ODI debut **Bangladesh v India at Sharjah 1994-95**

THE PROFILE A tidy, unflashy wicketkeeper, Khaled Mashud can also be a free-striking batsman whose matchwinning six against Kenya in the final of the 1997 ICC Trophy did much to raise his country's profile. But he is also capable of digging in, as shown by his stand of 93 with Aminul Islam in the inaugural Test against India in 2000-01, and, as Bangladesh's baptismal struggles continued, his doughty presence at No. 7 was often the saving grace of an innings. He is a good keeper standing up, and though he drops the odd ball off the seamers, he was once described as the best in Asia by his former coach Dav Whatmore. Mashud – also known as "Pilot" – was saddled with the captaincy when Naimur Rahman was jettisoned after the home defeat by Zimbabwe late in 2001. However, he was powerless to halt Bangladesh's woeful run, and quit after their humiliations at the 2003 World Cup, but remained a pivotal figure in the side. His finest hour came in St Lucia in June 2004, when his unbeaten second-innings century secured Bangladesh a draw in their first Test in the Caribbean. He made an unbeaten 71 in the final match of the NatWest Series against Australia in England in 2005, but has now gone 29 Test innings without a half-century, although he did make 49 in Bangladesh's first Test win, over Zimbabwe in January 2005. Almost ever-present until early 2007, he was overlooked for the World Cup in favour of 18-year-old Mushfiqur Rahim, who is seen as a better batsman. Mashud then lost his Test place, too, leaving him on the outside at 31.

THE FACTS Khaled Mashud missed only three of Bangladesh's first 47 Tests ... He averages 30.75 in ODIs against New Zealand, but only 13 in 14 matches against Kenya ... He made 201 not out for Rajshahi against Khulna at Dhaka in 2001-02 ... Mashud and Mohammad Rafique are the last survivors in the current squad from the team that won the ICC Trophy in Kuala Lumpur in April 1997 ...

THE FIGURES

Batting and fielding   www.cricinfo.com

	M	Inns	NO	Runs	HS	Avge	S/R	100	50	4s	6s	Ct	St
Tests *to 10.9.07*	44	84	10	1409	103*	19.04	34.06	1	3	147	1	78	9
ODIs *to 10.9.07*	126	110	27	1818	71*	21.90	54.84	0	7	–	–	91	35
First-class *to 10.9.07*	85	151	18	3163	201*	23.78	–	3	12	–	–	146	15

Bowling

	M	Balls	Runs	Wkts	BB	Avge	RpO	S/R	5i	10m
Tests *to 10.9.07*	144	0	–	–	–	–	–	–	–	–
ODIs *to 10.9.07*	126	0	–	–	–	–	–	–	–	–
First-class *to 10.9.07*	85	32	19	0	–	–	3.56	–	0	0

94

ZAHEER **KHAN**

Full name **Zaheer Khan**
Born **October 7, 1978, Shrirampur, Maharashtra**
Teams **Mumbai**
Style **Right-hand bat, left-arm fast-medium bowler**
Test debut **India v Bangladesh at Dhaka 1999-2000**
ODI debut **India v Kenya at Nairobi 2000-01**

THE PROFILE Like Waqar Younis a decade before, left-armer Zaheer Khan yorked his way into the collective consciousness of the cricket world: his performances at the Champions Trophy in Kenya in September 2000 announced the arrival of an all-too-rare star in the Indian fast-bowling firmament. He might just as easily have come from the Pakistani pace stable – well-built, quick and unfazed by a batsman's reputation, Zaheer could move the ball both ways off the pitch and swing the old ball at a decent pace. After initially struggling to establish himself as a new-ball bowler, he came of age in the West Indies in 2002, when he led the line with great heart. His subsequent displays in England and New Zealand – not to mention some eye-catching moments at the 2003 World Cup – established him at the forefront of India's new pace generation, but a hamstring injury saw him relegated to bit-part performer while Indian cricket scripted some of its finest moments away in Australia and Pakistan. In a bid to jump the queue of left-armers vying for a national spot, Zaheer put in the hard yards for Worcestershire in 2006, bowling a lot of overs and, in the match against Essex, taking the first nine wickets to fall in the first innings before Darren Gough's flailing bat – and a dropped catch behind the stumps – spoilt his figures and his chances of a rare all-ten. It worked: Zaheer reclaimed his Test place, survived the fallout from the World Cup, and led the line in England in 2007, where his nine wickets at Trent Bridge gave India the match – and the series.

THE FACTS Zaheer Khan's 75 against Bangladesh at Dhaka in December 2004 is the highest score by a No. 11 in Tests: he dominated a last-wicket stand of 133 with Sachin Tendulkar ... He took 9 for 138 for Worcestershire v Essex at Chelmsford in June 2006 – it included a spell of 9 for 28, but a last-wicket stand of 97 cost him the chance of taking all ten wickets ... Khan averages 23.33 with the ball in Tests against New Zealand, but 51.08 v Pakistan ... His record includes six ODIs for the Asia XI ...

THE FIGURES

Batting and fielding

www.cricinfo.com

	M	Inns	NO	Runs	HS	Avge	S/R	100	50	4s	6s	Ct	St
Tests to 10.9.07	50	66	16	608	75	12.16	50.75	0	1	64	14	12	0
ODIs to 10.9.07	133	74	32	583	34*	13.88	83.88	0	0	54	19	26	0
First-class to 10.9.07	109	143	31	1588	75	14.17	–	0	2	–	–	35	0

Bowling

	M	Balls	Runs	Wkts	BB	Avge	RpO	S/R	5i	10m
Tests to 10.9.07	50	9720	5334	160	5–29	33.33	3.29	60.75	5	0
ODIs to 10.9.07	133	6629	5370	188	5–42	28.56	4.86	35.26	1	0
First-class to 10.9.07	109	22232	12344	454	9–138	27.18	3.33	48.96	26	7

NUWAN **KULASEKARA**

Full name	**Kulasekara Mudiyanselage Dinesh Nuwan Kulasekara**
Born	**July 22, 1982, Nittambuwa**
Teams	**Colts**
Style	**Right-hand bat, right-arm fast-medium bowler**
Test debut	**Sri Lanka v New Zealand at Napier 2004-05**
ODI debut	**Sri Lanka v England at Dambulla 2003-04**

THE PROFILE From a bustling run-up and a whippy open-chested action, Nuwan Kulasekara generates a lively pace, and moves the ball off the seam at around 80mph. He can also maintain a tight line and length, which has seen him develop into something of a one-day specialist: he was part of the 2007 World Cup squad, although he only appeared in two matches and didn't take a wicket. Oddly, his biggest mark on international cricket so far has been with the bat: at Lord's in May 2006 Kulasekara hung on for more than three hours, scoring 64 – his maiden Test fifty – and putting on 105 for the ninth wicket with Chaminda Vaas, ensuring that Sri Lanka clung on for a draw after England made them follow on 359 behind. It was his second adhesive performance of the match, following 29 as he and Vaas pushed the first-innings total from 131 for 8 to a more respectable 192. After one more Test in England, though, he was dropped as his bowling lacked penetration (he has tried hard since to add a yard of pace, with some success). Kulasekara had made an instant impression in his first one-dayer, taking 2 for 19 in nine overs as England subsided for 88 at Dambulla in November 2003. That came soon after a fine first season, in which he took 61 wickets at 21.06 in domestic cricket for Colts. He started as a softball enthusiast before shifting his focus to cricket, first with Negegoda CC and then with Galle.

THE FACTS Playing for North Central Province at Dambulla in March 2005, Kulasekara dismissed the top six in the Central Province batting order, finishing with career-best figures of 6 for 71 ... Kulasekara made 95 for Galle against Nondescripts in Colombo in October 2003: he and Primal Buddika (80) doubled the score from 174 for 6 ... Earlier in 2003 he took 5 for 25 and 5 for 44 in the same fixture as Nondescripts were bowled out for 58 and 73 ...

THE FIGURES

Batting and fielding   www.cricinfo.com

	M	Inns	NO	Runs	HS	Avge	S/R	100	50	4s	6s	Ct	St
Tests to 10.9.07	4	7	0	115	64	16.42	49.35	0	1	14	2	1	0
ODIs to 10.9.07	20	12	7	34	11	6.80	35.05	0	0	1	0	4	0
First-class to 10.9.07	54	74	19	1000	95	18.18	–	0	3	–	–	16	0

Bowling

	M	Balls	Runs	Wkts	BB	Avge	RpO	S/R	5i	10m
Tests to 10.9.07	4	612	302	4	2–45	75.50	2.96	153.00	0	0
ODIs to 10.9.07	20	848	600	12	2–17	50.00	4.24	70.66	0	0
First-class to 10.9.07	54	7331	4054	175	6–71	23.16	3.31	41.89	7	1

ANIL **KUMBLE**

Full name	**Anil Kumble**
Born	**October 17, 1970, Bangalore**
Teams	**Karnataka**
Style	**Right-hand bat, legspinner**
Test debut	**India v England at Manchester 1990**
ODI debut	**India v Sri Lanka at Sharjah 1989-90**

THE PROFILE   No bowler has won more Test matches for India than Anil Kumble. Unorthodox, he trades the legspinner's usual yo-yo for a spear, as the ball hacks through the air rather than hanging in it, then comes off the pitch with a kick rather than a kink. He does not beat the bat as much as hit the splice, but has enjoyed stunning success, particularly on Indian soil, where his deliveries burst like water-bombs on the merest crack. Resilient and untiring, for most of his career Kumble struggled to make an impact outside India, but turned that around magnificently in Australia in 2003-04, with 24 wickets in three Tests. Then his 6 for 71 on a flat Multan track helped India win their first Test in Pakistan. Kumble is a handy batsman, although nervous running hindered him in one-dayers: at The Oval in 2007 he finally reached a century in his 118th Test. He catches well, usually in the gully, despite once being described as moving like "a man on stilts". In December 2001, at home at Bangalore, Kumble became the first Indian spinner to take 300 Test wickets. A year later he passed 300 in one-dayers too, although he retired from the shorter game after the disappointments of the 2007 World Cup. Against Australia in 2004-05 he pushed his Test tally past 400 – also at Bangalore – then skittled the Aussies in the next Test at Chennai with 13 wickets. And in March 2006, he was India's first to 500. Superstardom has somehow eluded the low-profile Kumble, but his deeds – especially his "Perfect Ten" in an innings against Pakistan at Delhi in February 1999 – speak for themselves.

THE FACTS   Kumble was only the second bowler (after Jim Laker) to take all ten wickets in a Test innings, with 10 for 74 v Pakistan at Delhi in 1998-99 ... He has taken 325 wickets at 23.71 in Tests in India, and 241 at 35.50 overseas: he has taken 272 in Tests that India have won – the next-best is 128, by Harbhajan Singh ... Kumble has taken 92 Test wickets against England, and 88 v Australia ... His highest first-class score of 154 not out came for Karnataka v Kerala at Bijapur in November 1991 ... His record includes two ODIs for the Asia XI ...

THE FIGURES

Batting and fielding

	M	Inns	NO	Runs	HS	Avge	S/R	100	50	4s	6s	Ct	St
Tests *to 10.9.07*	118	152	30	2212	110*	18.13	39.10	1	4	267	9	53	0
ODIs *to 10.9.07*	271	136	4/	938	26	10.53	61.06	0	0	57	6	85	0
First-class *to 10.9.07*	227	293	59	5259	154*	22.47	–	7	16	–	–	112	0

Bowling

	M	Balls	Runs	Wkts	BB	Avge	RpO	S/R	5i	10m
Tests *to 10.9.07*	118	36702	16262	566	10–74	28.73	2.65	64.84	33	8
ODIs *to 10.9.07*	271	14496	10412	337	6–12	30.89	4.30	43.01	2	0
First-class *to 10.9.07*	227	62297	26990	1071	10–74	25.20	2.59	58.16	70	19

SOUTH AFRICA

CHARL **LANGEVELDT**

Full name	**Charl Kenneth Langeveldt**
Born	**December 17, 1974, Stellenbosch, Cape Province**
Teams	**Lions, Leicestershire**
Style	**Right-hand bat, right-arm fast-medium bowler**
Test debut	**South Africa v England at Cape Town 2004-05**
ODI debut	**South Africa v Kenya at Kimberley 2001-02**

THE PROFILE For much of the early part of his career, Charl Langeveldt combined his first-class cricket with his job as a prison warder at Drakenstein prison, a short drive north of Cape Town. Langeveldt first came to prominence with his ability to swing the ball at genuine pace, and further work on his action allowed him to generate even more movement, bringing him to the attention of the national selectors. He made his ODI debut against Kenya in 2001-02, taking two top-order wickets. He followed that with career-best figures of 4 for 21 when the two sides met again at Cape Town shortly afterwards. Langeveldt was included in South Africa's 15-man squad for their ill-starred World Cup campaign in 2003, but played only in the pool match against Kenya. He returned to favour after South Africa experienced a dramatic slump in the middle of 2004, taking 3 for 31 in Sri Lanka and 3 for 17 against Bangladesh in the Champions Trophy in England. He made his Test debut in style against England at Cape Town in 2004-05, breaking his hand while batting but nonetheless taking 5 for 46. It was enough to win him selection for the series in the Caribbean which followed, and he came into his own there. In the third one-dayer in Barbados, he produced one of the most sensational finales in history, conjuring up a last-over hat-trick to steal a one-run win over West Indies which clinched the series. Test success proved more elusive, and he featured in only two of South Africa's matches in 2005-06. He retained his one-day place, though, and did well at the 2007 World Cup, finishing as his side's joint-top wicket-taker, failing to strike only once in eight games, and setting up the Super Eight victory over Sri Lanka, the eventual finalists, with 5 for 39.

THE FACTS Langeveldt's hat-trick against West Indies at Bridgetown in May 2005 was South Africa's first in ODIs ... He averages 20.81 with the ball in ODIs against Sri Lanka, but 82 against Australia ... Langeveldt took 5 for 7 when the SA Board President's XI bowled out the touring Bangladeshis for 51 at Pietermaritzburg in October 2000 ...

THE FIGURES

Batting and fielding

www.cricinfo.com

	M	Inns	NO	Runs	HS	Avge	S/R	100	50	4s	6s	Ct	St
Tests to 10.9.07	6	4	2	16	10	8.00	30.76	0	0	3	0	2	0
ODIs to 10.9.07	48	10	3	23	9	3.28	31.94	0	0	1	0	7	0
First-class to 10.9.07	68	85	32	780	56	14.71	–	0	1	–	–	19	0

Bowling

	M	Balls	Runs	Wkts	BB	Avge	RpO	S/R	5i	10m
Tests to 10.9.07	6	999	593	16	5–46	37.06	3.56	62.43	1	0
ODIs to 10.9.07	48	2251	1885	63	5–39	29.92	5.02	35.73	2	0
First-class to 10.9.07	68	12339	6077	212	6–48	28.66	2.95	58.20	6	1

VVS **LAXMAN**

Full name	**Vangipurappu Venkata Sai Laxman**
Born	**November 1, 1974, Hyderabad, Andhra Pradesh**
Teams	**Hyderabad Lancashire**
Style	**Right-hand bat, occasional offspinner**
Test debut	**India v South Africa at Ahmedabad 1996-97**
ODI debut	**India v Zimbabwe at Cuttack 1997-98**

THE PROFILE At his sublime best, VVS Laxman is a sight for the gods. Wristy, willowy and sinuous, he can match – sometimes even better – Tendulkar for strokeplay. His on-side game is comparable to his idol Azharuddin's, and yet he is decidedly more assured on the off side, and has the rare gift of being able to hit the same ball to either side. The Australians, who have suffered more than most, paid him the highest compliment after India's 2003-04 tour Down Under by admitting they did not know where to bowl to him. Laxman, a one-time medical student, finally showed signs of coming to terms with his considerable gifts in March 2001, as he tormented Steve Waugh's thought-to-be-invincible Aussies with a majestic 281 to stand the Kolkata Test on its head. But then he returned to mortality, suffering the frustrations of numerous twenties and thirties, and struggling to hold his one-day place. An uncharacteristic grinding century in Antigua in May 2002 marked his second coming, and he has been a picture of consistency since, often dazzling, but less prone to collaborating in his own dismissal. After the acute disappointment of being left out of the 2003 World Cup he made an emphatic return with a string of hundreds in Australia, and followed that with a matchwinning 107 in the deciding one-dayer of India's ice-breaking tour of Pakistan in March 2004. By 2006, though, he was largely confined to the five-day arena, and collected his tenth Test ton in St Kitts, before passing 5000 runs during a languid 51 that helped India draw the match – and win the series – at The Oval in 2007.

THE FACTS Laxman's 281 against Australia at Kolkata in March 2001 was the highest Test score by an Indian at the time (since passed by Virender Sehwag), and included a Indian-record stand of 376 for the fifth wicket with Rahul Dravid ... He averages 52.03 against Australia, and his highest three scores (281, 178 and 167) have all come against them ... Laxman has scored two first-class triple-centuries for Hyderabad – 353 v Karnataka at Bangalore in April 2000, and 301 not out v Bihar at Jamshedpur in February 1998 ...

THE FIGURES
Batting and fielding

www.cricinfo.com

	M	Inns	NO	Runs	HS	Avge	S/R	100	50	4s	6s	Ct	St
Tests to 10.9.07	83	135	16	5083	281	42.76	48.43	10	29	706	4	90	0
ODIs to 10.9.07	86	83	7	2338	131	30.76	71.23	6	10	222	4	39	0
First-class to 10.9.07	191	309	33	14194	353	51.42	–		40	64	–	–	208	1

Bowling

	M	Balls	Runs	Wkts	BB	Avge	RpO	S/R	5i	10m
Tests to 10.9.07	83	258	105	1	1-32	105.00	2.44	258.00	0	0
ODIs to 10.9.07	86	42	40	0	–	–	5.71	–	0	0
First-class to 10.9.07	191	1685	707	20	3–11	35.35	2.51	84.25	0	0

BRETT **LEE**

Full name **Brett Lee**
Born **November 8, 1976, Wollongong, New South Wales**
Teams **New South Wales**
Style **Right-hand bat, right-arm fast bowler**
Test debut **Australia v India at Melbourne 1999-2000**
ODI debut **Australia v Pakistan at Brisbane 1999-2000**

THE PROFILE If Brett Lee were a Ferrari ... No. There is no if. He's already the fastest in the world, equal with Shoaib Akhtar at a flicker above or below 100mph. When Lee releases the throttle and begins that smooth acceleration, anything could happen: that leaping, classical delivery might produce a devastating yorker, a slower ball or a young-Donald outswinger. Add a dash of peroxide, a fruity vocabulary, a trademark jump for joy, and a pop group (Six And Out), and you have the 21st century's first designer cricketer. Steve Waugh unleashed Lee at first, but Ricky Ponting gave him a blueprint for lasting success that doesn't rely solely on speed. Lee's career hasn't always been easy. He struggled with injury and accusations of throwing, and had a strangely barren first Ashes series in 2001 (nine wickets at 55). Three years later he overcame ankle surgery, but was 12th man for nine successive Tests. He returned for the 2005 Ashes, and earned plaudits for his never-say-die attitude with ball and bat, nearly conjuring victory at Edgbaston with a battling 43. Andrew Flintoff's consoling of Lee at the end was the defining image of that epic series. His 2006 brightened further when he partnered Michael Kasprowicz in a nailbiting win at Johannesburg that eased the pain of that previous near-miss. And when Glenn McGrath first struggled for impact then withdrew to care for his sick wife, Lee became leader of the attack – a position he had craved since first crashing onto the Test scene. He claimed 20 wickets in the Ashes rematch, but picked up another ankle injury in New Zealand which kept him out of the 2007 World Cup.

THE FACTS Lee took a hat-trick against Kenya in 2002-03, one of only five in the World Cup ... His older brother Shane played 45 ODIs for Australia between 1995 and 2001 ... Lee averages 22.71 with the ball against West Indies, but almost double that (40.61) against England ... He was on the winning side in each of his first ten Tests, a sequence ended by England's win at Leeds in 2001 ... Lee took 5 for 47 in his first Test innings, but did not improve on that until his 44th match ...

THE FIGURES

Batting and fielding   www.cricinfo.com

	M	Inns	NO	Runs	HS	Avge	S/R	100	50	4s	6s	Ct	St
Tests to 10.9.07	59	65	13	1098	64	21.11	55.96	0	3	132	15	17	0
ODIs to 10.9.07	150	68	27	739	57	18.02	82.01	0	2	37	22	35	0
First-class to 10.9.07	94	108	20	1644	79	18.68	55.48	0	5	–	–	28	0

Bowling

	M	Balls	Runs	Wkts	BB	Avge	RpO	S/R	5i	10m
Tests to 10.9.07	59	12279	7300	231	5–30	31.60	3.56	53.15	7	0
ODIs to 10.9.07	150	7729	6048	267	5–22	22.65	4.69	28.94	6	0
First-class to 10.9.07	94	18862	10844	392	7–114	27.66	3.44	48.11	16	2

KAUSHAL **LOKUARACHCHI**

Full name	**Kaushal Samaraweera Lokuarachchi**
Born	**May 20, 1982, Colombo**
Teams	**Sinhalese Sports Club**
Style	**Right-hand bat, legspinner**
Test debut	**Sri Lanka v New Zealand at Colombo 2002-03**
ODI debut	**Sri Lanka v Kenya at Sharjah 2002-03**

THE PROFILE The feisty, combative Kaushal Lokuarachchi is unlucky that he has come to prominence at a time when there are two other legspinners (Malinga Bandara and Upul Chandana) in contention for a berth in the national team, as well as the ever-present multi-faceted slow-bowling genius that is Muttiah Muralitharan. "Loku" seems to have decided that his best chance of making the national team is in one-day cricket, which he prefers anyway: "It is more difficult to play one-day cricket than Test cricket because the intensity is greater. I love the challenge." He is not a huge spinner of the ball, from a slightly round-arm action, but his batting makes him a handy one-day proposition – he has two first-class centuries under his belt and an overall average in the upper twenties. Lokuarachchi had disciplinary problems in 2003, when he was involved in a car crash in which a woman pedestrian was sadly killed: he was banned from cricket for four months as a result. But he put that behind him, winning his fourth (and last to date) Test cap against the Australians at Kandy in March 2004. Two years later he stepped in for the absent Murali for the two one-dayers in Holland which followed the successful tour of England. Against admittedly modest opposition Lokuarachchi took seven wickets to remind the selectors of his existence, and although he missed the 2007 World Cup he was recalled after it for the one-day series against Pakistan in Abu Dhabi.

THE FACTS Lokuarachchi took 4 for 44 and 3 for 41 in two matches against Holland in 2006, the only ODIs he has played outside Asia ... He took 7 for 17 as Sinhalese Sports Club bowled out Singha for 36 in Colombo in February 2006 ... A month later he took 7 for 66 and 5 for 29 – and scored 101 – for SSC against Colts ... He also made 101 not out for SSC against Kurunegala in Colombo in January 2006 ...

THE FIGURES
Batting and fielding
www.cricinfo.com

	M	Inns	NO	Runs	HS	Avge	S/R	100	50	4s	6s	Ct	St
Tests *to 10.9.07*	4	5	1	94	28*	23.50	58.02	0	0	14	1	1	0
ODIs *to 10.9.07*	19	16	3	201	69	15.46	80.72	0	1	9	5	4	0
First-class *to 10.9.07*	71	99	10	2476	101*	27.82	–	2	9	–	–	36	0

Bowling

	M	Balls	Runs	Wkts	BB	Avge	RpO	S/R	5i	10m
Tests *to 10.9.07*	4	594	295	5	2–47	590.00	2.97	118.80	0	0
ODIs *to 10.9.07*	19	921	656	30	4–44	21.86	4.27	30.70	0	0
First-class *to 10.9.07*	71	11215	4852	208	7–17	23.32	2.59	53.91	7	1

BRENDON **McCULLUM**

Full name	**Brendon Barrie McCullum**
Born	**September 27, 1981, Dunedin, Otago**
Teams	**Canterbury**
Style	**Right-hand bat, wicketkeeper**
Test debut	**New Zealand v South Africa at Hamilton 2003-04**
ODI debut	**New Zealand v Australia at Sydney 2001-02**

THE PROFILE Brendon McCullum has stepped up to the national side as a wicketkeeper-batsman after an outstanding career in international youth cricket, where he proved capable of dominating opposition attacks. He found it hard to replicate that at the highest level at first, although there were occasional fireworks at domestic level. But he finally made his mark in England in 2004, with 200 runs in the Test series, including an entertaining 96 at Lord's. After that near-miss he finally brought up his maiden century in Bangladesh in October, with 143 at Dhaka, and added another hundred in the two-day victory over Zimbabwe in August 2005. He first made the New Zealand one-day side as a batsman, in the 2001-02 VB Series in Australia, where he made the acquaintance of Brett Lee, who has since let him have more than one beamer, to widespread outrage. Two years later McCullum, by now keeping wicket, forced his way past Robbie Hart into the Test side for the 2003-04 series against South Africa. With some onlookers murmuring the name "Gilchrist", McCullum hammered 86 from 91 balls as New Zealand overhauled Australia's 346 at Hamilton in February 2007 with one wicket to spare. At his best down the order after a flirtation with one-day opening, McCullum is now one of his side's trump cards. A feisty fighter, he raised a few hackles when he ran Muttiah Muralitharan out at Christchurch in December 2006 as he wandered up the pitch to congratulate Kumar Sangakkara on reaching his century.

THE FACTS McCullum has made five dismissals in an ODI innings three times: the only other New Zealander to do this is Adam Parore (once) ... His 101 against the Rest of South Africa at Benoni in April 2006 included seven sixes ... McCullum hit 186 (out of 311) in an Under-19 Test against South Africa at Lincoln in 2000-01, and made 160 against Leicestershire on his debut for Glamorgan in July 2006 ... His father Stuart and brother Nathan have also played for Otago ...

THE FIGURES

Batting and fielding   www.cricinfo.com

	M	Inns	NO	Runs	HS	Avge	S/R	100	50	4s	6s	Ct	St
Tests to 10.9.07	25	39	3	1157	143	32.13	62.91	2	6	145	10	64	6
ODIs to 10.9.07	114	90	19	1636	86*	23.04	82.70	0	6	126	40	134	11
First-class to 10.9.07	59	98	6	3071	160	33.38	–	6	16	–	–	142	12

Bowling

	M	Balls	Runs	Wkts	BB	Avge	RpO	S/R	5i	10m
Tests to 10.9.07	25	0	–	–	–	–	–	–	–	–
ODIs to 10.9.07	114	0	–	–	–	–	–	–	–	–
First-class to 10.9.07	59	0	–	–	–	–	–	–	–	–

STUART **MacGILL**

Full name	**Stuart Charles Glyndwr MacGill**
Born	**February 25, 1971, Mount Lawley, Perth, W Australia**
Teams	**New South Wales**
Style	**Right-hand bat, legspinner**
Test debut	**Australia v South Africa at Adelaide 1997-98**
ODI debut	**Australia v Pakistan at Sydney 1999-2000**

THE PROFILE The praise lavished on his decision to boycott Zimbabwe in 2004 continued an unwelcome pattern for Stuart MacGill: he has long generated headlines for being out of the Australian team rather than for his performances in it. An old-fashioned operator with a gargantuan legbreak and a majestic wrong'un, MacGill has the best strike rate and worst luck of any modern spinner. His misfortune has been to play alongside Shane Warne. After showing they could work in tandem with 13 wickets against Pakistan at Sydney in January 2005, MacGill hoped – almost pleaded – for more double-act opportunities. In seven Tests in 2005-06, he dismantled the World XI, and finished with 16 wickets in two games against Bangladesh – but sat on the sidelines during the 2006-07 Ashes series, Warne's last hurrah. He has stayed philosophical, eagerly running in and usually running amok. A batting duffer and increasingly feckless fielder, he has played only three ODIs despite collecting his domestic scalps at a stupefying rate of one every 27 balls. MacGill seldom smiles after taking a wicket: instead he lets out a roar of accomplishment. It is only one of his quirks. He is a wine buff who only recently learned to enjoy beer, and he once read 24 novels on tour in Pakistan. The son and grandson of Western Australian players, he socialises with non-cricketers, and is often portrayed as a thinker, the odd man out. And finally, with Warne out of the way, MacGill might expect a longish run in the Test side, unless the selectors go for Brad Hogg, or Cullen Bailey, or ...

THE FACTS MacGill collected 53 wickets in 11 Tests during Shane Warne's 2003-04 drugs ban, yet was often maligned for bowling one boundary-ball per over ... In the 16 Tests they played together, MacGill took 82 wickets at 22.4, to Warne's 74 at 29.57 ... MacGill has taken 55 wickets against West Indies, 39 (in only six Tests) v England, and 33 at 15.75 v Bangladesh: 53 of his wickets have come in eight Tests at Sydney ... He is married to the former *Neighbours* actress and TV presenter Rachel Friend ...

THE FIGURES
Batting and fielding

www.cricinfo.com

	M	Inns	NO	Runs	HS	Avge	S/R	100	50	4s	6s	Ct	St
Tests *to 10.9.07*	40	45	11	347	43	10.20	49.43	0	0	38	2	16	0
ODIs *to 10.9.07*	3	2	1	1	1	1.00	33.33	0	0	0	0	2	0
First-class *to 10.9.07*	174	207	55	1529	56*	10.05	–	0	2	–	–	73	0

Bowling

	M	Balls	Runs	Wkts	BB	Avge	RpO	S/R	5i	10m
Tests *to 10.9.07*	40	10211	5387	198	8–108	27.20	3.16	51.57	12	2
ODIs *to 10.9.07*	3	180	105	6	4–19	17.50	3.50	30.00	0	0
First-class *to 10.9.07*	174	39085	22086	739	8–108	29.88	3.39	52.88	42	6

CRAIG McMILLAN

NEW ZEALAND

Full name	**Craig Douglas McMillan**
Born	**September 13, 1976, Christchurch, Canterbury**
Teams	**Canterbury**
Style	**Right-hand bat, right-arm medium-pacer**
Test debut	**New Zealand v Australia at Brisbane 1997-98**
ODI debut	**New Zealand v Sri Lanka at Hyderabad 1996-97**

THE PROFILE Strokemaker Craig McMillan, almost an automatic selection from the age of 21, found himself on the outer after a poor World Cup in 2003. It was the first hiccup in what had been a productive career until then – there was a century in his fourth Test and six in all, and a world record when he clubbed 26 off one over from Pakistan's Younis Khan. He was recalled to tour India in 2003-04, making 83 at Ahmedabad and 100 in the next Test at Chandigarh, both not out. He was in good form for Canterbury in 2004-05 – tempting Hampshire to sign him – but was not a success in the Tests, and was dropped again after a highest score of 23 in five innings against Australia. He remained in the one-day shake-up, but only two fifties in 13 matches at the start of 2005-06 cost him his place. That looked like it: he did not even make the 30-man preliminary squad for the Champions Trophy, and looked for work outside the game, without much luck. But he was surprisingly recalled for the tri-series in Australia, after a crop of injuries. He smacked 89 in a narrow defeat to Australia at Sydney, and repeated the dose with 52 and 117 as the shocked Aussies were whitewashed in a three-match series in New Zealand. Helped by Nathan Astle's retirement, McMillan retained his place for the 2007 World Cup, where he did well, playing the finisher in victories over West Indies and South Africa. His bowling, which had tailed off, claimed a few wickets too. Rarely has a second coming been more enjoyable.

THE FACTS McMillan hit 26 (444464) off Younis Khan's only over in the Hamilton Test against Pakistan in March 2001: it was a Test record until Brian Lara (28) broke it in 2003-04 ... He averages 58.81 in Tests against India, but only 20.60 against West Indies: he averages 49.60 in ODIs against Pakistan, but only 20.40 against Sri Lanka ... McMillan's highest first-class score of 168 not out came against the Indian Board President's XI at Jodhpur in October 1999 ...

THE FIGURES

Batting and fielding   www.cricinfo.com

	M	Inns	NO	Runs	HS	Avge	S/R	100	50	4s	6s	Ct	St
Tests to 10.9.07	55	91	10	3116	142	38.46	54.95	6	19	367	54	22	0
ODIs to 10.9.07	197	183	16	4707	117	28.18	75.94	3	28	373	84	44	0
First-class to 10.9.07	138	226	27	7817	168*	39.28	–		16	42	–	–	58	0

Bowling

	M	Balls	Runs	Wkts	BB	Avge	RpO	S/R	5i	10m
Tests to 10.9.07	55	2502	1257	28	3–48	44.89	3.01	89.35	0	0
ODIs to 10.9.07	197	1879	1717	49	3–20	35.04	5.48	38.34	0	0
First-class to 10.9.07	138	6572	3167	88	6–71	35.98	2.89	74.68	1	0

104

FARVEEZ **MAHAROOF**

SRI LANKA

Full name	**Mohamed Farveez Maharoof**
Born	**September 7, 1984, Colombo**
Teams	**Bloomfield**
Style	**Right-hand bat, right-arm fast-medium bowler**
Test debut	**Sri Lanka v Zimbabwe at Harare 2003-04**
ODI debut	**Sri Lanka v Zimbabwe at Harare 2003-04**

THE PROFILE Farveez Maharoof is a young fast-bowling allrounder of exciting potential, and bowls lively seamers from an upright, open-chested action. The selectors fast-tracked him into the national squad for the Zimbabwe tour early in 2004, as they looked towards the future. Faced with weak opposition, the 19-year-old Maharoof picked up a bunch of wickets – including 3 for 3 in his first ODI – but then came up against better players during the Asia Cup. He still performed reasonably well, and made a mark with his swinging deliveries when South Africa toured. He had worked his way up through the representative ranks, playing for Sri Lanka's Under-15, U17 and U19 teams, and enjoyed a prolific school career for Wesley College, with a highest score of 243 and best bowling figures of 8 for 20. He has found Test wickets hard to come by, but his occasionally ferocious hitting has helped him survive in the one-day side. A mean display during the Champions Trophy in England in 2004, when he exploited the end-of-summer conditions expertly, suggested he could be especially useful when Sri Lanka play in seamer-friendly conditions, although his major contribution to the 5-0 clean sweep of the one-dayers in England in 2006 was a rapid half-century at Headingley. Most importantly, he has also shown that he is comfortable under pressure, all too often the Achilles heel of Sri Lanka's recent fast-bowling allrounders. He was unlucky to miss the 2007 World Cup final after doing well in the lead-up games, although admittedly eight of his nine wickets came against Bermuda and Ireland. But he was back in favour afterwards, grabbing six wickets in three games against Pakistan.

THE FACTS Maharoof had figures of 3-1-3-3 on his ODI debut, as Zimbabwe were bowled out for 35 at Harare in April 2004 ... He took 6 for 14 against West Indies at Mumbai during the 2006-07 Champions Trophy ... Maharoof captained Sri Lanka in the 2004 Under-19 World Cup, and won the Man of the Match award against Australia ... He took 7 for 73 for Bloomfield against Ragama in Colombo in November 2006 ...

THE FIGURES

Batting and fielding   www.cricinfo.com

	M	Inns	NO	Runs	HS	Avge	S/R	100	50	4s	6s	Ct	St
Tests to 10.9.07	18	27	4	476	72	20.69	39.63	0	3	58	3	6	0
ODIs to 10.9.07	72	47	12	716	69*	20.45	87.42	0	2	62	18	16	0
First-class to 10.9.07	36	52	6	908	72	19.73	42.19	0	4	–	–	18	0

Bowling

	M	Balls	Runs	Wkts	BB	Avge	RpO	S/R	5i	10m
Tests to 10.9.07	18	2286	1269	74	4–52	52.87	3.33	95.25	0	0
ODIs to 10.9.07	72	2901	2293	90	6–14	25.47	4.74	32.23	1	0
First-class to 10.9.07	36	4602	2494	85	7–73	29.34	3.25	54.14	1	0

SAJID **MAHMOOD**

Full name	**Sajid Iqbal Mahmood**
Born	**December 21, 1981, Bolton, Lancashire**
Teams	**Lancashire**
Style	**Right-hand bat, right-arm fast-medium bowler**
Test debut	**England v Sri Lanka at Lord's 2006**
ODI debut	**England v New Zealand at Bristol 2004**

THE PROFILE A former supermarket shelf-stacker, Saj Mahmood was spotted in the Bolton League and joined Lancashire in 2002. From there, he rose rapidly through the ranks, and, despite having only six first-class wickets to his name, he was selected for the England A tour of India in 2003-04. His full England debut the following summer was a chastening experience – his seven overs disappeared for 56 against New Zealand in a one-dayer at Bristol. Mahmood is tall and decidedly rapid, and bowls a fuller length than many of his pace-bowling peers. For a while, he made his name at the expense of his team-mates – in 2003, he put Andrew Flintoff out of action with a beamer in the Old Trafford nets. But three years later he was inflicting the damage on his opponents instead, as he announced his Test arrival against Sri Lanka at Lord's with a fiery three-wicket burst, including another debutant, Chamara Kapugedera, who received the perfect inswinger first ball. But it got harder after that: he tended to fire one down the leg side every over, and proved horrendously expensive in the one-dayers that followed. Another injury to Flintoff (not Mahmood-induced this time) gave him another chance against Pakistan, and after failing to take a wicket in front of his home crowd he got it right at Headingley, with four wickets on the final day. It earned him a trip to Australia, but he never looked at home, and was equally hit-and-miss at the 2007 World Cup, when a couple of wicket-taking bursts were mixed with some exasperatingly wayward spells. The home season of 2007 was punctuated by a hernia operation, and when he returned Mahmood found himself well down the list of potential England fast men.

THE FACTS Mahmood took a wicket (Kumar Sangakkara) in his second over in Tests, at Lord's in May 2006, and soon had 3 for 6 – but finished with 3 for 50 ... His figures of 7-0-80-2 v Sri Lanka at The Oval in June 2006 are among England's most expensive in ODIs ... Mahmood struck 94 from 66 balls for Lancashire v Sussex at Manchester in June 2004 ... Amir Khan, the young boxer who won a silver medal at the 2004 Athens Olympics, is his cousin ...

THE FIGURES

Batting and fielding   www.cricinfo.com

	M	Inns	NO	Runs	HS	Avge	S/R	100	50	4s	6s	Ct	St
Tests to 10.9.07	8	11	1	81	34	8.10	50.31	0	0	10	0	0	0
ODIs to 10.9.07	25	15	4	85	22*	7.72	84.15	0	0	8	1	1	0
First-class to 10.9.07	52	68	10	823	94	14.18	62.16	0	2	–	–	8	0

Bowling

	M	Balls	Runs	Wkts	BB	Avge	RpO	S/R	5i	10m
Tests to 10.9.07	8	1130	762	20	4–22	38.10	4.04	56.50	0	0
ODIs to 10.9.07	25	1155	1128	29	4–50	38.89	5.85	39.82	0	0
First-class to 10.9.07	52	7197	4504	139	5–37	32.40	3.75	51.77	3	0

MAHMUDULLAH

Full name	**Mohammad Mahmudullah**
Born	**February 4, 1986, Mymensingh**
Teams	**Dhaka**
Style	**Right-hand bat, offspinner**
Test debut	**No Tests yet**
ODI debut	**Bangladesh v Sri Lanka at Colombo 2007**

THE PROFILE An offspinning allrounder who is also an assured close-in fielder, Mahmudullah was something of a surprise inclusion in the Bangladesh side for the one-day leg of their chastening tour of Sri Lanka in mid-2007 (all three Tests were lost by an innings, and all three ODIs ended in defeat too). Mahmudullah, who can be a free-flowing batsman, made his international debut in the second one-dayer, scoring 36 and picking up two wickets in his five overs, the first when Tillakaratne Dilshan missed an attempted reverse sweep, and the second when Upul Chandana was brilliantly caught by Tamim Iqbal on the long-on boundary. As a bowler he does turn the ball, and can also keep the runs down. Bangladesh have a lot of left-arm spinners, but not many offbreak bowlers have made a mark yet: Mahmudullah's batting may help him secure a more regular place in the squad. He spent the 2005 summer on the groundstaff at Lord's: MCC's head coach, the former Middlesex and England batsman Clive Radley, remembers him as "a top cricketer, who struck the ball well with wristy cuts and pulls. He got out too often on the long-leg boundary, but on the whole scored some useful runs for us against some good attacks (he made 55 against Surrey Seconds, who included Martin Bicknell). He's an offspin bowler who bowled from quite wide of the crease – he spun it a lot and bowled a good doosra."

THE FACTS Mahmudullah sometimes appears on scorecards under his nickname "Riyad" ... He spent some time on the MCC groundstaff in 2005, playing alongside future World Cup players in Daan van Bunge, Kevin O'Brien and William Porterfield ... He took 5 for 42 for the Bangladesh Academy against their Pakistani counterparts at Savar in April 2007, and a week later took 5 for 68 against the Sri Lanka Academy at Khulna ...

THE FIGURES
Batting and fielding
www.cricinfo.com

	M	Inns	NO	Runs	HS	Avge	S/R	100	50	4s	6s	Ct	St
Tests to 10.9.07	0	0	–	–	–	–	–	–	–	–	–	–	–
ODIs to 10.9.07	1	1	0	36	36	36.00	66.66	0	0	1	0	0	0
First-class to 10.9.07	20	35	3	911	70	28.46	48.87	0	5	–	–	19	0

Bowling

	M	Balls	Runs	Wkts	BB	Avge	RpO	S/R	5i	10m
Tests to 10.9.07	0	0	–	–	–	–	–	–	–	–
ODIs to 10.9.07	1	30	28	2	2–28	14.00	5.60	15.00	0	0
First-class to 10.9.07	20	1409	747	20	4–64	37.35	3.18	70.45	0	0

LASITH **MALINGA**

Full name	**Separamadu Lasith Malinga Swarnajith**
Born	**August 28, 1983, Galle**
Teams	**Nondescripts, Kent**
Style	**Right-hand bat, right-arm fast bowler**
Test debut	**Sri Lanka v Australia at Darwin 2004**
ODI debut	**Sri Lanka v United Arab Emirates at Dambulla 2004**

THE PROFILE A rare Sri Lankan cricketer from the south, Lasith Malinga hardly played any proper cricket until he was 17, preferring the softball version in the coconut groves near his home in Rathgama, a village near Galle. But after he was spotted by the former Test fast bowler Champaka Ramanayake, he was hurried into the Galle team, took 4 for 40 and 4 for 37 on his first-class debut, and has hardly looked back since. He bowls with a distinctive and explosive round-arm action – which earned him the nickname "Slinga Malinga" – and generates genuine pace, often disconcerting batsmen who struggle to pick up the ball's trajectory. Malinga was a surprise selection for the 2004 tour of Australia, and soon showed his speed, starting with 6 for 90 against the Northern Territory Chief Minister's XI at Darwin. That paved the way for his inclusion in the Test team, and he acquitted himself well, with six wickets in his first match and four in the second: he added 5 for 80 (nine in the match) against New Zealand at Napier in April 2005. With a propensity for no-balls he was originally seen as too erratic for the one-day side, but buried that reputation with 13 wickets in the 5-0 whitewash of England in 2006. He continued his progress during 2006-07, collecting 18 wickets during the World Cup, including four in four balls against South Africa. He was the best of the bowlers in the final, too, while his ever-changing exotic hairstyles make him stand out on and off the park.

THE FACTS Malinga is the only bowler to take four wickets in four balls in international cricket, doing so against South Africa at Providence during the 2007 World Cup ... After he took a Test-best 5 for 80 (9 for 210 in the match) with his low-slung action against New Zealand at Napier in April 2005, Stephen Fleming unsuccessfully asked the umpires to change their clothing: "There's a period there where the ball gets lost in their trousers" ... Malinga took 6 for 17, as Galle bowled out the Police for 51 in Colombo in November 2003 ...

THE FIGURES

Batting and fielding   www.cricinfo.com

	M	Inns	NO	Runs	HS	Avge	S/R	100	50	4s	6s	Ct	St
Tests to 10.9.07	24	28	11	132	26	7.76	35.38	0	0	17	1	7	0
ODIs to 10.9.07	40	17	8	70	15	7.77	65.42	0	0	4	1	5	0
First-class to 10.9.07	75	90	38	426	30	8.19	36.22	0	0	–	–	22	0

Bowling

	M	Balls	Runs	Wkts	BB	Avge	RpO	S/R	5i	10m
Tests to 10.9.07	24	3919	2551	83	5–68	30.73	3.90	47.21	2	0
ODIs to 10.9.07	40	1867	1461	61	4–44	23.95	4.69	30.60	0	0
First-class to 10.9.07	75	10277	6788	230	6–17	29.51	3.96	44.68	6	0

NEW ZEALAND

CHRIS **MARTIN**

Full name	**Christopher Stewart Martin**
Born	**December 10, 1974, Christchurch, Canterbury**
Teams	**Auckland**
Style	**Right-hand bat, right-arm fast-medium bowler**
Test debut	**New Zealand v South Africa at Bloemfontein 2000-01**
ODI debut	**New Zealand v Zimbabwe at Taupo 2000-01**

THE PROFILE Chris Martin is an angular fast-medium bowler who receives almost as much attention for his inept batting as for his nagging bowling, which has produced more than 100 Test wickets, including 11 in the match as New Zealand whipped South Africa at Auckland in March 2004. Seven more scalps followed in the next game. It was all the more remarkable as they were his first Tests in almost two years – he had been overlooked since Pakistan piled up 643 at Lahore in May 2002 (Martin 1 for 108). He got his original chance after a crop of injuries, but did not disgrace himself in the first portion of his Test career, taking 34 wickets at 34 in his first 11 Tests, including six as Pakistan were crushed by an innings at Hamilton in 2000-01. Since his return he has maintained that average of 34, happy to bowl long spells *à la* Ewen Chatfield – he took 5 for 152 at Brisbane in November 2004, after a surprisingly unproductive England tour. A back number in one-day cricket, Martin received a surprise summons to the 2007 World Cup when Daryl Tuffey injured his shoulder – but he never made the starting XI as New Zealand battled to the semi-final. But Martin is likely to be remembered more for his clueless batting: after 44 Test innings he has 17 ducks and is yet to reach double figures, although he did once manage 25 for his former province, Canterbury, sharing a stand of 75 with Chris Harris.

THE FACTS Very few Test players approach Martin's negative ratio of runs (52) to wickets (106): two that do are England's Bill Bowes (28 runs, 68 wickets) and David Larter (15 runs, 37 wickets) ... Martin shares the Test record of four pairs of ducks with Marvan Atapattu, Bhagwat Chandrasekhar, Merv Dillon and Courtney Walsh ... He has played only two ODIs since 2000-01, but took six of his 11 wickets in those two games, in 2005-06 ... In Tests Martin averages 23.13 with the ball against South Africa, but 102.12 v Australia ...

THE FIGURES

Batting and fielding   www.cricinfo.com

	M	Inns	NO	Runs	HS	Avge	S/R	100	50	4s	6s	Ct	St
Tests to 10.9.07	33	44	21	52	7	2.26	19.18	0	0	7	0	9	0
ODIs to 10.9.07	9	6	1	6	3	1.20	25.00	0	0	0	0	3	0
First-class to 10.9.07	110	137	65	310	25	4.30	–	0	0	–	–	22	0

Bowling

	M	Balls	Runs	Wkts	BB	Avge	RpO	S/R	5i	10m
Tests to 10.9.07	33	6188	3636	106	6–54	34.30	3.52	58.37	7	1
ODIs to 10.9.07	9	438	397	11	3–62	36.09	5.43	39.81	0	0
First-class to 10.9.07	110	21066	10598	343	6–54	30.89	3.01	61.41	16	1

DIMITRI **MASCARENHAS**

Full name **Adrian Dimitri Mascarenhas**
Born **October 30, 1977, Chiswick, Middlesex**
Teams **Hampshire**
Style **Right-hand bat, right-arm medium-pace bowler**
Test debut **No Tests yet**
ODI debut **England v West Indies at Lord's 2007**

THE PROFILE Dimitri Mascarenhas is just about the ultimate cosmopolitan cricketer: born in London, to Sri Lankan parents, he was brought up in Western Australia, and still returns there in the English winters (he turned down a chance to join the WA state squad, to remain available for England). Charging in off a shortish run, large ear-rings jangling, he bends the ball about at just above medium-pace, and is hard to get away: he can also be a fierce striker of the ball. He returned to England in 1996 to try his hand at county cricket, and has become a very handy allrounder. He made an immediate impact on his Hampshire debut, with 6 for 88 against Glamorgan, but has been more of a hit in one-day cricket: an early highlight was an awardwinning performance in the 1998 NatWest Trophy semi-final, when he added a brisk 73 to figures of 3 for 28. He made the first century at the new Rose Bowl, in 2001, and also took the first hat-trick in Twenty20 cricket. In 2004 Shane Warne, his county captain, expressed surprise that England hadn't tried Mascarenhas in ODIs – and continued to push his case until he finally did get the call, in the middle of 2007, his benefit year. His early matches were unspectacular: he failed to take a wicket in three games against West Indies, although he did keep the runs down. But he kept his place for the one-dayers against India, when his rapid 52 nearly conjured an unlikely victory at Edgbaston, and was called up for the inaugural World Twenty20 championships after being left out of the original squad.

THE FACTS Mascarenhas took the first hat-trick in a Twenty20 match, for Hampshire against Sussex at Hove in July 2004, on his way to figures of 5 for 14 ... He hit five successive sixes off Yuvraj Singh in an ODI against India at The Oval in September 2007 ... Mascarenhas was part of the England side that won the Hong Kong Sixes tournament in November 2004 ... His 104 against Worcestershire in May 2001 was the first first-class century scored at the new Rose Bowl ground in Southampton ...

THE FIGURES

Batting and fielding   www.cricinfo.com

	M	Inns	NO	Runs	HS	Avge	S/R	100	50	4s	6s	Ct	St
Tests to 10.9.07	0	0	–	–	–	–	–	–	–	–	–	–	–
ODIs to 10.9.07	7	5	1	98	52	24.50	116.66	0	1	1	10	1	0
First-class to 10.9.07	156	236	26	5258	131	25.03	–	7	19	–	–	60	0

Bowling

	M	Balls	Runs	Wkts	BB	Avge	RpO	S/R	5i	10m
Tests to 10.9.07	0	0	–	–	–	–	–	–	–	–
ODIs to 10.9.07	7	336	214	6	3–23	35.66	3.82	56.00	0	0
First-class to 10.9.07	156	22367	10223	364	6–25	28.08	2.74	61.44	14	0

MASHRAFE MORTAZA

Full name **Mashrafe bin Mortaza**
Born **October 5, 1983, Norail, Jessore, Khulna**
Teams **Khulna**
Style **Right-hand bat, right-arm fast-medium bowler**
Test debut **Bangladesh v Zimbabwe at Dhaka 2001-02**
ODI debut **Bangladesh v Zimbabwe at Chittagong 2001-02**

THE PROFILE Young, quick and aggressive, Mashrafe Mortaza has emerged as the leader of Bangladesh's pack of young pacemen, although fitness remains a problem. He made great strides under the tutelage of Andy Roberts, working on his stamina, and won his first Test cap against Zimbabwe at Dhaka in 2001-02, in what was his first-class debut – indeed, by mid-2007 he had played only eight first-class matches outside Tests. Though banging it in is his preferred style, "Koushik" proved adept at reining in his attacking instincts to concentrate on line and length. He excelled in the second Test against England in 2003-04, taking 4 for 60 in the first innings to keep Bangladesh in touch, but suffered a twisted knee that kept him out of Tests for over a year. He was recalled towards the end of 2004, and subsequently enhanced his reputation in England, standing head and shoulders above his team-mates in a torrid series. He is not a complete mug with the bat, and almost a quarter of his ODI runs have come in sixes. A persistent back injury caused him to return home early and miss the Test series in Sri Lanka in September 2005 – the sixth time he had failed to last throughout a tour – but he was back to face the Australians in April 2006. His 4 for 38 in the following year's World Cup was key in the defeat of India that propelled Bangladesh into the Super Eights, although he did little of note after that.

THE FACTS Mashrafe Mortaza was the first Bangladeshi (Nazmul Hossain in 2004-05 was the second) to make his first-class debut in a Test match: only three others have done this since 1899 – Graham Vivian of New Zealand (1964-65), Zimbabwe's Ujesh Ranchod (1992-93) and Yasir Ali of Pakistan in 2003-04 ... He started the famous ODI victory over Australia at Cardiff in 2005 by dismissing Adam Gilchrist second ball for 0 ... Mortaza's 6 for 26 against Kenya in Nairobi in August 2006 are Bangladesh's best bowling figures in ODIs ... He scored 132 not out for Khulna to help stave off defeat after following on against Sylhet at Khulna in 2004-05 ... His record includes two ODIs for the Asia XI ...

THE FIGURES
Batting and fielding
www.cricinfo.com

	M	Inns	NO	Runs	HS	Avge	S/R	100	50	4s	6s	Ct	St
Tests to 10.9.07	25	46	4	457	79	10.88	69.55	0	2	51	13	7	0
ODIs to 10.9.07	69	54	10	727	51*	16.52	95.65	0	1	56	29	22	0
First-class to 10.9.07	33	58	6	820	132*	15.76	73.08	1	4	–	–	9	0

Bowling

	M	Balls	Runs	Wkts	BB	Avge	RpO	S/R	5i	10m
Tests to 10.9.07	25	4385	2378	59	4–60	40.30	3.25	74.32	0	0
ODIs to 10.9.07	69	3558	2733	92	6–26	29.70	4.60	38.67	1	0
First-class to 10.9.07	33	5622	2999	82	4–27	36.57	3.13	68.42	0	0

MICHAEL **MASON**

NEW ZEALAND

Full name	**Michael James Mason**
Born	**August 27, 1974, Carterton, Wairarapa**
Teams	**Central Districts**
Style	**Right-hand bat, right-arm fast-medium bowler**
Test debut	**New Zealand v South Africa at Wellington 2003-04**
ODI debut	**New Zealand v Pakistan at Lahore 2003-04**

THE PROFILE   Michael Mason earned his place in the New Zealand side the old-fashioned way – by sheer hard work. Mason hails from Mangatainoka, not one of the more prolific development centres of the country's cricket, but he brings a long-valued work ethic associated with many country bowlers before him, including the likes of Ewen Chatfield, Harry Cave, Richard Collinge and Lance Cairns. Like them, Mason is a solid and reliable performer, a workhorse for whom no task is too great. He has been dogged by injuries, but has kept lining up for more. Once described by John Bracewell as "the best line-and-length bowler in the country", Mason was first called up by New Zealand late in 2003, after one of Shane Bond's several injuries and doubts about the availability of Chris Cairns. He toured India without playing a Test, although he did win his first – and so far only – cap at home against South Africa the following March. He has had more chances in ODIs, and after a period out of favour returned to the team in 2006-07, when his 4 for 24 against Sri Lanka won him the match award at Christchurch. He only made one appearance in the tri-series in Australia at the start of the 2007, but nonetheless made the cut for the World Cup, where he faded after being on the receiving end of John Davison's opening salvo for Canada. At 33, Mason does not have time on his side.

THE FACTS   At Queenstown on New Year's Eve 2006 Mason started the last over of an ODI, from Sri Lanka's Sanath Jayasuriya, needing one run from six balls to win the match for New Zealand – he didn't manage to score from the first five balls, then, with the tension sky-high, stepped down the pitch and lofted the last one back over the bowler's head for four ... Mason has taken 1 for 179 in three ODIs in Pakistan ... He took 6 for 56, and 11 for 115 in the match, for Central Districts against Canterbury at Timaru in January 2003 ...

THE FIGURES

Batting and fielding   www.cricinfo.com

	M	Inns	NO	Runs	HS	Avge	S/R	100	50	4s	6s	Ct	St
Tests *to 10.9.07*	1	2	0	3	3	1.50	9.09	0	0	0	0	0	0
ODIs *to 10.9.07*	19	5	2	22	13*	7.33	50.00	0	0	3	0	4	0
First-class *to 10.9.07*	62	80	22	938	64*	16.17	–	0	1	–	–	18	0

Bowling

	M	Balls	Runs	Wkts	BB	Avge	RpO	S/R	5i	10m
Tests *to 10.9.07*	1	132	105	0	–	–	4.77	–	0	0
ODIs *to 10.9.07*	19	819	767	21	4–24	36.52	5.16	42.42	0	0
First-class *to 10.9.07*	62	11983	4941	202	6–56	24.46	2.47	59.32	8	1

MEHRAB HOSSAIN

Full name	**Mehrab Hossain**
Born	**July 8, 1987, Dhaka**
Teams	**Dhaka**
Style	**Left-hand bat, slow left-arm orthodox spinner**
Test debut	**Bangladesh v Sri Lanka at Colombo 2007**
ODI debut	**Bangladesh v Zimbabwe at Jaipur 2006-07**

THE PROFILE Mehrab Hossain is a solid left-hand batsman, who has already made four first-class hundreds, including two in the same match for Bangladesh's A team against Zimbabwe A at Mutare in June 2006. He was opening in that game, but often goes in at No. 4 or 5 for his domestic team, Dhaka, where he is the unwitting cause of confusion sometimes when batting with a team-mate who is also called Mehrab Hossain. The junior Mehrab is a resolute batsman, who rarely looks hurried, and is capable of spending a long time at the crease if he gets set: he is a good timer of the ball on the off side. He is also a handy left-arm spinner, although Bangladesh is not exactly short of those, with Mohammad Rafique and Abdur Razzak the current favourites. Mehrab captained the national Academy side, then performed decently, without setting the world alight, when he had a run in the one-day team against Zimbabwe at the end of 2006. He finally made his Test debut in the second Test of Bangladesh's miserable tour of Sri Lanka in mid-2007. He took two wickets in three balls in his fourth over, but was among a host of batting failures as Bangladesh succumbed for 62 in the first innings, their lowest total in Tests. He is the philosopher of the team, but there's another side to his character – he plays the drums in a rock band!

THE FACTS Mehrab Hossain took 6 for 80 (10 for 130 in the match) for Dhaka at Barisal in April 2005 ... He made 120 and 100 not out for Bangladesh A against Zimbabwe A at Mutare in June 2006 ... Mehrab's highest score is 196, for Dhaka at Barisal in March 2006 ... He is usually shown on scorecards as "Mehrab Hossain junior", to distinguish him from his Dhaka team-mate Mehrab Hossain, an opener (born 1978) who played nine Tests and 18 ODIs for Bangladesh between 1998 and 2003 ... Eight of his ODIs have been against Zimbabwe, the other two against Scotland ...

THE FIGURES

Batting and fielding

www.cricinfo.com

	M	Inns	NO	Runs	HS	Avge	S/R	100	50	4s	6s	Ct	St
Tests to 10.9.07	1	2	0	14	8	7.00	63.63	0	0	2	0	0	0
ODIs to 10.9.07	10	9	0	200	54	22.22	43.76	0	1	18	0	2	0
First-class to 10.9.07	27	49	4	1434	196	31.86	–		4	5	–	–	13	0

Bowling

	M	Balls	Runs	Wkts	BB	Avge	RpO	S/R	5i	10m
Tests to 10.9.07	1	47	29	2	2–29	14.50	3.70	23.50	0	0
ODIs to 10.9.07	10	139	108	3	2–30	36.00	4.66	46.33	0	0
First-class to 10.9.07	27	2280	1323	30	6–80	44.10	3.48	76.00	1	1

KYLE **MILLS**

NEW ZEALAND

Full name **Kyle David Mills**
Born **March 15, 1979, Auckland**
Teams **Auckland**
Style **Right-hand bat, right-arm fast-medium**
Test debut **New Zealand v England at Nottingham 2004**
ODI debut **New Zealand v Pakistan at Sharjah 2000-01**

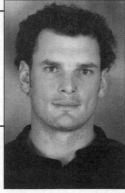

THE PROFILE   Injuries at inopportune times have affected Kyle Mills's prospects of building a substantial international career. While he was recovering, Shane Bond, Ian Butler and Jacob Oram seized their opportunities, making it harder for Mills, a genuine swing bowler, to force his way back. In and out of the team after the 2003 World Cup, in which he made only one fleeting, wicketless appearance – he marked another comeback, against Pakistan in 2003-04, by picking up a reprimand for excessive appealing. However, he did enough to earn a call-up for the tour of England in 2004, and made his Test debut in the third match at Trent Bridge. But he picked up a side strain during that game, and was forced to fly home and miss the NatWest Series. That was a shame, as one-day cricket is really his forte: he played throughout the 2005-06 season, chipping in with wickets in almost every game, even if his once-promising batting had diminished to the point that he managed double figures only once in 16 matches. A feisty temper remains, though: Stephen Fleming had to pull him away from Graeme Smith during a bad-tempered one-day series towards the end of 2005. Mills returned to South Africa for the Tests early in 2006, and picked up eight wickets in the two matches he played, almost doubling his career tally. But injuries impinged again: he had ankle surgery in May 2006, then broke down with knee trouble – which necessitated another op – in Australia in January 2007. He missed the World Cup, and was not expected to be fit again until the new domestic season.

THE FACTS   Mills spanked his only first-class century from No. 9 at Wellington in 2000-01, helping Auckland recover from 109 for 7 to reach 347 ... He averages 20.50 with the ball against West Indies in ODIs, but 38.73 v Australia ... Mills achieved the first ten-wicket haul of his career, and in the process reached 100 first-class wickets, for Auckland against Canterbury in December 2004 ...

THE FIGURES
Batting and fielding   www.cricinfo.com

	M	Inns	NO	Runs	HS	Avge	S/R	100	50	4s	6s	Ct	St
Tests to 10.9.07	7	12	3	120	31	13.33	41.95	0	0	17	2	2	0
ODIs to 10.9.07	65	37	18	261	44*	13.73	63.04	0	0	15	7	21	0
First-class to 10.9.07	48	68	19	1504	117*	30.69	–	1	9	–	–	18	0

Bowling

	M	Balls	Runs	Wkts	BB	Avge	RpO	S/R	5i	10m
Tests to 10.9.07	7	1041	534	17	4–43	31.41	3.07	61.23	0	0
ODIs to 10.9.07	65	3227	2511	89	4–14	28.21	4.66	36.25	0	0
First-class to 10.9.07	48	7625	3711	140	5–33	26.50	2.92	54.46	3	1

MISBAH-UL-HAQ

Full name	**Misbah-ul-Haq Khan Niazi**
Born	**May 28, 1974, Mianwali, Punjab**
Teams	**Faisalabad, Punjab, Sui Northern Gas Pipelines**
Style	**Right-hand bat, occasional legspinner**
Test debut	**Pakistan v New Zealand at Auckland 2000-01**
ODI debut	**Pakistan v New Zealand at Lahore 2001-02**

THE PROFILE An orthodox right-hander with a tight technique, Misbah-ul-Haq (who is no relation to Inzamam) caught the eye with his unflappable temperament in the triangular one-day tournament in Nairobi in September 2002, making 50 against Kenya and repeating that in the rain-ruined final against Australia. But before Pakistan could hail him as a possible middle-order mainstay, Misbah's form slumped: his highest score in three Tests against Australia was 17, and he was duly dumped. Pakistan's abysmal 2003 World Cup campaign – and the wholesale changes to the team in its aftermath – gave Misbah another chance to redeem himself, but he did little of note in his limited opportunities, and he seemed to have been forgotten. He has been overlooked for the senior side since another forgettable one-day outing against Zimbabwe in October 2004, although he has played quite a bit for Pakistan's A team, often as captain. He remained a consistent domestic performer, making 951 runs at 50 in 2004-05, 882 the following season, and capping that with 1108 at 61 in 2006-07, but it was nonetheless a shock when – by now 33 and hardly an investment for the future – Misbah was given a national contract for the 2007-08 season and called up for the World Twenty20 championships (where he was a surprise hit), following Inzamam's one-day retirement and the subsequent decision not to award him a contract at all.

THE FACTS Misbah-ul-Haq has made three first-class double-centuries: 202 and 204 not out for Sargodha against Hyderabad and Bahawalpur in 2001-02, and 205 for Sui Northern Gas Pipelines v Customs in December 2005 ... In 2006-07 Misbah (1108 runs) and Hasan Raza (1081) were the only batsmen to score 1000 first-class runs in Pakistan's domestic season ... He averages 44.50 in ODIs against Australia, but only 11.50 in Tests against them ... Misbah hit 107 not out for Pakistan A in a Twenty20 game against New Zealand A at Darwin in July 2006 ...

THE FIGURES

Batting and fielding   www.cricinfo.com

	M	Inns	NO	Runs	HS	Avge	S/R	100	50	4s	6s	Ct	St
Tests to 10.9.07	5	9	0	120	28	13.33	31.91	0	0	17	0	1	0
ODIs to 10.9.07	12	11	2	305	50*	33.88	67.18	0	2	22	5	5	0
First-class to 10.9.07	119	191	18	8514	205	49.21	–		25	42	–	–	106	0

Bowling

	M	Balls	Runs	Wkts	BB	Avge	RpO	S/R	5i	10m
Tests to 10.9.07	5	0	–	–	–	–	–	–	–	–
ODIs to 10.9.07	12	0	–	–	–	–	–	–	–	–
First-class to 10.9.07	119	192	149	3	1–2	49.66	4.65	64.00	0	0

MOHAMMAD ASHRAFUL

BANGLADESH

Full name	**Mohammad Ashraful**
Born	**July 7, 1984, Dhaka**
Teams	**Dhaka**
Style	**Right-hand bat, legspinner**
Test debut	**Bangladesh v Sri Lanka at Colombo 2001-02**
ODI debut	**Bangladesh v Zimbabwe at Bulawayo 2000-01**

THE PROFILE On September 8, 2001, at the Sinhalese Sports Club in Colombo, Mohammad Ashraful turned a terrible mismatch into a slice of history by becoming the youngest man – or boy – to make a Test century. Bangladesh still crashed to heavy defeat, but "Matin" brought hope and consolation with a sparkling hundred, repeatedly dancing down to hit the Sri Lankan spinners, including Muralitharan, back over their heads ... and on his debut, too. It was the day before his 17th birthday according to some sources, and 63 days after it according to most others: either way, he broke the long-standing record set by Mushtaq Mohammad (17 years 82 days) in 1960-61. Inevitably, such a heady early achievement proved hard to live up to, and after a prolonged poor run Ashraful was dropped for England's first visit in October 2003. He returned to the side a better player, but no less flamboyant, as he demonstrated with a glorious unbeaten 158 in defeat against India at Chittagong late in 2004. Still not 21 when Bangladesh made their maiden tour of England the following year, Ashraful confirmed his status as one for the future at Cardiff, when his brilliantly paced century set Bangladesh up for their astonishing victory over Australia in the NatWest Series. He continued to fire spasmodically, a superb 87 bringing victory over South Africa in the 2007 World Cup, but that was surrounded by more low scores. When Habibul Bashar stood down in May 2007 Ashraful assumed the captaincy at 22 – but the results stayed the same, as Sri Lanka completed a clean sweep of Tests and ODIs at home.

THE FACTS Only 12 players have made their Test debuts when younger than Ashraful: four of them are from Bangladesh ... He made 263, putting on 420 with Marshall Ayub, for Dhaka v Chittagong in November 2006 ... Ashraful averages 58.60 in Tests v India – and only 5.75 v England ... He took the catch that sealed Bangladesh's first Test win, over Zimbabwe at Chittagong in January 2005 ... His record includes two ODIs for the Asia XI ...

THE FIGURES
Batting and fielding   www.cricinfo.com

	M	Inns	NO	Runs	HS	Avge	S/R	100	50	4s	6s	Ct	St
Tests to 10.9.07	38	74	4	1801	158*	25.72	46.02	4	7	217	19	13	0
ODIs to 10.9.07	104	97	9	1918	100	21.79	72.26	1	11	199	20	17	0
First-class to 10.9.07	75	140	5	4136	263	30.63	–	12	15	–	–	32	0

Bowling

	M	Balls	Runs	Wkts	BB	Avge	RpO	S/R	5i	10m
Tests to 10.9.07	38	1080	820	9	2–42	91.11	4.55	120.00	0	0
ODIs to 10.9.07	104	348	353	11	3–26	32.09	6.08	31.63	0	0
First-class to 10.9.07	75	4792	2878	85	7–99	33.85	3.60	53.67	5	0

MOHAMMAD ASIF

Full name	**Mohammad Asif**
Born	**December 20, 1982, Sheikhupura, Punjab**
Teams	**Sialkot, National Bank**
Style	**Left-hand bat, right-arm fast-medium bowler**
Test debut	**Pakistan v Australia at Sydney 2004-05**
ODI debut	**Pakistan v England at Rawalpindi 2005-06**

THE PROFILE When Mohammad Asif made his Test debut at Sydney in January 2005, there was little to suggest that Pakistan's long and happy tradition of unearthing blitzing fast bowlers was about to continue: he bowled 18 innocuous overs as Australia completed a whitewash. Towards the end of 2005, though, Bob Woolmer called Asif the most improved player around the national squad, and he responded with ten wickets as Pakistan A embarrassed England at the start of their tour in November 2005. Asif didn't feature in the Tests, but did make an impressive one-day debut the day after his 23rd birthday, dismissing Marcus Trescothick with his third ball and ending up with 2 for 14 from seven incisive overs. Tall and lean, and slightly more muscular these days, he generates good pace. His action isn't pure, and now involves a Shoaib Akhtar-ish position of the left arm in his jump, but it earned him seven plum wickets at Karachi as Pakistan clinched a famous win over India early in 2006, then 11 for 71 in a three-day win over Sri Lanka at Kandy. An elbow injury kept him out of the first three Tests in England in 2006, but he looked dangerous when he returned at The Oval, taking four wickets in England's first innings before the ball-tampering row blew up. More controversy followed when he failed a drug test: initially banned for a year, he was eventually cleared, and returned with 19 wickets in three Tests in South Africa. He missed the 2007 World Cup with an elbow injury. The doping taint apart, he remains arguably the world's most promising bowling talent.

THE FACTS Mohammad Asif took 11 for 71 (6 for 44 and 5 for 27) against Sri Lanka at Kandy in April 2006 ... For Pakistan A against the England tourists in Lahore in November 2005 he took 7 for 62 in the first innings (10 for 106 in the match) ... At The Oval in 2006 Asif collected his fifth consecutive Test duck, equalling the unwanted record of Australia's Bob Holland and Ajit Agarkar of India ... Asif took 7 for 35 as Sialkot bowled Multan out for 67 in October 2004 ... His record includes three ODIs for the Asia XI ...

THE FIGURES

Batting and fielding

www.cricinfo.com

	M	Inns	NO	Runs	HS	Avge	S/R	100	50	4s	6s	Ct	St
Tests *to 10.9.07*	9	13	6	40	12*	5.71	24.53	0	0	5	0	2	0
ODIs *to 10.9.07*	28	9	3	28	6	4.66	37.83	0	0	2	0	4	0
First-class *to 10.9.07*	68	91	37	448	42	8.29	–	0	0	–	–	26	0

Bowling

	M	Balls	Runs	Wkts	BB	Avge	RpO	S/R	5i	10m
Tests *to 10.9.07*	9	1914	986	49	6–44	20.12	3.09	39.06	4	1
ODIs *to 10.9.07*	28	1383	1064	31	3–28	34.32	4.61	44.61	0	0
First-class *to 10.9.07*	68	12169	6713	280	7–35	23.97	3.30	43.46	17	5

MOHAMMAD HAFEEZ

Full name **Mohammad Hafeez**
Born **October 17, 1980, Sargodha, Punjab**
Teams **Faisalabad, Sui Gas Pipelines**
Style **Right-hand bat, offspinner**
Test debut **Pakistan v Bangladesh at Karachi 2003-04**
ODI debut **Pakistan v Zimbabwe at Sharjah 2002-03**

THE PROFILE Mohammad Hafeez was one of the young players the selectors tried after Pakistan's abysmal display in the 2003 World Cup. Some good one-day performances followed, in Sharjah, Sri Lanka and England: he showed good technique and temperament at the top of the order and bowled his Saqlainish offspinners tidily, but was arguably at his most impressive in the field, where he patrolled the point-cover region with feverish alertness. His organised approach to batting earned him a Test cap when Bangladesh toured shortly afterwards, and he started brightly, scoring a half-century on debut then stroking a maiden hundred in his second Test. However, his form dipped alarmingly in the ODIs that followed against South Africa – only 33 runs in five innings. He lost his Test place, and was then dumped from the one-day team as well. Consistent domestic form kept him in contention, but he seemed to be a back number after being dropped again early in 2005. Hafeez was not originally chosen for the 2006 tour of England, but a spanking 180 against Australia A at Darwin in July, while Pakistan struggled to find an opening combination worth the name in England, led to a surprise call-up for the final Test at The Oval. Before the ball-tampering row overshadowed everything, Hafeez contributed a tidy 95, then spanked 46 in the Twenty20 bunfight that followed. From nowhere, a regular place loomed, and he consolidated in 2006-07, scoring another Test century against West Indies before struggling a little in South Africa, where all six of his Test innings ranged between 10 and 32.

THE FACTS Mohammad Hafeez scored 50 in his first Test, v Bangladesh at Karachi in August 2003, and added 102 not out in his second, at Peshawar a week later ... He averages 35.80 with the bat in ODIs v Sri Lanka – but only 6.87 in eight matches v South Africa ... Hafeez took 8 for 57 (10 for 87 in the match) for Faisalabad v Quetta in December 2004 ...

THE FIGURES

Batting and fielding
www.cricinfo.com

	M	Inns	NO	Runs	HS	Avge	S/R	100	50	4s	6s	Ct	St
Tests to 10.9.07	10	19	1	642	104	35.66	45.02	2	3	85	3	3	0
ODIs to 10.9.07	47	47	1	868	92	18.86	58.68	0	4	101	8	20	0
First-class to 10.9.07	90	153	5	4875	180	32.93	–	10	24	–	–	69	0

Bowling

	M	Balls	Runs	Wkts	BB	Avge	RpO	S/R	5i	10m
Tests to 10.9.07	10	636	236	3	1–11	88.66	2.50	212.00	0	0
ODIs to 10.9.07	47	1661	1234	38	3–17	32.47	4.45	43.71	0	0
First-class to 10.9.07	90	6079	2716	83	8–57	32.72	2.68	73.24	3	1

MOHAMMAD RAFIQUE

Full name	**Mohammad Rafique**
Born	**May 9, 1970, Dhaka**
Teams	**Dhaka**
Style	**Left-hand bat, slow left-arm orthodox spinner**
Test debut	**Bangladesh v India at Dhaka 2000-01**
ODI debut	**Bangladesh v India at Sharjah 1994-95**

THE PROFILE   An accurate, rhythmical slow left-armer, Rafique played in Bangladesh's inaugural Test in November 2000, and was far from outclassed, producing his side's most economical figures. His career hit the rocks shortly afterwards, when his bowling action was reported, but he bounced back in May 2003, with 6 for 77 against South Africa at Dhaka. It was the best bowling performance by a Bangladeshi in 19 Tests at the time, and it spurred Rafique on to greater things. Later in 2003 he was the leading wicket-taker in the series against England. He can bat a bit too, usually employing the long handle, although his returns have diminished with age. His 77 at Hyderabad in May 1998 was instrumental in Bangladesh's victory over Kenya – surprisingly, their first in seven attempts – while in May 2004 he carved an astonishing 111 from No. 9 to help secure a rare first-innings lead over West Indies in St Lucia. His 5 for 65 helped Bangladesh win their first Test, against Zimbabwe at Chittagong early in 2005, and he also played a vital role in turning around the one-day series that followed. He survived a public training-ground argument with then-coach Dav Whatmore to play a role in the national side past his 37th birthday. Nine wickets as Bangladesh almost upset Australia at Fatullah in April 2006 edged him towards a notable double of 1000 runs and 100 wickets in Tests, although he got some fearful tap early in 2007 – 2 for 181 against India at Dhaka, then 1 for 344 in three Tests in Sri Lanka. He's already reached that double in ODIs.

THE FACTS   Mohammad Rafique has taken 17 Test wickets at 23.82 against India, but only nine at 85.55 v Sri Lanka ... He had played only one first-class match before his Test debut in 2000-01 ... 29 (31%) of his 94 Test wickets have been left-handers ... Rafique and Khaled Mashud are the last survivors in the current squad of the team that won the ICC Trophy in Kuala Lumpur in April 1997 ... His record includes two ODIs for the Asia XI ...

THE FIGURES

Batting and fielding   www.cricinfo.com

	M	Inns	NO	Runs	HS	Avge	S/R	100	50	4s	6s	Ct	St
Tests to 10.9.07	31	59	6	1035	111	19.52	65.01	1	4	107	34	7	0
ODIs to 10.9.07	125	106	17	1191	77	13.38	71.61	0	2	110	29	28	0
First-class to 10.9.07	54	94	10	1557	111	18.53	–	1	8	–	–	19	0

Bowling

	M	Balls	Runs	Wkts	BB	Avge	RpO	S/R	5i	10m
Tests to 10.9.07	31	8162	3835	94	6–77	40.79	2.81	86.82	7	0
ODIs to 10.9.07	125	6414	4739	125	5–47	37.91	4.43	51.31	1	0
First-class to 10.9.07	54	14132	5763	212	7–52	27.18	2.44	66.66	12	2

MOHAMMAD SAMI

Full name	**Mohammad Sami**
Born	**February 24, 1981, Karachi, Sind**
Teams	**Karachi, Sind, National Bank**
Style	**Right-hand bat, right-arm fast-medium bowler**
Test debut	**Pakistan v New Zealand at Auckland 2000-01**
ODI debut	**Pakistan v Sri Lanka at Sharjah 2000-01**

THE PROFILE Mohammad Sami shouldered his way into Test cricket with outstanding domestic performances, and had an immediate impact on his debut with eight wickets against New Zealand in March 2001. Then, in only his third match, he took a hat-trick, prising out the last three Sri Lankans in the Asian Test Championship final: he has a one-day hat-trick too. But since that promising start, and especially after the 2003 World Cup, when he was expected to become Pakistan's spearhead after the retirements of Wasim Akram and Waqar Younis, his story has been a fitful and disappointing one. He is occasionally threatening, as he was against India early in 2005, especially in the Kolkata Test and some of the ODIs. But mostly he has been surprisingly ineffective, and prone to leaking runs. Sami was finally dropped after a poor home series against India early in 2006, missed the Sri Lankan tour, and was lucky to be recalled for the trip to England – but he was wayward there too, and only stayed in the side as others were injured. It was the same story in 2006-07: he only made the World Cup squad after Shoaib Akhtar dropped out. Nobody is sure where the problem lies: he's fit; he's athletic; he generates surprising pace from a shortish run-up; he does outswing, reverse-swing and yorkers; he has been given licence to attack with the new ball ... but still that Test average is nudging 50. Some say it's a confidence thing, but opportunities will be limited when other fast bowlers regain fitness.

THE FACTS Mohammad Sami took a Test hat-trick against Sri Lanka at Lahore in March 2002 ... He had also taken a hat-trick in an ODI against West Indies at Sharjah the previous month: neither one involved a fielder, as all the victims were bowled or lbw ... Among bowlers who have taken more than 50 Test wickets, only Carl Hooper (49.42) and Greg Matthews (48.22) have worse averages ... Sami's 5 for 36 on debut, v New Zealand at Auckland in March 2001, remain his best figures in Tests ... He has played county cricket for Kent, and took his career-best figures of 8 for 64 for them against Nottinghamshire in 2003 ...

THE FIGURES
Batting and fielding   www.cricinfo.com

	M	Inns	NO	Runs	HS	Avge	S/R	100	50	4s	6s	Ct	St
Tests to 10.9.07	30	46	11	382	49	10.91	31.03	0	0	43	2	7	0
ODIs to 10.9.07	83	46	19	314	46	11.62	64.08	0	0	16	10	18	0
First-class to 10.9.07	82	109	34	1071	49	14.28	–	0	0	–	–	32	0

Bowling

	M	Balls	Runs	Wkts	BB	Avge	RpO	S/R	5i	10m
Tests to 10.9.07	30	6252	3686	77	5–36	47.87	3.53	81.19	2	0
ODIs to 10.9.07	83	4094	3357	118	5–10	28.44	4.91	34.69	1	0
First-class to 10.9.07	82	15070	8781	283	8–64	31.02	3.49	53.25	14	2

MOHAMMAD SHARIF

Full name **Mohammad Sharif**
Born **December 12, 1985, Narayanganj, Dhaka**
Teams **Dhaka**
Style **Right-hand bat, right-arm fast-medium bowler**
Test debut **Bangladesh v Zimbabwe at Bulawayo 2000-01**
ODI debut **Bangladesh v Zimbabwe at Harare 2000-01**

THE PROFILE Tall and lanky, and on the faster side of fast-medium, Mohammad Sharif forced his way into the national side in Zimbabwe early in 2001 on the back of some impressive club performances in the National League. He was only 15 at the time, the third-youngest of all Test players and the youngest from Bangladesh. Perhaps not surprisingly, he proved a little expensive, conceding more than 100 runs in an innings in each of his first six Tests, but he did impress with 4 for 98 as Pakistan made 465 at Chittagong in January 2002. After that Sharif disappeared off the radar, mainly thanks to a persistent ankle injury and a groin strain that needed surgery. Injuries to some senior bowlers paved the way for him to return to the national side in 2007, as a veteran of 21, more than five years after his previous appearances, following an impressive domestic season that brought him 42 wickets at 20.02 apiece. His first two Tests back, predictably heavy losses against India and Sri Lanka, did not bring him a wicket, and he needs to build on his undoubted promise and make an impact soon if he is to survive at international level. But he is capable of finding reverse swing, and can move the ball both ways: he's also a handy lower-order hitter, and a jaunty fielder.

THE FACTS Mohammad Sharif made his Test debut against Zimbabwe at Bulawayo in April 2001, aged 15 years and 128 days – only Hasan Raza and Mushtaq Mohammad of Pakistan have played Test cricket at an allegedly more tender age ... Sharif took 6 for 43 and 6 for 31 for Biman Airlines against Dhaka at Faridpur in December 2000, a week after his 15th birthday ... His highest score is 75 not out, for Dhaka against Khulna at Dhaka in March 2006 ...

THE FIGURES
Batting and fielding www.cricinfo.com

	M	Inns	NO	Runs	HS	Avge	S/R	100	50	4s	6s	Ct	St
Tests to 10.9.07	10	20	3	122	24*	7.17	43.26	0	0	10	4	5	0
ODIs to 10.9.07	9	9	5	53	13ᴬ	13.25	51.96	0	0	1	0	1	0
First-class to 10.9.07	50	84	16	1012	75*	14.88	–	0	1	–	–	24	0

Bowling

	M	Balls	Runs	Wkts	BB	Avge	RpO	S/R	5i	10m
Tests to 10.9.07	10	1651	1106	14	4–98	79.00	4.01	117.92	0	0
ODIs to 10.9.07	9	499	424	10	3–40	42.40	5.09	49.90	0	0
First-class to 10.9.07	50	8261	4733	151	6–31	31.34	3.43	54.70	8	3

BANGLADESH

MOHAMMAD YOUSUF

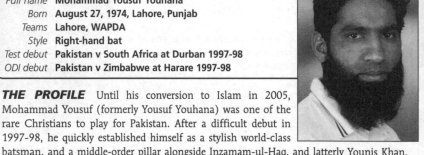

Full name	**Mohammad Yousuf Youhana**
Born	**August 27, 1974, Lahore, Punjab**
Teams	**Lahore, WAPDA**
Style	**Right-hand bat**
Test debut	**Pakistan v South Africa at Durban 1997-98**
ODI debut	**Pakistan v Zimbabwe at Harare 1997-98**

THE PROFILE Until his conversion to Islam in 2005, Mohammad Yousuf (formerly Yousuf Youhana) was one of the rare Christians to play for Pakistan. After a difficult debut in 1997-98, he quickly established himself as a stylish world-class batsman, and a middle-order pillar alongside Inzamam-ul-Haq, and latterly Younis Khan. Since becoming a Muslim, he has turned into a run machine, shattering Viv Richards's 30-year-old record for Test runs in a calendar year during a stellar 2006. Yousuf gathers his runs through composed, orthodox strokeplay: he is particularly strong driving through the covers and flicking wristily off his legs, and has a backlift as decadent and delicious as any, although a tendency to overbalance when playing across his front leg can get him into trouble. He is quick between the wickets, although not the best judge of a single, and there have recently been signs of increasing sluggishness in the field. Some initially questioned his temperament under pressure, but he began to silence those critics late in 2004. First came a spellbindingly languid century against Australia at Melbourne, as stand-in captain, when he ripped into Shane Warne as few Pakistanis have done before or since. A century followed in the Kolkata cauldron, and he ended 2005 with an easy-on-the-eye 223 against England at Lahore, eschewing the waftiness that had previously blighted him. His batting (and his beard) burgeoned in 2006, and it was a surprise when he jeopardised his international future the following year by signing up for the breakaway Indian Cricket League.

THE FACTS Since becoming a Muslim in September 2005 Mohammad Yousuf has averaged 84.48 in 16 Tests: in 59 matches beforehand he averaged 47.46 ... He scored 1788 Test runs in 2006, breaking Viv Richards's old calendar-year record of 1710 in 1976 ... Yousuf made double-centuries in successive matches against England, 223 at Lahore in December 2005, and 202 at Lord's in July 2006: he has scored two more double-hundreds in Tests, but no others in first-class cricket ... His record includes seven ODIs for the Asia XI ...

THE FIGURES

Batting and fielding   www.cricinfo.com

	M	Inns	NO	Runs	HS	Avge	S/R	100	50	4s	6s	Ct	St
Tests to 10.9.07	75	126	9	6553	223	56.00	52.82	23	27	841	47	59	0
ODIs to 10.9.07	242	229	32	8081	141*	41.02	74.41	12	54	650	82	52	0
First-class to 10.9.07	115	190	16	8833	223	50.76	–		27	42	–	–	76	0

Bowling

	M	Balls	Runs	Wkts	BB	Avge	RpO	S/R	5i	10m
Tests to 10.9.07	75	6	3	0	–	–	3.00	–	0	0
ODIs to 10.9.07	242	2	1	1	1–0	1.00	3.00	2.00	0	0
First-class to 10.9.07	115	18	24	0	–	–	8.00	–	0	0

ALBIE **MORKEL**

Full name **Johannes Albertus Morkel**
Born **June 10, 1981, Vereeniging, Transvaal**
Teams **Titans**
Style **Left-hand bat, right-arm fast-medium bowler**
Test debut **No Tests yet**
ODI debut **South Africa v New Zealand at Wellington 2003-04**

THE PROFILE Albie Morkel, a right-arm fast-medium bowler and left-handed batsman, was lumbered with the tag of being the "new Lance Klusener", and was touted early in his career by Ray Jennings – his provincial coach, and a former national coach too – as someone who could become a world-class allrounder. It hasn't quite happened yet, although he does average over 40 with the bat in first-class cricket, with a double-century to his name, and Twenty20 cricket seems to be tailor-made for his style of play. There have been glimpses of his talent: he rose to prominence for his provincial side Easterns (now the Titans) against the touring West Indians at Benoni in 2003-04, defying food poisoning to score a century – putting on 141 for the ninth wicket with his brother, Morne, with whom he often opens the bowling too – and also took five wickets in the match. Albie was picked for the senior tour of New Zealand shortly after that, and made his ODI debut there early in 2004: he performed solidly, if unspectacularly, in seven further one-dayers up till November 2005, after which the selectors looked elsewhere for a while. Morkel was back – again alongside his brother, who had appeared in a Test in the meantime – for the Afro-Asia Cup in India in June 2007. In the second match at Chennai, Albie and Morne opened the bowling together for the African XI, the first instance of brothers sharing the new ball in an ODI since Kenya's Martin and Tony Suji did so during the 1999 World Cup. Shortly after that he hit 97 against the outclassed Zimbabweans.

THE FACTS Albie Morkel made 204 not out, putting on 264 with Justin Kemp, as Titans drew with Western Province Boland at Paarl in March 2005 after following on ... He took 6 for 36 for Easterns against Griqualand West at Kimberley in December 1999 ... Morkel's brother Morne has also played for South Africa, while another brother, Malan, played for SA Schools ... His record includes two ODIs for the Africa XI, in one of which he opened the bowling with Morne ...

THE FIGURES
Batting and fielding   www.cricinfo.com

	M	Inns	NO	Runs	HS	Avge	S/R	100	50	4s	6s	Ct	St
Tests to 10.9.07	0	0	–	–	–	–	–	–	–	–	–	–	–
ODIs to 10.9.07	12	9	1	182	97	22.75	83.10	0	1	17	5	1	0
First-class to 10.9.07	50	71	13	2347	204*	40.46	–	3	16	–	–	18	0

Bowling

	M	Balls	Runs	Wkts	BB	Avge	RpO	S/R	5i	10m
Tests to 10.9.07	0	0	–	–	–	–	–	–	–	–
ODIs to 10.9.07	12	408	376	11	2–23	34.18	5.52	37.09	0	0
First-class to 10.9.07	50	8165	4172	140	6–36	29.80	3.06	58.32	3	0

SOUTH AFRICA

MORNE **MORKEL**

Full name	**Morne Morkel**
Born	**October 6, 1984, Vereeniging, Transvaal**
Teams	**Titans, Kent**
Style	**Left-hand bat, right-arm fast bowler**
Test debut	**South Africa v India at Durban 2006-07**
ODI debut	**Africa XI v Asia XI at Bangalore 2007**

THE PROFILE Morne Morkel, the brother of Easterns allrounder Albie, has been a hot property on the South African domestic scene ever since his first-class debut in 2003-04, when he made 44 not out in a ninth-wicket stand of 141 with his brother, who hit 132, against the touring West Indians at Benoni. An out-and-out fast bowler, the lanky Morne did well in 2004-05, taking 20 wickets at 18.20 apiece, but then sat out most of the following season with injuries. But he impressed Allan Donald at a fast-bowlers' camp when he was fit again: "He gets serious bounce, and he's got really great pace – genuine pace. He has a great attitude to go with his physical strengths." Morkel shook up the Indians while playing for the Rest of South Africa at Potchefstroom in December 2006, bowling Virender Sehwag with his first ball, and adding the wickets of Laxman, Tendulkar and Dhoni as the tourists lurched to 69 for 5. That got him into the national frame, and he played in the second Test at Durban when Dale Steyn was ruled out, although three wickets and some handy runs in a crushing victory weren't quite enough to keep him in for the final Test, when Steyn was fit again. Morkel played his first ODIs in the Afro-Asia Cup in India in June 2007, and impressed again, taking eight wickets in three matches and opening the bowling with Albie in one game. Then he nipped over to England to play for Kent, the eventual winners, in the qualifying rounds of the Twenty20 Cup.

THE FACTS Morne Morkel took 6 for 66 for a Combined XI against the Zimbabweans at Benoni in February 2005 ... His brother Albie has also played for South Africa, while another brother, Malan, played for SA Schools ... Morkel's first three ODIs were for the Africa XI: in one he opened the bowling with Albie, the first instance of brothers sharing the new ball in an ODI since Kenya's Martin and Tony Suji did it during the 1999 World Cup ...

THE FIGURES
Batting and fielding

www.cricinfo.com

	M	Inns	NO	Runs	HS	Avge	S/R	100	50	4s	6s	Ct	St
Tests *to 10.9.07*	1	2	1	58	31*	58.00	62.36	0	0	7	0	0	0
ODIs *to 10.9.07*	6	3	2	52	25	52.00	118.18	0	0	5	2	2	0
First-class *to 10.9.07*	19	26	6	379	57	18.95	48.65	0	1	–	–	13	0

Bowling

	M	Balls	Runs	Wkts	BB	Avge	RpO	S/R	5i	10m
Tests *to 10.9.07*	1	144	111	3	3–86	37.00	4.62	48.00	0	0
ODIs *to 10.9.07*	6	360	282	12	3–50	23.50	4.70	30.00	0	0
First-class *to 10.9.07*	19	3327	1948	66	6–66	29.51	3.51	50.40	3	0

RUNAKO **MORTON**

Full name	**Runako Shakur Morton**
Born	**July 22, 1978, Nevis**
Teams	**Leeward Islands**
Style	**Right-hand bat, occasional offspinner**
Test debut	**West Indies v Sri Lanka at Colombo 2005**
ODI debut	**West Indies v Pakistan at Sharjah 2001-02**

THE PROFILE Runako Morton is fiery on and off the pitch. His career looked to be over before it had properly started when he was expelled from the West Indian Academy in 2001 for a series of disciplinary breaches. He refused to be bowed, and continued to accumulate runs for the Leeward Islands. In February 2002, his penance complete, he was called into an injury-plagued squad. But he threw away his opportunity when he pulled out of the Champions Trophy in September 2002, pretending that his grandmother had died. His career slipped further down the pan when he was arrested in January 2004, in connection with a stabbing incident, but he was given a third chance at redemption in May 2005, when he was recalled to the one-day squad when South Africa toured, although he didn't actually play. After moving to live in Trinidad – and calming down, he says – he finally made his debut (becoming only the fifth Test player from the tiny island of Nevis) in Sri Lanka in 2005, in a side decimated by a damaging contracts dispute, and also toured New Zealand early in 2006, making two handy scores in the Tests, and adding a defiant one-day century at Napier. He struggled against spin, though, and was pushed up to open in the home one-day series against Zimbabwe, helping himself to 79 and 109. But the Indians were an altogether stiffer proposition, and he was dropped after innings of 23, 1 and 0 against them in May 2006. He played a few good-looking cameos in England in 2007, although he always gave the impression that a wild swing was never too far away, and he needs to knuckle down more to become a genuine Test No. 4.

THE FACTS Morton made 201 for the West Indians against MCC at Durham in 2007 ... He withdrew from the 2002 Champions Trophy in Sri Lanka, claiming that his grandmother had died: it later turned out that one of his grandmothers had been dead for 16 years, and the other was still alive ... Morton averages 57.25 in ODIs against New Zealand, but 0.00 v South Africa ...

THE FIGURES

Batting and fielding   www.cricinfo.com

	M	Inns	NO	Runs	HS	Avge	S/R	100	50	4s	6s	Ct	St
Tests *to 10.9.07*	10	17	1	381	70*	23.81	48.22	0	3	48	5	13	0
ODIs *to 10.9.07*	40	35	4	986	110*	31.80	64.31	2	6	86	8	16	0
First-class *to 10.9.07*	68	112	6	3818	201	36.01	–	8	24	–	–	81	0

Bowling

	M	Balls	Runs	Wkts	BB	Avge	RpO	S/R	5i	10m
Tests *to 10.9.07*	10	66	50	0	–	–	4.54	-	0	0
ODIs *to 10.9.07*	20	6	2	0	–	–	2.00	–	0	0
First-class *to 10.9.07*	68	467	289	8	3–17	36.12	3.71	58.37	0	0

JEHAN **MUBARAK**

Full name	**Jehan Mubarak**
Born	**January 10, 1981, Washington, USA**
Teams	**Colombo Cricket Club**
Style	**Left-hand bat, occasional offspinner**
Test debut	**Sri Lanka v Bangladesh at Colombo 2002**
ODI debut	**Sri Lanka v South Africa at Johannesburg 2002-03**

THE PROFILE A graceful left-hander, Jehan Mubarak has something of David Gower about him. Like Gower, he plays the game as though it was his birthright – and after representing Sri Lanka at Under-15, U17 and U19 levels, maybe it is. After some middling domestic seasons, he was spotted at a training camp by Arjuna Ranatunga and Aravinda de Silva, who liked what they saw: Mubarak made his Test debut in 2002, even before he had scored a first-class hundred. He also made the squad for the 2003 World Cup, despite not passing 15 in his first five ODI appearances – and played only once in South Africa, being one of five players to collect ducks in a crushing defeat by India. A fluid driver, he remains a favourite of the selectors, and is a serial A-team representative, but finds the final step up a hard one: he still hasn't managed a Test fifty, although he does have three one-day half-centuries to his name, the highest 72 against Bangladesh in July 2007, which won him a place at the World Twenty20 championships in September. Marvan Atapattu's decision to turn down a central contract may give him another chance at the top of the order. He was born in Washington DC, the son of Aziz Mubarak, a respected scientist and a Cambridge cricket Blue, but returned to Sri Lanka to attend Colombo's prestigious Royal College. Mubarak is a useful offspinner and an excellent fielder ... and a top-class swimmer, who has represented Sri Lanka at water polo.

THE FACTS Mubarak is only the second Test player to have been born in the United States: the other was Kenneth "Bam Bam" Weekes, who played two Tests for West Indies in 1939, scoring 137 at The Oval ... Mubarak made 169 for Colombo CC against Ragama in November 2003 ... He averages 39.50 in ODIs against New Zealand, but 0.00 v India ... Mubarak's father, Aziz, was a Cambridge Blue from 1978 to 1980 ...

THE FIGURES
Batting and fielding   www.cricinfo.com

	M	Inns	NO	Runs	HS	Avge	S/R	100	50	4s	6s	Ct	St
Tests *to 10.9.07*	8	14	1	236	48	18.15	42.59	0	0	31	1	10	0
ODIs *to 10.9.07*	23	22	2	409	72	20.45	64.40	0	3	42	3	8	0
First-class *to 10.9.07*	89	157	14	4307	169	30.11	–	4	24	–	–	80	0

Bowling

	M	Balls	Runs	Wkts	BB	Avge	RpO	S/R	5i	10m
Tests *to 10.9.07*	8	78	42	0	–	–	3.23	–	0	0
ODIs *to 10.9.07*	23	51	50	1	1–10	50.00	5.88	51.00	0	0
First-class *to 10.9.07*	89	2465	1283	28	4–59	45.82	3.12	88.03	0	0

MUTTIAH **MURALITHARAN**

Full name	**Muttiah Muralitharan**
Born	**April 17, 1972, Kandy**
Teams	**Tamil Union, Lancashire**
Style	**Right-hand bat, offspinner**
Test debut	**Sri Lanka v Australia at Colombo 1992-93**
ODI debut	**Sri Lanka v India at Colombo 1993-94**

THE PROFILE Muttiah Muralitharan is one of the most successful bowlers the game has seen, Sri Lanka's greatest player ... and without doubt the most controversial cricketer of the modern age. Murali's rise from humble beginnings – the Tamil son of a hill-country confectioner – to the top of the wicket-taking lists has divided opinion because of his weird bent-armed delivery. From a loose-limbed, open-chested action, his chief weapons are the big-turning offbreak and two top-spinners, one of which goes straight on and the other, his doosra, which spins from a rubbery wrist in the opposite direction to his stock ball. However, suspicions about his action surfaced when he was no-balled for throwing in Australia, first on Boxing Day 1995 at Melbourne, then in the subsequent one-day series. He was cleared by ICC after biomechanical analysis concluded that his action, and a deformed elbow which he can't fully straighten, create the "optical illusion of throwing". But the controversy did not die: Murali was called again in Australia in 1998-99, had more tests, and was cleared again. Then his new doosra prompted further suspicion, and he underwent more high-tech tests in 2004, which ultimately forced ICC to revise their rules on chucking. On the field, Murali continued to pile up the wickets, overtaking Courtney Walsh's Test-record 519 in May 2004: only shoulder trouble, which required surgery, allowed Shane Warne to pass him. Murali returned, potent as ever, and flummoxed England with 8 for 70 at Nottingham to square the 2006 series.

THE FACTS Muralitharan was the second bowler (after Shane Warne) to take 700 Test wickets, and the first to take 1,000 in all international cricket, reaching that landmark in March 2006 ... His 60 Test five-fors is easily a record (next comes Warne with 37) ... Murali has taken nine wickets in a Test innings twice, and his 16 for 220 at The Oval in 1998 is the fifth-best haul in all Tests ... He reached 200 County Championship wickets during 2007, in only 27 games ... His record includes one Test and three ODIs for the World XI, and four ODIs for the Asia XI ...

THE FIGURES

Batting and fielding   www.cricinfo.com

	M	Inns	NO	Runs	HS	Avge	S/R	100	50	4s	6s	Ct	St
Tests to 10.9.07	113	144	49	1117	67	11.75	69.24	0	1	129	24	64	0
ODIs to 10.9.07	297	135	50	491	27	5.77	70.74	0	0	33	6	117	0
First-class to 10.9.07	212	256	76	2048	67	11.37	–	0	1	–	–	115	0

Bowling

	M	Balls	Runs	Wkts	BB	Avge	RpO	S/R	5i	10m
Tests to 10.9.07	113	37382	14931	700	9-51	21.33	2.39	53.40	60	20
ODIs to 10.9.07	297	16094	10321	455	7-30	22.68	3.84	35.37	8	0
First-class to 10.9.07	212	60276	23748	1274	9-51	18.64	2.36	47.31	112	32

MUSHFIQUR RAHIM

BANGLADESH

Full name	**Mohammad Mushfiqur Rahim**
Born	**September 1, 1988, Bogra**
Teams	**Rajshahi**
Style	**Right-hand bat, wicketkeeper**
Test debut	**Bangladesh v England at Lord's 2005**
ODI debut	**Bangladesh v Zimbabwe at Harare 2006**

THE PROFILE A wild-card inclusion for Bangladesh's maiden tour of England in 2005, Mushfiqur Rahim was just 16 when he was selected for that daunting trip – two Tests in May, followed by six ODIs against England and Australia – even though he hadn't been named in the preliminary squad of 20. Mushfiqur was principally chosen as an understudy to the long-serving wicketkeeper, Khaled Mashud, but his inclusion was further evidence of Bangladesh's determination to build for a better future. He had done well on an A-team tour of Zimbabwe earlier in 2005, scoring a century in the first Test at Bulawayo, and also enjoyed some success in England the previous year with the Under-19s, making 88 in the second Test at Taunton. He showed more evidence of grit with the full team, with a maiden first-class half-century to soften the pain of defeat against Sussex, followed by a hundred against Northamptonshire. That earned him a call-up – as a batsman – to become the youngest player to appear in a Test at Lord's. He was one of only three players to reach double figures in a disappointing first innings, but a twisted ankle kept him out of the second Test. He also featured in Bogra's inaugural Test, against Sri Lanka the following month, but could make little of the spin of Murali and Malinga Bandara. He supplanted Mashud for the 2007 World Cup, anchoring the win over India with 56 not out, then nicked Mashud's Test place too – and a defiant 80 in Colombo showed he meant to keep it.

THE FACTS Mushfiqur Rahim's hundred for Bangladesh against Northamptonshire in 2005 made him the youngest century-maker in English first-class cricket, beating Sachin Tendulkar's record: Rahim was 16 years 261 days old, 211 days younger than Tendulkar was in 1990; the youngest Englishman was 17-year-old Stephen Peters for Essex in 1996 ... Rahim played two Tests – and eight other matches for Bangladesh representative teams – before appearing in a first-class match at home, for Rajshahi ...

THE FIGURES

Batting and fielding   www.cricinfo.com

	M	Inns	NO	Runs	HS	Avge	S/R	100	50	4s	6s	Ct	St
Tests to 10.9.07	4	8	1	125	80	17.85	36.33	0	1	15	1	1	0
ODIs to 10.9.07	25	19	5	346	57	24.71	53.72	0	2	23	3	18	6
First-class to 10.9.07	16	28	5	700	115*	30.43	41.10	2	4	–	–	24	1

Bowling

	M	Balls	Runs	Wkts	BB	Avge	RpO	S/R	5i	10m
Tests to 10.9.07	4	0	–	–	–	–	–	–	–	–
ODIs to 10.9.07	25	0	–	–	–	–	–	–	–	–
First-class to 10.9.07	16	0	–	–	–	–	–	–	–	–

PHIL **MUSTARD**

Full name	**Philip Mustard**
Born	**October 8, 1982, Sunderland, Co. Durham**
Teams	**Durham**
Style	**Left-hand bat, wicketkeeper**
Test debut	**No Tests yet**
ODI debut	**No ODIs yet**

THE PROFILE   Phil Mustard, born and bred in Durham, is an improving wicketkeeper-batsman who was called up to England's one-day side for the tour of Sri Lanka late in 2007. Mustard's one-day form – he made 893 runs at a shade under 50 in the 2007 domestic season, including his first one-day century, to help Durham to their first two trophies – clinched his place ahead of a clutch of other fancied keepers after Matt Prior broke a finger during the World Twenty20 championships in South Africa. Mustard played for England Under-19s in 2002, after scoring 75 on his first-class debut earlier that season. For a couple of years he jostled with Andrew Pratt for the Durham wicketkeeping spot, but made the place his own with 578 first-class runs in 2005, followed by around 800 in each of the following two seasons. A big hitter with all the shots (including a reverse slog-sweep), he set up Durham's matchwinning 312 in the Friends Provident Trophy final at Lord's in August 2007 with a rapid 49: Shane Warne, the opposing captain that day, rated him the best one-day keeper-batsman in England, saying he reminded him of Adam Gilchrist. But Durham's skipper, Dale Benkenstein, was more cautious: "I think he has a few steps to go before he is ready for international cricket. It can also crucify you." A talented allround sportsman, Mustard was on Manchester United's books for two years until he was 13, and then with Middlesbrough for two more. He still plays football in the winter to keep fit.

THE FACTS   Mustard made 75 on his first-class debut, for Durham against the Sri Lankans in May 2002 ... He scored two first-class hundreds in 2006, and hit a one-day ton in 2007 ... Mustard's nickname is "Colonel", after the Cluedo character: Durham scorecards often feature the entry "caught Mustard bowled Onions" (Graham Onions, a fast-medium bowler, has been close to England selection too) ... His brother, Alan, is a handy batsman who plays for Sunderland ...

THE FIGURES

Batting and fielding   www.cricinfo.com

	M	Inns	NO	Runs	HS	Avge	S/R	100	50	4s	6s	Ct	St
Tests *to 10.9.07*	0	0	–	–	–	–	–	–	–	–	–	–	–
ODIs *to 10.9.07*	0	0	–	–	–	–	–	–	–	–	–	–	–
First-class *to 10.9.07*	50	79	4	2103	130	28.04	71.02	2	9	–	–	151	7

Bowling

	M	Balls	Runs	Wkts	BB	Avge	RpO	S/R	5i	10m
Tests *to 10.9.07*	0	0	–	–	–	–	–	–	–	–
ODIs *to 10.9.07*	0	0	–	–	–	–	–	–	–	–
First-class *to 10.9.07*	50	0	–	–	–	–	–	–	–	–

RANA **NAVED-UL-HASAN**

PAKISTAN

Full name	**Rana Naved-ul-Hasan**
Born	**February 28, 1978, Sheikhupura, Punjab**
Teams	**Sialkot, WAPDA, Sussex**
Style	**Right-hand bat, right-arm fast-medium bowler**
Test debut	**Pakistan v Sri Lanka at Karachi 2004-05**
ODI debut	**Pakistan v Sri Lanka at Sharjah 2002-03**

THE PROFILE Naved-ul-Hasan made his debut in Sharjah immediately after the disastrous 2003 World Cup, when he seemed to be competing with Abdul Razzaq, Azhar Mahmood and Shoaib Malik for the allrounder's spot. Few backed him then, despite some impressive early performances, and he was dropped soon after, supposedly because of some unspecified disciplinary problems. But, helped by the continuing doubts about Shoaib Akhtar's fitness and injuries to other bowlers, Naved worked his way up to become the one-day team's spearhead, although he can be expensive on a bad day – as at Centurion in February 2007 when his eight overs cost 92. As with most Pakistan pace bowlers, he can bowl a reverse-swinging yorker, and his change of pace is another useful weapon. But his nous, his control over line and length, and his refusal to give anything less than his all in the field have stood out. He was Pakistan's leading one-day bowler in 2005, impressing first in the VB Series in Australia and then on the flatter, less responsive pitches of India and the Caribbean. So far it has been a different story in Tests, although he was badly missed in 2006 in England – where he has done well for Sussex – when he missed the entire Test series with a troublesome groin injury. He is a hard-hitting lower-order batsman, with centuries for Sheikhupura and Sussex, although he hasn't had much chance to display this skill at international level yet, despite his insistence that he is, in fact, a natural wicketkeeper/batsman. He gave up his first love, hockey, for cricket.

THE FACTS Naved-ul-Hasan has taken 31 wickets at 23.67 in ODIs against India – but only two at 96.00 against South Africa ... He took 6 for 27 against India at Jamshedpur in April 2005 ... Naved made his highest score of 139 for Sussex against Middlesex at Lord's in 2005, and then took seven wickets, including four in one over in the second innings ... He took 91 wickets in Pakistan in 2000-01: the following season he took 7 for 49, still his best figures, for Sheikhupura against Sialkot at Muridke ...

THE FIGURES

Batting and fielding   www.cricinfo.com

	M	Inns	NO	Runs	HS	Avge	S/R	100	50	4s	6s	Ct	St
Tests *to 10.9.07*	9	15	3	239	42*	19.91	84.15	0	0	32	5	3	0
ODIs *to 10.9.07*	62	41	14	359	29	13.29	74.63	0	0	28	8	13	0
First-class *to 10.9.07*	100	142	15	2917	139	22.96	–	3	9	–	–	52	0

Bowling

	M	Balls	Runs	Wkts	BB	Avge	RpO	S/R	5i	10m
Tests *to 10.9.07*	9	1565	1044	18	3–30	58.00	4.00	86.94	0	0
ODIs *to 10.9.07*	62	2854	2630	95	6–27	27.68	5.52	30.04	1	0
First-class *to 10.9.07*	100	19033	10705	454	7–49	23.57	3.37	41.92	26	4

ANDRE **NEL**

Full name	**Andre Nel**
Born	**July 15, 1977, Germiston, Transvaal**
Teams	**Titans, Essex**
Style	**Right-hand bat, right-arm fast bowler**
Test debut	**South Africa v Zimbabwe at Harare 2001-02**
ODI debut	**South Africa v West Indies at Port-of-Spain 2000-01**

SOUTH AFRICA

THE PROFILE Andre Nel is a muscular fast bowler who has belied his conservative Afrikaans upbringing by amassing a chequered disciplinary record. He was sent home from the A-team tour of Australia in 2003 after being found to be driving under the influence of alcohol. It was only his latest misdemeanour, but he was nonetheless chosen for the one-day portion of the 2003 tour of England, where he was already playing for Northamptonshire. Nel was tipped early on as a future international, and he first made the headlines early in 2001 when he felled Allan Donald – his hero – with a fierce bouncer. Nel burst into tears as Donald tottered off, and it later emerged that he was following instructions from his coach, Ray Jennings, to target South Africa's premier fast bowler. Further controversy followed when Nel was one of five players caught smoking marijuana during a tour of the Caribbean. However, it was during the home West Indies series of 2003-04, during which he got married, that Nel established himself – and he was only in trouble once, for making facial gestures at Chris Gayle. Back trouble curtailed his progress, but he returned with wickets – and more gurning – against England in 2004-05. He came into his own in Australia in 2005-06, where he was an intimidating presence with 14 wickets and an attacking approach. Four Boxing Day dismissals preceded a strong showing at Sydney, and the Aussie crowds – sensing a kindred spirit to their own Merv Hughes – loved to hate him. Nel is charming and humorous off the field: he calls his snarling alter ego "Gunther the mountain boy".

THE FACTS Nel has taken 39 of his 97 wickets in seven Tests against West Indies, at an average of 20.61: against New Zealand he averages 76.00 ... He took 10 for 88 in the match in South Africa's innings win over West Indies at Bridgetown in April 2005 ... Nel dismissed Brian Lara eight times in Tests (and three more times in ODIs) ... He has never made a first-class fifty, but did hit 64 in a three-day game against a Western Australia XI in December 2005, sharing a ninth-wicket stand of 175 with Jacques Rudolph ...

THE FIGURES

Batting and fielding

www.cricinfo.com

	M	Inns	NO	Runs	HS	Avge	S/R	100	50	4s	6s	Ct	St
Tests *to 10.9.07*	27	31	7	200	23*	8.33	39.29	0	0	26	2	12	0
ODIs *to 10.9.07*	65	17	9	61	22*	7.02	50.41	0	0	6	1	17	0
First-class *to 10.9.07*	93	105	34	929	44	13.08	–	0	0	–	–	34	0

Bowling

	M	Balls	Runs	Wkts	BB	Avge	RpO	S/R	5i	10m
Tests *to 10.9.07*	27	5935	3023	97	6–32	31.16	3.05	61.18	3	1
ODIs *to 10.9.07*	65	3190	2459	89	5–45	27.62	4.62	35.84	1	0
First-class *to 10.9.07*	93	18560	8611	327	6–25	26.33	2.78	56.75	12	1

MAKHAYA **NTINI**

SOUTH AFRICA

Full name	**Makhaya Ntini**
Born	**July 6, 1977, Mdingi, Cape Province**
Teams	**Warriors**
Style	**Right-hand bat, right-arm fast bowler**
Test debut	**South Africa v Sri Lanka at Cape Town 1997-98**
ODI debut	**South Africa v New Zealand at Perth 1997-98**

THE PROFILE Makhaya Ntini has had a fair bit to contend with during his young life. A product of the United Cricket Board's development programme, Ntini was discovered as a cattleherd in the Eastern Cape, given a pair of boots and packed off to Dale College, one of South Africa's best-regarded cricketing nurseries. With an action consciously modelled on Malcolm Marshall's, Ntini found himself touring Australia in 1997-98 when Roger Telemachus failed a fitness test. He made his one-day international debut on that tour, bowling well in helpful conditions at Perth, and his Test debut – the first black African to play for South Africa – came later the same year. He was then convicted of rape, but cleared on appeal. After that ordeal he returned for the Sharjah tournament in 2000, impressing observers with greater control than before. Although he is a little short of the pace of a Brett Lee or a Shoaib Akhtar, he steadily improved, getting closer to the stumps but maintaining his high pace and occasional dangerous late inswing, and in 2003 became the first South African to take ten wickets in a Test at Lord's, before devastating West Indies in Trinidad in 2005 with 13 for 132, the best match figures for South Africa. Ntini steamed on, relishing his new role as the pace spearhead, and hurtled past 300 Test wickets during a destructive spell of 6 for 59 against Pakistan at Port Elizabeth in January 2007. Shortly after that, though, he failed to spark during the World Cup, and was dropped for South Africa's last two games. He'll be back.

THE FACTS Ntini's 13 for 132 (6 for 95 and 7 for 37) at Port-of-Spain in April 2005 are South Africa's best match figures in Tests, surpassing Hugh Tayfield's 13 for 165 at Melbourne in 1952-53 ... He has taken 54 Test wickets against England, and 53 v West Indies ... Ntini has taken 210 (68%) of his Test wickets in 41 matches at home ... Only 21 (7%) of his Test wickets have been lbws ... Ntini's record includes one ODI for the World XI ...

THE FIGURES
Batting and fielding

www.cricinfo.com

	M	Inns	NO	Runs	HS	Avge	S/R	100	50	4s	6s	Ct	St
Tests to 10.9.07	75	86	24	619	32*	9.98	54.58	0	0	93	8	20	0
ODIs to 10.9.07	158	39	19	174	42*	8.70	64.92	0	0	15	5	29	0
First-class to 10.9.07	140	164	48	1107	34*	9.54	–	0	0	–	–	34	0

Bowling

	M	Balls	Runs	Wkts	BB	Avge	RpO	S/R	5i	10m
Tests to 10.9.07	75	15826	8465	308	7–37	27.48	3.20	51.38	17	4
ODIs to 10.9.07	158	7931	5812	242	6–22	24.01	4.39	32.77	4	0
First-class to 10.9.07	140	26145	14333	499	7–37	28.72	3.28	52.39	22	4

JACOB **ORAM**

Full name	**Jacob David Philip Oram**
Born	**July 28, 1978, Palmerston North, Manawatu**
Teams	**Central Districts**
Style	**Left-hand bat, right-arm fast-medium bowler**
Test debut	**New Zealand v India at Wellington 2002-03**
ODI debut	**New Zealand v Zimbabwe at Wellington 2000-01**

THE PROFILE It's hard to miss Jacob Oram, and not just because of his height of 6ft 6ins (1.98m). He is agile in the field, especially at gully – his skills were developed as a schoolboy soccer goalkeeper – and he complements that with solid fast-medium bowling and aggressive batting. Foot problems during 2001-02 cost him a season at a vital stage, but he came back strongly the following year and sealed a place in both the Test and one-day sides. He narrowly missed a century against Pakistan in the Boxing Day Test at Wellington in 2003, but made up for that in the next match by carving 119 not out against South Africa, then 90 in the second Test, which earned him a spot for the England tour of 2004. By then his bowling was starting to lose its sting, and he went down with a back injury shortly after pounding 126, again not out, against Australia at Brisbane in November. After nearly 18 months out of the Test side Oram showed in April 2006 what New Zealand's middle order had been missing, coming in at 38 for 4 in the first match at Centurion and making his highest score of 133. He missed the start of the 2006-07 one-day series in Australia with a hamstring injury, but bucked the team up with some stirring performances when he did get there, including a 71-ball century – New Zealand's fastest, and his first in ODIs – against Australia in Perth. A badly broken finger threatened to keep him out of the 2007 World Cup, but he made it – he said he'd have the offending digit amputated if that would help – and played his part as New Zealand advanced to the semi-finals.

THE FACTS Oram averages 62.00 in Tests against Australia, 60.50 v South Africa – and 10.25 v India ... With the ball he averages 19.69 v India, and 106.00 v England ... Oram scored his maiden century in only his fourth first-class match, for Central Districts v Canterbury at Christchurch in 1998-99, and his 155 remains his highest score ...

THE FIGURES

Batting and fielding

www.cricinfo.com

	M	Inns	NO	Runs	HS	Avge	S/R	100	50	4s	6s	Ct	St
Tests to 10.9.07	22	39	8	1221	133	39.38	50.41	3	4	141	16	13	0
ODIs to 10.9.07	102	78	10	1547	101*	22.75	79.31	1	6	116	46	29	0
First-class to 10.9.07	64	101	15	3147	155	36.59	–		6	16	–	–	32	0

Bowling

	M	Balls	Runs	Wkts	BB	Avge	RpO	S/R	5i	10m
Tests to 10.9.07	22	3370	1443	42	4–41	34.35	2.56	80.23	0	0
ODIs to 10.9.07	102	4465	3364	110	5–26	30.58	4.52	40.59	2	0
First-class to 10.9.07	64	7553	3026	106	6–45	28.54	2.40	71.25	2	0

MONTY **PANESAR**

Full name	**Mudhsuden Singh Panesar**
Born	**April 25, 1982, Luton, Bedfordshire**
Teams	**Northamptonshire**
Style	**Left-hand bat, slow left-arm orthodox spinner**
Test debut	**England v India at Nagpur 2005-06**
ODI debut	**England v Australia at Melbourne 2006-07**

THE PROFILE Monty Panesar made his Test debut early in 2006, and by the middle of that year had made himself a cult hero to English crowds enchanted by his enthusiastic wicket celebrations and his endearingly erratic fielding. That, and equally amateurish batting, had threatened to hold him back, but when Ashley Giles was ruled out of the 2005-06 Indian tour Panesar received a late summons. He's a throwback to an earlier Northamptonshire slow left-armer, Bishan Bedi, who also twirled away in a patka at the County Ground, teasing and tempting with flight and guile, although Panesar, who has huge hands, gives it more of a rip than Bedi did. Panesar took eight wickets on his first-class debut, against Leicestershire in 2001, including 4 for 11 in the second innings. University intruded, but despite only two first-class games in 2001, and six in 2002, he did enough to earn a place in the Academy squad in Australia. Finally free from studies, he had a fine season in 2005, with 46 Championship wickets at 21.54, and was a late addition for the Indian tour. He made his debut at Nagpur, picking up Sachin Tendulkar as his first Test wicket. He captivated crowds at home in 2006, sending down the ball of the season to bowl Younis Khan to set up victory at Leeds. Despite his near-cult status Panesar missed the first two Ashes Tests in 2006-07 – the returning Giles was unaccountably preferred – then showed what England were missing with 5 for 92 at Perth. He even became indispensable to the one-day side. Back home in 2007 he claimed 31 wickets in seven Tests, and remained the crowd's favourite as Montymania showed no sign of running out of steam.

THE FACTS Panesar took 7 for 181 for Northamptonshire v Essex at Chelmsford in July 2005 ... He was the first Sikh to play Test cricket for anyone other than India: when Panesar opposed Harbhajan Singh during his debut at Nagpur in 2005-06 it was the first instance of one Sikh bowling to another in a Test ... He was the first Luton-born Test cricketer, and only the seventh to have been born in Bedfordshire, the previous one being Wayne Larkins ...

THE FIGURES

Batting and fielding   www.cricinfo.com

	M	Inns	NO	Runs	HS	Avge	S/R	100	50	4s	6s	Ct	St
Tests to 10.9.07	20	28	11	124	26	7.29	32.46	0	0	16	1	3	0
ODIs to 10.9.07	25	7	3	23	13	5.75	29.48	0	0	2	0	3	0
First-class to 10.9.07	64	83	30	430	39*	8.11	31.71	0	0	–	–	16	0

Bowling

	M	Balls	Runs	Wkts	BB	Avge	RpO	S/R	5i	10m
Tests to 10.9.07	20	4593	2249	73	6–129	30.80	2.93	62.91	6	1
ODIs to 10.9.07	25	1248	949	23	3–25	41.26	4.56	54.26	0	0
First-class to 10.9.07	64	15053	7244	246	7–181	29.44	2.88	61.19	16	3

MICHAEL **PAPPS**

Full name	**Michael Hugh William Papps**
Born	**July 2, 1979, Christchurch, Canterbury**
Teams	**Canterbury**
Style	**Right-hand bat, occasional wicketkeeper**
Test debut	**New Zealand v South Africa at Hamilton 2003-04**
ODI debut	**New Zealand v South Africa at Auckland 2003-04**

THE PROFILE After a successful junior career Michael Papps – an shortish, unflashy opener with an enviable ability to work the bowlers around and convert length balls into half-volleys – was selected to play against South Africa at home in 2003-04, after a prolific domestic season that brought him well over 1000 runs in all matches, in another attempt to solve New Zealand's long-running search for a capable opening batsman to partner Stephen Fleming. He impressed in the one-dayers, and was duly selected for the accompanying Test series. He made 59 on his debut, but struggled afterwards. Nevertheless, the selectors kept faith, and picked him for the 2004 tour of England, where an injury to Craig McMillan handed him a spot in the second Test at Headingley. He scored a battling 86, opening in difficult conditions, but at some price: he broke a finger, and was forced to bat down the order in the second innings as New Zealand sunk to a series defeat. After a couple of injury-marred seasons – there was a broken finger, a dislocated shoulder, and a bang on the head from Brett Lee – he was recalled for the South African tour early in 2006. He failed to pass 22 in four attempts in the Tests, but kept his name in the selectors' minds with a superb domestic season in 2006-07, racking up 1005 runs at 91.36, nearly 250 more than anyone else. He can also keep wicket, adding some flexibility to the squad.

THE FACTS Papps won the Redpath Cup, as New Zealand's "most meritorious batsman in first-class cricket" after his 1005 runs for Canterbury in 2006-07 ... His highest score of 192 was for Canterbury against Northern Districts in Christchurch in December 2003 ... Papps hit 201 not out for the NZ Academy against their Australian counterparts in October 1999, putting on 257 for the seventh wicket with James Franklin ... His brother Tim has also played for Canterbury ...

THE FIGURES
Batting and fielding   www.cricinfo.com

	M	Inns	NO	Runs	HS	Avge	S/R	100	50	4s	6s	Ct	St
Tests to 10.9.07	6	12	1	229	86	20.81	35.89	0	2	34	0	7	0
ODIs to 10.9.07	6	6	2	207	92*	51.75	60.52	0	2	24	0	1	0
First-class to 10.9.07	82	144	9	4919	192	36.43	–	12	22	–	–	93	4

Bowling

	M	Balls	Runs	Wkts	BB	Avge	RpO	S/R	5i	10m
Tests to 10.9.07	6	0	–	–	–	–	–	–	–	–
ODIs to 10.9.07	6	0	–	–	–	–	–	–	–	–
First-class to 10.9.07	82	12	6	0	–	–	3.00	–	0	0

JEETAN **PATEL**

Full name	**Jeetan Shashi Patel**
Born	**May 7, 1980, Wellington**
Teams	**Wellington**
Style	**Right-hand bat, offspinner**
Test debut	**New Zealand v South Africa at Cape Town 2005-06**
ODI debut	**New Zealand v Zimbabwe at Harare 2005-06**

THE PROFILE The son of Indian parents, but born and brought up in Wellington's eastern suburbs, offspinner Jeetan Patel was fast-tracked into the New Zealand one-day side after John Bracewell, the coach, identified him as the sort of slow bowler who could be effective at the death. Patel first played for Wellington in 1999-2000, bowling 59 overs and taking 5 for 145 against Auckland on his debut. Three middling seasons followed, and he seemed to be heading nowhere, with an average in the mid-forties. But then he took 6 for 32 against Otago in the last State Championship match of 2004-05, propelling Wellington into the final against Auckland, which they lost. Suddenly good judges were noting his ability to make the ball loop and drift, not unlike a right-handed Daniel Vettori. Bracewell took him to Zimbabwe in August 2005, and he played nine ODIs during the season, in eight being either the super-sub or the subbed-out player, as his batting – although better than when he began – is underwhelming. At home his 2 for 23 from ten overs throttled Sri Lanka at Wellington, then three wickets at Christchurch helped subdue West Indies too. All this put Patel in line for a first Test cap, which came against South Africa at Cape Town in April 2006. And he had a nice long bowl, wheeling down 42 overs and removing Graeme Smith, Boeta Dippenaar and AB de Villiers at a cost of 117 runs. In 2006-07 he was often used as a foil to Vettori on spinning tracks, and usually succeeded in keeping the runs down – not least in most of his six outings in the 2007 World Cup.

THE FACTS Patel won the Man of the Match award for his tight spell of 2 for 23 against Sri Lanka at Wellington in 2005-06 after being super-subbed into the game ... He also won the match award in his first international Twenty20 match, after taking 3 for 20 v South Africa at Johannesburg in October 2005 ... Patel hit his highest score of 58 not out for Wellington v Otago at Dunedin in 2000-01, after going in as nightwatchman ...

THE FIGURES

Batting and fielding   www.cricinfo.com

	M	Inns	NO	Runs	HS	Avge	S/R	100	50	4s	6s	Ct	St
Tests to 10.9.07	1	1	1	27	27*	–	87.09	0	0	3	0	1	0
ODIs to 10.9.07	23	7	2	56	34	11.20	53.84	0	0	4	1	8	0
First-class to 10.9.07	58	71	30	775	58*	18.90	–	0	2	–	–	19	0

Bowling

	M	Balls	Runs	Wkts	BB	Avge	RpO	S/R	5i	10m
Tests to 10.9.07	1	252	117	3	3–117	39.00	2.78	84.00	0	0
ODIs to 10.9.07	23	1206	1009	32	3–11	31.53	5.01	37.68	0	0
First-class to 10.9.07	58	9799	4493	113	6–32	39.76	2.75	86.71	3	0

MUNAF **PATEL**

Full name	**Munaf Musa Patel**
Born	**July 12, 1983, Ikhar, Gujarat**
Teams	**Maharashtra**
Style	**Right-hand bat, right-arm fast-medium bowler**
Test debut	**India v England at Mohali 2005-06**
ODI debut	**India v England at Goa 2005-06**

THE PROFILE   Few fast men generated as much hype before bowling a ball in first-class – let alone international – cricket as Munaf Patel, the young boy from the little town of Ikhar in Gujarat, did early in 2003. Kiran More spotted him in the nets and sent him straight to Chennai to train under Dennis Lillee. Soon he was being hailed as the fastest man in Indian cricket. Then, as Baroda and Gujarat jostled for his signature, Patel chose Mumbai, after Sachin Tendulkar had a word with the authorities there. Even then Patel's first-class career was anything but smooth, as he spent more time recovering from injuries than actually playing, and he later moved to play for Maharashtra. He's strongly built, though not overly tall; a wild mane flows behind him as he bustles up to the bowling crease, gathering momentum before releasing the ball with a windmill-whirl of hands. Patel's priority is to bowl quick, but he has added reverse swing to his repertoire, and also has a well-directed yorker. In March 2006 he finally received a call from the selectors – now chaired by Patel's old pal More – for the second Test against England, after taking 10 for 91 against them for the Board President's XI. He ended the Mohali Test with 7 for 97, the best performance by an Indian fast bowler on debut, and continued to take wickets consistently in the West Indies later in 2006. Things got harder after that. He picked up a niggling ankle injury in South Africa, and was criticised by his own Board when it bothered him in the final Test – but he regained full fitness in time for the World Cup, where he did as well as anyone. Then it was a back injury, and he returned to the Chennai academy – which he calls his "second home" – to remodel his action.

THE FACTS   Patel's match figures of 7 for 97 were the best on Test debut by an Indian fast bowler, beating Mohammad Nissar's 6 for 135 in India's inaugural Test, against England at Lord's in 1932 (Abid Ali, more of a medium-pacer, took 7 for 116 on debut against Australia at Adelaide in 1967-68) ... Patel's best first-class figures are 6 for 50, for Maharashtra against Railways at Delhi in January 2006 ...

THE FIGURES

Batting and fielding   www.cricinfo.com

	M	Inns	NO	Runs	HS	Avge	S/R	100	50	4s	6s	Ct	St
Tests to 10.9.07	7	9	3	32	13	5.33	31.37	0	0	3	1	4	0
ODIs to 10.9.07	25	10	5	32	15	6.40	62.74	0	0	3	0	3	0
First-class to 10.9.07	31	36	10	385	78	14.80	–	0	1	–	–	9	0

Bowling

	M	Balls	Runs	Wkts	BB	Avge	RpO	S/R	5i	10m
Tests to 10.9.07	7	1500	725	25	4–25	29.00	2.90	60.00	0	0
ODIs to 10.9.07	25	1189	944	32	4–49	29.50	4.76	37.15	0	0
First-class to 10.9.07	31	5634	2580	113	6–50	22.83	2.74	49.85	4	1

IRFAN **PATHAN**

Full name	**Irfan Khan Pathan**
Born	**October 27, 1984, Baroda, Gujarat**
Teams	**Baroda**
Style	**Left-hand bat, left-arm medium-fast bowler**
Test debut	**India v Australia at Adelaide 2003-04**
ODI debut	**India v Australia at Melbourne 2003-04**

THE PROFILE   Left-armer Irfan Pathan was initially rated the most talented swing and seam bowler to emerge from India since Kapil Dev. Within a couple of years in international cricket, he was being thought of as a possible successor for Kapil in the allround department, too. When he made his Test debut in Australia late in 2003, it was with the energy of a 19-year-old, but with a composed air striking even for one who had been specifically readied for the purpose via the A-team and age-group sides. His instinct is not just what to bowl to who and when, but also to keep learning new tricks. Already he possesses perhaps the most potent left-armer's outswinger in world cricket – which helped him to a Test hat-trick in the first over of the Karachi Test in January 2006 – he's adept at reverse-swinging the ball, and enjoys long spells. He played a big part in India's one-day and Test series wins in Pakistan early in 2004. His batting also took off, and he was regularly pushed up the order, sometimes even opening in one-dayers. His first stint at No. 3 produced a spectacular 83 against Sri Lanka at Nagpur – and he has often bailed India out in the Test arena as well, with successive innings of 93 and 82 against Sri Lanka late in 2005, and 90 as India piled up 603 against Pakistan at Faisalabad early in 2006. He struggled after that with a shoulder niggle, which may have contributed to a loss of rhythm when bowling. He went to the World Cup but didn't play, them missed the England tour as he tried to rediscover the spark. He was recalled for the World Twenty20 championship in September 2007 – alongside his brother.

THE FACTS   Pathan was the first bowler to take a hat-trick in the first over of a Test match, when he dismissed Salman Butt, Younis Khan and Mohammad Yousuf at Karachi in January 2006: from 0 for 3, Pakistan recovered to win by 341 runs ... He took 12 for 126 in the match v Zimbabwe at Harare in September 2005 ... Pathan hit 111 not out for the Indians v Rest of South Africa in December 2006 ... His brother Yusuf Pathan plays for Baroda too, and was also called up for the inaugural World Twenty20 championship in September 2007 ...

THE FIGURES

Batting and fielding   www.cricinfo.com

	M	Inns	NO	Runs	HS	Avge	S/R	100	50	4s	6s	Ct	St
Tests to 10.9.07	25	32	2	835	93	27.83	49.97	0	6	99	13	8	0
ODIs to 10.9.07	73	54	14	1006	83	25.15	80.09	0	5	99	25	12	0
First-class to 10.9.07	68	88	19	1899	111*	27.52	–	1	10	–	–	21	0

Bowling

	M	Balls	Runs	Wkts	BB	Avge	RpO	S/R	5i	10m
Tests to 10.9.07	25	5078	2802	91	7–59	30.79	3.31	55.80	7	2
ODIs to 10.9.07	73	3555	2980	115	5–27	25.91	5.02	30.91	1	0
First-class to 10.9.07	68	12800	6885	223	7–59	30.87	3.22	57.39	10	3

ROBIN **PETERSON**

Full name	**Robin John Peterson**
Born	**August 4, 1979, Port Elizabeth, Cape Province**
Teams	**Warriors**
Style	**Left-hand bat, slow left-arm orthodox spinner**
Test debut	**South Africa v Bangladesh at Dhaka 2002-03**
ODI debut	**South Africa v India at Colombo 2002-03**

THE PROFILE Spin bowlers of genuine potential are rare in South Africa, more so the jewels who can bat and field well, but Robin Peterson, a left-arm finger-spinner, ticks all three boxes. He has four centuries and nearly 200 first-class wickets, and is a lurking presence square of the wicket in the field. At first glance his left-arm spin looks a little too plain, but he does turn it given help from the pitch. He also has a doosra, which turns in to the right-hander. After a glittering youth career Peterson made his Test debut against Bangladesh in May 2003, taking five wickets and scoring 61, but since then has been seen mainly as a one-day specialist – especially after Brian Lara carted him for a Test-record 28 in an over at the end of 2003. He was back for some one-dayers in India late in 2005, but had little success, a pattern repeated when the Australians toured early the following year, when he managed only one wicket in three matches. Still, Peterson was the only specialist spinner chosen for the 2006 Champions Trophy and, despite continuing modest returns, for the 2007 World Cup. Again he contributed little with the ball, although his thick-edged four did complete a last-gasp victory over Sri Lanka, after Lasith Malinga's four wickets in four balls had detonated what seemed a routine run-chase. The suspicion remains that Peterson does not do enough with the ball in international cricket, but he did well in an Emerging Players tournament in Australia in mid-2007, to keep himself in the selectors' thoughts.

THE FACTS Peterson's unlucky 13th over against West Indies at Johannesburg in December 2003 was the most expensive in Test history: Brian Lara hit it for 28 (466444) ... Peterson's highest score is 130, for Eastern Province v Gauteng at Johannesburg in October 2002 ... He also made 108 for South Africa A v India A at Bloemfontein in April 2002 ... Peterson took 6 for 67 for Eastern Province v Border at East London in December 1999, and 6 for 16 in a one-day game for EP v Namibia in November 2002 ...

THE FIGURES

Batting and fielding   www.cricinfo.com

	M	Inns	NO	Runs	HS	Avge	S/R	100	50	4s	6s	Ct	St
Tests to 10.9.07	5	6	1	159	61	31.80	72.27	0	1	18	1	4	0
ODIs to 10.0.07	35	15	4	147	36	13.36	75.77	0	0	14	2	7	0
First-class to 10.9.07	72	117	15	2591	130	25.40	–	4	9	–	–	31	0

Bowling

	M	Balls	Runs	Wkts	BB	Avge	RpO	S/R	5i	10m
Tests to 10.9.07	5	785	403	8	3–46	50.37	3.08	98.12	0	0
ODIs to 10.9.07	35	1252	992	17	2–26	58.35	4.75	73.64	0	0
First-class to 10.9.07	72	13423	6919	195	6–67	35.48	3.09	68.83	8	1

VERNON **PHILANDER**

Full name	**Vernon Darryl Philander**
Born	**June 24, 1985, Bellville, Cape Province**
Teams	**Cape Cobras**
Style	**Right-hand bat, right-arm fast-medium bowler**
Test debut	**No Tests yet**
ODI debut	**South Africa v Ireland at Belfast 2007**

THE PROFILE The possessor of one of international cricket's more remarkable surnames (Brian Johnston would have loved it, and his initials), Vernon Philander is a powerful allrounder who has done consistently well for the Cape Cobras since breaking into first-class cricket in 2003-04. Before that he toured England with the Under-19s in 2003, and returned there the following year to play for Devon, helping them to a famous C&G Trophy win over Leicestershire, dismissing Brad Hodge in a low-scoring game that eventually finished with the scores level. His nippy, accurate bowling is backed up with some muscular batting, as he demonstrated in only his fourth first-class game when he flogged 168 (out of 283) for Western Province against Griqualand West at Kimberley. In 2006-07 he produced an impressive one-day season for the Cobras, averaging 72 with the bat and 30 with the ball. It was enough to earn him a place in South Africa's squad for their mid-2007 one-day tour of Ireland – a team he'd been lined up to play for before a shin stress fracture ruled him out – and he starred on his ODI debut, which was also his 22nd birthday, taking 4 for 12 to make sure the Irish did not approach South Africa's modest total of 173 from 31 overs in a rain-hit game. Philander then also did well in an Emerging Players tournament in Australia, and was called up for the Twenty20 World Championships in South Africa in September 2007.

THE FACTS In his first ODI, against Ireland in June 2007 on his 22nd birthday, Philander took 4 for 12, the second-best figures by a South African on ODI debut after Allan Donald's 5 for 29 in 1991-92 ... He scored 168 for Western Province against Griqualand West at Kimberley in November 2004, in only his fourth first-class match ... Philander scored 59 and then took 3 for 20 to help South Africa beat New Zealand in the final of Cricket Australia's Emerging Players tournament in Brisbane in July 2007...

THE FIGURES

Batting and fielding   www.cricinfo.com

	M	Inns	NO	Runs	HS	Avge	S/R	100	50	4s	6s	Ct	St
Tests to 10.9.07	0	0	–	–	–	–	–	–	–	–	–	–	–
ODIs to 10.9.07	5	3	2	40	17*	40.00	90.90	0	0	4	0	1	0
First-class to 10.9.07	26	42	2	1046	168	26.15	47.45	1	4	–	–	9	0

Bowling

	M	Balls	Runs	Wkts	BB	Avge	RpO	S/R	5i	10m
Tests to 10.9.07	0	0	–	–	–	–	–	–	–	–
ODIs to 10.9.07	5	197	129	6	4–12	21.50	3.92	32.83	0	0
First-class to 10.9.07	26	4038	1718	71	5–49	24.19	2.55	56.87	1	0

KEVIN **PIETERSEN**

Full name	**Kevin Peter Pietersen**
Born	**June 27, 1980, Pietermaritzburg, Natal, South Africa**
Teams	**Hampshire**
Style	**Right-hand bat, offspinner**
Test debut	**England v Australia at Lord's 2005**
ODI debut	**England v Zimbabwe at Harare 2004-05**

THE PROFILE Expansive with bat and explosive with bombast, Kevin Pietersen is not one for the quiet life. Bold-minded and big-hitting, he first ruffled feathers by quitting South Africa – he was disenchanted with the race-quota system – in favour of England, his eligibility coming courtesy of an English mother. He never doubted he would play Test cricket: he has self-confidence in spades but, fortunately, sackfuls of talent too. Sure enough, as soon as he was eligible for England, in September 2004, he was chosen for a one-day series in Zimbabwe, where he averaged 104, earning him a late call-up to play ... South Africa. Undeterred by hostile crowds, he announced his arrival with a robust century in the second match at Bloemfontein. On reaching his ton, he kissed the England badge with unreserved fervour. Test cricket was next on the to-do list, and it was only a matter of time. In 2005 he replaced Graham Thorpe, against Australia, at Lord's ... and coolly blasted a couple of fifties in a losing cause, then, with the Ashes at stake, again showed his eye for the limelight by clubbing 158 on the final day at The Oval, to secure the draw England needed. "KP" had arrived – and how. He played for the World XI less than a year after his one-day debut, and hammered 158 and 142 in successive home Tests against Sri Lanka in 2006. The runs kept coming: 158 at Adelaide and 226 against West Indies at Headingley sandwiching two tons in the 2007 World Cup, where he was the star of England's lame campaign with 444 runs at 55. Ricky Ponting wrote that Pietersen could be "the next superstar of world cricket", and the man himself is unlikely to disagree – or to stop until he is.

THE FACTS Pietersen reached his hundred v South Africa at East London in Feb 2005 from 69 balls, the fastest for England in ODIs ... After 25 Tests he had scored 2448 runs, more than anyone else except Don Bradman (3194) ... He averages 114.25 in ODIs against South Africa – and 16.50 v Bangladesh ... Pietersen was out for 158 three times in Tests before going on to 226 v West Indies at Leeds in May 2007 ... His record includes two ODIs for the World XI ...

THE FIGURES

Batting and fielding

www.cricinfo.com

	M	Inns	NO	Runs	HS	Avge	S/R	100	50	4s	6s	Ct	St
Tests *to 10.9.07*	30	57	2	2898	226	52.69	65.49	10	10	336	37	19	0
ODIs *to 10.9.07*	61	55	11	2277	116	51.75	89.32	5	16	213	44	24	0
First-class *to 10.9.07*	111	185	14	8917	254*	52.14	–	31	35	–	–	99	0

Bowling

	M	Balls	Runs	Wkts	BB	Avge	RpO	S/R	5i	10m
Tests *to 10.9.07*	30	336	262	2	1–11	131.00	4.67	168.00	0	0
ODIs *to 10.9.07*	61	101	106	2	1–4	53.00	6.29	50.50	0	0
First-class *to 10.9.07*	111	5050	2904	58	4–31	50.06	3.45	87.06	0	0

LIAM **PLUNKETT**

Full name	**Liam Edward Plunkett**
Born	**April 6, 1985, Middlesbrough, Yorkshire**
Teams	**Durham**
Style	**Right-hand bat, right-arm fast-medium bowler**
Test debut	**England v Pakistan at Lahore 2005-06**
ODI debut	**England v Pakistan at Lahore 2005-06**

THE PROFILE Liam Plunkett's selection for England's tours of Pakistan and India in 2005-06 represented the culmination of a two-year rise to prominence. He had made his first-class debut for Durham in 2003, taking on immediate responsibilities in the absence of Steve Harmison and the injured Mark Davies, and in 2005 reached 50 wickets in a season for the first time. Not dissimilar to the young Harmison in build or bowling style, Plunkett also has the makings of a useful allrounder, as he demonstrated with a composed half-century in only his second ODI in Pakistan. Earlier on that tour, following the withdrawal of Simon Jones with an ankle injury, Plunkett also made his Test debut, acquitting himself well in the ruins of a thumping defeat at Lahore. His second Test, against India at Mohali in March 2006, was less successful, but at the age of 20, he had undoubtedly marked himself out as one for the future. Injuries to Jones, Andrew Flintoff and James Anderson meant that Plunkett was in the frame throughout the 2006 home season, but although he picked up a few wickets – six of them in the demolition of Sri Lanka at Birmingham late in May – there was a frustrating looseness about some of his bowling, and he looked overplaced at No. 8 in the batting order. After a frustrating Ashes tour, when he suddenly emerged from the woodwork to star in a couple of one-dayers, that inconsistency returned in the home Tests against West Indies: he was consigned back to county cricket after some wayward displays.

THE FACTS Plunkett took three wickets in his first ODI, and scored 56 in his second, both against Pakistan in December 2005 ... He took 5 for 53 on his County Championship debut, for Durham v Yorkshire at Leeds in 2003 ... Plunkett's best bowling figures are 6 for 74, for Durham v Hampshire at Chester-le-Street in August 2004 ... His highest score is 74 not out, for Durham v Somerset at Stockton in May 2005, when he shared a ninth-wicket stand of 124 with Mark Davies ... Plunkett took 13 wickets in three Under-19 Tests in Australia in 2002-03, when England lost a closely contested series 2–1 ...

THE FIGURES

Batting and fielding

www.cricinfo.com

	M	Inns	NO	Runs	HS	Avge	S/R	100	50	4s	6s	Ct	St
Tests to 10.9.07	9	13	2	126	44*	11.45	39.62	0	0	16	0	3	0
ODIs to 10.9.07	27	24	10	295	56	21.07	85.26	0	1	21	5	7	0
First-class to 10.9.07	53	81	19	1234	74*	19.90	45.30	0	4	–	–	22	0

Bowling

	M	Balls	Runs	Wkts	BB	Avge	RpO	S/R	5i	10m
Tests to 10.9.07	9	1538	916	23	3–17	39.82	3.57	66.86	0	0
ODIs to 10.9.07	27	1291	1260	37	3–24	34.05	5.85	34.89	0	0
First-class to 10.9.07	53	8648	5299	165	6–74	32.11	3.67	52.41	5	0

KIERON **POLLARD**

Full name	**Kieron Adrian Pollard**
Born	**May 12, 1987, Cacariqua, Trinidad**
Teams	**Trinidad & Tobago**
Style	**Right-hand bat, right-arm medium-pacer**
Test debut	**No Tests yet**
ODI debut	**West Indies v South Africa at St George's 2006-07**

THE PROFILE Kieron Pollard shot to prominence in 2006-07 when still only 19, with his muscular batting doing much to take Trinidad & Tobago to the final of the inaugural Stanford 20/20 competition: in the semi-final, against Nevis, he clobbered 83 in only 38 balls, and then grabbed a couple of wickets with his medium-pacers. That won him a first-class start against Barbados, and it was a memorable one: he got off the mark with a six, and cleared the boundary six more times on his way to 117. Another hundred, and six more sixes, followed in his third match, and in between he hit 87 off 58 balls – seven sixes this time – in a one-dayer against Guyana. That was ... in West Indies' World Cup squad. The cometary rise tailed off ... ed his first Carib Beer season with 420 runs at 42, and played ... up itself, as a rather surprise selection in the Super Eight match ... ust-win encounter which West Indies lost, thus putting them ... for the future, and if he can make the final step up to the ... which big hitters like Andrew Symonds took some time to do ... or Caribbean cricket for a long time to come.

... made 126 on his first-class debut, for Trinidad & Tobago ... Hill in January 2007: his innings included 11 fours and seven ... im off the mark ... In his second match (against Guyana) he hit 69 in 31 balls, with one four and six sixes, and in his third (against the Leeward Islands) he made 117 from 87 balls with 11 fours and six more sixes ... Pollard was the only player from any country to make his international debut at the 2007 World Cup ...

THE FIGURES

Batting and fielding

	M	Inns	NO	Runs	HS	Avge	S/R	100	50	4s	6s	Ct	St
Tests to 10.9.07	0	0	–	–	–	–	–	–	–	–	–	–	–
ODIs to 10.9.07	1	1	0	10	10	10.00	58.82	0	0	1	0	0	0
First-class to 10.9.07	6	10	0	420	126	42.00	–	2	1	–	–	9	0

Bowling

	M	Balls	Runs	Wkts	BB	Avge	RpO	S/R	5i	10m
Tests to 10.9.07	0	0	–	–	–	–	–	–	–	–
ODIs to 10.9.07	1	18	20	0	–	–	6.66	–	0	0
First-class to 10.9.07	6	73	51	2	2–29	25.50	4.19	36.50	0	0

SHAUN **POLLOCK**

Full name	**Shaun Maclean Pollock**
Born	**July 16, 1973, Port Elizabeth, Cape Province**
Teams	**Dolphins**
Style	**Right-hand bat, right-arm fast-medium bowler**
Test debut	**South Africa v England at Centurion 1995-96**
ODI debut	**South Africa v England at Cape Town 1995-96**

THE PROFILE It would have been surprising if Shaun Pollock had not been an international cricketer. Father Peter led the South African attack through the 1960s, while uncle Graeme was arguably the finest left-hand batsman of them all. It is as an immaculate line-and-length seamer that Shaun will be remembered. At first he was slippery and aggressive, and his Natal team-mates totted up the number of batsmen he hit. He was brought into the Test side against England in 1995-96 by his father, the chairman of selectors at the time. Pollock junior settled in quickly, and his testing new-ball partnership with Allan Donald was the springboard of much of South Africa's success during the late 1990s. Pollock moves the ball both ways, and also has stamina and courage, as he proved in 1997-98 when he toiled in blazing heat to take 7 for 87 in 41 overs on a flat Adelaide track. He was handed the captaincy in 2000 when Hansie Cronje was booted out, and faced the huge challenge of lifting a shocked and demoralised side. However, he lost credibility after a drubbing in Australia, and was later blamed for South Africa's disastrous 2003 World Cup, when they failed to qualify for the Super Sixes by one run: Pollock was replaced by Graeme Smith. With 100 Test caps under his belt, "Polly" is approaching the veteran stage; his nagging brilliance around off stump remains, but his pace has dipped, relegating him to first change. But he answered questions about his right to a place with 21 wickets in five Tests in 2006-07, and proved as economical as ever in ODIs.

THE FACTS Pollock and Jacques Kallis were the first South Africans to play 100 Tests, reaching the mark at Centurion in April 2006 ... He is SA's leading wicket-taker in Tests and ODIs ... 88 (21%) of his Test wickets have been lbws ... On his debut for Warwickshire, in a one-day match in 1996, Pollock took four wickets in four balls v Leicestershire ... His record includes three ODIs for the World XI, and six for the Africa XI (he scored his maiden ODI hundred for them in 2007, in his 285th such match)...

THE FIGURES

Batting and fielding   www.cricinfo.com

	M	Inns	NO	Runs	HS	Avge	S/R	100	50	4s	6s	Ct	St
Tests to 10.9.07	107	156	39	3781	111	32.31	52.52	2	16	412	35	72	0
ODIs to 10.9.07	290	194	68	3279	130	26.02	86.63	1	12	228	56	107	0
First-class to 10.9.07	183	265	55	6952	150*	33.10	–	6	34	–	–	129	0

Bowling

	M	Balls	Runs	Wkts	BB	Avge	RpO	S/R	5i	10m
Tests to 10.9.07	107	24185	9648	416	7–87	23.19	2.39	58.13	16	1
ODIs to 10.9.07	290	14962	9250	383	6–35	24.15	3.70	39.06	5	0
First-class to 10.9.07	183	38521	15318	656	7–33	23.35	2.38	58.72	22	2

RICKY **PONTING**

Full name **Ricky Thomas Ponting**
Born **December 19, 1974, Launceston, Tasmania**
Teams **Tasmania**
Style **Right-hand bat, right-arm medium-pace bowler**
Test debut **Australia v Sri Lanka at Perth 1995-96**
ODI debut **Australia v South Africa at Wellington 1994-95**

THE PROFILE Ricky Ponting began with Tasmania at 17 and Australia at 20, and was unluckily given out for 96 on his Test debut. He remains the archetypal modern cricketer, playing all the shots with a full flourish and knowing only attack – and his dead-eye fielding is a force by itself. A gambler and a buccaneer, Ponting is a one-day natural. He has had setbacks, against probing seam and high-class finger-spin, which he plays with hard hands when out of form. In the '90s there were off-field indiscretions that forced him to address an alcohol problem, but his growing maturity was acknowledged when he succeeded Steve Waugh as one-day captain in 2002. It was a seamless transition: Ponting led the 2003 World Cup campaign from the front, clouting a coruscating century in the final, and acceded to the Test crown when Waugh finally stepped down early in 2004. But things changed in 2005. A humiliating one-day defeat by Bangladesh caused the first ripples of dissent against his leadership style, and more followed as the Ashes series progressed. A heroic 156 saved the Manchester Test, but he couldn't save the urn. The result hurt, and the pain lingered. Ponting bounced back by winning 11 of 12 Tests in 2005-06, which was just a warm-up for the Ashes rematch. He led that off with 196 at Brisbane – and was furious to miss his double-century – and remained tight-lipped until the 5-0 whitewash was sealed at Sydney. His batting never wavered, and after retaining the World Cup he is within touching distance of 20,000 international runs.

THE FACTS The only Australians with higher Test batting averages than Ponting's are Don Bradman (99.94) and Michael Hussey (79.85) ... Ponting is the only player to score two hundreds in his 100th Test, v South Africa at Sydney in Jan 2006 ... His 242 at Adelaide in 2003-04, v India, is the highest by a player on the losing side in a Test (in the next game he made 257, and they won) ... When he was 8, Ponting's grandmother gave him a T-shirt that read "Under this shirt is a Test player" ... Ponting's record includes one ODI for the World XI ...

THE FIGURES

Batting and fielding   www.cricinfo.com

	M	Inns	NO	Runs	HS	Avge	S/R	100	50	4s	6s	Ct	St
Tests *to 10.9.07*	110	183	25	9368	257	59.29	58.95	33	36	1059	57	124	0
ODIs *to 10.9.07*	280	272	32	10395	164	43.31	80.27	23	62	898	132	124	0
First-class *to 10.9.07*	205	345	50	17750	257	60.16	–	66	71	–	–	208	0

Bowling

	M	Balls	Runs	Wkts	BB	Avge	RpO	S/R	5i	10m
Tests *to 10.9.07*	110	527	231	5	1–0	46.20	2.62	105.40	0	0
ODIs *to 10.9.07*	280	150	104	3	1–12	34.66	4.16	50.00	0	0
First-class *to 10.9.07*	205	1422	757	14	2–10	54.07	3.19	101.57	0	0

RAMESH **POWAR**

Full name	**Ramesh Rajaram Powar**
Born	**May 20, 1978, Bombay**
Teams	**Mumbai**
Style	**Right-hand bat, offspinner**
Test debut	**India v Bangladesh at Chittagong 2006-07**
ODI debut	**India v Pakistan at Rawalpindi 2003-04**

THE PROFILE A stocky offspinner who is more than handy with the bat, Ramesh Powar has been a consistent performer in domestic cricket, and was crucial to Mumbai's 2002-03 Ranji Trophy success. His 20 wickets with his flighted stuff was useful enough, but even more crucial were his runs. He never batted higher than No. 7 – sometimes going in as low as No. 10 – but ended up with Mumbai's second-highest aggregate, scoring 418 runs at more than 46, most of those coming when his team was in trouble. His domestic exploits soon caught the selectors' attention, and he made the Indian squad for the Pakistan tour early in 2004. His offspin and his batting both stood up in the couple of ODIs he played, but even more impressive was his combative attitude, as he bravely tossed the ball up on batting shirtfronts, and didn't bat an eyelid while striking some lusty blows against the pace of Shoaib Akhtar and Mohammad Sami. An ideal bits-and-pieces player, Powar returned to the one-day side early in 2006, now armed with a new delivery – a drifter – which helped him to 63 domestic wickets in 2005-06, after 54 the previous season. Again he impressed with both bat and ball, although some critics made disparaging remarks about his waistline, causing him to tempt fate: "I've never missed a game owing to fitness problems." Almost inevitably, he then twisted an ankle and missed the first two ODIs in the West Indies in June 2006. He missed the World Cup – possibly a blessing in disguise – but made his Test debut in Bangladesh shortly afterwards, taking three wickets in both matches, and retained his place for the 2007 England tour, where although he could not force his way into the Test side he teased away in the one-dayers.

THE FACTS Powar has made four hundreds in first-class cricket, the highest of them 131 against Railways at Mumbai in December 2003 ... His best bowling figures of 7 for 44 came for West Zone v South Zone at Hyderabad in February 2005 ... Powar made 54 in the Jamshedpur ODI against England in April 2006 ...

THE FIGURES

Batting and fielding

	M	Inns	NO	Runs	HS	Avge	S/R	100	50	4s	6s	Ct	St
Tests *to 10.9.07*	2	2	0	13	7	6.50	72.22	0	0	2	0	0	0
ODIs *to 10.9.07*	29	18	5	146	54	11.23	60.33	0	1	11	1	3	0
First-class *to 10.9.07*	80	100	14	2683	131	31.19	–	0	4	14	–	–	37	0

Bowling

	M	Balls	Runs	Wkts	BB	Avge	RpO	S/R	5i	10m
Tests *to 10.9.07*	2	252	118	6	3–33	19.66	2.80	42.00	0	0
ODIs *to 10.9.07*	29	1470	1111	34	3–24	32.67	4.53	43.23	0	0
First-class *to 10.9.07*	80	16320	7647	286	7–44	26.73	2.81	57.06	15	2

DAREN **POWELL**

Full name **Daren Brent Lyle Powell**
Born **April 15, 1978, Jamaica**
Teams **Jamaica, Hampshire**
Style **Right-hand bat, right-arm fast bowler**
Test debut **West Indies v New Zealand at Bridgetown 2001-02**
ODI debut **West Indies v Bangladesh at Dhaka 2002-03**

THE PROFILE Daren Powell began his cricketing life at school in Jamaica as a No. 3 batsman and offspinner, but then came across a concrete pitch that he thought wouldn't suit his spin bowling, so decided to try some medium-pace instead. Seam-up turned out to be the way forward for Powell, and he has developed into a slippery fast bowler with a rhythmic, high action. But his international career has been less smooth. A solitary Test against New Zealand at home in 2002 was followed by one in India and two in Bangladesh, but pitches in the subcontinent were never going to suit his style of bowling, and he was dropped – without really doing much wrong – and sat on the sidelines for two years. Powell continued to pick up wickets in domestic cricket, and returned for the first Test against South Africa in March 2005, when several players were unavailable owing to a bitter contracts dispute, and did enough to retain his place throughout that season when the others returned. He picked up 5 for 25 on the first day of the second Test against Sri Lanka at Kandy later that year (West Indies still lost heavily), and retained his place for the tour of Australia at the end of 2005. After a spell out of the side, Powell was probably the pick of the faster bowlers in England in 2007 – particularly in the one-dayers, when he seemed to gain a yard of pace. After that Hampshire pipped Glamorgan in a race for his signature.

THE FACTS Powell was West Indies' leading wicket-taker at the 2007 World Cup with 14, one more than Dwayne Bravo, and often made early inroads into the opponents' innings ... Powell's best bowling figures of 6 for 49 were for Derbyshire against Durham University at Derby in 2004 ... He has also played for Gauteng in South Africa ...

THE FIGURES

Batting and fielding

www.cricinfo.com

	M	Inns	NO	Runs	HS	Avge	S/R	100	50	4s	6s	Ct	St
Tests to 10.9.07	22	34	1	216	36*	6.54	32.72	0	0	26	3	1	0
ODIs to 10.9.07	30	14	3	73	48*	6.63	70.87	0	0	2	3	5	0
First-class to 10.9.07	75	106	15	11330	62	12.45	–	0	3	–	–	22	0

Bowling

	M	Balls	Runs	Wkts	BB	Avge	RpO	S/R	5i	10m
Tests to 10.9.07	22	4341	2443	56	5–25	43.62	3.37	77.51	1	0
ODIs to 10.9.07	30	1578	1206	40	4–27	30.15	4.58	39.45	0	0
First-class to 11.9.06	75	12389	6677	219	6–49	30.48	3.23	56.57	6	0

SOUTH AFRICA

ASHWELL **PRINCE**

Full name **Ashwell Gavin Prince**
Born **May 28, 1977, Port Elizabeth, Cape Province**
Teams **Cape Cobras**
Style **Left-hand bat, occasional left-arm spinner**
Test debut **South Africa v Australia at Johannesburg 2001-02**
ODI debut **South Africa v Bangladesh at Kimberley 2002-03**

THE PROFILE A crouching left-hander with a high-batted stance and a Gooch-like grimace, Ashwell Prince was helped into the national team by South Africa's controversial race-quota system, although he quickly justified his selection by top-scoring with a gutsy debut 49 against Australia in 2001-02. That, and a matchwinning 48 in the third Test, seemed to have buried his reputation as a one-day flasher. But by the following season his form had fallen away horribly, and he failed in four successive Tests against Bangladesh and Sri Lanka. Domestic runs won his place back, and valuable knocks against West Indies and England at home also made him more of a one-day regular. Test hundreds followed, against outclassed Zimbabwe and almost-outclassed West Indies, but his 119 at Sydney in January 2006 was an altogether better performance. Prince had struggled against Shane Warne, falling to him in his first four innings of that series, and although he eventually succumbed again it was only after an important stand of 219 with Jacques Kallis. Warne troubled him again in the return series, when Prince's only substantial contribution was a splendid 93 in the third Test at Johannesburg. Free of Warne's wiles, Prince smacked a cathartic century against New Zealand in April 2006. Shortly after that an ankle injury to Graeme Smith meant that Prince was named as South Africa's first black captain, for a tough Test tour of Sri Lanka. He made Test centuries against India and Pakistan in 2006-07, but a poor one-day run found him left out after a largely anonymous World Cup. Long rated highly by Ali Bacher, Prince is strong through the off side, and although his throwing has been hampered by a long-term shoulder injury, he remains a brilliant shot-stopping fielder in the covers.

THE FACTS Prince averages 66.33 in Test against West Indies – and 1.00 v Bangladesh ... In 18 Test innings against Australia, Prince was dismissed 11 times by Shane Warne ... Prince's highest first-class score is 184, for Western Province Boland against the Lions at Paarl in 2004-05 ... His record includes three ODIs for the Africa XI ...

THE FIGURES

Batting and fielding

www.cricinfo.com

	M	Inns	NO	Runs	HS	Avge	S/R	100	50	4s	6s	Ct	St
Tests *to 10.9.07*	29	47	5	1800	139*	42.85	41.92	6	5	196	3	16	0
ODIs *to 10.9.07*	52	41	12	1018	89*	35.10	67.77	0	3	77	4	26	0
First-class *to 10.9.07*	120	188	22	7014	184	42.25	–	17	34	–	–	74	0

Bowling

	M	Balls	Runs	Wkts	BB	Avge	RpO	S/R	5i	10m
Tests *to 10.9.07*	29	78	31	1	1–2	31.00	2.38	78.00	0	0
ODIs *to 10.9.07*	52	12	3	0	–	–	1.50	–	0	0
First-class *to 10.9.07*	120	192	101	2	1–2	50.50	3.15	96.00	0	0

MATT **PRIOR**

Full name **Matthew James Prior**
Born **February 26, 1982, Johannesburg, South Africa**
Teams **Sussex**
Style **Right-hand bat, wicketkeeper**
Test debut **England v West Indies at Lord's 2007**
ODI debut **England v Zimbabwe at Bulawayo 2004-05**

THE PROFILE Sussex wicketkeeper Matt Prior represented England at several junior levels, and completed his set by making his Test debut in May 2007, against West Indies at Lord's. He repaid the faith of Peter Moores, his former county boss turned national coach, with a cracking century – the first by a keeper on debut for England. It was full of solid drives and clumping pulls, and seemed to announce a readymade star, especially when Prior added some acrobatic takes behind the stumps. He finished that series with 324 runs – but there were already some rumbles about his keeping technique, which didn't seem to matter while England were winning. But then India arrived, and Prior's fumbles were magnified as the visitors stole the series: he dropped Sachin Tendulkar and VVS Laxman as India piled up 664 at The Oval. Prior's runs dried up, too, and suddenly his talkativeness behind the stumps, and his footwork, were called into question. He retained his place, but it was a harsh reality check. Prior was born in South Africa, but his family moved to England when he was 11 – he says he lost his accent within a week – and he soon joined Sussex, making his debut in 2001. For a while he shared the gloves with Tim Ambrose, but won that particular battle when Ambrose decamped to Edgbaston. His early ODIs for England were unconvincing, firm hands making placement for quick singles problematic, but he does seem ideal for one-dayers: the jury is out about Test cricket, though.

THE FACTS Prior was the 17th man to score a century on Test debut for England, but the first to keep wicket in the same match: he was the fifth person to score a century on Test debut at Lord's, after Australia's Harry Graham, John Hampshire and Andrew Strauss of England, and India's Sourav Ganguly ... Prior scored 201 not out for Sussex v Loughborough UCCE at Hove in May 2004 ... In successive weeks in March 2005 he made hundreds for England A against the United Arab Emirates in Sharjah and Sri Lanka A in Colombo ...

THE FIGURES
Batting and fielding

www.cricinfo.com

	M	Inns	NO	Runs	HS	Avge	S/R	100	50	4s	6s	Ct	St
Tests *to 10.9.07*	7	12	2	397	126*	39.70	64.86	1	2	50	4	20	0
ODIs *to 10.9.07*	22	22	0	469	52	21.31	72.93	0	1	58	2	23	2
First-class *to 10.9.07*	115	182	17	6321	201*	38.30	67.56	15	32	–	–	262	20

Bowling

	M	Balls	Runs	Wkts	BB	Avge	RpO	S/R	5i	10m
Tests *to 10.9.07*	7	0	–	–	–	–	–	–	–	–
ODIs *to 10.9.07*	22	0	–	–	–	–	–	–	–	–
First-class *to 10.9.07*	115	0	–	–	–	–	–	–	–	–

RAJIN SALEH

Full name	**Khondokar Mohammad Rajin Saleh Alam**
Born	**November 20, 1983, Sylhet, Bangladesh**
Teams	**Sylhet**
Style	**Right-hand bat, occasional offspinner**
Test debut	**Bangladesh v Pakistan at Karachi 2003-04**
ODI debut	**Bangladesh v Pakistan at Multan 2003-04**

THE PROFILE Rajin Saleh is one of the most talented batsmen in Bangladesh, and, as a man who takes pride in his physical fitness as well, he was also a favourite of his former coach, Dav Whatmore. Saleh, a No. 3 batsman on the domestic circuit, first attracted attention when he averaged 56 in the National League in 2000-01. He had played only five matches for Sylhet when he was included in the Bangladesh Cricket Board XI which took on the Australian Cricket Academy the following year, but made 81 in the first match, a knock which drew high praise from the Aussie press. Technically sound, Saleh is equally solid forward or back, and rapidly became a mainstay of the Bangladesh batting line-up. And before he had turned 21 he was elevated to the captaincy for the Champions Trophy in England in 2004, after Habibul Bashar broke his thumb. Back in the ranks, he cracked 89 in the historic victory over Zimbabwe at Chittagong early in 2005, but lost his place after making only 2 and 7 against England at Chester-le-Street. An undefeated 108 against Kenya at Fatullah in March 2006 – on the 35th anniversary of Bangladesh's independence from Pakistan – forced Saleh back into the Test reckoning, and he distinguished himself with innings of 67, 33 and 71 against the Australians. Leaner times followed, and he found himself dumped from the one-day team – before, oddly, being recalled for the 2007 World Cup but not actually getting a game. He remained in the Test frame, although three successive ducks in Sri Lanka in July 2007 threatened his place there too.

THE FACTS Rajin Saleh captained Bangladesh in the Champions Trophy in England in 2004 when only 20 ... His 108 not out against Kenya at Fatullah in March 2006 was only Bangladesh's third century in ODIs, and their highest score at the time ... Saleh averages 35.57 in ODIs against Pakistan, and 0.00 v South Africa ... He has two brothers who have also played first-class cricket ...

THE FIGURES

Batting and fielding   www.cricinfo.com

	M	Inns	NO	Runs	HS	Avge	S/R	100	50	4s	6s	Ct	St
Tests *to 10.9.07*	22	43	2	1115	89	27.19	36.83	0	7	137	5	13	0
ODIs *to 10.9.07*	43	43	1	1005	108*	23.92	54.82	1	6	94	3	9	0
First-class *to 10.9.07*	60	108	9	3448	130*	34.82	–	–	7	16	–	–	47	0

Bowling

	M	Balls	Runs	Wkts	BB	Avge	RpO	S/R	5i	10m
Tests *to 10.9.07*	22	438	268	2	1–9	134.00	3.67	219.00	0	0
ODIs *to 10.9.07*	43	539	459	15	4–16	30.60	5.10	35.93	0	0
First-class *to 10.9.07*	60	1220	685	5	2–44	137.00	3.36	244.00	0	0

DENESH **RAMDIN**

Full name	**Denesh Ramdin**
Born	**March 13, 1985, Couva, Trinidad**
Teams	**Trinidad & Tobago**
Style	**Right-hand bat, wicketkeeper**
Test debut	**West Indies v Sri Lanka at Colombo 2005**
ODI debut	**West Indies v India at Dambulla 2005**

THE PROFILE Denesh Ramdin is a wicketkeeper-batsman of great potential, viewed by many in the Caribbean as the long-term solution to the void which has never really been satisfactorily filled since the retirement of Jeff Dujon in 1991. Originally a fast bowler who then kept wicket when he had finished his stint with the ball, Ramdin decided at 13 to concentrate on keeping, honing his reflexes and working on his agility. He led both the Trinidad & Tobago and West Indies Under-19 sides before being selected, still only 19 and with just 13 first-class games behind him, as the first-choice keeper for the senior squad's tour of Sri Lanka in 2005. He impressed everyone with his work behind and in front of the stumps, and continued to do so in the series in Australia later in 2005. A plucky 71 – he shared a fine partnership of 182 in the second Test at Hobart with his fellow Trinidadian Dwayne Bravo, just after they'd heard that T&T had qualified for the soccer World Cup – was his best moment Down Under. Carlton Baugh was preferred for some of the home one-dayers early in 2006, and it was something of a surprise when Ramdin returned for the Tests against India. But he justified his selection with some smooth keeping, and a gritty unbeaten 62 that took West Indies frustratingly close to victory in the series-deciding fourth Test in Jamaica. He started the 2007 series in England with a bright 60 at Lord's, but struggled with the bat after that, while his keeping was patchy. He faces a battle to keep his place, although he still has time on his side.

THE FACTS Ramdin played in the West Indies side that won the Under-15 World Challenge in 2000, beating Pakistan in the final at Lord's: four years later he captained West Indies in the Under-19 World Cup, when they lost the final at Dhaka – to Pakistan ... His highest score is 131 for the West Indians against MCC at Durham in June 2007 ... Ramdin was one of only eight players offered central contracts by the cash-strapped West Indian board in June 2006 ...

THE FIGURES
Batting and fielding   www.cricinfo.com

	M	Inns	NO	Runs	HS	Avge	S/R	100	50	4s	6s	Ct	St
Tests to 10.9.07	19	34	5	704	71	24.27	45.80	0	5	95	1	49	2
ODIs to 10.9.07	37	28	8	444	74*	22.20	80.28	0	2	44	1	51	2
First-class to 10.9.07	45	75	8	1728	131	25.79	–	3	9	–	–	116	16

Bowling

	M	Balls	Runs	Wkts	BB	Avge	RpO	S/R	5i	10m
Tests to 10.9.07	19	0	–	–	–	–	–	–	–	–
ODIs to 10.9.07	37	0	–	–	–	–	–	–	–	–
First-class to 10.9.07	45	0	–	–	–	–	–	–	–	–

WEST INDIES

RAVI **RAMPAUL**

Full name	**Ravindranath Rampaul**
Born	**October 15, 1984, Preysal, Trinidad**
Teams	**Trinidad & Tobago**
Style	**Left-hand bat, right-arm fast-medium bowler**
Test debut	**No Tests yet**
ODI debut	**West Indies v Zimbabwe at Bulawayo 2003-04**

THE PROFILE Ravi Rampaul is a tall and well-built fast bowler, but his career has been hamstrung by injuries. Of East Indian descent, he first came to notice as West Indies won the World Under-15 Challenge in England in 2000. Two years later he made his Trinidad debut, and 18 wickets in six matches in 2003 – and some impressive performances for the West Indian Under-19s – propelled him to the verge of full international selection. It was his aggressive approach that really caught the eye: in a one-dayer against Antigua & Barbuda he unleashed four successive bouncers at the opener, then finished him off with an unplayable yorker. He was picked to tour southern Africa in 2003-04, and made his ODI debut in Zimbabwe. Rampaul was a consistent selection, rarely getting collared but not running through sides either – in 14 matches in Africa and the Caribbean that season he took nine wickets, only once managing more than one. Nonetheless he was retained for the 2004 England tour, and played three more one-dayers before he broke down and returned home before the Tests. Shin splints sidelined him for more than a year, and he did not play another first-class match until 2006-07, taking 7 for 51 as T&T beat Barbados in the Carib Beer final. That won him a recall for another England tour. Restricted by a groin tear, he missed the Tests, but helped West Indies turn the one-day series around by demolishing England's middle order with 4 for 41 in the pivotal second match at Edgbaston.

THE FACTS Rampaul took 7 for 51 as Trinidad & Tobago beat Barbados in the final of the Carib Beer International Challenge at Pointe-a-Pierre in February 2007 ... His highest score of 64 not out was for West Indies A against Sri Lanka A at Basseterre in December 2006 ... In the World Under-15 Challenge in England in 2000, Rampaul took 7 for 11 against Holland, and opened both the bowling and the batting in the final at Lord's, as West Indies beat Pakistan ...

THE FIGURES

Batting and fielding   www.cricinfo.com

	M	Inns	NO	Runs	HS	Avge	S/R	100	50	4s	6s	Ct	St
Tests to 10.9.07	0	0	–	–	–	–	–	–	–	–	–	–	–
ODIs to 10.9.07	23	5	1	59	24	14.75	56.73	0	0	6	0	2	0
First-class to 10.9.07	21	27	3	314	64*	13.08	–	0	1	–	–	8	0

Bowling

	M	Balls	Runs	Wkts	BB	Avge	RpO	S/R	5i	10m
Tests to 10.9.07	0	0	–	–	–	–	–	–	–	–
ODIs to 10.9.07	23	852	714	21	4-41	34.00	5.02	40.57	0	0
First-class to 10.9.07	21	2943	1702	57	7-51	29.85	3.46	51.63	3	0

ADIL **RASHID**

Full name **Adil Usman Rashid**
Born **February 17, 1988, Bradford, Yorkshire**
Teams **Yorkshire**
Style **Right-hand bat, legspinner**
Test debut **No Tests yet**
ODI debut **No ODIs yet**

THE PROFILE Yorkshire have rarely had much truck with legspinners, but a funny thing happened in 2006: they suddenly started playing two of them, often at the same time. The first was Mark Lawson, and he was joined towards the end of the season by 18-year-old Adil Rashid, a product of the young-spinner programme set up by Terry Jenner, Shane Warne's Australian mentor. Rashid, who bowls with a high action and has all the legspin variations, plus the priceless virtue of accuracy, bowled Yorkshire to victory over Warwickshire with 6 for 67 in his first match, then had purists licking their lips as he and Lawson shared all ten Middlesex wickets in an innings at Scarborough. The first home-grown player of Asian descent to appear regularly for Yorkshire, Rashid finished his first season with 25 wickets in six matches – plus 14 in three Under-19 Tests against India, traditionally good players of spin – then toured Bangladesh with England A. He consolidated in 2007, finishing as a shoo-in for the Cricket Writers' Club's prestigious Young Cricketer of the Year award, and made a strong claim for the second spinner's spot on the winter tour of Sri Lanka. Rashid is also a wristy batsman, regularly going in at No. 6 or 7 for Yorkshire: he narrowly missed a maiden century against Surrey at Headingley in July 2007, being left stranded on 91, but made not mistake a couple of weeks later with 108 against Worcestershire. The only fly in the ointment so far has been a stress fracture of the back, which forced him to remodel his action over the winter of 2006-07: he is now more side-on.

THE FACTS Rashid took 6 for 67 on his first-class debut, for Yorkshire against Warwickshire at Scarborough in July 2006 ... He scored 114, and then took 8 for 157, for England Under-19s against India at Taunton in August 2006 ... Rashid improved his highest score several times during 2007 – 86 then 91 not out against Surrey, then 108 v Worcestershire ... He was the Cricket Writers' Club's Young Cricketer of the Year in 2007 ...

THE FIGURES

Batting and fielding   www.cricinfo.com

	M	Inns	NO	Runs	HS	Avge	S/R	100	50	4s	6s	Ct	St
Tests *to 10.9.07*	0	0	–	–	–	–	–	–	–	–	–	–	–
ODIs *to 10.9.07*	0	0		–	–	–	–	–	–	–	–	–	–
First-class *to 10.9.07*	22	29	5	947	108	39.45	56.84	1	8	–	–	11	0

Bowling

	M	Balls	Runs	Wkts	BB	Avge	RpO	S/R	5i	10m
Tests *to 10.9.07*	0	0	–	–	–	–	–	–	–	–
ODIs *to 10.9.07*	0	0	–	–	–	–	–	–	–	–
First-class *to 10.9.07*	22	3921	2464	69	6–67	35.71	3.77	56.82	4	0

WEST INDIES

AUSTIN **RICHARDS**

Full name	**Austin Conroy Lenroy Richards junior**
Born	**November 14, 1983, Freetown, Antigua**
Teams	**Leeward Islands**
Style	**Left-hand bat**
Test debut	**No Tests yet**
ODI debut	**West Indies v Scotland at Dublin 2007**

THE PROFILE If you're a batsman from Antigua called Richards, there's only one man you're going to be compared with. But comparisons between Austin and Sir Viv Richards don't get very far, as the unrelated Austin is a left-hander, for a start, and usually opens. His achievements are rather more modest, too – in four seasons after his debut in 2003-04, he played only ten first-class games, four of them for West Indies B. He finally made a mark in the tenth of those matches, hitting 183 for the Leeward Islands against the Windwards on the tiny island of St Maarten in February 2007, when he opened and put on 225 for the second wicket with Runako Morton. A good fielder, he is considered more of a one-day specialist, although his record with the bat in that is hardly spectacular either – three half-centuries in 20 matches, with a highest score of 77 against Guyana in October 2005. Changes were inevitable in the fallout from the 2007 World Cup, after West Indies failed to crash the later stages of their own party, but it was still a surprise when Richards was one of those called up for the one-day portion of the England tour. He didn't get many opportunities, but did make play in one of the Twenty20 internationals against England at The Oval, and then made his official ODI debut against Scotland during the quadrangular series in Ireland.

THE FACTS Richards made 183 for Leeward Islands against Windward Islands in St Maarten in February 2007: his next-highest first-class score is 74 ... He hit 71 for Antigua & Barbuda against England A at St John's in February 2006 ... His father – also Austin Conroy Lenroy Richards – is an umpire in Antigua ...

THE FIGURES
Batting and fielding

www.cricinfo.com

	M	Inns	NO	Runs	HS	Avge	S/R	100	50	4s	6s	Ct	St
Tests *to 10.9.07*	0	0	–	–	–	–	–	–	–	–	–	–	–
ODIs *to 10.9.07*	1	1	0	2	2	2.00	100.00	0	0	0	0	1	0
First-class *to 10.9.07*	10	18	0	682	183	37.88	–	1	4	–	–	4	0

Bowling

	M	Balls	Runs	Wkts	BB	Avge	RpO	S/R	5i	10m
Tests *to 10.9.07*	0	0	–	–	–	–	–	–	–	–
ODIs *to 10.9.07*	1	0	–	–	–	–	–	–	–	–
First-class *to 10.9.07*	10	48	23	0	–	–	2.87	–	0	0

154

CHRIS **ROGERS**

Full name	**Christopher John Llewellyn Rogers**
Born	**August 31, 1977, St George, Sydney, NSW**
Teams	**Western Australia, Northamptonshire**
Style	**Left-hand batsman, occasional legspinner**
Test debut	**No Tests yet**
ODI debut	**No ODIs yet**

AUSTRALIA

THE PROFILE A tenacious left-hander, Chris Rogers holds the rare record of scoring a double-century against his own country. Playing for Leicestershire in 2005 against the touring Australians, he toasted them for 56 and 219 despite Matthew Hayden telling him he should get out to support his national team. He followed that fine English summer by topping Western Australia's run-makers with 794 at 41.78, including two hundreds and four fifties, which earned him an Australia A call-up. Like Michael Hussey before him, Rogers was probably more highly rated in England than at home, at least until a stellar 2006-07 season that brought him 1202 runs at 70 for WA and the award of State Player of the Year. That followed another prolific summer for Northamptonshire, his third English county, which included an innings of 319 – threatening Hussey's county-record 331 – against Gloucestershire. He had come close to 1000 runs in 2003-04 as well, making four hundreds, but was hampered for a while after that by shoulder and hamstring troubles. He is also short-sighted and colour-blind, which means he sometimes struggles to focus on the red ball when it mixes with the background colours. Ginger-haired Rogers is now among the favourites to succeed Justin Langer, a similar type of player, at the top of the order in Tests. He possesses a fine cricketing pedigree: his father John represented New South Wales in the Sheffield Shield in the 1960s, and later became a highly respected administrator, ultimately becoming general manager of the Western Australian Cricket Association.

THE FACTS Rogers scored 279 for Western Australia v Victoria at Perth in October 2006, sharing a third-wicket stand of 459 with Marcus North (239 not out) ... He made 319 for Northamptonshire, his third English county, v Gloucestershire at Northampton in August 2006: a month later he made 128 and 222 not out against Somerset at Taunton ... For WA v South Australia at Perth in March 2002 Rogers made 101 (his maiden first-class century) and 102, both not out ... His father John played for New South Wales ...

THE FIGURES

Batting and fielding   www.cricinfo.com

	M	Inns	NO	Runs	HS	Avge	S/R	100	50	4s	6s	Ct	St
Tests to 10.9.07	0	0	–	–	–	–	–	–	–	–	–	–	–
ODIs to 10.9.07	0	0		–	–	–	–	–	–	–	–	–	–
First-class to 10.9.07	97	174	10	7964	319	48.56	–	21	40	–	–	100	0

Bowling

	M	Balls	Runs	Wkts	BB	Avge	RpO	S/R	5i	10m
Tests to 10.9.07	0	0	–	–	–	–	–	–	–	–
ODIs to 10.9.07	0	0	–	–	–	–	–	–	–	–
First-class to 10.9.07	97	184	106	1	1–16	106.00	3.45	184.00	0	0

SALMAN BUTT

Full name	**Salman Butt**
Born	**October 7, 1984, Lahore, Punjab**
Teams	**Lahore, National Bank**
Style	**Left-hand bat, occasional offspinner**
Test debut	**Pakistan v Bangladesh at Multan 2003-04**
ODI debut	**Pakistan v West Indies at Southampton 2004**

THE PROFILE Because he's left-handed, with supple wrists, it is easy to compare Salman Butt with the delectable Saeed Anwar. His drives and cuts through extra cover and backward point are flicked or scooped: it is a high-scoring region for him, as it was for Anwar. He doesn't mind pulling, and off his toes he's efficient, rather than whippy as Anwar was. But in attitude and temperament he is more like Anwar's long-time opening partner, Aamer Sohail. He has a confident air, a certain spikiness, and is a rare young Pakistan player at ease speaking English. Butt first made headlines by smashing 233 during an Under-19 tour of South Africa, and his breakthrough at the highest level came late in 2004. After a maiden one-day century, at Eden Gardens, he made 70 at Melbourne and 108 in the New Year Test at Sydney. Then came the fall: he failed to build on that during 2005, despite another one-day hundred against India, and was dropped as doubts crept in about his defence and his dash. He responded by unveiling startling restraint against England late in the year, grinding out a hundred and two fifties in the Tests, followed by another ton at India's expense. He was dropped again after an uninspiring England tour, and did not feature in 2006-07, which at least meant he was spared the misery of the World Cup – in the aftermath of which he found himself promoted to vice-captain, responding with 74 in a one-dayer against Sri Lanka in Abu Dhabi. Salman Butt could be one half of the solution to the opening conundrum that has haunted Pakistan since ... well, since Anwar and Sohail retired.

THE FACTS All three of Salman Butt's ODI hundreds to date have come against India: he averages 45.70 against them, but only 14.83 against West Indies (and 1.00 v Scotland) ... Butt's highest score is 206, for Lahore Whites against Karachi Whites at Lahore in November 2004 ... He captained Pakistan in the Under-19 World Cup in New Zealand early in 2002 ...

THE FIGURES
Batting and fielding   www.cricinfo.com

	M	Inns	NO	Runs	HS	Avge	S/R	100	50	4s	6s	Ct	St
Tests to 10.9.07	14	26	0	777	122	29.88	51.42	2	4	109	1	7	0
ODIs to 10.9.07	36	36	1	1072	108*	30.62	71.13	3	4	138	1	11	0
First-class to 10.9.07	57	99	5	3582	206	38.10	–	9	17	–	–	23	0

Bowling

	M	Balls	Runs	Wkts	BB	Avge	RpO	S/R	5i	10m
Tests to 10.9.07	14	24	18	0	–	–	4.50	–	0	0
ODIs to 10.9.07	36	36	42	0	–	–	7.00	–	0	0
First-class to 10.9.07	57	813	558	10	4–82	55.80	4.11	81.30	0	0

THILAN **SAMARAWEERA**

SRI LANKA

Full name	Thilan Thusara Samaraweera
Born	September 22, 1976, Colombo
Teams	Sinhalese Sports Club
Style	Right-hand bat, offspinner
Test debut	Sri Lanka v India at Colombo 2001-02
ODI debut	Sri Lanka v India at Sharjah 1998-99

THE PROFILE As an offspinner, Thilan Samaraweera lived in the shadow of Muttiah Muralitharan early on in his career, only occasionally getting a one-day outing. But after scoring 103 not out on Test debut against India in August 2001, an innings that helped Sri Lanka to a 2-1 series win, he carved out a reputation as a specialist batsman, and the departure of Aravinda de Silva and Hashan Tillakaratne allowed him to cement a place in the middle order, where his patient no-risks approach makes him a very valuable foil for some of his more flamboyant colleagues. An adhesive and well-organised player, he took a particular liking to his home ground, the Sinhalese Sports Club in Colombo, where he scored three centuries in his first six Tests. Until Sri Lanka toured India at the end of 2005 he maintained a Test batting average of over 50, but a low-key run – including difficulties against the moving ball in England in 2006 – pushed that down a few points. He has been branded a Test specialist by the selectors, and seldom features in ODIs. His steady offspin is rarely used now, although he has a developing reputation as a partnership-breaker and clearly has the talent to become a useful support bowler. He did not feature in senior internationals in 2006-07, but kept his name in the frame by leading Sri Lanka's A side. He scored 162 for them against Bangladesh A in Colombo in March 2007, putting on 376 with Malinda Warnapura, whose 242 helped him into the Test side.

THE FACTS Samaraweera was the third Sri Lankan, after Brendon Kuruppu and Romesh Kaluwitharana, to score a century on Test debut, against India in August 2001 ... That innings, and his next two Test centuries as well, was scored at the Sinhalese Sports Club, his home ground in Colombo, where he averages 77.90 in Tests ... Only one of his five Test centuries was scored outside Colombo: 100 v Pakistan at Faisalabad in October 2004 ... Samaraweera's brother Dulip played seven Tests for Sri Lanka in the early 1990s ...

THE FIGURES
Batting and fielding

www.cricinfo.com

	M	Inns	NO	Runs	HS	Avge	S/R	100	50	4s	6s	Ct	St
Tests to 10.9.07	39	58	8	2089	142	41.78	41.53	5	13	223	1	30	0
ODIs to 10.9.07	17	13	1	199	33	16.58	52.50	0	0	15	0	3	0
First-class to 10.9.07	182	244	46	8474	206	42.79	–	17	49	–	–	152	0

Bowling

	M	Balls	Runs	Wkts	BB	Avge	RpO	S/R	5i	10m
Tests to 10.9.07	39	1285	671	14	4–49	47.49	3.13	91.78	0	0
ODIs to 10.9.07	17	672	509	10	3–34	50.90	4.54	67.20	0	0
First-class to 10.9.07	182	17445	8121	348	6–55	23.33	2.79	50.12	15	2

DARREN **SAMMY**

Full name	**Darren Julius Garvey Sammy**
Born	**December 20, 1983, Micoud, St Lucia**
Teams	**Windward Islands**
Style	**Right-hand bat, right-arm fast-medium bowler**
Test debut	**West Indies v England at Manchester 2007**
ODI debut	**West Indies v New Zealand at Southampton 2004**

THE PROFILE Darren Julius Garvey Sammy has names invoking images of great leadership. He is the first international cricketer to emerge from St Lucia, an island rediscovering its cricket culture as the new Beausejour Stadium has captured imaginations, so it is a major feat that he has cracked the regional squad. Sammy, who spent some time at Lord's with the MCC cricket staff, is a handy batsman and a tall, nagging medium-pacer. He won a one-day cap in England in 2004, although the match was abandoned, and was called up late to the Champions Trophy squad that September after Jermaine Lawson pulled out with a stress fracture in the back. In July 2006 he was named as St Lucia's captain for the inaugural Stanford 20/20 tournament, and a decent first-class season – 269 runs at 44 in five matches, plus 16 wickets at less than 20 – earned him a recall for the 2007 England tour. He was drafted into the side for the third Test at Old Trafford, and celebrated with seven wickets in the second innings – three of them in one over. His pace is unthreatening, but he brings the ball down from quite a height and wobbles it around enough to unsettle the batsmen. "I want to be the workhorse of the team," he pronounced after his dream debut – but sadly he didn't get the chance again on that tour, as he picked up a groin strain while batting during his debut and missed the final Test and the one-dayers that followed.

THE FACTS Sammy took 7 for 66 in his first Test, against England at Old Trafford in 2007: only Alf Valentine, with 8 for 104 against England at Old Trafford in 1950, has returned better figures on Test debut for West Indies ... No play was possible in his first ODI, against New Zealand at Southampton in July 2004, but because the toss was made it counts as an appearance ... Sammy is believed to be the only Seventh Day Adventist ever to have played Test cricket ...

THE FIGURES

Batting and fielding   www.cricinfo.com

	M	Inns	NO	Runs	HS	Avge	S/R	100	50	4s	6s	Ct	St
Tests *to 10.9.07*	1	2	0	26	25	13.00	40.62	0	0	5	0	1	0
ODIs *to 10.9.07*	5	1	1	18	18*	–	138.46	0	0	1	0	3	0
First-class *to 10.9.07*	35	58	5	1287	87	24.28	–	0	10	–	–	49	0

Bowling

	M	Balls	Runs	Wkts	BB	Avge	RpO	S/R	5i	10m
Tests *to 10.9.07*	1	231	98	8	7–66	12.25	2.54	28.87	1	0
ODIs *to 10.9.07*	5	74	44	3	2–2	14.66	3.56	24.66	0	0
First-class *to 10.9.07*	35	4232	1772	87	7–66	20.36	2.51	48.64	6	2

MARLON **SAMUELS**

Full name	**Marlon Nathaniel Samuels**
Born	**January 5, 1981, Kingston, Jamaica**
Teams	**Jamaica**
Style	**Right-hand bat, offspinner**
Test debut	**West Indies v Australia at Adelaide 2000-01**
ODI debut	**West Indies v Sri Lanka at Nairobi 2000-01**

THE PROFILE Marlon Samuels is a classy right-hander whose composed start in Tests prompted comparisons with Viv Richards. When he flew into Australia for the third Test of the 2000-01 series, Samuels was only 19 and had played just one first-class match for Jamaica. But he showed a beautifully balanced technique, standing still at the crease and moving smoothly into his strokes off either foot. His undistinguished offspin also claimed a couple of wickets. Samuels exudes a bull-headed confidence – he used to skip his schoolwork, saying that exams were irrelevant for future Test cricketers. That confidence/arrogance almost got him sent home from India late in 2002, after he defied a team curfew – but he was kept on, and responded with a disciplined maiden Test century at Kolkata, and followed that with 91 against Bangladesh. Attitude – or perhaps naivete – has been a problem since: he was investigated for links with a bookmaker shortly before the 2007 World Cup. He was allowed to play – and ran Brian Lara out in his last international innings. Samuels then missed out on selection for the England tour, although he was called up after Ramnaresh Sarwans's injury. He had already been crocked himself – an injured knee kept him out for more than a year. He was back for the 2005-06 Australian tour, and warmed up for the first Test by hammering 257 against Queensland, and followed that with 5 for 87. But just as he seemed to have cemented his place in the side he injured his knee again, and had to fly home. Knees – and attitude – permitting, he should be a regular.

THE FACTS Samuels scored 257 and then took 5 for 87 – both career-bests – for the West Indians against Queensland in Brisbane in October 2005 ... He scored his maiden first-class century in a Test – 104 v India at Kolkata in October 2002: he was the fifth West Indian to do this, following Clifford Roach, Clairmonte Depeiaza, Gerry Alexander and Bernard Julien ... His brother Robert Samuels, older by ten years, played six Tests and eight ODIs as a left-hand opener, and scored 125 against New Zealand in his second Test ...

THE FIGURES

Batting and fielding　　　　　　　　　　　　　　　　　　www.cricinfo.com

	M	Inns	NO	Runs	HS	Avge	S/R	100	50	4s	6s	Ct	St
Tests to 10.9.07	24	43	4	1065	104	27.30	44.26	1	7	145	5	10	0
ODIs to 10.9.07	96	188	14	1512	108*	29.82	74.30	2	15	231	31	27	0
First-class to 10.9.07	59	100	7	3272	257	35.18	–	5	20	–	–	32	0

Bowling

	M	Balls	Runs	Wkts	BB	Avge	RpO	S/R	5i	10m
Tests to 10.9.07	24	1362	750	5	2–49	150.00	3.30	272.40	0	0
ODIs to 10.9.07	96	2863	2319	54	3–25	42.94	4.85	53.01	0	0
First-class to 10.9.07	59	4204	2091	35	5–87	59.74	2.98	120.11	1	0

KUMAR **SANGAKKARA**

Full name	**Kumar Chokshanada Sangakkara**
Born	**October 27, 1977, Matale**
Teams	**Nondescripts, Warwickshire**
Style	**Left-hand bat, wicketkeeper**
Test debut	**Sri Lanka v South Africa at Galle 2000**
ODI debut	**Sri Lanka v Pakistan at Galle 2000**

THE PROFILE Within months of making the side at 22, Kumar Sangakkara had become one of Sri Lanka's most influential players: a talented left-hand strokemaker, a slick wicketkeeper, a sharp-eyed strategist and an even sharper-tongued sledger, capable of riling even the most unflappable. His success was unexpected, for his domestic performances had been relatively modest, but the selectors' judgment was immediately justified as he starred in his first one-day tournament, in July 2000. Early on his keeping could be ragged, but his effortless batting oozed class from the start. He possesses the grace of David Gower, but the attitude of an Australian. At the outset he was happier on the back foot, but a fierce work ethic and a deep interest in the theory of batsmanship helped him, and he is now as comfortable driving through the covers as cutting behind point. He was briefly relieved of keeping duties after the 2003 World Cup: he made more runs, but got the job back when Australia visited early in 2004. This time the extra burden had no discernible effect on his batting: he made 185 against Pakistan in March 2006, and scored consistently in England too. But there was a sea-change after that, and Prasanna Jayawardene was given the gloves. Sangakkara responded with five centuries, among them three doubles, in the next seven Tests, including 287 as he and Mahela Jayawardene put on a worldrecord 624 against South Africa. A charismatic personality and an astute thinker – he is training as a lawyer – Sangakkara is tipped as a future captain.

THE FACTS Sangakkara scored 287, and put on 624 – the highest stand in first-class cricket – with Mahela Jayawardene (374) v South Africa in Colombo in July 2006 ... He also made 270, putting on 438 with Marvan Atapattu, v Zimbabwe at Bulawayo in May 2004 ... Sangakkara averages 82.66 in Tests v Pakistan, but 25.40 v Australia ... Against Bangladesh in July 2007 he became only the fourth man to score back-to-back double-centuries in Tests, with 200 and 222, both not out ... His record includes three ODIs for the World XI and four for the Asia XI ...

THE FIGURES

Batting and fielding   www.cricinfo.com

	M	Inns	NO	Runs	HS	Avge	S/R	100	50	4s	6s	Ct	St
Tests to 10.9.07	67	110	9	5492	287	54.37	55.67	14	22	735	18	147	20
ODIs to 10.9.07	203	187	23	5866	138*	35.76	74.42	6	40	585	27	183	52
First-class to 10.9.07	150	237	19	9417	287	43.19	–	20	46	–	–	302	33

Bowling

	M	Balls	Runs	Wkts	BB	Avge	RpO	S/R	5i	10m
Tests to 10.9.07	67	6	4	0	–	–	4.00	–	0	0
ODIs to 10.9.07	203	0	–	–	–	–	–	–	–	–
First-class to 10.9.07	150	132	74	1	1–13	74.00	3.36	132.00	0	0

WEST INDIES

RAMNARESH **SARWAN**

Full name **Ramnaresh Ronnie Sarwan**
Born **June 23, 1980, Wakenaam Island, Essequibo, Guyana**
Teams **Guyana**
Style **Right-hand bat, legspinner**
Test debut **West Indies v Pakistan at Bridgetown 1999-2000**
ODI debut **West Indies v England at Nottingham 2000**

THE PROFILE A light-footed right-hander, Ramnaresh Sarwan was brought up in the South American rainforest around the Essequibo River. After his first Test innings – 84 against Pakistan – the former England captain Ted Dexter was moved to predict a Test average of 50, an unfair millstone to hang around any young player's neck. But on his first tour, to England in 2000, Sarwan lived up to the hype by topping the averages: his footwork was strikingly confident and precise. It was a surprise when a horror run of three runs in five innings followed in Australia, but he did better against India at home in 2002. It still took him 28 matches to post his maiden Test century, 119 against Bangladesh in December 2002. He has scored consistently since: he made 392 runs in four Tests against South Africa in 2003-04 then, after a lean run at home against England, stroked a stunning unbeaten 261 against Bangladesh at Kingston in June 2004. Then came another England tour: he began and ended it on a low note, but was prolific in between. He also played a big part as West Indies reached the final of the one-day NatWest Series then won the Champions Trophy and carried on his good form in Australia the following year. After Brain Lara's enforced retirement, "Reggie" Sarwan took on the captaincy for the 2007 England tour – but that ended in tears with an injured shoulder during the second Test. West Indies need him back to full fitness – although not necessarily as captain, after Chris Gayle's stirring one-day displays.

THE FACTS Sarwan's 261 not out at Kingston in June 2004 is the highest score against Bangladesh, and also the highest Test score by a Guyanese batsman, beating Rohan Kanhai's 256 for West Indies v India at Calcutta in 1958-59 ... In ODIs Sarwan averages 69.69 v India – but only 21.87 v Sri Lanka ... He was out for 199 when Guyana played Kenya at Georgetown in February 2004 ... Sarwan made 100 and 111 for the West Indies Board President's XI against the touring Zimbabweans at Pointe-à-Pierre in March 2000 ...

THE FIGURES
Batting and fielding   www.cricinfo.com

	M	Inns	NO	Runs	HS	Avge	S/R	100	50	4s	6s	Ct	St
Tests *to 10.9.07*	67	119	8	4303	261*	38.76	44.97	9	26	570	8	46	0
ODIs *to 10.9.07*	124	116	24	4099	115*	44.55	76.90	3	26	346	41	34	0
First-class *to 10.9.07*	161	272	20	9358	261*	37.13	–	21	52	–	–	119	0

Bowling

	M	Balls	Runs	Wkts	BB	Avge	RpO	S/R	5i	10m
Tests *to 10.9.07*	67	1896	1075	23	4–37	46.73	3.40	82.43	0	0
ODIs *to 10.9.07*	124	485	472	12	3–31	39.33	5.83	40.41	0	0
First-class *to 10.9.07*	161	3921	2034	51	6–62	39.88	3.11	76.88	1	0

161

VIRENDER **SEHWAG**

INDIA

Full name	**Virender Sehwag**
Born	**October 20, 1978, Delhi**
Teams	**Delhi**
Style	**Right-hand bat, offspinner**
Test debut	**India v South Africa at Bloemfontein 2001-02**
ODI debut	**India v Pakistan at Mohali 1998-99**

THE PROFILE Virender Sehwag is a primal talent whose rough edges make him all the more appealing. By the time he had scored his first centuries in ODIs (off 70 balls, against New Zealand) and Tests (on debut, against South Africa, from 68 for 4), he was already eliciting comparisons with his idol Sachin Tendulkar. It is half-true. Like Tendulkar, he is short and square with curly hair, and plays the straight drive, back-foot punch and whip off the hips identically – but he leaves Tendulkar standing when it comes to audacity. Asked to open in England in 2002, Sehwag proved an instant hit, cracking 84 and 106 in the first two Tests. And he kept conjuring up pivotal innings, none as significant as India's first triple-century (brought up, characteristically, with a six), against Pakistan at Multan early in 2004. Sehwag bowls effective, loopy offspin, and is a reliable catcher in the slips. Surprisingly, he struggled in one-day cricket after his electric start, and endured a run of 60 games from January 2004 in which he averaged below 30. His fitness levels also dropped, but he continued to sparkle in Tests, with a magnificent 254 – and an opening stand of 410 with Rahul Dravid – against Pakistan at Lahore in January 2006. Then, in June, he came excruciatingly close to scoring a century before lunch on the first day in St Lucia, a feat never yet accomplished by an Indian. Despite hammering 114 against Bermuda in the 2007 World Cup, Sehwag got the chop afterwards – from Tests (not surprising after a modest run) and one-dayers too (more of a shock). He missed both legs of the England tour, but practised hard, lost a stone, and vowed to be back soon: "It hurts when you're dropped."

THE FACTS Sehwag's 309 against Pakistan at Multan in March 2004 was India's highest score (and first triple-century) in Tests ... He made 105 on his Test debut, against South Africa at Bloemfontein in November 2001 ... Sehwag averages 91.14 in Tests against Pakistan, with three double-centuries, but only 11.50 v Bangladesh ... His record includes one Test and three ODIs for the World XI, and seven ODIs for the Asia XI ...

THE FIGURES

Batting and fielding   www.cricinfo.com

	M	Inns	NO	Runs	HS	Avge	S/R	100	50	4s	6s	Ct	St
Tests to 10.9.07	52	87	3	4155	309	49.46	75.75	12	12	612	42	44	0
ODIs to 10.9.07	175	170	7	5153	130	31.61	97.11	8	25	712	73	71	0
First-class to 10.9.07	108	175	7	8434	309	50.20	–	–	26	30	–	–	102	0

Bowling

	M	Balls	Runs	Wkts	BB	Avge	RpO	S/R	5i	10m
Tests to 10.9.07	52	1286	674	14	3–33	48.14	3.14	91.85	0	0
ODIs to 10.9.07	175	3494	3060	76	3–25	40.26	5.25	45.97	0	0
First-class to 10.9.07	108	5485	2857	76	4–32	37.59	3.12	72.17	0	0

OWAIS **SHAH**

ENGLAND

Full name	**Owais Alam Shah**
Born	**October 22, 1978, Karachi, Pakistan**
Teams	**Middlesex**
Style	**Right-hand bat, occasional offspinner**
Test debut	**England v India at Mumbai 2005-06**
ODI debut	**England v Australia at Bristol 2001**

THE PROFILE Owais Shah was a schoolboy prodigy, making 64 for Middlesex in a one-dayer against Yorkshire when only 16, and captaining England to victory in the Youth World Cup in February 1998. A silky strokemaker, strong on the leg side, he seemed set for a stellar career, and after a couple of low-key seasons played for England in 2001, scoring 28 not out against Australia in his first ODI and 62 against Pakistan in his second. So far, so good ... but then he dropped off the radar, amid suggestions that his fielding wasn't up to scratch. He was in and out of the one-day side until the 2002-03 Australian VB Series, when he made only one decent contribution, and was then forgotten for three years. It seemed to be a classic case of wasted talent, but he was revitalised by Twenty20 cricket, and finished 2005 with more first-class runs than anyone else. When England had personnel problems in India that winter Shah was summoned, and lit up his Test debut at Mumbai with two cocky innings of 88 and 38 ... before being forgotten again. He got another chance early in 2007, but struggled, and was dumped as soon as Michael Vaughan regained fitness. However, he kept his name in the frame with a sparkling Twenty20 innings against West Indies, which ensured him another run in the one-day side and a place in the inaugural World Twenty20 championships in September 2007, just after he scored a fine maiden one-day hundred against India. It's hard to believe that Shah is still only 29: his best days may still lie ahead.

THE FACTS Shah score 203 for Middlesex against Derbyshire at Southgate in 2001 ... He captained England Under-19 to victory in the Youth World Cup in February 1998, beating New Zealand in the final at Johannesburg: his team-mates included Robert Key and Chris Schofield ... Shah was the leading runscorer in English first-class cricket in 2005, with 1728 runs at 66.46 ... He hit 55 from 35 balls as England won their Twenty20 international against West Indies at The Oval in June 2007 ...

THE FIGURES

Batting and fielding   www.cricinfo.com

	M	Inns	NO	Runs	HS	Avge	S/R	100	50	4s	6s	Ct	St
Tests to 10.9.07	2	4	0	136	88	34.00	44.73	0	1	19	1	1	0
ODIs to 10.9.07	26	25	3	581	107*	26.40	74.29	1	3	44	5	6	0
First-class to 10.9.07	181	306	29	11913	203	43.00	–		32	60	–	–	139	0

Bowling

	M	Balls	Runs	Wkts	BB	Avge	RpO	S/R	5i	10m
Tests to 10.9.07	2	0	–	–	–	–	–	–	–	–
ODIs to 10.9.07	26	24	19	1	1–19	19.00	4.75	24.00	0	0
First-class to 10.9.07	181	1814	1235	21	3–33	58.80	4.08	86.38	0	0

SHAHADAT HOSSAIN

Full name **Kazi Shahadat Hossain**
Born **August 7, 1986, Dhaka**
Teams **Dhaka**
Style **Right-hand bat, right-arm fast-medium bowler**
Test debut **Bangladesh v England at Lord's 2005**
ODI debut **Bangladesh v Kenya at Bogra 2005-06**

THE PROFILE Shahadat Hossain was discovered during a talent-spotting camp in Narayanganj, and whisked away to the Bangladesh Institute of Sports for refinement. He was picked for the 2004 Under-19 World Cup, where he stood out as a promising fast bowler in a tournament which generally lacked firepower, and was rapidly called up for Bangladesh A. Shahadat – who's also known as "Rajib" – has all the necessary attributes for a genuine fast bowler. He is tall, comes in off a smooth run-up, and doesn't put unnecessary pressure on his body with a slightly open-chested delivery position. He has a strong frame, and endurance in abundance. He is naturally aggressive and, above everything, has raw pace. His Test debut at Lord's in 2005 was a chastening experience, as he conceded 101 runs in just 12 overs. But he was just 18: since then he impressed against Sri Lanka, taking four wickets in an innings in Colombo and again at Chittagong, before going one better in Bogra's inaugural Test, when his 5 for 86 confirmed him as the leading fast bowler on either side. He struggled against the Australians in April 2006, having only the wicket of Ricky Ponting to show for 67 overs of effort, and was in and out of the side in 2006-07, playing only once in the World Cup (and being hit around in the sobering defeat by Ireland). However, he is still only 21, and if he continues to progress, along with the left-armer Syed Rasel, he could be a force for Bangladesh in the years to come.

THE FACTS Shahadat Hossain's 5 for 86 against Sri Lanka at Bogra in 2005-06 was only the second five-wicket haul by a Bangladesh fast bowler in Tests, following Manjural Islam's 6 for 81 against Zimbabwe at Bulawayo in 2000-01 ... Shahadat took Bangladesh's first hat-trick in ODIs, against Zimbabwe at Harare in August 2006 ... He took only two wickets – both against Kenya – in his first six ODIs ... Shahadat took 5 for 63 and 5 for 53 (his first-class career-best) in successive A-team Tests in Zimbabwe in February 2005 ...

THE FIGURES

Batting and fielding   www.cricinfo.com

	M	Inns	NO	Runs	HS	Avge	S/R	100	50	4s	6s	Ct	St
Tests *to 10.9.07*	11	21	5	96	31	6.00	34.04	0	0	11	0	3	0
ODIs *to 10.9.07*	24	11	7	27	9*	6.75	45.76	0	0	1	0	1	0
First-class *to 10.9.07*	27	46	17	314	37*	10.82	48.98	0	0	–	–	6	0

Bowling

	M	Balls	Runs	Wkts	BB	Avge	RpO	S/R	5i	10m
Tests *to 10.9.07*	11	1551	1153	25	5–86	46.12	4.46	62.04	1	0
ODIs *to 10.9.07*	24	1066	883	27	3–34	32.70	4.96	39.48	0	0
First-class *to 10.9.07*	27	3923	2651	78	5–53	33.98	4.05	50.29	4	0

SHAHID AFRIDI

Full name	**Sahibzada Mohammad Shahid Khan Afridi**
Born	**March 1, 1980, Khyber Agency**
Teams	**Karachi, Habib Bank**
Style	**Right-hand bat, legspinner**
Test debut	**Pakistan v Australia at Karachi 1998-99**
ODI debut	**Pakistan v Kenya at Nairobi 1996-97**

THE PROFILE A flamboyant allrounder introduced to international cricket as a 16-year-old legspinner, Shahid Afridi astonished everyone except himself by pinch-hitting the fastest one-day hundred in his maiden innings. He's a compulsive shot-maker, and although until 2004 that was too often his undoing, a combination of growing maturity and a sympathetic coach (Bob Woolmer) allowed him blossom into one of the most dangerous players around. A string of incisive contributions culminated in a violent century against India in April 2005: the only faster ODI hundred was Afridi's own. A few weeks before, he had smashed 58 in 34 balls, and also grabbed three crucial wickets, as Pakistan memorably squared the Test series at Bangalore. And so it continued: a Test ton against West Indies, important runs against England, then, early in 2006, he went berserk on some flat pitches against India. He was a forlorn spectator at the World Cup, serving out a four-match ban after an altercation with a spectator in South Africa: he played only in Pakistan's inconsequential final game. An Afridi virtuoso is laced with lofted drives and short-arm jabs over midwicket. He's at his best when forcing straight, and at his weakest pushing at the ball just outside off. But perhaps the biggest improvement has been in his legspin. When conditions suit, he gets turn as well as lazy drift, but variety is the key: there's a vicious faster ball and an offbreak too. He shocked everyone when, after finally establishing himself, he announced his retirement from Tests early in 2006. To less surprise, he retracted his retirement a fortnight later.

THE FACTS In his second match (he hadn't batted in the first) Shahid Afridi hit the fastest hundred in ODIs, from only 37 balls, v Sri Lanka in Nairobi in October 1996 ... Afridi has the fastest strike rate – 109.38 runs per 100 balls – of anyone who has batted more than 20 times in ODIs ... In successive matches v India early in 2006 he hit 103 (from 80 balls) at Lahore, and 156, from 128 balls with six sixes, at Faisalabad ... Only Sanath Jayasuriya (242) has hit more sixes in ODIs ... His record includes three ODIs for the Asia XI and two for the World XI ...

THE FIGURES

Batting and fielding

www.cricinfo.com

	M	Inns	NO	Runs	HS	Avge	S/R	100	50	4s	6s	Ct	St
Tests to 10.9.07	26	46	1	1683	156	37.40	86.13	5	8	216	50	10	0
ODIs to 10.9.07	240	228	11	5072	109	23.37	109.38	4	28	476	229	83	0
First-class to 10.9.07	96	163	4	5105	164	32.10	–	12	25	–	–	61	0

Bowling

	M	Balls	Runs	Wkts	BB	Avge	RpO	S/R	5i	10m
Tests to 10.9.07	26	3092	1640	47	5–52	34.89	3.18	65.78	1	0
ODIs to 10.9.07	240	9375	7193	204	5–11	35.25	4.60	45.95	2	0
First-class to 10.9.07	96	11463	5958	216	6–101	27.58	3.11	53.06	7	0

SHAHRIAR NAFEES

Full name	**Shahriar Nafees Ahmed**
Born	**January 25, 1986, Dhaka**
Teams	**Barisal**
Style	**Left-hand bat**
Test debut	**Bangladesh v Sri Lanka at Colombo 2005-06**
ODI debut	**Bangladesh v England at Nottingham 2005**

THE PROFILE   As a left-hand opening batsman, Shahriar Nafees is a rarity among Bangladesh cricketers, and at the age of 19 he was thrust into the Test squad for their maiden tour of England with just five first-class matches behind him. He hadn't fared too badly in those, however, with 350 runs at 35, and his Under-19 coach Richard McInness reckoned he had the talent and temperament to become a future Test captain. With Nafees Iqbal and Javed Omar established as Bangladesh's opening pair, the England trip was a case of watching and learning for Shahriar. He did get an opportunity in the NatWest Series, and cashed in with 75 in the final one-dayer against Australia. He made his Test debut in Sri Lanka in September 2005, and made 51 in his second match. He also got starts in all the one-day games, but converted only one into a fifty. Then in April 2006 he exploded in sensational fashion against the might of Australia, stroking his way to a brilliant hundred, his maiden first-class ton as well as his first in Tests, at Fatullah. His stunning 138, with 19 fours, set up a scarcely believable first-day total of 355 for 5 as the Aussies reeled. He added 33 in the second innings, and a brisk 79 in the second Test to show that this was no flash in the pan. He cashed in against the minnows with three one-day hundreds off Zimbabwe and one against Bermuda, but found life harder after that against the big boys – he was dropped after six innings in the World Cup produced only 31 runs and a top score of only 12.

THE FACTS   Shahriar Nafees's 138 against Australia at Fatullah in 2005-06 was his maiden century in first-class cricket: his previous-highest score was 97, for the Board President's XI v the touring Zimbabweans in January 2005 ... Shahriar hit four of Bangladesh's first seven ODI hundreds ... He averages 62.41 in ODIs against Zimbabwe, with three hundreds, but only 10 v England (and 0 v Canada) ... Shahriar captained Bangladesh Under-19 in a one-day game against England, skippered by Alastair Cook, in 2004 ...

THE FIGURES

Batting and fielding   www.cricinfo.com

	M	Inns	NO	Runs	HS	Avge	S/R	100	50	4s	6s	Ct	St
Tests *to 10.9.07*	11	22	0	607	138	27.59	54.93	1	3	85	0	11	0
ODIs *to 10.9.07*	49	49	4	1565	123*	34.77	69.64	4	7	196	7	7	0
First-class *to 10.9.07*	27	53	1	1670	138	32.11	60.86	1	14	–	–	19	0

Bowling

	M	Balls	Runs	Wkts	BB	Avge	RpO	S/R	5i	10m
Tests *to 10.9.07*	11	0	–	–	–	–	–	–	–	–
ODIs *to 10.9.07*	49	0	–	–	–	–	–	–	–	–
First-class *to 10.9.07*	27	18	20	0	–	–	6.66	–	0	0

SHAKIB AL HASAN

Full name	**Shakib Al Hasan**
Born	**March 24, 1987, Magura, Khulna**
Teams	**Khulna**
Style	**Left-hand bat, slow left-arm orthodox spinner**
Test debut	**Bangladesh v India at Chittagong 2006-07**
ODI debut	**Bangladesh v Zimbabwe at Harare 2006**

THE PROFILE   Shakib Al Hasan first came to prominence in Bangladesh's Under-19 team late in 2005, when he blasted 83 not out from only 62 balls to take his side to victory over England in a one-day tournament in Dhaka. A fortnight later he was at it again, with an 82-ball century against Sri Lanka, after taking three wickets with his slow left-armers. He was reportedly only 15 at the time, although when his birthdate eventually emerged he turned out to be 18. Soon Shakib was in the A team, smashing 55 not out in 32 balls then grabbing four wickets as Zimbabwe A were swept aside at Kwekwe in July 2006. A full debut was not far off, and it duly came against the full Zimbabwe side (such as it is) the following month: he took a wicket and then strolled in at No. 4 to make 30 not out in the matchwinning partnership. He proved remarkably consistent with the bat, being dismissed in single figures only once in 18 one-dayers leading up to the 2007 World Cup: that run included 134 not out against Canada, Bangladesh's highest score in ODIs. The heady start continued in the Caribbean with a half-century in the famous win over India, and another against England. After the World Cup came his first taste of personal failure – only 17 runs in three innings in Sri Lanka. His bowling has rarely been collared, and he maintains an impressively low one-day economy rate, although he might struggle to take regular wickets in Tests.

THE FACTS   Shakib Al Hasan made 134 not out against Canada at St John's in February 2007, Bangladesh's highest score in ODIs ... He averages 37.25 in ODIs against Zimbabwe – and 0.00 against West Indies ... Shakib is yet to make a first-class century, his highest score being 85 for Bangladesh A against Sri Lanka A at Bogra in March 2006 ... He took 6 for 79 for Khulna at Sylhet in April 2005 ... His name is sometimes spelt "Saqibul Hasan" on scorecards ...

THE FIGURES
Batting and fielding

www.cricinfo.com

	M	Inns	NO	Runs	HS	Avge	S/R	100	50	4s	6s	Ct	St
Tests *to 10.9.07*	3	5	0	96	30	19.20	50.00	0	0	13	0	1	0
ODIs *to 10.9.07*	34	33	9	937	134*	39.04	67.45	1	5	87	3	7	0
First-class *to 10.9.07*	16	29	3	721	85	27.73	–	0	3	–	–	11	0

Bowling

	M	Balls	Runs	Wkts	BB	Avge	RpO	S/R	5i	10m
Tests *to 10.9.07*	3	288	148	0	–	–	3.08	–	0	0
ODIs *to 10.9.07*	34	1556	1062	32	3–18	33.18	4.09	48.62	0	0
First-class *to 10.9.07*	16	2657	1173	35	6–79	33.51	2.64	75.91	2	0

ISHANT **SHARMA**

Full name	**Ishant Sharma**
Born	**September 2, 1988, Delhi**
Teams	**Delhi**
Style	**Right-hand bat, right-arm fast-medium bowler**
Test debut	**India v Bangladesh at Dhaka 2006-07**
ODI debut	**India v South Africa at Belfast 2007**

THE PROFILE   Tall fast bowlers have always been a much-prized rarity in Indian cricket. Their earliest Tests featured Mohammad Nissar, a few years ago Abey Kuruvilla flitted across the international scene ... and now there's Ishant Sharma, who is 6ft 4ins tall and still growing. He's regularly above 80mph (130kph), and possesses a sharp and deceptive bouncer, delivered from a high-arm action. He started to play seriously at 14, rose quickly, and played one-dayers for Delhi in 2005-06, when he was 17. The following season he took 4 for 65 from 34 overs on his first-class debut, against Tamil Nadu, and finished his first term with 29 wickets at 20.10. He also played for India's Under-19s, taking 21 wickets in six Tests and setting up a big win in New Zealand with 5 for 55 in January 2007. Just before that he had been on the verge of reinforcing the full Indian squad in South Africa – flights had been booked and visa arrangements made – but in the end he was left to concentrate on domestic cricket and that youth tour. However, when Munaf Patel was injured again in Bangladesh in May, Sharma finally did get on the plane, and took one wicket in a landslide victory at Dhaka. The learning process continued with a place on the tour of England. His relatively frail physique is a worry, so the selectors need to make sure he is not overbowled – but if he can stay fit and healthy he looks set for a successful career.

THE FACTS   Ishant Sharma took 4 for 34 in his first senior match for Delhi, a one-day game against Jammu & Kashmir at Delhi in February 2006 ... He took 5 for 35 for Delhi v Baroda at Delhi in December 2006 ... In 2006-07, his first season of first-class cricket, Sharma took 29 wickets at 20.10 for Delhi, then made his Test debut in only his seventh match ...

THE FIGURES
Batting and fielding

www.cricinfo.com

	M	Inns	NO	Runs	HS	Avge	S/R	100	50	4s	6s	Ct	St
Tests *to 10.9.07*	1	0	–	–	–	–	–	0	0	0	0	0	0
ODIs *to 10.9.07*	1	0	–	–	–	–	–	0	0	0	0	0	0
First-class *to 10.9.07*	9	7	6	11	7*	11.00	25.00	0	0	–	–	1	0

Bowling

	M	Balls	Runs	Wkts	BB	Avge	RpO	S/R	5i	10m
Tests *to 10.9.07*	1	78	49	1	1–19	49.00	3.76	78.00	0	0
ODIs *to 10.9.07*	1	42	38	0	–	–	5.42	–	0	0
First-class *to 10.9.07*	9	1844	839	32	5–35	25.93	2.70	57.62	1	0

ROHIT **SHARMA**

Full name	**Rohit Gurunathan Sharma**
Born	**April 30, 1987, Bansod, Nagpur, Maharashtra**
Teams	**Mumbai**
Style	**Right-hand bat, offspinner**
Test debut	**No Tests yet**
ODI debut	**India v Ireland at Belfast 2007**

THE PROFILE Rohit Sharma made a stellar start to his first-class career, hitting 205 against Gujarat in only his fourth match for Mumbai, in December 2006, after a near-miss of 95 in his previous game, against Hyderabad. He actually made his first-class debut for India A, in the Top End Series in Australia a few months before, and had also represented West Zone in the Duleep Trophy. He had exuded class in the Youth World Cup in Sri Lanka earlier in 2006, cracking three half-centuries in six days in mid-tournament before missing out in the low-scoring final, when India were shot out for 71 in response to Pakistan's unimposing 109. Brian Murgatroyd, the ICC's media manager, watched throughout and observed: "Rohit stood apart with his solid play and classic style." Sharma was at No. 3 then, which may well turn out to be his best position in the long run, as he is an adaptable batsman, strong off the back foot, equally happy as accumulator or aggressor. He finished the 2006-07 Indian season with 600 runs at 40, plus 356 in one-dayers and a 49-ball Twenty20 century against Gujarat, which was enough to earn him a national call as the dust settled on India's disastrous 2007 World Cup campaign. He made his ODI debut in Ireland, and retained his place for the one-day leg of the tour of England that followed, and the World Twenty20 championship. Sharma is also a handy offspinner, and is trying to improve his bowling to give him another string to his bow.

THE FACTS Rohit Sharma extended his maiden first-class century to 205, for Mumbai against Gujarat at Mumbai in December 2006... He also hit 101 not out, off only 45 balls, against Gujarat in a Twenty20 match in April 2007 ... In 2006-07, his maiden first-class season at home (he played two matches for India A in Australia earlier in 2006), Sharma made 600 first-class runs at 40 ... He hit 142 not out for West Zone against North Zone in a one-day Deodhar Trophy match at Udaipur in March 2006 ...

THE FIGURES

Batting and fielding www.cricinfo.com

	M	Inns	NO	Runs	HS	Avge	S/R	100	50	4s	6s	Ct	St
Tests to 10.9.07	0	0	–	–	–	–	–	–	–	–	–	–	–
ODIs to 10.9.07	2	1	0	8	8	8.00	88.88	0	0	0	0	2	0
First-class to 10.9.07	15	22	1	851	205	40.52	–	1	5	–	–	14	0

Bowling

	M	Balls	Runs	Wkts	BB	Avge	RpO	S/R	5i	10m
Tests to 10.9.07	0	0	–	–	–	–	–	–	–	–
ODIs to 10.9.07	2	6	3	0	–	–	3.00	–	0	0
First-class to 10.9.07	15	168	96	1	1–12	96.00	3.42	168.00	0	0

SHOAIB AKHTAR

PAKISTAN

Full name	**Shoaib Akhtar**
Born	**August 13, 1975, Rawalpindi, Punjab**
Teams	**Islamabad, Khan Research Laboratories**
Style	**Right-hand bat, right-arm fast bowler**
Test debut	**Pakistan v West Indies at Rawalpindi 1997-98**
ODI debut	**Pakistan v Zimbabwe at Harare 1997-98**

THE PROFILE Shoaib Akhtar electrified the 1999 World Cup with his spectacular run-up and blistering speed. Star status was sealed by a flop of unruly hair, a talent for showboating and a vivid nickname – "The Rawalpindi Express". But it was too much, too young. Breaking the 100mph barrier seemed to matter more than cementing his place. He was twice sidelined after throwing allegations, and although his action was cleared – tests showed a hyper-extensible elbow – injuries often impinged. He was back in 2002, shaking up the Aussies with five-fors in Brisbane and Colombo. He promised much in the 2003 World Cup, but came a cropper, especially in a needle encounter with Sachin Tendulkar. Then Pakistan lost a series to India, and Shoaib felt the heat as his commitment was questioned. He blew hot and cold in Australia in 2004–05, by turns Pakistan's most incisive threat and their most disinterested player. Worries about fitness and attitude kept him out for most of 2005, but he bounced back at the end with 17 England wickets, mixing yorkers and bouncers with lethal slower balls. But just when he seemed to be back there were further whispers about his action, then he missed most of the 2006 England tour with ankle trouble, and next he was banned for two years after a positive drug test. The ban was lifted on appeal, but it and various injuries confined him to one Test in 2006–07 – he took four wickets to set up a win at Port Elizabeth, then limped off with a sore hamstring – and kept him out of the World Cup. He was back late in 2007 – briefly, being sent home from the World Twenty20 championships after a dressing-room spat left Mohammad Asif with a bat-bruised thigh, which might be one controversy too far.

THE FACTS Shoaib was clocked at 100.04mph by an unofficial speed-gun during a one-dayer v New Zealand in April 2002: he also recorded 100.23mph (161.3kph) at the 2003 World Cup ... His best figures in Tests and ODIs both came against New Zealand ... Against England in the 2003 World Cup Shoaib was the fifth No. 11 to top-score in an ODI innings, with 43 ... His record includes three ODIs for the Asia XI and two for the World XI ...

THE FIGURES

Batting and fielding

www.cricinfo.com

	M	Inns	NO	Runs	HS	Avge	S/R	100	50	4s	6s	Ct	St
Tests to 10.9.07	43	63	12	541	47	10.60	41.87	0	0	53	22	11	0
ODIs to 10.9.07	133	65	31	344	43	10.11	73.50	0	0	22	10	17	0
First-class to 10.9.07	123	171	47	1536	59*	12.38	–	0	1	–	–	37	0

Bowling

	M	Balls	Runs	Wkts	BB	Avge	RpO	S/R	5i	10m
Tests to 10.9.07	43	7556	4276	169	6–11	25.30	3.39	44.71	12	2
ODIs to 10.9.07	133	6276	4854	208	6–16	23.33	4.64	30.17	4	0
First-class to 10.9.07	123	19018	11484	440	6–11	26.10	3.62	43.22	28	2

SHOAIB MALIK

Full name	**Shoaib Malik**
Born	**February 1, 1982, Sialkot, Punjab**
Teams	**Sialkot, Pakistan International Airlines**
Style	**Right-hand bat, offspinner**
Test debut	**Pakistan v Bangladesh at Multan 2001-02**
ODI debut	**Pakistan v West Indies at Sharjah 1999-2000**

THE PROFILE Short of wicketkeeping, there are few roles Shoaib Malik hasn't tried. He has batted everywhere from 1 to 10 in one-dayers, though he has now settled at 3 or 4. He began in Tests in the lower order, but lately has been opening. As an offspinner, everything about his bowling, from the short-stepping run-up to the doosra, bears a striking similarity to Saqlain Mushtaq's. His action isn't clean, though: he has been reported twice, first in October 2004, after which he played primarily as a batsman for the next six months before undergoing elbow surgery. He was reported again in November 2005, and had another operation early in 2006, which kept him out of the Tests in England. And now he faces his biggest challenge: captaincy, in the wake of the disasters of the 2007 World Cup. If anyone can follow Inzamam-ul-Haq and Bob Woolmer, and make Pakistan proud again, it could be the versatile and intelligent Shoaib. Under Woolmer, he became a one-day linchpin, regularly marshalling run-chases or setting up platforms for big totals. He is an uncomplicated batsman, free with checked drives and cuts, or slogging when needed. Against India, in both the 2005 and 2006 series, he produced all these – but he can still come in at No. 6, as he did against South Africa in October 2003, and blast 82 from 41 balls. His finest performance so far in Tests came when he defied Murali with an unbeaten eight-hour 148 to earn a draw in Colombo in March 2006.

THE FACTS Shoaib Malik extended his first Test century, against Sri Lanka in Colombo in March 2006, to 148 not out in 448 minutes as Pakistan forced a draw ... He made 90, 95 and 106 in successive one-day innings against India in February 2006 ... Shoaib has batted in every position except No. 11 in ODIs, averaging 59.88 from No. 4 and 39.90 at No. 3 (and 7.50 at No. 10) ... He took 7 for 81 for Pakistan International Airlines against WAPDA at Faisalabad in February 2001 ...

THE FIGURES

Batting and fielding   www.cricinfo.com

	M	Inns	NO	Runs	HS	Avge	S/R	100	50	4s	6s	Ct	St
Tests to 10.9.07	18	29	4	941	148*	37.64	44.13	1	5	130	8	8	0
ODIs to 10.9.07	140	124	17	3641	143	34.02	77.50	5	22	303	44	48	0
First-class to 10.9.07	73	111	13	2766	148*	28.22	–	6	12	–	–	36	0

Bowling

	M	Balls	Runs	Wkts	BB	Avge	RpO	S/R	5i	10m
Tests to 10.9.07	18	1429	820	13	4–42	63.07	3.44	109.92	0	0
ODIs to 10.9.07	140	4858	3630	105	4–19	34.57	4.48	46.26	0	0
First-class to 10.9.07	73	9842	4905	163	7–81	30.09	2.99	60.38	5	1

RYAN **SIDEBOTTOM**

Full name	**Ryan Jay Sidebottom**
Born	**January 15, 1978, Huddersfield, Yorkshire**
Teams	**Nottinghamshire**
Style	**Left-hand bat, left-arm fast-medium bowler**
Test debut	**England v Pakistan at Lord's 2001**
ODI debut	**England v Zimbabwe at Harare 2001-02**

THE PROFILE Although Ryan Sidebottom's long, curly ginger hair made him one of the most recognisable faces on the county circuit, for six years he seemed destined to be an England one-cap wonder, just like his father, Arnie, who played once in 1985. The junior Sidebottom (who like his dad was also a useful footballer, having trials for Sheffield United) did well on the England A tour of West Indies with his brisk left-armers early in 2001, and made his Test debut against Pakistan at Lord's later that year: he didn't move it much, failed to take a wicket, and was promptly returned to county cricket. He was playing for Yorkshire then, but a move to Trent Bridge in 2004 revitalised him. He took 50 wickets for the first time in 2005, and repeated the dose the following year, and when Matthew Hoggard was injured at the start of 2007 Sidebottom was the surprise packet unveiled by the selectors – nudged by some wise words from his county captain, Stephen Fleming. He was an instant success back on his old stamping ground of Headingley, taking eight wickets (five of them lbw) as West Indies were blown away. Crucially for a bowler who rarely nudges the speedo above 80mph, he now swung the ball in, as well as away – the first left-armer to do this regularly for England since John Lever a generation earlier. Sidebottom kept his place, taking 24 wickets in six Tests despite suffering more than most from fallible catching behind the stumps and in the slips.

THE FACTS Sidebottom took 7 for 97 for Yorkshire against Derbyshire at Leeds in May 2003 ... His father, Arnie, played one Test for England against Australia in 1985 ... Sidebottom took 6 for 16 (and 5 for 27) for Yorkshire against Kent at Leeds in June 2000 ... One of his nicknames is "Sexual Chocolate", after a fictional band in an Eddie Murphy film who all had long, flowing hair ... Sidebottom took 7 for 30 for England Under-19s (captained by Andrew Flintoff) in a Test against Zimbabwe at Birmingham in August 1997 ...

THE FIGURES

Batting and fielding

www.cricinfo.com

	M	Inns	NO	Runs	HS	Avge	S/R	100	50	4s	6s	Ct	St
Tests to 10.9.07	7	10	5	111	26*	22.20	55.50	0	0	17	0	2	0
ODIs to 10.9.07	3	2	1	17	15	17.00	188.88	0	0	2	0	1	0
First-class to 10.9.07	112	141	42	1189	54	12.01	–	0	1	–	–	42	0

Bowling

	M	Balls	Runs	Wkts	BB	Avge	RpO	S/R	5i	10m
Tests to 10.9.07	7	1482	682	24	5–88	28.41	2.76	61.75	1	0
ODIs to 10.9.07	3	138	140	4	2–56	35.00	6.08	34.50	0	0
First-class to 10.9.07	112	18792	8830	348	7–97	25.37	2.81	54.00	12	1

CHAMARA **SILVA**

Full name	**Lindamlilage Prageeth Chamara Silva**
Born	**December 14, 1979, Panadura**
Teams	**Sebastianites**
Style	**Right-hand bat, occasional legspinner**
Test debut	**Sri Lanka v New Zealand at Christchurch 2006-07**
ODI debut	**Sri Lanka v Australia at Colombo 1999-2000**

SRI LANKA

THE PROFILE Chamara Silva arrived on the international scene as a slightly built 19-year-old in 1999, a beneficiary of the youth policy championed by the then chairman of selectors Sidath Wettimuny, and started well with 55 against Australia on his one-day debut. His batting style – particularly his bow-legged stance and flamboyant cover-drives – attracted immediate comparisons with the great Aravinda de Silva. Wristy, and quick on his feet, he is a good sweeper and cutter, and loves to loft the ball over the covers. But Silva failed to nail down a regular place despite his obvious talent, and was quietly dropped after the 2002 England tour. Over the next four years he was a prolific domestic runscorer, and eventually caught the eye of Tom Moody, Sri Lanka's coach, who couldn't understand why he was not in the national squad. Silva did well for the A team in India, and duly won a long-overdue recall for the senior tour of New Zealand at the end of 2006. He won his first Test cap at Christchurch, but bagged a pair in a five-wicket defeat. However, the management kept faith for the second Test at Wellington, and he rewarded them handsomely, scoring 61 in the first innings and a magnificent unbeaten 152 in the second. A maiden one-day century followed in India, just three weeks before the 2007 World Cup, where he was consistently in the runs, peeling off three successive half-centuries at the start and only once failing to reach double figures in Sri Lanka's march to the final.

THE FACTS Silva made 152 not out in his second Test, against New Zealand at Wellington in December 2006, after bagging a pair in his first: he is only the seventh batsman ever to score a Test century after a debut pair, and the first one to atone immediately in his second match ... Silva's 55 against Australia in August 1999 is the highest by any Sri Lankan on ODI debut: the only other half-century was by Sunil Wettimuny, with 53 not out against Australia at The Oval in the 1975 World Cup ...

THE FIGURES

Batting and fielding

www.cricinfo.com

	M	Inns	NO	Runs	HS	Avge	S/R	100	50	4s	6s	Ct	St
Tests to 10.9.07	5	7	1	272	152*	45.33	68.17	1	1	33	1	3	0
ODIs to 10.9.07	30	26	3	859	107*	37.34	73.92	1	7	79	6	10	0
First-class to 10.9.07	103	173	12	6072	152*	37.71	–	13	36	–	–	79	0

Bowling

	M	Balls	Runs	Wkts	BB	Avge	RpO	S/R	5i	10m
Tests to 10.9.07	5	0	–	–	–	–	–	–	–	–
ODIs to 10.9.07	30	0	–	–	–	–	–	–	–	–
First-class to 10.9.07	103	1741	1193	34	4–85	35.08	4.11	51.20	0	0

LENDL **SIMMONS**

Full name	**Lendl Mark Platter Simmons**
Born	**January 25, 1985, Port-of-Spain, Trinidad**
Teams	**Trinidad & Tobago**
Style	**Right-hand bat, right-arm medium-pace bowler**
Test debut	**No Tests yet**
ODI debut	**West Indies v Pakistan at Faisalabad 2006-07**

THE PROFILE Like his compatriots Denesh Ramdin and Ravi Rampaul, Trinidad's Lendl Simmons (the nephew of the former Test opener Phil) first made a mark at the Under-15 World Challenge event in England in 2000, which West Indies won. He made a steady rise through the junior ranks, playing in the Youth World Cups of 2002 (when they lost in the semi-final) and 2004 (beaten finalists). An opener, and a fine fielder who sometimes keeps wicket, Simmons – who is named after the top 1980s tennis player Ivan Lendl – made his first-class debut six weeks after his 17th birthday. He passed 500 runs in the home season of 2004-05, and did so again the following year, which won him a place in the West Indies A team for their tour of England later in 2006, the highlight of which was an unbeaten 108 in a one-dayer against the Pakistan tourists: he also scored 100 against Leicestershire. He stepped up to the full ODI side in Pakistan late in 2006, picking up a duck in his first match but making a mature 70 in his second. He struggled a little after that, collecting only 42 runs in four innings, but retained his place in the World Cup squad. He made one only appearance, though, in rather peculiar circumstances: called up as a extra batsman in place of a fast bowler for the vital Super Eight match against New Zealand, he batted at No. 8 and didn't bowl.

THE FACTS Simmons made 200 – his maiden first-class century – for Trinidad & Tobago v Jamaica at Scarborough in Tobago in February 2006, after being out for 0 in the first innings ... He was part of the West Indian side that won the Under-15 World Challenge at Lord's in 2000, and was on the losing side in the 2004 Youth World Cup final at Dhaka, in both matches alongside future West Indian team-mates Denesh Ramdin and Ravi Rampaul ... His uncle, Phil Simmons, won 26 Test caps for West Indies between 1988 and 1997...

THE FIGURES

Batting and fielding   www.cricinfo.com

	M	Inns	NO	Runs	HS	Avge	S/R	100	50	4s	6s	Ct	St
Tests *to 10.9.07*	0	–	–	–	–	–	–	–	–	–	–	–	–
ODIs *to 10.9.07*	8	8	1	126	70	18.00	56.00	0	1	15	0	3	0
First-class *to 10.9.07*	41	72	6	1962	200	29.72	–	3	10	–	–	49	4

Bowling

	M	Balls	Runs	Wkts	BB	Avge	RpO	S/R	5i	10m
Tests *to 10.9.07*	0	0	–	–	–	–	–	–	–	–
ODIs *to 10.9.07*	8	6	9	0	–	–	9.00	–	0	0
First-class *to 10.9.07*	41	186	94	6	3–6	15.66	3.03	31.00	0	0

MATHEW **SINCLAIR**

Full name	**Mathew Stuart Sinclair**
Born	**November 9, 1975, Katherine, Australia**
Teams	**Central Districts**
Style	**Right-hand bat, occasional right-arm medium-pacer**
Test debut	**New Zealand v West Indies at Wellington 1999-2000**
ODI debut	**New Zealand v Australia at Christchurch 1999-2000**

THE PROFILE Two double-centuries in his first 12 Tests, including one on debut, suggested that Mathew Sinclair should be a fixture in the New Zealand side – but he has been inconsistent since, and was close to leaving the country for good after losing his central contract for 2005-06. A correct right-hander, Sinclair made 214 against West Indies at Wellington in December 1999, and followed that with an unbeaten 204 against Pakistan at Christchurch in March 2001. In between there was 150 against South Africa at Port Elizabeth. But he struggled after that fine start, and lost his place. He was recalled for the third Test against South Africa at Wellington in March 2004, but an impressive 74 wasn't enough to get him picked for the tour of England later that year, although he was whistled up from club cricket in East Anglia after Craig McMillan broke a finger. Similarly, that October he was rushed to Bangladesh when Michael Papps dislocated his shoulder, and collected 76 in the first Test, followed by a dogged 69 against Australia at Brisbane – but after one more Test he was out of the side again. Speculation about his future was rekindled when he was originally left off the 2007-08 contracts list, but he was saved for the nation when Hamish Marshall decided to stay in England as a Kolpak player. He was born in Australia's Northern Territory, but his mother moved to New Zealand after Sinclair's father was killed in a car crash when he was only five.

THE FACTS Sinclair is one of only five people to score a double-century on Test debut: the others are "Tip" Foster, Lawrence Rowe, Brendon Kuruppu and Jacques Rudolph ... He averages 108.33 in Tests against Pakistan, but 13.00 v Sri Lanka ... Sinclair has never played a Test or an ODI against England ... His highest first-class score is 268 for New Zealand A v South Africa A at Potchefstroom in 2004-05 ...

THE FIGURES

Batting and fielding www.cricinfo.com

	M	Inns	NO	Runs	HS	Avge	S/R	100	50	4s	6s	Ct	St
Tests to 10.9.07	27	46	5	1448	214	35.31	43.23	3	4	169	7	26	0
ODIs to 10.9.07	45	44	2	1100	110*	26.09	60.76	2	7	101	4	15	0
First-class to 10.9.07	131	223	22	9327	268	46.40	–	22	50	–	–	124	1

Bowling

	M	Balls	Runs	Wkts	BB	Avge	RpO	S/R	5i	10m
Tests to 10.9.07	27	24	13	0	–	–	3.25	–	0	0
ODIs to 10.9.07	45	0	–	–	–	–	–	–	–	–
First-class to 10.9.07	131	861	382	8	2–24	47.75	2.66	107.62	0	0

RUDRA PRATAP **SINGH**

Full name **Rudra Pratap Singh**
Born **December 6, 1985, Rae Bareli, Uttar Pradesh**
Teams **Uttar Pradesh, Leicestershire**
Style **Right-hand bat, left-arm fast-medium bowler**
Test debut **India v Pakistan at Faisalabad 2005-06**
ODI debut **India v Zimbabwe at Harare 2005-06**

INDIA

THE PROFILE Rudra Pratap Singh first made the headlines in the Under-19 World Cup in Bangladesh in 2004, taking eight wickets at 24.75 apiece and bowling well in the slog overs at the end of the innings. Later that year he joined the conveyor belt of Indian left-arm seamers, taking 34 wickets in six Ranji Trophy games for Uttar Pradesh, the joint-highest for the summer. He made the national one-day squad at the end of 2005, and took two wickets in his second over of international cricket, against Zimbabwe at Harare in September. He took four wickets (and the match award) against Sri Lanka in his third game, and three more in his fourth, before a run of four wicketless matches cost him his place after the first match of the West Indies tour in May 2006. He also won a couple of Test caps, winning the match award on his debut for some persistent bowling on a shirtfront at Faisalabad, where Pakistan ran up 588. He drifted out of contention after that, but was well respected in the Indian set-up, as Virender Sehwag confirmed: "RP is a very talented bowler – his specialty is that he can bring the ball into the right-handers and swing it both ways." He put an early-season stint with Leicestershire to good use in 2007, forcing his way into the side for the three-Test series against England. He took 5 for 59 in a tidy display of swing bowling at Lord's, knocking over Michael Vaughan in both innings, troubling him with a round-the-wicket approach and whistling the ball in.

THE FACTS RP Singh won the Man of the Match award on his Test debut – even though there were six centuries in the match, at Faisalabad in January 2006: Singh took 4 for 89 in Pakistan's first innings of 588 ... He averages 15.25 with the ball in ODIs against Sri Lanka, and 17.62 v Pakistan ... Singh took 2 for 25 in the semi-final of the Under-19 World Cup in February 2004 – but Pakistan still won by two wickets ...

THE FIGURES
Batting and fielding

www.cricinfo.com

	M	Inns	NO	Runs	HS	Avge	S/R	100	50	4s	6s	Ct	St
Tests to 10.9.07	7	7	2	36	17	7.20	33.96	0	0	4	0	3	0
ODIs to 10.9.07	30	12	7	39	12*	7.80	43.82	0	0	1	0	8	0
First-class to 10.9.07	32	41	10	279	41*	9.00	–	0	0	–	–	13	0

Bowling

	M	Balls	Runs	Wkts	BB	Avge	RpO	S/R	5i	10m
Tests to 10.9.07	7	1305	822	27	5–59	30.44	3.77	48.33	0	0
ODIs to 10.9.07	30	1344	1099	37	4–35	29.70	4.90	36.32	0	0
First-class to 10.9.07	32	5885	3167	127	5–33	24.93	3.22	46.33	7	1

DEVON **SMITH**

Full name **Devon Sheldon Smith**
Born **Oct 21, 1981, Hermitage, Sauters, St Patrick, Grenada**
Teams **Windward Islands**
Style **Left-hand bat, occasional offspinner**
Test debut **West Indies v Australia at Georgetown 2002-03**
ODI debut **West Indies v Australia at Kingston 2002-03**

THE PROFILE A belligerent left-handed opener whose eye makes up for a lack of footwork, Grenada's Devon Smith was drafted into the Test squad for the home series against India early in 2002, after making 750 runs for Windward Islands in the Busta Cup. He didn't play, though, and made his debut against Australia the following year. Smith blazed 62 in his first Test, but bagged a pair in the next one. Early in 2004 he dragged West Indies out of a hole with a stroke-filled century against England on the first day of the series at Kingston. But just as he began to settle in, he fractured a thumb in the nets: he missed the next two Tests, then was dropped after three failures in the return series in England. He started the 2005-06 Australian tour well, making a hundred against Queensland then 88 in the first Test at Brisbane, but five single-figure scores followed, and the axe fell again. In one-dayers he has been rather overshadowed by another Smith, the unrelated Dwayne, but both played in the 2007 World Cup, Devon making 61 in West Indies' last match, the thriller against England, which ensured him another English tour. He made several starts in the Tests there, crunching some classy cover-drives, but too often got out when set, making five scores between 16 and 42 before a double failure at The Oval. He remains another under-achiever in a West Indian side rather too full of them.

THE FACTS Smith scored 61 (in 34 balls) in his only Twenty20 international, against England at The Oval in June 2007 ... His highest first-class score is 181, for West Indies A against Lancashire at Liverpool in July 2002: he also made 180 for the Windward Islands against Kenya at Kingstown in February 2004, when he shared an opening stand of 309 with Romel Currency ... Smith has never played a Test or an ODI against Sri Lanka or Zimbabwe ...

THE FIGURES
Batting and fielding www.cricinfo.com

	M	Inns	NO	Runs	HS	Avge	S/R	100	50	4s	6s	Ct	St
Tests to 10.9.07	20	37	1	882	108	24.55	46.45	1	3	131	0	18	0
ODIs to 10.9.07	19	17	2	394	61	26.26	65.77	0	1	43	1	7	0
First-class to 10.9.07	95	171	6	6014	181	36.44	–	13	30	–	–	81	0

Bowling

	M	Balls	Runs	Wkts	BB	Avge	RpO	S/R	5i	10m
Tests to 10.9.07	20	0	–	–	–	–	–	–	–	–
ODIs to 10.9.07	19	0	–	–	–	–	–	–	–	–
First-class to 10.9.07	95	354	172	2	1–2	86.00	2.91	177.00	0	0

DWAYNE **SMITH**

Full name	**Dwayne Romel Smith**
Born	**April 12, 1983, Storey Gap, St Michael, Barbados**
Teams	**Barbados**
Style	**Right-hand bat, right-arm medium-pace bowler**
Test debut	**West Indies v South Africa at Cape Town 2003-04**
ODI debut	**West Indies v South Africa at Cape Town 2003-04**

THE PROFILE Tall, aggressive and powerful, Dwayne Smith shares his name with the wide receiver for the Wisconsin Badgers, and the 2002 world champion of Public Speaking – and when he was called up to join the West Indian Test squad in South Africa in December 2003, he was about as well known in cricket circles as either of them. All that changed, however, on the final day of the third Test at Cape Town, where he put the calypso back into Caribbean cricket with a wonderful debut century. Smith had been given a surprise opportunity – ahead of his Grenadian namesake Devon – when Marlon Samuels flew home with a knee injury. It was rumoured that Viv Richards had recognised something of himself in the stance of the young Barbadian and, sure enough, he needed just 93 balls to justify his selection, bringing up only the second century of his first-class career with a crashing cover-drive. It was enough to stem West Indies' run of seven consecutive defeats in South Africa. His batting reflects both his temperament and his youth: he's still inclined to lose his wicket through careless strokeplay, and he made starts, but no more, in his next few Tests before the selectors lost patience. He has had more one-day opportunities, maintaining a strike rate that is healthier than his average: he struggled with the bat at the 2007 World Cup, and by June had gone 43 ODIs – over more than two years – without passing 38. But his one-day case is boosted by his athletic fielding, and his handy medium-pacers, with which he grabbed 5 for 45 against New Zealand at Auckland in March 2006.

THE FACTS Smith was the 11th West Indian to make a century on his Test debut, but only the third from Barbados (after Conrad Hunte and Gordon Greenidge) and the first to do it against South Africa: his 93-ball effort is believed to be the fastest ton on debut in Tests ... He has the best strike rate (101.54) of any West Indian who has scored more than 500 runs in ODIs ... Smith hit 103 not out off just 70 balls for the West Indies Board XI v Bangladesh in Grenada in May 2004 ...

THE FIGURES
Batting and fielding

www.cricinfo.com

	M	Inns	NO	Runs	HS	Avge	S/R	100	50	4s	6s	Ct	St
Tests *to 10.9.07*	10	14	1	320	105*	24.61	70.02	1	0	47	6	9	0
ODIs *to 10.9.07*	71	56	3	791	68	14.92	101.54	0	2	62	40	24	0
First-class *to 10.9.07*	55	91	5	2306	114	26.81	–		5	6	–	–	59	0

Bowling

	M	Balls	Runs	Wkts	BB	Avge	RpO	S/R	5i	10m
Tests *to 10.9.07*	10	651	344	7	3–71	49.14	3.17	93.00	0	0
ODIs *to 10.9.07*	71	2264	1813	49	5–45	37.00	4.80	46.20	1	0
First-class *to 10.9.07*	55	4403	2154	78	4–22	27.61	2.93	56.44	0	0

GRAEME **SMITH**

Full name	**Graeme Craig Smith**
Born	**February 1, 1981, Johannesburg, Transvaal**
Teams	**Cape Cobras**
Style	**Left-hand bat, occasional offspinner**
Test debut	**South Africa v Australia at Cape Town 2001-02**
ODI debut	**South Africa v Australia at Bloemfontein 2001-02**

THE PROFILE In March 2003, at just 22, Graeme Smith became South Africa's youngest captain, when Shaun Pollock was dumped after a disastrous World Cup. A tall, aggressive left-hand opener, Smith had few leadership credentials – and only a handful of caps – but the selectors' faith was instantly justified: in England in 2003 he collected back-to-back double-centuries. Reality bit back in 2004, with Test series defeats to India and Sri Lanka. There was also a run of 11 losses in 12 ODIs, the start of an ultimately fruitless Test series with England, and personal humiliation after some Stephen Fleming mind games in Auckland. Yet Smith continued to crunch runs aplenty, and his 125 to square the series in New Zealand was a minor epic. He yields to no-one physically, but can be subdued by more insidious means: by the end of 2004, as Matthew Hoggard's inswinger had him frequently fumbling around his front pad, even the runs started to dry up. But he roared back in the West Indies in 2005, with hundreds in three successive Tests. Then, early in 2006, he orchestrated a 3-2 home win over Australia in probably the greatest one-day series ever played. Smith kick-started his side's reply to 434 for 4 in the decider at Johannesburg with 90 from 55 balls, adding 187 with Herschelle Gibbs in just 20.1 overs. South Africa eventually won with a ball to spare. He did well at the 2007 World Cup, except when it really mattered – a wild stroke gifted Nathan Bracken his wicket as South Africa subsided to Australia in the semi, ensuring that their reputation as "chokers" (one that Smith detests, and denies) lives on.

THE FACTS In the first Test against England in 2003 Smith scored 277 at Birmingham, the highest score by a South African in Tests: in the second he made 259, the highest Test score by a visiting player at Lord's, beating Don Bradman's 254 in 1930 ... He averages 76.91 in Tests against West Indies – but only 22.25 against Australia ... Smith played four matches for Somerset in 2005, scoring 311 against Leicestershire in one of them ... His record includes one Test for the World XI (as captain), and one ODI for the Africa XI ...

THE FIGURES

Batting and fielding   www.cricinfo.com

	M	Inns	NO	Runs	HS	Avge	S/R	100	50	4s	6s	Ct	St
Tests to 10.9.07	54	96	5	4285	277	47.08	60.36	11	18	562	14	65	0
ODIs to 10.9.07	117	115	7	4296	134*	39.77	82.61	6	29	508	27	58	0
First-class to 10.9.07	89	156	10	7114	311	48.72	–		19	27	–	–	119	0

Bowling

	M	Balls	Runs	Wkts	BB	Avge	RpO	S/R	5i	10m
Tests to 10.9.07	54	1265	750	8	2-145	93.75	3.55	158.12	0	0
ODIs to 10.9.07	117	1026	951	18	3-30	52.83	5.56	57.00	0	0
First-class to 10.9.07	89	1633	997	11	2-145	90.63	3.66	148.45	0	0

SREESANTH

INDIA

Full name	**Shanthakumaran Sreesanth**
Born	**February 6, 1983, Kothamangalam, Kerala**
Teams	**Kerala**
Style	**Right-hand bat, right-arm fast-medium bowler**
Test debut	**India v England at Nagpur 2005-06**
ODI debut	**India v Sri Lanka at Nagpur 2005-06**

THE PROFILE For three seasons, Sreesanth was little more than an answer to a trivia question: who's the only Kerala bowler to have taken a Ranji Trophy hat-trick? He started as a legspinner, idolising Anil Kumble, then once he turned to pace his rise was rapid but, since he played for a weak side, unnoticed. Not too many bowlers are selected for the Duleep Trophy in their first season, but Sreesanth was, in 2002-03 after taking 22 wickets in his first seven games. His progress was halted by a hamstring injury the following year, but he returned stronger, with a more side-on action and increased pace, and a superb display at the 2005 Challenger Trophy – trial matches for the national squad – propelled him into the side for the Sri Lanka series. Later he snapped up 6 for 55 against England, the best one-day figures by an Indian fast bowler at home. Idiosyncratic, with an aggressive approach – to the stumps and the game – he can be expensive in one-dayers, but is also a wicket-taking bowler. He does it in Tests, too – in Antigua in June 2006 he fired out Ramnaresh Sarwan and Brian Lara (for 0) in successive overs. "People think I am high-strung," he says of his whole-hearted approach. "In fact, it's been a habit with me for a long time, this constant revving-up, something like brushing my teeth." He rubbed a few of his opponents up the wrong way in England in 2007, sending down a beamer to Kevin Pietersen then overstepping by a yard for a bouncer at Paul Collingwood, while a barge on Michael Vaughan earned him a fine from the referee. But there is talent among the tantrums: he took nine wickets in the series, which England won.

THE FACTS Sreesanth took a hat-trick for Kerala against Himachal Pradesh in the Ranji Trophy in November 2004 ... He is only the second man from Kerala to play for India, after Tinu Yohannan, another fast-medium bowler ... Sreesanth did not score a run in ODIs until his 16th match, although that was only his fourth innings ... Over a quarter (26%) of his Test wickets have been lbws, including Paul Collingwood and Monty Panesar twice ...

THE FIGURES

Batting and fielding   www.cricinfo.com

	M	Inns	NO	Runs	HS	Avge	S/R	100	50	4s	6s	Ct	St
Tests to 10.9.07	11	17	6	167	35	15.18	64.47	0	0	22	3	2	0
ODIs to 10.9.07	29	9	4	7	3	1.40	25.00	0	0	0	0	3	0
First-class to 10.9.07	39	53	18	338	35	9.65	44.82	0	0	–	–	7	0

Bowling

	M	Balls	Runs	Wkts	BB	Avge	RpO	S/R	5i	10m
Tests to 10.9.07	11	2387	1299	46	5–40	28.23	3.26	51.89	1	0
ODIs to 10.9.07	29	1407	1328	38	6–55	34.94	5.66	37.02	1	0
First-class to 10.9.07	39	7163	3891	124	5–40	31.37	3.25	57.76	3	0

SOUTH AFRICA

DALE **STEYN**

Full name	**Dale Willem Steyn**
Born	**June 27, 1983, Phalaborwa, Limpopo Province**
Teams	**Titans, Warwickshire**
Style	**Right-hand bat, right-arm fast bowler**
Test debut	**South Africa v England at Port Elizabeth 2004-05**
ODI debut	**Africa XI v Asia XI at Centurion 2005-06**

THE PROFILE Dale Steyn's rise to the South African side was as rapid as his bowling: he was picked for the first Test against England in December 2004 little more than a season after his first-class debut. He is genuinely fast, and moves the ball away from the right-hander. He sprints up to the wicket and hurls the ball down aggressively, often following up with a snarl for the batsman, *à la* Allan Donald. He took eight wickets in three Tests against England before returning to the finishing school of domestic cricket. He missed the massacres that followed against Zimbabwe, and the West Indian tour. He was recalled in April 2006, and responded with his first five-wicket haul as New Zealand were routed in the first Test at Centurion. Seven more wickets followed in the third match at Johannesburg, which South Africa also won, as the partnership of Steyn and Makhaya Ntini looked ever more promising. He couldn't quite nail down a regular spot, though, despite six wickets in a win over India at Cape Town in January 2007. He had half a season of county cricket with Essex in 2005, after being recommended by Darren Gough, and although his wickets were expensive he took the chance to polish his previously negligible batting, improving his highest score from 11 to 82 after going in as a nightwatchman against Durham. He also rattled a few helmets during a stint with Warwickshire in 2007. Steyn is a rare first-class cricketer from the far north of South Africa, close to the Zimbabwean border – he was born in Phalaborwa, just two miles from the Kruger National Park in Limpopo Province.

THE FACTS Steyn improved his highest first-class score by 745% when he scored 82 for Essex v Durham in July 2005: his previous-highest was 11 ... He was the leading wicket-taker in South African first-class cricket in 2005-06, with 68 at 20.95 ... Steyn made his official ODI debut for the Africa XI, and his record includes two matches for them ...

THE FIGURES

Batting and fielding

www.cricinfo.com

	M	Inns	NO	Runs	HS	Avge	S/R	100	50	4s	6s	Ct	St
Tests to 10.9.07	11	17	6	80	13	7.27	32.00	0	0	9	1	2	0
ODIs to 10.9.07	7	2	0	4	3	2.00	26.66	0	0	0	0	0	0
First-class to 10.9.07	48	59	17	514	82	12.23	52.18	0	2	–	–	7	0

Bowling

	M	Balls	Runs	Wkts	BB	Avge	RpO	S/R	5i	10m
Tests to 10.9.07	11	2040	1375	42	5–47	31.54	3.89	48.57	2	0
ODIs to 10.9.07	7	247	262	9	3–65	29.11	6.36	27.44	0	0
First-class to 10.9.07	48	9069	5080	178	5–27	28.53	3.36	50.94	8	1

ANDREW **STRAUSS**

Full name	**Andrew John Strauss**
Born	**March 2, 1977, Johannesburg, South Africa**
Teams	**Middlesex**
Style	**Left-hand bat**
Test debut	**England v New Zealand at Lord's 2004**
ODI debut	**England v Sri Lanka at Dambulla 2003-04**

THE PROFILE Andrew Strauss, a fluid and attractive left-hand opener, had a rapid rise to prominence. His stock rose after Angus Fraser stood down as Middlesex's captain to write for *The Independent*. Strauss filled the breach admirably: 1400 runs in 2003, his first full season in charge, proved he was unfazed by responsibility. He was born in Johannesburg, but – schooled at Radley College and Durham University – is a very English product. At the crease, there is something of Graham Thorpe about his ability to accumulate runs without recourse to big shots, and it was this that first earned him a one-day place in 2003-04. He confirmed his star quality – and his affinity for Lord's – with a century on Test debut against New Zealand (hastening Nasser Hussain's retirement) in May 2004, and added another in his first ODI there, against West Indies two months later. But that was only a warm-up: in South Africa that winter, Strauss won the first Test almost single-handedly with 126 and 94 not out, and added two further hundreds on his way to 656 runs in the series. In 2005 he overcame initial uncertainties against McGrath and, especially, Warne to record two more tons in England's historic Ashes victory. Things have gone less swimmingly since: after seven hundreds in his first 19 Tests, the next 24 produced only three, as bowlers probed outside off and fed a penchant for a rather uppish pull/hook. The one-day runs dried up, too, and by the end of 2007 Straus had been returned for a refresher course in county cricket.

THE FACTS Strauss was the 15th Englishman (but the first for 11 years) to score a century on Test debut, with 112 v New Zealand at Lord's in May 2004: he was run out for 83 in the second innings ... In July 2006 he became only the third man to make a century on debut as England captain, following Archie MacLaren (1897-98) and Allan Lamb (1989-90) ... England have never lost a Test in which Strauss has scored a century ... Strauss opened with Ben Hutton – who was also born in Johannesburg – for school (Radley), university (Durham) and county (Middlesex) ...

THE FIGURES

Batting and fielding

	M	Inns	NO	Runs	HS	Avge	S/R	100	50	4s	6s	Ct	St
Tests *to 10.9.07*	43	81	2	3223	147	40.79	50.36	10	11	411	6	51	0
ODIs *to 10.9.07*	78	77	7	2239	152	31.98	75.82	2	14	240	8	28	0
First-class *to 10.9.07*	140	249	12	9625	176	40.61	–		23	44	–	–	107	0

Bowling

	M	Balls	Runs	Wkts	BB	Avge	RpO	S/R	5i	10m
Tests *to 10.9.07*	43	0	–	–	–	–	–	–	–	–
ODIs *to 10.9.07*	78	6	3	0	–	–	3.00	–	0	0
First-class *to 10.9.07*	140	84	74	2	1–16	37.00	5.28	42.00	0	0

SCOTT **STYRIS**

Full name	**Scott Bernard Styris**
Born	**July 10, 1975, Brisbane, Australia**
Teams	**Auckland, Durham**
Style	**Right-hand bat, right-arm medium-pacer**
Test debut	**New Zealand v West Indies at St George's 2001-02**
ODI debut	**New Zealand v India at Rajkot 1999-2000**

THE PROFILE Scott Styris, who was born in Australia but moved to New Zealand when he was six, had a long apprenticeship in domestic cricket, playing almost ten years for Northern Districts before finally making the Test side. By the time of his debut, in Grenada in June 2002, he had been a one-day regular for three years, and had done nothing to suggest that he was a Test batsman – he had 418 runs at 16 in 40 ODIs, and was regarded more as a containing medium-pacer. But he thumped an uncomplicated 107 in his first Test innings, added 69 not out in the second, and has been a fixture ever since, latterly adding solidity at the giddy heights of No. 4 – from where, in March 2004, his 170 set up a winning total against South Africa at Auckland. On that 2002 tour of the Caribbean Styris took 6 for 25 at Port-of-Spain, New Zealand's best ODI bowling analysis at the time (since beaten by Shane Bond, twice). Coach John Bracewell has encouraged him to work on his offspin, as an option that would put less strain on his body than his energetic military mediums, but this has yet to be unveiled outside the nets. Styris continued to score consistently – for Middlesex, for his new province Auckland, and for New Zealand. A back injury kept him out of the home series against Sri Lanka in December 2006, but he was fit in time for the World Cup, where he never failed to reach double figures in nine visits to the crease, including 87 against England, 80 against West Indies and 111 against Sri Lanka – all not out – and he finished with 499 runs at 83.16.

THE FACTS Styris was the seventh New Zealander to score a century on Test debut, following Jackie Mills, Bruce Taylor, Rodney Redmond, Mark Greatbatch, Mathew Sinclair and Lou Vincent ... He averages only 16.83 in ODIs against Australia, despite making 101 against them at Christchurch in 2005-06 ... He has made two centuries in the World Cup, but finished on the losing side both times ... Styris was actually awarded his first cap on the eve of the Karachi Test against Pakistan in May 2002, only for it to be taken back when the match was cancelled after a bomb blast ...

THE FIGURES

Batting and fielding

www.cricinfo.com

	M	Inns	NO	Runs	HS	Avge	S/R	100	50	4s	6s	Ct	St
Tests *to 10.9.07*	27	44	4	1527	170	38.17	51.83	5	6	196	13	23	0
ODIs *to 10.9.07*	133	114	15	3158	141	31.89	78.65	4	19	245	51	52	0
First-class *to 10.9.07*	114	189	18	5391	212*	31.52	–	9	26	–	–	88	0

Bowling

	M	Balls	Runs	Wkts	BB	Avge	RpO	S/R	5i	10m
Tests *to 10.9.07*	27	1906	981	20	3–28	49.04	3.08	95.29	0	0
ODIs *to 10.9.07*	133	4803	3784	116	6–25	32.62	4.72	41.40	1	0
First-class *to 10.9.07*	114	12436	6223	203	6–32	30.65	3.00	61.26	9	1

GRAEME **SWANN**

Full name	**Graeme Peter Swann**
Born	**March 24, 1979, Northampton**
Teams	**Nottinghamshire**
Style	**Right-hand bat, offspinner**
Test debut	**No Tests yet**
ODI debut	**South Africa v England at Bloemfontein 1999-2000**

THE PROFILE Self-confident and gregarious, Graeme Swann is an aggressive offspinner, not afraid to give the ball a real tweak, and a hard-hitting middle-order batsman. He made his maiden century for Northamptonshire in 1998, his first season, and was often promoted in one-dayers to provide oomph. Fast-tracked into the England A team in southern Africa, he took 21 wickets at 25.61, and averaged 22 with the bat. *Wisden* pronounced: "Swann did spin the ball appreciably ... he had the potential to become a genuine allrounder, with a wide range of attractive strokes, though he needs to use them more selectively." Called up for the final Test of England's inglorious summer of 1999, against New Zealand, he was eventually left out of the starting XI, but was rewarded with a place in the revamped England squad which toured South Africa that winter under new coach Duncan Fletcher. Swann found life outside the Test side frustrating, but did play an ODI, when he bravely continued to give the ball a rip. However, he was less impressive off the field – what some saw as confidence, others interpreted as arrogance or cheek – and slid out of the international reckoning. After marking time with Northants for a while, not helped by Monty Panesar's arrival, Swann packed his bags for Trent Bridge in 2005 – a decision immediately justified when he helped Nottinghamshire win the Championship that year. Improved returns in 2007 earned him an England recall for the winter tour on what were expected to be spinning tracks in Sri Lanka.

THE FACTS Swann took 7 for 33 (after not bowling in the first innings) for Northamptonshire against Derbyshire at Northampton in June 2003 ... He took 8 for 118 for England in an Under-19 Test against Pakistan at Taunton in 1998 ... Swann made 183 for Northants against Gloucestershire at Bristol in August 2002, helping Michael Hussey (310 not out) put on 318 for the sixth wicket ... Swann's brother Alec played for Northamptonshire and Lancashire ...

THE FIGURES

Batting and fielding   www.cricinfo.com

	M	Inns	NO	Runs	HS	Avge	S/R	100	50	4s	6s	Ct	St
Tests to 10.9.07	0	0	–	–	–	–	–	–	–	–	–	–	–
ODIs to 10.9.07	1	0	–	–	–	–	–	–	–	–	–	0	0
First-class to 10.9.07	157	222	15	5448	183	26.31	–	4	26	–	–	109	0

Bowling

	M	Balls	Runs	Wkts	BB	Avge	RpO	S/R	5i	10m
Tests to 10.9.07	0	0	–	–	–	–	–	–	–	–
ODIs to 10.9.07	1	30	24	0	–	–	4.80	–	0	0
First-class to 10.9.07	157	26284	13254	400	7–33	33.13	3.02	65.71	15	3

SYED RASEL

Full name	**Syed Rasel**
Born	**July 3, 1984, Jessore, Khulna**
Teams	**Khulna**
Style	**Left-hand bat, left-arm fast-medium bowler**
Test debut	**Bangladesh v Sri Lanka at Colombo 2005-06**
ODI debut	**Bangladesh v Sri Lanka at Colombo 2005-06**

THE PROFILE   A sensational spell of swing bowling for Bangladesh A against Kent at Canterbury in August 2005 propelled Syed Rasel into the international reckoning at the age of 21. He had missed the senior tour earlier in the season, but, having steadily developed his trade on a difficult five-week trip, Rasel tore through Kent's defences with 7 for 50 in the first innings, and finished with 10 for 91 in the match. It wasn't enough to win the game, but he was immediately drafted into the senior squad for the tour of Sri Lanka that followed in September, and he made his Test and one-day debuts there. With shades of Chaminda Vaas in his left-arm approach, he took six wickets in his first two matches, including 4 for 129 in the second Test in Colombo, a match that Bangladesh lost by an innings. Nevertheless, he soon had his revenge on home soil, taking 2 for 28 at Bogra the following February, as Sri Lanka slumped to their first-ever one-day defeat at Bangladesh's hands. Rasel rose through the ranks from divisional cricket in his home province of Khulna, and his ability to swing the ball at a decent pace sets him apart from many of his rivals. He injured his foot in a motorbike accident shortly before the Champions Trophy in India in October 2006, but recovered to play, and did enough over the season to claim a World Cup place. He troubled many batsmen in the Caribbean with his left-arm approach – he only once failed to take a wicket in seven starts – and seems set for a promising career.

THE FACTS   Fourteen of Syed Rasel's ODI wickets have come against Kenya (at 15.21), and 16 (at 28.25) against Sri Lanka ... He took 7 for 55 (11 for 109 in the match) for Khulna against Dhaka in Dhaka, and 8 for 67 against Barisal at Barisal, both in 2003-04 ... His first four Tests – and his sixth – were against Sri Lanka: he hasn't yet played an ODI against Pakistan ...

THE FIGURES

Batting and fielding

www.cricinfo.com

	M	Inns	NO	Runs	HS	Avge	S/R	100	50	4s	6s	Ct	St
Tests *to 10.9.07*	6	12	4	37	19	4.62	38.94	0	0	6	0	0	0
ODIs *to 10.9.07*	31	16	5	56	15	5.09	43.41	0	0	5	0	4	0
First-class *to 10.9.07*	36	54	14	394	33	10.10	43.87	0	0	–	–	6	0

Bowling

	M	Balls	Runs	Wkts	BB	Avge	RpO	S/R	5i	10m
Tests *to 10.9.07*	6	879	573	12	4–129	47.75	3.91	73.25	0	0
ODIs *to 10.9.07*	31	1647	1139	44	4–22	25.88	4.14	37.43	0	0
First-class *to 10.9.07*	36	5916	2957	95	8–67	31.12	2.99	62.27	3	2

ANDREW **SYMONDS**

AUSTRALIA

Full name	**Andrew Symonds**
Born	**June 9, 1975, Birmingham, Warwickshire, England**
Teams	**Queensland**
Style	**Right-hand bat, right-arm medium-pace or offbreaks**
Test debut	**Australia v Sri Lanka at Galle 2004**
ODI debut	**Australia v Pakistan at Lahore 1998-99**

THE PROFILE Andrew Symonds brings gusto to whatever he does, whether firing down offbreaks or medium-pacers, hurling his bulk around the outfield, or ruffling the bowler's hair after a wicket. He saves his loudest grunt for batting, where he is an unabashed six-hitter. For Gloucestershire, when only 20, he scythed a world-record 16 in an innings against Glamorgan, and 20 in the match (another record). His flaw has been to attempt one six too many: during four years in and out of the one-day side he wasted opportunities galore. But one day changed everything: striding out with Australia sinking against Pakistan during the 2003 World Cup – a tournament he never expected to play in – Symonds sculpted a masterly 143 from 125 balls. Until then, he had just 762 one-day runs at 23: ever since he has averaged around 50. He had more trouble cementing a Test place. He struggled in Sri Lanka in 2004, and was dumped after two Tests. Almost two years later he received an extended run as Australia tried to find a Flintoff, but couldn't reproduce that one-day consistency. Faced with the axe, he cracked a huge six – the first of five – against South Africa at the MCG to open his account in a pressure-relieving 72, but remained a borderline selection until, recalled after Damien Martyn's sudden retirement, he dug Australia out of a hole against England at Melbourne in December 2006 with a forthright 156, putting on 279 with his Queensland buddy Matthew Hayden. At last he looked at home in the Test side. There were concerns that a bicep injury would unbalance Australia in the shake-up for the 2007 World Cup – but Symonds regained full fitness and played his part as the Cup was retained.

THE FACTS Birmingham-born Symonds was voted *England's* Young Cricketer of the Year in 1995, but turned down a place on an England A tour that winter and pledged his future to Australia, where he grew up ... He played 71 ODIs before winning his first Test cap, a record at the time ... Symonds first came to notice in Queensland as a 13-year-old, after a partnership of 466 with Matthew Mott, who also went on to play first-class cricket ...

THE FIGURES

Batting and fielding   www.cricinfo.com

	M	Inns	NO	Runs	HS	Avge	S/R	100	50	4s	6s	Ct	St
Tests *to 10.9.07*	13	19	0	518	156	27.26	60.94	1	2	50	14	13	0
ODIs *to 10.9.07*	170	136	29	4226	156	39.49	92.31	5	22	378	84	72	0
First-class *to 10.9.07*	203	336	28	13124	254*	42.61	–	39	54	–	–	145	0

Bowling

	M	Balls	Runs	Wkts	BB	Avge	RpO	S/R	5i	10m
Tests *to 10.9.07*	13	1080	488	11	3–50	44.36	2.71	98.18	0	0
ODIs *to 10.9.07*	170	5588	4659	124	5–18	37.57	5.00	45.06	1	0
First-class *to 10.9.07*	203	15869	7900	218	6–105	36.23	2.98	72.79	2	0

SHAUN **TAIT**

Full name	**Shaun William Tait**
Born	**Feb 22, 1983, Bedford Park, Adelaide, South Australia**
Teams	**South Australia**
Style	**Right-hand bat, right-arm fast bowler**
Test debut	**Australia v England at Nottingham 2005**
ODI debut	**Australia v England at Sydney 2006-07**

THE PROFILE Shaun Tait's shoulder-strong action slung him on to the 2005 Ashes tour, where he played in two of the Tests, but it soon disrupted his quest for further impact. With a muscular but unrefined method that seems to invite pain, Tait returned from England only to hurt himself in a grade match. Shoulder surgery forced him out for the rest of the year, but fortunately there seemed to be no reduction in his frightening pace, which has sometimes been clocked above 99mph (160kph). An abbreviated 2005-06 season featured 6 for 41 in the domestic one-day final, an amazing combination of spot-on speed and 14 wides. His old-fashioned approach of yorkers and bumpers, mixed with a modern dose of reverse-swing, had brought him 65 wickets in 2004-05, his first full home season, earning him that Ashes trip and exciting followers to believe that Tait and Brett Lee might be the 21st century's version of Lillee and Thomson. A hamstring twang delayed Tait's ODI entry until February 2007, but despite mixed results (much speed, less accuracy) in his first four games he made the World Cup squad and, helped when Lee pulled out injured, was one of the stars in the Caribbean, blowing away 23 wickets, more than anyone except Glenn McGrath. Again there was a cost: he had to have elbow surgery in mid-2007. Another Lee injury had given Tait his first taste of international cricket, when he introduced himself to Ricky Ponting in the nets in Sri Lanka in 2003-04 by hitting him on the head with a bouncer.

THE FACTS Tait took 8 for 43 for South Australia v Tasmania at Adelaide in January 2004, the best figures in Australian domestic one-day cricket ... He played for Durham in 2004, bowling 21 no-balls in his first match, against Somerset, in figures of 12-0-113-0: in his second (and last) game the damage was 6-0-63-0 ... Tait took 23 wickets in the 2007 World Cup, equal with Muttiah Muralitharan and behind only Glenn McGrath (26) ... His best first-class figures are 7 for 99, for SA v Queensland at Adelaide in November 2004 ...

THE FIGURES

Batting and fielding   www.cricinfo.com

	M	Inns	NO	Runs	HS	Avge	S/R	100	50	4s	6s	Ct	St
Tests *to 10.9.07*	2	3	2	8	4	8.00	29.62	0	0	1	0	0	0
ODIs *to 10.9.07*	15	1	0	11	11	11.00	110.00	0	0	1	1	1	0
First-class *to 10.9.07*	43	61	26	443	68	12.65	50.97	0	2	–	–	10	0

Bowling

	M	Balls	Runs	Wkts	BB	Avge	RpO	S/R	5i	10m
Tests *to 10.9.07*	2	288	210	5	3–97	42.00	4.37	57.60	0	0
ODIs *to 10.9.07*	15	741	685	28	4–39	24.46	5.54	26.46	0	0
First-class *to 10.9.07*	43	7838	4756	174	7–99	27.33	3.64	45.04	6	0

TAMIM IQBAL

Full name	**Tamim Iqbal Khan**
Born	**March 20, 1989, Chittagong**
Teams	**Chittagong**
Style	**Left-hand bat**
Test debut	**No Tests yet**
ODI debut	**Bangladesh v Zimbabwe at Harare 2006-07**

THE PROFILE The flamboyant left-hander Tamim Iqbal is one of Bangladesh's most assured young batsmen, and one of their hardest hitters. Included in the 2007 World Cup squad after just four ODIs – in which he amassed only 57 runs against Zimbabwe, Bermuda and Canada – Tamim proceeded to light up the start of the competition with 51 off only 53 balls to ensure that Bangladesh's pursuit of India's modest 191 got off to a flying start. Shrugging off a blow on the neck when he missed a hook at Zaheer Khan, Tamim jumped down the wicket and smashed him over midwicket for six. Bangladesh duly administered the victory which virtually ensured that they, not India, would progress to the Super Eights. All this came three days before the 18th birthday of a player with cricket in his veins: Tamim, who is also a fine fielder, has recently overshadowed his older brother, Nafees Iqbal, who has also opened for Bangladesh, while their uncle Akram Khan was a former national captain. Tamim, who hates to get bogged down, has struggled to reproduce this form since – it wasn't until his 18th ODI, in Sri Lanka in July 2007, that he reached 50 again. Before his World Cup adventures, his most notable innings came for the Under-19s against England at the end of 2005, when he flayed 112 from just 71 balls, with six sixes. He is particularly strong square of the wicket, and has a good flick shot, but his almost premeditated charges down the track – while spectacular – sometimes bring his downfall.

THE FACTS Tamim Iqbal scored 112 in 71 balls for Bangladesh Under-19s v England in a one-day game at Fatullah in December 2005 ... His two first-class centuries came within a week in March 2006, 118 and 113 for Chittagong against Dhaka and Sylhet ... Tamim's brother, Nafees Iqbal, has played 11 Tests and 18 ODIs for Bangladesh, while their uncle, Akram Khan, played eight Tests and 44 ODIs, and captained them in pre-Test days ...

THE FIGURES
Batting and fielding   www.cricinfo.com

	M	Inns	NO	Runs	HS	Avge	S/R	100	50	4s	6s	Ct	St
Tests *to 10.9.07*	0	0	–	–	–	–	–	–	–	–	–	–	–
ODIs *to 10.9.07*	18	18	0	349	54	19.38	62.65	0	2	42	5	8	0
First-class *to 10.9.07*	12	20	1	824	118	43.36	80.70	2	5	–	–	4	0

Bowling

	M	Balls	Runs	Wkts	BB	Avge	RpO	S/R	5i	10m
Tests *to 10.9.07*	0	0	–	–	–	–	–	–	–	–
ODIs *to 10.9.07*	18	0	–	–	–	–	–	–	–	–
First-class *to 10.9.07*	12	24	15	0	–	–	3.75	–	0	0

JEROME **TAYLOR**

Full name	**Jerome Everton Taylor**
Born	**June 22, 1984, St Elizabeth, Jamaica**
Teams	**Jamaica, Leicestershire**
Style	**Right-hand bat, right-arm fast bowler**
Test debut	**West Indies v Sri Lanka at Gros Islet 2002-03**
ODI debut	**West Indies v Sri Lanka at Kingstown 2002-03**

THE PROFILE Jerome Taylor was just 18, with a solitary limited-overs game for Jamaica to his name, when he was called into the squad for the final one-dayer of West Indies' home series against Sri Lanka in June 2003. It was the culmination of an explosive first season for Taylor, who was named the most promising fast bowler in the 2003 Carib Beer Series after picking up 21 wickets at 20.14 in six first-class matches. That haul included a second-innings 8 for 59 in Jamaica's five-wicket victory over Trinidad & Tobago. After a persistent back injury, he bounced back with 26 more wickets at 16.61 in the 2004-05 Carib Beer Cup, which – along with the prolonged contracts dispute which opened up places in the squad – helped him force his way back into international contention. He had a quiet tour of New Zealand early in 2006, bowling tightly in the one-dayers but playing only one Test. However, the inexperienced Zimbabweans found Taylor's pace too hot to handle in the Caribbean shortly afterwards: he took 2 for 19 and 4 for 24 in the first two games, winning the match award in both. He continued his good form when the Indians arrived, taking three wickets as West Indies picked up a consolation victory at the end of the one-day series, then collecting nine – including his first five-wicket haul – in vain in the deciding Test at Kingston in July 2006. He impressed in one-dayers in 2006-07, with 13 wickets in the Champions Trophy, and showed occasional signs of fire in the Tests in England in 2007, but without much success: he was left out of the squad for the one-day series that followed.

THE FACTS Taylor was 18 years 363 days old when he made his Test debut in June 2003: only six men have played for West Indies at a younger age, the most recent of them Garry Sobers in 1953-54 and Alfie Roberts two years later ... Taylor took 8 for 59 (10 for 81 in the match) in only his third first-class game, for Jamaica v Trinidad & Tobago at Port-of-Spain in March 2003 ... He also took 10 for 104 as the West Indians drew with Zimbabwe A in Harare in 2003-04 ...

THE FIGURES

Batting and fielding

www.cricinfo.com

	M	Inns	NO	Runs	HS	Avge	S/R	100	50	4s	6s	Ct	St
Tests *to 10.9.07*	13	21	4	164	23*	9.64	50.15	0	0	21	1	1	0
ODIs *to 10.9.07*	35	13	5	65	13	8.12	73.86	0	0	6	0	9	0
First-class *to 10.9.07*	42	63	14	535	40	10.91	–	0	0	–	–	10	0

Bowling

	M	Balls	Runs	Wkts	BB	Avge	RpO	S/R	5i	10m
Tests *to 10.9.07*	13	2266	1389	35	5–50	39.68	3.67	64.74	2	0
ODIs *to 10.9.07*	35	1796	1455	49	4–24	29.69	4.86	36.65	0	0
First-class *to 10.9.07*	42	6401	3412	134	8–59	25.46	3.19	47.76	9	2

ROSS **TAYLOR**

Full name	**Ross Luteru Taylor**
Born	**March 8, 1984, Lower Hutt, Wellington**
Teams	**Central Districts**
Style	**Right-hand bat, offspinner**
Test debut	**No Tests yet**
ODI debut	**New Zealand v West Indies at Napier 2005-06**

THE PROFILE Ross Taylor was singled out for attention from an early age – he captained New Zealand in the 2001-02 Under-19 World Cup – but it was only in 2005 that he made the breakthrough to the senior ranks. He started the year by extending his maiden first-class century to 184, then began the following season with such a bang that the selectors were bound to come calling. An innings of 107 – with five sixes – in a warm-up game against Otago was followed by an identical score in a State Shield one-dayer, also against Otago, in January 2006. He then cracked 121 against Wellington, 114 (yes, Otago again) in the semi-final, then 50 in the final against Canterbury. Taylor rounded off a fine season with 106 as CD won the State Championship final at Wellington. He finished with 537 first-class runs at 38, and 649 in one-dayers at an average of 59 and a breakneck strike rate. "The way he's batting he could bludgeon any attack," said Mathew Sinclair, a provincial team-mate. It all led to a call-up for the final two one-dayers of West Indies' tour early in 2006, and a regular one-day place the following season. He flogged Sri Lanka – Murali and all – for an unbeaten 128 in only his third ODI, and showed that was no fluke with an equally muscular 117 against Australia at Auckland in February 2007. All of this made him a cert for the World Cup, but he was a disappointment there, with his only score above 10 being 85 against Kenya. But time is on his side if he can resist the urge to go large too early in an innings.

THE FACTS Taylor has scored three of his four limited-overs centuries against Otago, and averages 87.20 against them ... He made his highest score of 217 for CD v Otago at Napier in December 2006 ... He hit 66 from 22 balls in a Twenty20 match against Otago in January 2006 ... Taylor won the 2002 New Zealand Young Player to Lord's scholarship, following the likes of Martin Crowe and Ken Rutherford ...

THE FIGURES
Batting and fielding

www.cricinfo.com

	M	Inns	NO	Runs	HS	Avge	S/R	100	50	4s	6s	Ct	St
Tests to 10.9.07	0	–	–	–	–	–	–	–	–	–	–	–	–
ODIs to 10.9.07	24	22	1	706	128*	33.61	81.05	2	3	77	10	15	0
First-class to 10.9.07	35	54	2	1914	217	36.80	–	3	11	–	–	29	0

Bowling

	M	Balls	Runs	Wkts	BB	Avge	RpO	S/R	5i	10m
Tests to 10.9.07	0	0	–	–	–	–	–	–	–	–
ODIs to 10.9.07	24	12	16	0	–	–	8.00	–	0	0
First-class to 10.9.07	35	510	298	4	2–34	74.50	3.50	127.50	0	0

SACHIN **TENDULKAR**

Full name	**Sachin Ramesh Tendulkar**
Born	**April 24, 1973, Bombay**
Teams	**Mumbai**
Style	**Right-hand bat, occasional medium-pace/legspin**
Test debut	**India v Pakistan at Karachi 1989-90**
ODI debut	**India v Pakistan at Gujranwala 1989-90**

THE PROFILE You only have to attend a one-dayer at the Wankhede Stadium, and watch the lights flicker and the floor tremble as the massive wave of applause echoes around the ground when he comes in, to realise what Sachin Tendulkar means to Mumbai ... and India. Age, and troublesome elbow and shoulder injuries, may have dimmed the light a little – he's now more of a accumulator than an artist – but he's still light-footed with bat in hand, the nearest thing to Bradman, as The Don himself recognised before his death. Sachin seems to have been around for ever: that's because he made his Test debut at 16 in 1989, shrugging off a blow on the head against Pakistan; captivated England in 1990, with a maiden Test century; and similarly enchanted Australians in 1991-92. He leads the list of ODI and World Cup run-scorers by a country mile, and owns the records for most centuries in Tests and one-dayers too. Fitness and desire permitting, he could reach 100 hundreds in international cricket before he's done. Until he throttled back in his thirties, he usually looked to attack, but although Dravid may average more now, and Sehwag is more explosive, Tendulkar's is the wicket the opposition want. Small, steady at the crease before a decisive move forward or back, he remains a master, and his whipped flick to fine leg is an object of wonder. He could have starred as a bowler, as he can do offbreaks, legbreaks, or dobbly medium-pacers, and remains a handy option, especially in one-dayers.

THE FACTS Tendulkar passed his childhood idol Sunil Gavaskar's record of 34 Test centuries in December 2005, with 109 v Sri Lanka at Delhi: in seven Tests afterwards his highest score was 34 ... No one is close to his record of 41 ODI centuries – Sanath Jayasuriya is next with 25 ... He has hit seven centuries against Australia and Sri Lanka in both Tests and ODIs ... Tendulkar's first mark on the record books came when he was 14, in an unbroken stand of 664 with another future Test batsman, Vinod Kambli, in a school game ... He was Yorkshire's first official overseas player, in 1992 ...

THE FIGURES

Batting and fielding

www.cricinfo.com

	M	Inns	NO	Runs	HS	Avge	S/R	100	50	4s	6s	Ct	St
Tests *to 10.9.07*	140	226	23	11150	248*	54.92	–	37	45	–	42	93	0
ODIs *to 10.9.07*	395	385	37	15425	186*	44.32	85.63	41	83	1669	163	116	0
First-class *to 10.9.07*	239	373	38	19894	248*	59.38	–	63	91	–	–	160	0

Bowling

	M	Balls	Runs	Wkts	BB	Avge	RpO	S/R	5i	10m
Tests *to 10.9.07*	140	3718	2135	42	3–10	50.83	3.44	88.52	0	0
ODIs *to 10.9.07*	395	7859	6645	152	5–32	43.70	5.07	51.70	2	0
First-class *to 10.9.07*	239	7077	4024	67	3–10	60.05	3.41	105.62	0	0

UPUL **THARANGA**

Full name	**Warushavithana Upul Tharanga**
Born	**February 2, 1985, Balapitiya**
Teams	**Nondescripts**
Style	**Left-hand bat, occasional wicketkeeper**
Test debut	**Sri Lanka v India at Ahmedabad 2005-06**
ODI debut	**Sri Lanka v West Indies at Dambulla 2005-06**

THE PROFILE   Upul Tharanga's call-up to Sri Lanka's one-day squad in July 2005 brightened a year marred by the Indian Ocean tsunami, which washed away his family home in Ambalangoda, a fishing town on the west coast. From an early age Tharanga, a wispy left-hander blessed with natural timing, had been tipped for the big time, playing premier-league cricket at 15 and passing seamlessly through the various national age-group squads. He first caught the eye during the Under-19 World Cup in Bangladesh early in 2004, with 117 against South Africa and 61 in 42 balls against India in the next game. Then, after a successful Under-19 tour of Pakistan, the Sri Lankan board sent him to play league cricket in Essex, where he did well for Loughton. In August 2005 he won his first one-day cap, and hit 105 against Bangladesh in only his fifth match – he celebrated modestly, aware that stiffer challenges lay ahead – and then pummelled 165 against them in his third Test. Another one-day hundred followed at Christchurch in January 2006, then he lit up Lord's with 120 in the first of what became five successive defeats of England: he added 109 in the fifth of those, at Headingley, sharing an ODI record opening stand with Sanath Jayasuriya. The feature of those innings was the way he made room to drive through the off side. Other opponents might not be so accommodating, but a bright future beckons for Tharanga, who can also keep wicket. He scored consistently during 2006-07, playing throughout the World Cup, scoring 73 in the semi-final against New Zealand.

THE FACTS   Tharanga and Sanath Jayasuriya put on 286 in 31.5 overs against England at Leeds in July 2006, a new first-wicket record for all ODIs: Tharanga made 109, his fourth one-day century ... He averages 68.16 in ODIs against England, but 9.75 v West Indies ... Tharanga made 165 and 71 not out in the ten-wicket defeat of Bangladesh at Bogra in March 2006 ... His record includes one ODI for the Asia XI ...

THE FIGURES

Batting and fielding   www.cricinfo.com

	M	Inns	NO	Runs	HS	Avge	S/R	100	50	4s	6s	Ct	St
Tests to 10.9.07	13	24	1	687	165	29.86	49.89	1	3	95	5	11	0
ODIs to 10.9.07	61	58	0	1928	120	33.24	73.16	6	9	231	5	11	0
First-class to 10.9.07	48	83	1	2431	165	29.64	–	4	12	–	–	44	0

Bowling

	M	Balls	Runs	Wkts	BB	Avge	RpO	S/R	5i	10m
Tests to 10.9.07	13	0	–	–	–	–	–	–	–	–
ODIs to 10.9.07	61	0	–	–	–	–	–	–	–	–
First-class to 10.9.07	48	0	–	–	–	–	–	–	–	–

CHRIS **TREMLETT**

Full name	**Christopher Timothy Tremlett**
Born	**September 2, 1981, Southampton, Hampshire**
Teams	**Hampshire**
Style	**Right-hand bat, right-arm fast bowler**
Test debut	**England v India at Lord's 2007**
ODI debut	**England v Bangladesh at Nottingham 2005**

THE PROFILE Chris Tremlett has the silent, simmering looks – and impressive sideburns – of a baddie in a spaghetti western, and bangs the ball down from an impressive height at an impressive speed. He has a fine cricket pedigree: his grandfather captained Somerset and played for England, while his father also played for Hampshire and is now their coach. But this Tremlett needed no nepotism: he took 4 for 16 on his first-class debut, for Hampshire against New Zealand A in 2000, and has rarely looked back since, halted only occasionally by niggling injuries (growing pains, perhaps – he's now 6ft 7ins tall). As he matured he was one of the first selected by then-coach Rod Marsh for the England Academy, and narrowly missed out on selection for the Champions Trophy in 2004. The following year he almost marked his ODI debut with a hat-trick at Lord's – the vital ball fell on the stumps without dislodging a bail – then was 12th man in the first four Tests of the epic Ashes series, before a loss of rhythm led to a loss of form. Another injury made him miss the start of the 2007 season, but as England's pacemen hit the treatment table Tremlett got the call. He used his height well, and collected 13 wickets in three Tests against India, including VVS Laxman three times, Rahul Dravid and Sachin Tendulkar. Tremlett is also a handy batsman, although he looked a little overplaced at No. 8 for England and bagged a pair on debut.

THE FACTS Tremlett's grandfather, Maurice, played three Tests for England in 1948: his father, Tim, also played for Hampshire and is now their coach ... Tremlett took two wickets in successive balls on his ODI debut, against Bangladesh at Trent Bridge in June 2005: the hat-trick ball bounced on top of the stumps but didn't dislodge the bails ... He bagged a pair on his Test debut in July 2007, the first person ever to do this at Lord's ... Tremlett took 6 for 44 for Hampshire against Sussex at Hove in April 2005 ...

THE FIGURES

Batting and fielding

www.cricinfo.com

	M	Inns	NO	Runs	HS	Avge	S/R	100	50	4s	6s	Ct	St
Tests *to 10.9.07*	3	5	1	50	25*	12.50	43.85	0	0	5	0	1	0
ODIs *to 10.9.07*	8	5	2	35	19*	11.66	70.00	0	0	2	1	1	0
First-class *to 10.9.07*	71	94	28	1247	64*	18.89	–	0	3	–	–	19	0

Bowling

	M	Balls	Runs	Wkts	BB	Avge	RpO	S/R	5i	10m
Tests *to 10.9.07*	3	859	386	13	3–12	29.69	2.69	66.07	0	0
ODIs *to 10.9.07*	8	419	395	8	4–32	49.37	5.65	52.37	0	0
First-class *to 10.9.07*	71	11935	6586	243	6–44	27.10	3.31	49.11	6	0

MARCUS **TRESCOTHICK**

ENGLAND

Full name	**Marcus Edward Trescothick**
Born	**December 25, 1975, Keynsham, Somerset**
Teams	**Somerset**
Style	**Left-hand bat, right-arm medium-pace bowler**
Test debut	**England v West Indies at Manchester 2000**
ODI debut	**England v Zimbabwe at The Oval 2000**

THE PROFILE There was something biblical about Marcus Trescothick's early career: seven years of schoolboy plenty, seven years of famine when he started with Somerset. And lo, it came to pass that he batted on a pacy pitch at Taunton while Duncan Fletcher was Glamorgan's coach in 1999, and hit 167. When England needed a one-day opener in 2000, Fletcher remembered Trescothick. Hefty, knock-kneed and genial, he was described by Nasser Hussain as a left-handed Gooch, but his ease on the big stage and his blazing strokeplay – a mixture of expert leaves, crisp cover-drives, spanking pulls and fearless slog-sweeps – were just as reminiscent of David Gower. All that held him back was a tendency to get out when well set. He seemed to have conquered this at home in 2002, but it reappeared – like so many English frailties – in Australia the following winter: Trescothick still has not made a Test hundred against them. He showed glimpses of his blazing best against South Africa in 2003, biffing 219 in the astonishing series-levelling victory at The Oval, but struggled in the Caribbean that winter. The selectors never lost faith, and Trescothick repaid them with twin tons against West Indies at Birmingham, and a brutal 180 at Johannesburg early in 2005. After bullying the Bangladeshis he spearheaded the batting against Australia with 431 runs. But then his career hit the buffers: a stress-related illness forced him home early from India in 2005-06 and then the Ashes rematch, and despite a prolific season for Somerset in 2007 he declared himself not ready for an international return that winter. If that really is the end, it is a sad misfortune for English cricket, as well as for the troubled Trescothick.

THE FACTS Trescothick averages 59.16 in Tests against India, but 33.76 v Australia ... Six of his 12 ODI hundreds have come in matches which England lost ... Like his England team-mates Simon Jones and Alastair Cook, Trescothick was born on Christmas Day ... He hit 284 for Somerset at Northampton in May 2007 ... Trescothick's modest bowling haul includes a first-class hat-trick, for Somerset v Young Australia in 1995: the first victim was Adam Gilchrist ...

THE FIGURES

Batting and fielding

www.cricinfo.com

	M	Inns	NO	Runs	HS	Avge	S/R	100	50	4s	6s	Ct	St
Tests *to 10.9.07*	76	143	10	5825	219	43.79	54.51	14	29	831	42	95	0
ODIs *to 10.9.07*	123	122	6	4335	137	37.37	85.21	12	21	528	41	49	0
First-class *to 10.9.07*	222	383	20	13458	284	37.07	–	27	68	–	–	271	0

Bowling

	M	Balls	Runs	Wkts	BB	Avge	RpO	S/R	5i	10m
Tests *to 10.9.07*	76	300	155	1	1–34	155.00	3.10	300.00	0	0
ODIs *to 10.9.07*	123	232	219	4	2–7	54.75	5.66	58.00	0	0
First-class *to 10.9.07*	222	2674	1541	36	4–36	42.80	3.45	74.27	0	0

SOUTH AFRICA

THANDI **TSHABALALA**

Full name **Thandi Tshabalala**
Born **November 19, 1984, Welkom, Free State**
Teams **Eagles**
Style **Right-hand bat, offspinner**
Test debut **No Tests yet**
ODI debut **South Africa v Ireland at Belfast 2007**

THE PROFILE Thandi Tshabalala initially caught the eye as
a top-order batsman when he played for Free State Schools in
2001. He has had less success in that role at senior level, but has
showed much promise as a finger-spinner. He first made his
name in limited-overs cricket, especially Twenty20, in which he was the leading wicket-
taker after the first two seasons of domestic competition in South Africa. Few doubt that
he has what it takes to perform as an international offspinner, but there are differing
opinions about just when he will be ready for the big step up. Helped by the continued push
for "transformation" of the national side – the positive-discrimination process that Kevin
Pietersen blamed for his decision to quit South Africa – Tshabalala had his first taste of
international cricket when he was named in the squad for the Twenty20 international
against Australia early in 2006, although he did not play in the end. He also twiddled his
thumbs during the tour of Sri Lanka in mid-2006, but finally made his one-day debut in
Ireland in June 2007. Understandably nervous, he bowled a few full-tosses in his first game,
but claimed the big scalp of Sachin Tendulkar (for 93) in his second, in the shadow of
Stormont Palace. Tshabalala, who is quite short, does turn the ball, and has enough
variation to keep batsmen guessing ... but he is still very much learning his trade. The sorry
state of South Africa's spin reserves has meant that his development is undoubtedly being
rushed.

THE FACTS Tshabalala took 5 for 68 (while Nicky Boje took 2 for 112) for Eagles v
Warriors at Port Elizabeth in December 2006: he also took 5 for 72 for Free State v Border
at Bloemfontein in October 2004 ... His first international wicket was Kevin O'Brien of
Ireland, but his second was Sachin Tendulkar ... In 2003-04, the first season of Twenty20
cricket in South Africa, Tshabalala took 10 wickets for the Eagles at 7.70 apiece, and 10
more (at 13.60) in 2004-05 ..

THE FIGURES
Batting and fielding   www.cricinfo.com

	M	Inns	NO	Runs	HS	Avge	S/R	100	50	4s	6s	Ct	St
Tests to 10.9.07	0	0	–	–	–	–	–	–	–	–	–	–	–
ODIs to 10.9.07	4	1	1	2	2*	–	66.66	0	0	0	0	0	0
First-class to 10.9.07	26	35	9	294	34	11.30	34.38	0	0	–	–	10	0

Bowling

	M	Balls	Runs	Wkts	BB	Avge	RpO	S/R	5i	10m
Tests to 10.9.07	0	0	–	–	–	–	–	–	–	–
ODIs to 10.9.07	4	150	151	3	1–30	50.33	6.04	50.00	0	0
First-class to 10.9.07	26	3657	2222	56	5–68	39.67	3.64	65.30	2	0

PAKISTAN

UMAR GUL

Full name	**Umar Gul**
Born	**April 14, 1984, Peshawar, North-Western Frontier Province**
Teams	**Peshawar, Habib Bank**
Style	**Right-hand bat, right-arm fast-medium bowler**
Test debut	**Pakistan v Bangladesh at Karachi 2003-04**
ODI debut	**Pakistan v Zimbabwe at Sharjah 2002-03**

THE PROFILE Umar Gul had played only nine first-class games when he was drafted into the Pakistan side at 19, in the wake of a miserable 2003 World Cup campaign. He performed admirably on Sharjah's flat tracks, maintaining good discipline and obtaining appreciable outswing with the new ball. He can also nip the ball back from outside off. He had a gentle introduction to Test cricket, collecting 15 wickets against Bangladesh later in 2003, including four in each innings at Multan. Sterner challenges followed, but he starred in his only Test of India's historic "comeback" tour of Pakistan, at Lahore in April 2004. Gul, who had been disparaged by some as the "Peshawar Rickshaw" to Shoaib Akhtar's "Rawalpindi Express", tore through India's imposing top order, moving the ball both ways off the seam at a sharp pace. His 5 for 31 in the first innings gave Pakistan the early initiative, which they drove home to level the series. Stress fractures in the back kept him out of the third Test, and it was two years before he returned. He managed only two wickets in the Tests in Sri Lanka, but was retained for the subsequent tour of England – where, in the absence of several senior seamers, he looked the best of the rest, particularly enjoying the conditions at Headingley, taking five wickets in the first innings as the others struggled. He maintained his progress in 2006-07, taking nine wickets in the first Test against West Indies at Lahore before missing the series in South Africa with a knee injury. He was back for the World Cup, and was one of the few to return with reputation intact.

THE FACTS Umar Gul took 6 for 96 in his only Test against India, but averages 106.00 with the ball against Sri Lanka ... His best bowling figures are 8 for 78, for Peshawar v Karachi Urban at Peshawar in October 2005 ... Gul claimed 5 for 46 on his first-class debut, for Pakistan International Airlines v ADBP at Karachi in his only match in 2000-01, then took 45 wickets at 18.62 in 2001-02, his first full season of domestic cricket ...

THE FIGURES

Batting and fielding   www.cricinfo.com

	M	Inns	NO	Runs	HS	Avge	S/R	100	50	4s	6s	Ct	St
Tests *to 10.9.07*	14	17	2	116	26	7.73	38.28	0	0	15	3	4	0
ODIs *to 10.9.07*	30	8	2	45	17*	7.50	49.45	0	0	6	0	4	0
First-class *to 10.9.07*	39	43	7	404	46	11.22	–	0	0	–	–	10	0

Bowling

	M	Balls	Runs	Wkts	BB	Avge	RpO	S/R	5i	10m
Tests *to 10.9.07*	14	3141	1868	61	5–31	30.62	3.56	51.49	3	0
ODIs *to 10.9.07*	30	1374	1054	39	5–17	27.02	4.60	35.23	1	0
First-class *to 10.9.07*	39	7974	4605	184	8–78	25.02	3.46	43.33	12	1

ROBIN **UTHAPPA**

Full name **Robin Venu Uthappa**
Born **November 11, 1985, Coorg, Karnataka**
Teams **Karnataka**
Style **Right-hand bat, occasional right-arm medium-pacer**
Test debut **No Tests yet**
ODI debut **India v England at Indore 2005-06**

THE PROFILE The son of Venu Uthappa, an international hockey referee, the tall and robust Robin Uthappa was long spoken of as a batsman with an international future. Although his record in domestic cricket was modest before a stellar 2006-07 season (1084 runs at 57.05, with five centuries), his limited-overs figures were better to start with: he averages a touch under 40, with a highest score of 160, and his runs come at a strike rate of over 90. Originally a wicketkeeper-batsman, Uthappa gave up the big gloves to concentrate on batting, and now occasionally bowls some medium-pace. As a batsman he has always been attractive to watch – hard-hitting, with all the shots and unafraid to hit the ball in the air. Uthappa first caught the eye with a brilliant 66 in a losing cause for India B against India A in the Challenger Trophy (trial matches for the national squad) at Mumbai early in 2005, against an attack that included Zaheer Khan, Murali Kartik and Rudra Pratap Singh. But it was in the next edition of the same tournament, at Mohali in October 2005, when he really arrived in the big league. After VVS Laxman made a century for India A, Uthappa cracked a matchwinning 116 from only 93 balls. It won him a place instead of Virender Sehwag in the final one-dayer against England early in 2006, and he capitalised with a well-paced 86 at Indore. His next few outings were less spectacular, apart from a matchwinning half-century at The Oval in September 2007, but time is very much on his side.

THE FACTS Uthappa's 86 against England at Indore in April 2006 was the highest score by an Indian making his ODI debut, beating Brijesh Patel's 82 against England at Leeds in 1974 ... He made 162 for Karnataka v Madhya Pradesh at Bangalore in November 2004: he also thumped 160 in a one-day game against Kerala at Margao in January 2005 ... After only one first-class century in his first four seasons Uthappa hit five in ten weeks in 2006-07 ... For India B against India A at Mohali in October 2005 he sped from 61 to 101 in the space of 14 balls ...

THE FIGURES
Batting and fielding

www.cricinfo.com

	M	Inns	NO	Runs	HS	Avge	S/R	100	50	4s	6s	Ct	St
Tests to 10.9.07	0	0	–	–	–	–	–	–	–	–	–	–	–
ODIs to 10.9.07	14	13	1	409	86	34.08	103.28	0	1	59	7	8	0
First-class to 10.9.07	35	60	2	2410	162	41.55	–	6	14	–	–	33	0

Bowling

	M	Balls	Runs	Wkts	BB	Avge	RpO	S/R	5i	10m
Tests to 10.9.07	0	0	–	–	–	–	–	–	–	–
ODIs to 10.9.07	14	0	–	–	–	–	–	–	–	–
First-class to 10.9.07	35	150	74	2	1–7	37.00	2.96	75.00	0	0

SRI LANKA

CHAMINDA **VAAS**

Full name	**Warnakulasuriya Patabendige Ushantha Joseph Chaminda Vaas**
Born	**January 27, 1974, Mattumagala**
Teams	**Colts, Middlesex**
Style	**Left-hand bat, fast-medium left-arm bowler**
Test debut	**Sri Lanka v Pakistan at Kandy 1994-95**
ODI debut	**Sri Lanka v India at Rajkot 1993-94**

THE PROFILE Waspish left-armer Chaminda Vaas – possessor of the most initials and longest name in Test cricket – is easily the most penetrative and successful new-ball bowler Sri Lanka have had. He swings and seams the ball with skill, his trademark delivery being the late indipper. However, he also bowls a well-disguised offcutter, and more recently added reverse-swing to his armoury, a skill that has made him a consistent wicket-taker even on bland subcontinental pitches. As long ago as March 1995 he outbowled New Zealand's seamers on a Napier greentop, taking ten wickets to give Sri Lanka their first Test win overseas. In 2001-02 he made a quantum leap, taking 26 wickets in the 3-0 rout of West Indies, and becoming only the second fast bowler, after Imran Khan, to take 14 wickets in a match on the subcontinent. He's consistent in one-dayers too, and given to spectacular bursts of wicket-taking: he was the first to take eight in an ODI, as Zimbabwe were blown away for 38 in Colombo in December 2001, and also uniquely claimed a hat-trick with the first three balls of the match against Bangladesh in the 2003 World Cup. Vaas has taken 300 wickets in both Tests and one-dayers, and is easily Sri Lanka's most successful bowler after Muttiah Muralitharan. His approach to his batting is equally whole-hearted: he made over 2500 runs in Tests before finally scoring a century in his 97th match, and faced more balls in the Tests in England in 2006 than any of Sri Lanka's specialist batsmen.

THE FACTS Vaas's figures of 8 for 19 against Zimbabwe in Colombo in December 2001 are the best in all ODIs ... That included a hat-trick, and he took another with the first three balls of the match against Bangladesh at Pietermaritzburg in the 2003 World Cup: at the end of the first over they were 5 for 4 ... Vaas finally made a century, in his 97th Test – the longest anyone had had to wait at the time (previously 71 Tests, by Jason Gillespie: Anil Kumble broke the record later in 2007) ... His record includes one ODI for the Asia XI ...

THE FIGURES

Batting and fielding

www.cricinfo.com

	M	Inns	NO	Runs	HS	Avge	S/R	100	50	4s	6s	Ct	St
Tests *to 10.9.07*	98	142	28	2684	100*	23.54	43.31	1	11	330	15	30	0
ODIs *to 10.9.07*	300	203	67	1910	50*	14.04	73.77	0	1	121	22	59	0
First-class *to 10.9.07*	175	235	49	4661	134	25.05	–	4	20	–	–	53	0

Bowling

	M	Balls	Runs	Wkts	BB	Avge	RpO	S/R	5i	10m
Tests *to 10.9.07*	98	20952	9321	319	7–71	29.21	2.66	65.68	11	2
ODIs *to 10.9.07*	300	14701	10260	383	8–19	26.78	4.18	38.38	4	0
First-class *to 10.9.07*	175	33359	15216	618	7–54	24.62	2.73	53.97	26	3

MICHAEL **VANDORT**

Full name	**Michael Graydon Vandort**
Born	**January 19, 1980, Colombo**
Teams	**Colombo Cricket Club**
Style	**Left-hand bat, occasional right-arm medium-pacer**
Test debut	**Sri Lanka v Bangladesh at Colombo 2001-02**
ODI debut	**Sri Lanka v Australia at Melbourne 2005-06**

THE PROFILE Michael Vandort, a 6ft 5ins tall left-hander fond of the off-drive, emerged in 2001 after a string of impressive performances for Colombo Cricket Club and Sri Lanka A. A late developer, he played only once for his school, St Joseph's College, but nonetheless quickly made an impression in first-class cricket. He was picked for the Board XI against the Indians in August 2001, and earned himself a berth in the Test squad with an impressive 116 against the proven new-ball attack of Javagal Srinath and Venkatesh Prasad. He sat on the sidelines throughout that series, but was given a chance against Bangladesh when the selectors rested some senior players. He duly scored a century in the second Test, but with the Jayasuriya-Atapattu opening combination seemingly unassailable he had to wait more than three years before another sniff. An injury to Jayasuriya paved the way for his one-day debut, at Melbourne in February 2006: he top-scored with a gritty 48, but Jayasuriya returned and Vandort missed the rest of the VB Series – he hasn't had an ODI since, although he did play two Tests against Bangladesh shortly afterwards. With Jayasuriya in short-lived retirement Vandort got his chance in England in 2006, and starred in defeat at Edgbaston, last out for a dogged 105 in the second innings. He failed to reach double figures in his other three knocks, though, and missed the one-day demolitions that followed – he's a good slip fielder but is rather ponderous in the field, and this counts against him in the one-day arena. When Atapattu missed the Tests against Bangladesh in mid-2007, pleading the "trauma" of sitting on the bench thoughout the World Cup, Vandort got another chance ... and another century.

THE FACTS Seven of Vandort's first nine Tests have been against Bangladesh: he averages 64.37 in them ... He scored 100 on his first-class debut, for Colombo Cricket Club v Kurunegala in Colombo in March 1999 ... When still only 18 Vandort made 226 and 225 in successive matches for Colombo Cricket Club in 1998-99, v Panadura and Singha ...

THE FIGURES

Batting and fielding   www.cricinfo.com

	M	Inns	NO	Runs	HS	Avge	S/R	100	50	4s	6s	Ct	St
Tests to 10.9.07	9	14	2	635	140	52.91	52.82	3	2	72	4	2	0
ODIs to 10.9.07	1	1	0	48	48	48.00	41.02	0	0	3	0	0	0
First-class to 10.9.07	109	182	13	5870	226	34.73	–		14	26	–	–	84	0

Bowling

	M	Balls	Runs	Wkts	BB	Avge	RpO	S/R	5i	10m
Tests to 10.9.07	9	0	–	–	–	–	–	–	–	–
ODIs to 10.9.07	1	0	–	–	–	–	–	–	–	–
First-class to 10.9.07	109	61	53	1	1–46	53.00	5.21	61.00	0	0

MICHAEL **VAUGHAN**

ENGLAND

Full name	**Michael Paul Vaughan**
Born	**October 29, 1974, Manchester, Lancashire**
Teams	**Yorkshire**
Style	**Right-hand bat, offspinner**
Test debut	**England v South Africa at Johannesburg 1999-2000**
ODI debut	**England v Sri Lanka at Dambulla 2000-01**

THE PROFILE   In September 2005 Michael Vaughan secured his place in English cricket's hall of fame, becoming the first captain to lift the Ashes since Mike Gatting in 1986-87. It was the culmination of a five-year journey for Vaughan, whose captaincy had become as classy and composed as the batting technique that briefly carried him to the top of the world rankings. He had faced his first ball in Test cricket with England 2 for 4 on a damp flyer at Johannesburg late in 1999, and drew immediate comparisons with Michael Atherton for his calm aura at the crease. But he soon demonstrated he was more than just a like-for-like replacement. He blossomed magnificently, playing with a freedom Atherton never dared to approach. He conjured 900 runs in seven Tests against Sri Lanka and India in 2002, the prelude to a formidable series in Australia – three tons, 633 runs. He inherited the Test captaincy in 2003 when Nasser Hussain abdicated, having spotted Vaughan's burgeoning man-management abilities. After a stutter in Sri Lanka, he confirmed the arrival of a new era by routing West Indies in the Caribbean. Returning home, England swept seven out of seven Tests in 2004, won in South Africa, then triumphed in the greatest Ashes series of them all. An old injury flared up, wrecking his 2006 season and keeping him out of the Ashes rematch, but he hung doggedly in there. He retired from ODIs after England's lacklustre World Cup, but was back to his silky best in the 2007 home Tests, stroking a superb 103 against West Indies at Leeds and an equally effortless 124 – ended by a freak dismissal – against India at Nottingham.

THE FACTS   Vaughan made 633 runs in the 2002-03 Ashes series: the last Englishman to score as many in Australia was Geoff Boycott, with 657 in 1970-71 ... Vaughan averages 72.57 in Tests against India, but only 14 v Zimbabwe: he averaged 50.98 before he was captain, and only 38.68 since ... Born in Manchester, Vaughan was the first Lancastrian to play for Yorkshire after the home-grown-only policy was relaxed in the 1990s ...

THE FIGURES
Batting and fielding
www.cricinfo.com

	M	Inns	NO	Runs	HS	Avge	S/R	100	50	4s	6s	Ct	St
Tests to 10.9.07	70	126	9	5141	197	43.94	52.14	17	15	670	22	39	0
ODIs to 10.9.07	86	83	10	1982	90*	27.15	68.39	0	16	204	13	25	0
First-class to 10.9.07	241	425	27	15281	197	38.39	–	41	64	–	–	109	0

Bowling

	M	Balls	Runs	Wkts	BB	Avge	RpO	S/R	5i	10m
Tests to 10.9.07	70	960	555	6	2–71	92.50	3.46	160.00	0	0
ODIs to 10.9.07	86	796	649	16	4–22	40.56	4.89	49.75	0	0
First-class to 10.9.07	241	9282	5189	114	4–39	45.51	3.35	81.42	0	0

DANIEL **VETTORI**

Full name	**Daniel Luca Vettori**
Born	**January 27, 1979, Auckland**
Teams	**Northern Districts**
Style	**Left-hand bat, left-arm orthodox spinner**
Test debut	**New Zealand v England at Wellington 1996-97**
ODI debut	**New Zealand v Sri Lanka at Christchurch 1996-97**

THE PROFILE Daniel Vettori is probably the best left-arm spinner around – an assessment reinforced by his selection in the World XI for the ICC Super Series in Australia late in 2005 – and the only cloud on his horizon is a susceptibility to injury, particularly in the bowler's danger area of the back. He seemed to have recovered from one stress fracture, which led to a dip in form in 2003, but after just a couple of matches in 2006 for Warwickshire, his second English county, Vettori was on the plane home nursing another one. When fit, he still exhibits the enticing flight and guile that made him New Zealand's youngest Test player in 1996-97. There were signs on the tour of England in 2004 that he was back to his best after his mini-slump, and he butchered the Bangladeshis shortly afterwards, taking 20 wickets in the two Tests. After starting at No. 11, blinking nervously through his glasses, he has improved his batting, to the point that he has made two centuries – one of them New Zealand's fastest in Tests, an 82-ball effort against the admittedly hopeless Zimbabweans at Harare in August 2005. He helped himself to his 200th Test wicket in the same two-day massacre. Vettori atoned for an underwhelming performance at the 2003 World Cup – two wickets for 259 – with 16 in 2007, the most for New Zealand as they marched to the semi-final. He still hasn't passed 14 with the bat in 17 World Cup matches, though. The selectors gave a sign of their future plans by making him captain in Stephen Fleming's absence for the Chappell-Hadlee one-day series against Australia in December 2005, and he was duly confirmed as Fleming's permanent successor late in 2007. As long as the back holds out ...

THE FACTS Vettori made his first-class debut in 1996-97, for Northern Districts against the England tourists: his maiden first-class victim was Nasser Hussain ... Three weeks later Vettori made his Test debut, New Zealand's youngest-ever player at 18 years 10 days: his first wicket was Hussain again ... Vettori has taken 52 Test wickets against Australia, but only four v Pakistan, costing 100.25 each ... His record includes one Test and four ODIs for the World XI ...

THE FIGURES

Batting and fielding

	M	Inns	NO	Runs	HS	Avge	S/R	100	50	4s	6s	Ct	St
Tests *to 10.9.07*	73	105	16	2250	137*	25.28	54.81	2	13	294	6	36	0
ODIs *to 10.9.07*	201	127	39	1284	83	14.59	78.82	0	3	96	6	53	0
First-class *to 10.9.07*	119	163	23	3649	137*	26.06	–	4	20	–	–	57	0

Bowling

	M	Balls	Runs	Wkts	BB	Avge	RpO	S/R	5i	10m
Tests *to 10.9.07*	73	17585	7851	229	7–87	34.28	2.67	76.79	13	3
ODIs *to 10.9.07*	201	9491	6689	203	5–30	32.95	4.22	46.75	1	0
First-class *to 10.9.07*	119	27346	12288	381	7–87	32.25	2.69	71.77	23	3

LOU **VINCENT**

Full name	**Lou Vincent**
Born	**November 11, 1978, Warkworth, Auckland**
Teams	**Auckland**
Style	**Right-hand bat, occasional wicketkeeper**
Test debut	**New Zealand v Australia at Perth 2001-02**
ODI debut	**New Zealand v Sri Lanka at Auckland 2000-01**

THE PROFILE Lou Vincent started with a bang – a memorable hundred on Test debut against Australia in 2001-02, followed by 54 in the second innings – then slipped back as he struggled for consistency, managing only one more century (106 against India on a shirtfront at Mohali) in his next 18 Tests. Part of the problem was finding a settled spot in the batting order: something of a reluctant opener, he was miffed when this led to his being left out of the Test team. "It was just a preference, I wasn't insisting on anything," he explained early in 2006. Before this setback Vincent, a stylish right-hander with a penchant for sixes, had worked his way back into both national sides, first re-establishing himself at Test level with a measured 224 (from No. 4) against the Murali-less Sri Lankans to set up an innings victory at Wellington in April 2005, then cementing his one-day spot with a national-record 172 – off 120 balls, with nine sixes – against the outclassed Zimbabweans at Bulawayo in August. He made 102 against West Indies at Napier in March 2006 not long after fracturing a finger, but was originally left out of the one-day series in Australia in 2006-07. He was called up when Nathan Astle announced his retirement in mid-tournament, and silenced the doubters with 66, 76 and 90 in his first three matches back. He started the World Cup with two ducks, recovered with a century against Canada ... and then broke his wrist in practice, forcing him home. His Test career seems to have stalled, although his Auckland coach Mark O'Donnell thinks he'll be back: "Lou's had to cope with failure, work his way back into favour, and figure out a method that would prove successful at Test level."

THE FACTS Vincent was the sixth of seven New Zealanders to score a century on Test debut: the others are Jackie Mills, Bruce Taylor, Rodney Redmond, Mark Greatbatch, Mathew Sinclair and Scott Styris ... He averages 92 v Sri Lanka in Tests, but only 11.50 v Bangladesh: he has not played against South Africa ... Vincent's 172 v Zimbabwe in August 2005 is NZ's highest ODI score, beating Glenn Turner's 171 v East Africa in the first World Cup in 1975 ...

THE FIGURES

Batting and fielding www.cricinfo.com

	M	Inns	NO	Runs	HS	Avge	S/R	100	50	4s	6s	Ct	St
Tests to 10.9.07	22	38	1	1295	224	35.00	46.93	3	9	156	11	19	0
ODIs to 10.9.07	97	94	10	2375	172	28.27	70.05	3	11	218	36	37	0
First-class to 10.9.07	84	135	10	4584	224	36.67	–	10	27	–	–	100	0

Bowling

	M	Balls	Runs	Wkts	BB	Avge	RpO	S/R	5i	10m
Tests to 10.9.07	22	6	2	0	–	–	2.00	–	0	0
ODIs to 10.9.07	97	14	25	0	–	–	10.71	–	0	0
First-class to 10.9.07	84	1003	527	10	2–37	52.70	3.15	100.30	0	0

ADAM **VOGES**

Full name	**Adam Charles Voges**
Born	**October 4, 1979, Subiaco, Perth, Western Australia**
Teams	**Western Australia, Hampshire**
Style	**Right-hand bat, slow left-arm unorthodox spinner**
Test debut	**No Tests yet**
ODI debut	**Australia v New Zealand at Hamilton 2006-07**

THE PROFILE Part of Western Australia's big-hitting middle order, Adam Voges (it's pronounced Vo-jes) is most famous for his maiden one-day century in 2004-05, a 62-ball effort against New South Wales – batting at No. 3, he didn't enter until the 30th over – which was the fastest in Australian domestic history at the time. He not only broke a record, but also clattered a sponsor's sign with one of his seven sixes. Voges collected many plaudits for that innings, and a $50,000 bonus for his superb aim ... but was left out for the next Pura Cup match. He did return later in the season, produced his first hundred, and finished with an eye-catching double of 362 four-day runs at 72.40, plus 287 in one-dayers. Next season he passed 600 first-class runs: his prize was a return to the Academy, after captaining them in India in 2004. The only blemish was a brief suspension for missing a training session, but that was forgotten the following season when, after Damien Martyn's unexpected retirement, Voges was called into Australia's squad for the third Ashes Test on his home turf at the WACA. He didn't play – Andrew Symonds got the place instead, and made it his own – but Voges kept his name in the frame by ending the season with 630 runs at 57. He made his ODI debut in New Zealand, but didn't quite do enough to win a World Cup spot. He is a fine fielder, but his left-arm wrist-spin hasn't had much chance yet in a state side which already boasts Brad Hogg.

THE FACTS Voges's 100 not out in 62 balls for Western Australia v NSW in the ING Cup in October 2004 was the fastest century in Australian domestic one-day cricket: he averages 87.25 in one-dayers against NSW ... His highest score is 178 for WA v Queensland at Perth in January 2006 ... Voges learnt of his call-up to the Australian Test squad in 2006-07 while playing for a Cricket Australia XI against the England tourists: he was tapped on the shoulder and asked to leave the field, and admitted "I thought I was in trouble" ...

THE FIGURES
Batting and fielding
www.cricinfo.com

	M	Inns	NO	Runs	HS	Avge	S/R	100	50	4s	6s	Ct	St
Tests to 10.9.07	0	0	–	–	–	–	–	–	–	–	–	–	–
ODIs to 10.9.07	1	1	1	16	16*	–	160.00	0	0	0	1	1	0
First-class to 10.9.07	29	49	8	1724	178	42.04	49.48	6	5	–	–	36	0

Bowling

	M	Balls	Runs	Wkts	BB	Avge	RpO	S/R	5i	10m
Tests to 10.9.07	0	0	–	–	–	–	–	–	–	–
ODIs to 10.9.07	1	18	33	0	–	–	11.00	–	0	0
First-class to 10.9.07	29	1128	672	15	4–92	44.80	3.57	75.20	0	0

MALINDA **WARNAPURA**

Full name **Basnayake Shalith Malinda Warnapura**
Born **May 26, 1979, Colombo**
Teams **Colts**
Style **Left-hand bat, offspinner**
Test debut **Sri Lanka v Bangladesh at Colombo 2007**
ODI debut **Sri Lanka v Pakistan at Abu Dhabi 2007**

THE PROFILE A nuggety left-hander, Malinda Warnapura took his time to make his mark in international cricket, despite an impressive pedigree (his uncle, Bandula Warnapura, captained Sri Lanka). This Warnapura started his first-class career in 1998, but it was not until late in 2006 that he really arrived. Chosen for the Sri Lanka A side that took part in India's Duleep Trophy tournament, he made 421 runs in three matches, including 65 and 149 not out in the final, won by North Zone. Despite this he missed the senior tour of New Zealand that followed, then struggled with illness when the A team visited the West Indies. But when Bangladesh A toured Sri Lanka early in 2007 he was back to his best, stroking a career-best 242 in the first unofficial Test, and followed that with a hundred in one of the one-dayers to show he was adept at the shorter game as well. At 28, he was handed a first Test cap when Bangladesh came calling in June 2007 ... and was dismissed by the only ball he received on his debut. But in the absence of Upul Tharanga (injured foot) and Marvan Atapattu (injured pride, after being kept on the bench throughout the World Cup) Warnapura retained his place, and made an assured 82 in another innings victory in the second Test. He is an accumulator of runs, particularly strong square on the off side, but needs to polish his footwork and free up his backlift, which is sometimes too close to his body.

THE FACTS Warnapura scored 242 for Sri Lanka A v Bangladesh A in Colombo in March 2007, sharing a stand of 376 with Thilan Samaraweera (162) ... On his Test debut, against Bangladesh in Colombo three months later, he was out first ball ... Warnapura was in the Sri Lankan squad for the Commonwealth Games in Kuala Lumpur in 1998, playing against Malaysia and the eventual gold medallists South Africa ... His uncle, Bandula Warnapura, captained Sri Lanka in their inaugural Test, against England in 1981-82 ...

THE FIGURES
Batting and fielding
www.cricinfo.com

	M	Inns	NO	Runs	HS	Avge	S/R	100	50	4s	6s	Ct	St
Tests to 10.9.07	2	2	0	82	82	41.00	58.15	0	1	9	0	3	0
ODIs to 10.9.07	1	1	0	5	5	5.00	35.71	0	0	1	0	0	0
First-class to 10.9.07	112	163	18	5265	242	36.31	–	12	24	–	–	74	0

Bowling

	M	Balls	Runs	Wkts	BB	Avge	RpO	S/R	5i	10m
Tests to 10.9.07	2	0	–	–	–	–	–	–	–	–
ODIs to 10.9.07	1	0	–	–	–	–	–	–	–	–
First-class to 10.9.07	112	6552	3043	114	6–22	26.69	2.78	57.47	4	0

SHANE **WATSON**

Full name	**Shane Robert Watson**
Born	**June 17, 1981, Ipswich, Queensland**
Teams	**Queensland**
Style	**Right-hand bat, right-arm fast-medium bowler**
Test debut	**Australia v Pakistan at Sydney 2004-05**
ODI debut	**Australia v South Africa at Centurion 2001-02**

THE PROFILE Hulklike, blond and spiky-haired, Shane Watson should be the shiny embodiment of modern-day Australian cricket ... if only that body didn't keep cracking up. He started young: Queensland Under-17s at 15, the Academy, nipping off at 19 to Tasmania, where he hit his maiden hundred in his fifth match. He missed the 2003 World Cup with stress fractures of the back: until then his batting lacked nothing in swagger, if a little in gap-finding artifice, while his bowling was willing if docile. He bounced back in 2003-04 with four hundreds for Tasmania. Watson remains the cleanest of hitters and, several remodelled actions later, decidedly sharp. Back home in Queensland (he hated the cold), he was tipped to become Australia's next champion allrounder – not least by their last one: "A fine physical specimen, good athlete – just give him time," said Alan Davidson in 2002. Watson was overlooked for the 2005 Ashes tour, but his stock rose afterwards, as Andrew Flintoff highlighted the benefits of a genuine allrounder. A dislocated shoulder in the field against West Indies at Brisbane ruined 2005-06, and he watched his mate Andrew Symonds fill in. Watson returned for the one-dayers in South Africa early in 2006, but missed the Tests – although 201 in the Pura Cup final eased the pain. There was more pain later in the year, as a persistent hamstring injury kept him out of the Ashes rematch, but he bounced back to play an allround role in the defence of the World Cup, and – after a few handy outings at the top of the order – announced that he wanted to replace the retired Justin Langer as Australia's Test opener.

THE FACTS Watson hit 201 for Queensland in the 2005-06 Pura Cup final demolition of Victoria before retiring hurt: uniquely, four batsmen passed 150 in Queensland's 900 for 6 ... He averaged 145 at the 2007 World Cup, thanks to five not-outs, but scored at a mind-boggling 170.58 runs per 100 balls ... Watson has played for Hampshire, alongside Shane Warne: in 2005 he scored 203 not out for them against Warwickshire at the Rose Bowl ...

THE FIGURES

Batting and fielding   www.cricinfo.com

	M	Inns	NO	Runs	HS	Avge	S/R	100	50	4s	6s	Ct	St
Tests *to 10.9.07*	3	4	0	81	31	20.25	38.20	0	0	8	0	0	0
ODIs *to 10.9.07*	65	47	18	1001	79	34.51	80.01	0	7	81	15	15	0
First-class *to 10.9.07*	55	94	14	3938	203*	49.22	–		11	19	–	–	37	0

Bowling

	M	Balls	Runs	Wkts	BB	Avge	RpO	S/R	5i	10m
Tests *to 10.9.07*	3	186	123	2	1–25	61.50	3.96	93.00	0	0
ODIs *to 10.9.07*	65	2593	2115	62	4–39	34.11	4.89	41.82	0	0
First-class *to 10.9.07*	55	5226	3106	103	6–32	30.15	3.56	50.73	2	1

CAMERON **WHITE**

Full name **Cameron Leon White**
Born **August 18, 1983, Bairnsdale, Victoria**
Teams **Victoria, Somerset**
Style **Right-hand bat, legspinner**
Test debut **No Tests yet**
ODI debut **Australia v World XI at Melbourne 2005-06**

AUSTRALIA

THE PROFILE Fair-haired and level-headed, Cameron "Bear" White long seemed destined to play a significant role in Australia's future. Only the precise nature of that role baffled his admirers. Nagging legspinner? Solid middle-order bat? Intuitive skipper? Or a bit of all three? The over-eager Shane Warne comparisons that accompanied his arrival have long since died away. Indeed, White is a peculiarly unAustralian leggie – tall and robust, relying on changes of pace and a handy wrong'un rather than prodigious turn or flight. He bowls a good line, and has a neat line in self-deprecation too: "There's no flippers or anything exciting like that," he once admitted. What is not in doubt is his cricket sense, nor his maturity. Victoria's youngest-ever captain at 20, he won rave reviews for his cool head and handling of more hardened colleagues. White made his ODI debut in the Super Series late in 2005. He made little impact, and lost his central contract after a mediocre season. But he had a wonderful time with the bat for Somerset in 2006 (David Hookes, the late Victorian coach, felt White's best chance of representing Australia was to earn a top-six spot). He feasted on county bowlers, and smashed a Twenty20 ton in 55 balls. That preceded a better home summer, although he was sometimes criticised for not bowling himself enough. He was recalled for the annual one-day triangular at the start of 2007: his bowling lacked control, and his batting opportunities were limited. He was overlooked for the World Cup, but there was some good news: he got his national contract back for 2007-08.

THE FACTS White made 260 not out for Somerset v Derbyshire in August 2006, the highest individual score in the fourth innings of any first-class match, beating a record formerly held by Hansie Cronje and Denis Compton ... White's 141 not out for Somerset v Worcestershire in 2006 is the highest innings in any senior Twenty20 match ... Nine of his 11 first-class centuries have been scored for Somerset ... In his only Twenty20 international, against England at Sydney in January 2007, White hit 40 not out in 20 balls ...

THE FIGURES

Batting and fielding   www.cricinfo.com

	M	Inns	NO	Runs	HS	Avge	S/R	100	50	4s	6s	Ct	St
Tests to 10.9.07	0	0	–	–	–	–	–	–	–	–	–	–	–
ODIs to 10.9.07	16	10	3	157	45	22.42	116.29	0	0	7	9	5	0
First-class to 10.9.07	81	133	16	4769	260*	40.76	–	12	19	–	–	76	0

Bowling

	M	Balls	Runs	Wkts	BB	Avge	RpO	S/R	5i	10m
Tests to 10.9.07	0	0	–	–	–	–	–	–	–	–
ODIs to 10.9.07	16	174	201	4	1–5	50.25	6.93	43.50	0	0
First-class to 10.9.07	81	9870	5786	153	6–66	37.81	3.51	64.50	2	1

LUKE **WRIGHT**

ENGLAND

Full name	**Luke James Wright**
Born	**March 7, 1985, Grantham, Lincolnshire**
Teams	**Sussex**
Style	**Right-hand bat, right-arm fast medium bowler**
Test debut	**No Tests yet**
ODI debut	**England v India at The Oval 2007**

THE PROFILE   Since he's an attacking batsman who can bowl medium-fast, it's no great surprise that Luke Wright admires similar players like Jacques Kallis and Andrew Flintoff, or that he hoped to emulate Freddie by playing for England. That ambition came closer when he was selected for the inaugural World Twenty20 championships in September 2007, and closer still when he was called up to cover for, among others, the injured Flintoff for the last part of the late-season one-day series against India. He made his debut at The Oval, and copied Flintoff exactly by scoring 50 – an exciting innings which started with a four and a six off Yuvraj Singh. Wright played for England Under-19s while at Loughborough University, and made his first-class debut for Leicestershire against Sussex in 2003. Although Mushtaq Ahmed nabbed him for a duck Sussex still signed him up for the following season. Wright made an instant impression with a century on debut, against his old mates from Loughborough, but he had played only ten first-class games when he was called up from the Academy squad to join England A in the West Indies early in 2006. Wright's career really took off in 2007, when he was the leading scorer in the Twenty20 Cup with 346 runs, including a pyrotechnic 103 in just 45 balls against Kent. That earned him his county cap – and that national Twenty20 call-up, which he celebrated by hammering 125 in 73 balls in a Pro40 match against Gloucestershire. He also biffed 56 in 40 balls for England Lions in a one-dayer against the Indians. His bowling has made less of an impression, and it's probably as a hard-hitting batsman that he will ultimately make his mark.

THE FACTS   Wright made 103 from 45 balls (with 11 fours and six sixes) in a Twenty20 Cup match against Kent at Canterbury in June 2007 ... He scored 100, his only first-class century so far, on his debut for Sussex (his second first-class match), v Loughborough UCCE in May 2004 ... Wright took a hat-trick for England Under-19s v South Africa in a one-day game at Hove in August 2003 ...

THE FIGURES

Batting and fielding   www.cricinfo.com

	M	Inns	NO	Runs	HS	Avge	S/R	100	50	4s	6s	Ct	St
Tests *to 10.9.0/*	0	0	–	–	–	–	–	–	–	–	–	–	–
ODIs *to 10.9.07*	2	2	0	50	50	25.00	121.95	0	1	7	1	1	0
First-class *to 10.9.07*	42	32	9	915	100	26.91	59.41	1	6	–	–	16	0

Bowling

	M	Balls	Runs	Wkts	BB	Avge	RpO	S/R	5i	10m
Tests *to 10.9.07*	0	0	–	–	–	–	–	–	–	–
ODIs *to 10.9.07*	2	12	11	0	–	–	5.50	–	0	0
First-class *to 10.9.07*	32	3062	1729	43	3–33	40.20	3.38	71.20	0	0

YASIR ARAFAT

Full name **Yasir Arafat Satti**
Born **March 12, 1982, Rawalpindi, Punjab**
Teams **Rawalpindi, National Bank, Kent**
Style **Right-hand bat, right-arm fast-medium bowler**
Test debut **No Tests yet**
ODI debut **Pakistan v Sri Lanka at Karachi 1999-2000**

THE PROFILE Yasir Arafat is a typical Pakistan allrounder: he's ideal for one-day cricket, but also looks capable of making a contribution in Tests, although he is yet to play in one. He is a useful lower-order plunderer, but his bowling remains much his stronger suit. His straight, full, skiddy bowling, from a slingy action, accounted for Andrew Flintoff in a one-dayer at Karachi in December 2005. It also helped him winkle out nine England wickets in a warm-up game earlier in that tour, and once brought him five wickets in six deliveries (the other one was a no-ball) in a domestic game. How straight he bowls is shown by four of those five being bowled or lbw. Arafat can generate pace and, when conditions are helpful, swing. He has wide experience of cricket in the UK: he represented Scotland before Sussex signed him up in 2006 to join one Pakistani, Mushtaq Ahmed, and replace another, Naved-ul-Hasan. Arafat took 24 wickets in his first four games for them, and was then called up himself by Pakistan, after injuries to other seamers, and put on standby for the second and third Tests. He earned a national contract for 2007-08 after some fine allround performances for his new county, Kent, despite playing only ODI the previous season (and top-scoring as Pakistan slumped to 89 all out against South Africa). He was a late replacement for the World Cup, but didn't play. Pakistan have a lot of allrounders, so Arafat still faces an uphill battle to win a regular place.

THE FACTS Yasir Arafat took five wickets in six balls for Rawalpindi against reigning champions Faisalabad in the Quaid-e-Azam Trophy in December 2004: only three other bowlers had previously done this – Derbyshire's Bill Copson (1937), William Henderson of Orange Free State (1937-38) and Surrey's Pat Pocock (1972) ... Arafat represented Scotland in 2004 and 2005, Sussex in 2006, and Kent in 2007 – making 122, his highest score, in his second game for them ...

THE FIGURES

Batting and fielding www.cricinfo.com

	M	Inns	NO	Runs	HS	Avge	S/R	100	50	4s	6s	Ct	St
Tests to 10.9.07	0	0	–	–	–	–	–	–	–	–	–	–	–
ODIs to 10.9.07	7	5	1	48	27	12.00	78.68	0	0	5	0	1	0
First-class to 10.9.07	120	183	23	4234	122	26.46	–	3	23	–	–	41	0

Bowling

	M	Balls	Runs	Wkts	BB	Avge	RpO	S/R	5i	10m
Tests to 10.9.07	0	0	–	–	–	–	–	–	–	–
ODIs to 10.9.07	7	234	233	4	1–28	58.25	5.97	58.50	0	0
First-class to 10.9.07	120	19659	11238	492	7–102	22.84	3.42	39.95	28	3

YASIR HAMEED

Full name **Yasir Hameed Qureishi**
Born **Feb 28, 1978, Peshawar, North-West Frontier Province**
Teams **Peshawar, Pakistan International Airlines**
Style **Right-hand bat, occasional offspinner**
Test debut **Pakistan v Bangladesh at Karachi 2003-04**
ODI debut **Pakistan v New Zealand at Dambulla 2002-03**

THE PROFILE Yasir Hameed announced himself in Test cricket with two centuries on debut, against Bangladesh in May 2003. He may look frail, but his game is built on timing and an easy elegance, and a technique more solid than some Pakistan have tried recently. His early one-day exploits were initially equally impressive, and he forged a superb combination with Imran Farhat: against New Zealand at home late in 2003 they put together a record four consecutive three-figure opening partnerships. But after this promising beginning Yasir developed a worrying tendency to waste his starts, making pretty twenties and then throwing it away, often flailing at wide ones outside off. Selectorial inconsistencies didn't help: he made 58 and 63 against McGrath and Warne at Sydney in January 2005, but was dropped for the next Test (against India) a couple of months later. For a while opportunities were limited to a few scattered ODIs, in most of which he made a contribution with the bat. However, domestic persistence paid off, and he returned to the one-day squad against West Indies at the end of 2006. He made 71 and 41, but still missed out on a World Cup spot (possibly a blessing in disguise). He was recalled for the post-Cup one-dayers against Sri Lanka in Abu Dhabi: he made 50 in the second match, and stretched his run of double-figure scores in ODIs to 12 in succession, which may be enough to embarrass the selectors into giving him a longer run.

THE FACTS Yasir Hameed made 170 and 105 (with 40 fours in all) on his Test debut against Bangladesh at Karachi in August 2003: the only other man to make twin centuries on Test debut is Lawrence Rowe, with 214 and 100 not out for West Indies v New Zealand at Kingston in 1971-72 ... In 2003-04 Yasir and Imran Farhat shared successive opening stands of 115, 142, 134 and 197 in ODIs against New Zealand ... He made 207 for PIA v Khan Research Laboratories at Karachi in February 2003 ... Yasir has played two ODIs against Zimbabwe and was caught behind for a duck in both, lasting a grand total of three balls ...

THE FIGURES

Batting and fielding   www.cricinfo.com

	M	Inns	NO	Runs	HS	Avge	S/R	100	50	4s	6s	Ct	St
Tests *to 10.9.07*	20	39	3	1292	170	35.88	57.91	2	8	189	3	16	0
ODIs *to 10.9.07*	53	53	1	1999	127*	38.44	61.80	3	12	217	6	13	0
First-class *to 10.9.07*	102	171	11	5780	207	36.12	–	12	29	–	–	79	0

Bowling

	M	Balls	Runs	Wkts	BB	Avge	RpO	S/R	5i	10m
Tests *to 10.9.07*	20	6	5	0	–	–	5.00	–	0	0
ODIs *to 10.9.07*	53	18	26	0	–	–	8.66	–	0	0
First-class *to 10.9.07*	102	765	588	6	2–46	98.00	4.61	127.50	0	0

YOUNIS KHAN

Full name **Mohammad Younis Khan**
Born **November 29, 1977, Mardan, North-West Frontier Province**
Teams **Peshawar, Habib Bank, Yorkshire**
Style **Right-hand bat, occasional legspinner**
Test debut **Pakistan v Sri Lanka at Rawalpindi 1999-2000**
ODI debut **Pakistan v Sri Lanka at Karachi 1999-2000**

THE PROFILE Younis Khan is a fearless middle-order batsman, as befits his Pathan ancestry. He plays with a flourish, and is especially strong in the arc from backward point to extra cover, and he is prone to getting down on one knee and driving extravagantly. But this flamboyance is coupled with grit. His main weaknesses are playing away from his body and leaving straight balls. He started with 107 on Test debut, against Sri Lanka early in 2000, and scored well in bursts after that, with 153 against West Indies in a Test in Sharjah the highlight. Younis was one of the few batsmen who retained his place after Pakistan's disastrous 2003 World Cup campaign, but he lost it soon afterwards after a string of low scores at home against Bangladesh and South Africa. Another century against Sri Lanka finally cemented that Test place, and he has been a heavy run-maker ever since, especially against India: in March 2005 he made 147 and 267 in successive Tests against them, and continued in that vein early in 2006, with 199, 83, 194, 0 and 77, before scoring consistently in England too, making 173 at Leeds, which became his home ground the following year during a successful spell with Yorkshire. He blotted his copybook by theatrically resigning as captain after being appointed to replace the banned Inzamam for the Champions Trophy late in 2006 – he then changed his mind and took the job after all. But after a miserable World Cup he announced he was not interested in the position full-time. He is a good fielder, and he displayed further versatility by keeping wicket – and winning the Man of the Match award – in a one-dayer against Zimbabwe in October 2004.

THE FACTS Younis Khan averages 106.10 in Tests against India – and more than 31 against everyone else ... He was the seventh of nine Pakistanis to score a century on Test debut, with 107 v Sri Lanka at Rawalpindi in February 2000 ... Against India at home early in 2006 Younis shared successive stands of 319, 142, 242, 0 and 158 with Mohammad Yousuf ... At Lahore in that series he became the sixth batsman to be out for 199 in a Test ...

THE FIGURES
Batting and fielding
www.cricinfo.com

	M	Inns	NO	Runs	HS	Avge	S/R	100	50	4s	6s	Ct	St
Tests *to 10.9.07*	53	95	6	4291	267	48.21	53.30	12	19	529	18	64	0
ODIs *to 10.9.07*	151	146	18	3988	144	31.15	73.78	2	26	310	35	80	0
First-class *to 10.9.07*	121	196	21	8713	267	49.78	–		27	35	–	–	133	0

Bowling

	M	Balls	Runs	Wkts	BB	Avge	RpO	S/R	5i	10m
Tests *to 10.9.07*	53	264	169	2	1–24	84.50	3.84	132.00	0	0
ODIs *to 10.9.07*	151	197	106	1	1–24	106.00	6.55	97.00	0	0
First-class *to 10.9.07*	121	1591	1011	20	4–52	50.55	3.81	79.55	0	0

YUVRAJ SINGH

INDIA

Full name **Yuvraj Singh**
Born **December 12, 1981, Chandigarh**
Teams **Punjab**
Style **Left-hand bat, slow left-arm orthodox spinner**
Test debut **India v New Zealand at Mohali 2003-04**
ODI debut **India v Kenya at Nairobi 2000-01**

THE PROFILE Generously gifted, Yuvraj Singh has long been looked upon as a strong, fearless natural destined for great things. Two months short of his 19th birthday he made a lordly entry into international cricket, toppling Australia in the ICC Knockout of October 2000 in Nairobi with a blistering 84 in his first innings (he hadn't batted in his first game) and some scintillating fielding. In time he was to supplement these skills with clever, loopy left-arm spin. While his ability to hit the ball long and clean was instantly recognised, he was soon found to be troubled by quality spin, and also perceived to lack commitment, traits for which he temporarily lost his one-day place. But he returned for the last two ODIs against Zimbabwe early in 2002, and swung the series India's way with a matchwinning innings in each game, then went to England and played key roles in three run-chases in the NatWest Series, culminating in the final, where his 69, and stand of 121 with Mohammad Kaif, set up India's memorable victory over England. It still took another 15 months, and an injury to Sourav Ganguly, for Yuvraj to get a Test look-in. But in his third match, against Pakistan on a greentop at Lahore, he stroked a stunning first-day century off 110 balls. The 2005-06 season was a good one for Yuvraj, with 1161 runs at 58 in one-dayers, and another Test century against Pakistan – but still he couldn't be sure of a Test place, not helped by a troublesome knee injury that briefly threatened to keep him out of the 2007 World Cup. He remained an automatic one-day selection, though, and showed why by smashing Stuart Broad for six sixes in an over during the inaugural World Twenty20 championships in September 2007.

THE FACTS Yuvraj played 73 ODIs before winning his first Test cap, in October 2003 ... He made 209 for North Zone v South Zone in March 2002 ... Yuvraj averages 46.09 in ODIs v South Africa, but only 17.66 v New Zealand ... His father Yograj Singh, a fast bowler, played one Test in 1980-81 ... Yuvraj's record includes three ODIs for the Asia XI ...

THE FIGURES
Batting and fielding   www.cricinfo.com

	M	Inns	NO	Runs	HS	Avge	S/R	100	50	4s	6s	Ct	St
Tests to 10.9.07	19	29	4	830	122	33.20	52.93	2	3	118	5	21	0
ODIs to 10.9.07	183	166	25	5109	139	36.23	87.03	/	30	531	71	59	0
First-class to 10.9.07	72	115	14	4410	209	43.66	–		14	20	–	–	77	0

Bowling

	M	Balls	Runs	Wkts	BB	Avge	RpO	S/R	5i	10m
Tests to 10.9.07	19	144	90	1	1–25	90.00	3.75	144.00	0	0
ODIs to 10.9.07	183	2296	1946	49	4–6	39.71	5.08	46.85	0	0
First-class to 10.9.07	72	1071	591	10	3–25	59.10	3.31	107.10	0	0

IRELAND

| *Trent Johnston:* | *Niall O'Brien:* | *Boyd Rankin:* |
| *inspirational captain* | *feisty wicketkeeper* | *rangy fast bowler* |

Cricket in Ireland was once so popular that Oliver Cromwell banned it in 1656. Since then, it has been something of a minority sport, although there have been occasional big days, such as the one in 1969 when the mighty West Indians were skittled for 25 on a boggy pitch at Sion Mills in County Tyrone (rumours that the visitors enjoyed lavish hospitality at a nearby Guinness brewery the night before are, sadly, thought to be unfounded). Cricket continued as an amateur pastime until the 1990s, when the Irish Cricket Union left the auspices of the English board and attained independent ICC membership. Ireland became eligible to play in the World Cup, and narrowly missed out on the 1999 tournament, when they lost a playoff to Scotland. They made no mistake for 2007, though, winning the ICC Trophy (handily, it was played in Ireland) to ensure qualification. A change of captain to the Australian-born Trent Johnston ushered in a new, more professional set-up, and Ireland travelled to the Caribbean hopeful of making a mark. No-one, though, was quite prepared for what happened – except perhaps Johnston, who packed enough for a seven-week stay when most were expecting a quiet return home in a week or two. In their first World Cup match, Ireland tied with Zimbabwe, then went one better on a Sabina Park greentop on St Patrick's Day, hanging on to beat Pakistan and eliminate one of the pre-tournament favourites. Ireland sailed on to the Super Eights, where they beat Bangladesh too. Back home, though, reality set in: the better Irish players are already with English counties (one, Dublin-born Ed Joyce, has already played for England, and others are trying to follow suit), and Ireland need a more professional domestic structure if the giant leap forward made by Johnston's merry men is to be anything more than a footnote in cricket history.

Ireland's ODI records

Highest total	308-7	v Canada at Nairobi 2006-07
Lowest total	77	v Sri Lanka at St George's 2006-07
Most runs	614	WTS Porterfield (avge. 34.11)
Highest score	142*	KJ O'Brien v Kenya at Nairobi 2006-07
Most wickets	23	AC Botha (avge. 22.43)
Best bowling	4-36	WK McCallan v Kenya at Nairobi 2006-07
Most matches	22	WK McCallan (2006-2007)
World Cup record		Reached Super Eight stage in only appearance, 2006-07
Overall ODI record		Played 22: Won 6, Lost 13, Tied 1, No result 2

IRELAND

BOTHA, Andre Cornelius September 12, 1975, Johannesburg, South Africa
LHB, RM: 18 ODIs, 263 runs at 18.78, HS 56; 23 wickets at 22.43, BB 4-42.
Former South African provincial player: made 186 for Ireland v Scotland in August 2007.

BRAY, Jeremy Paul November 30, 1973, Newtown, Sydney, Australia
LHB: 15 ODIs, 401 runs at 28.64, HS 116, 2×100.
Former Australian Under-19 player: carried his bat for 115 v Zimbabwe in 2007 World Cup.*

CARROLL, Kenneth Edward Desmond March 22, 1983, Dublin
RHB, occasional LB: 6 ODIs, 70 runs at 11.66, HS 28; 0 wickets.
Captain and opening bat for the Railway Union club in Dublin.

CUSACK, Alex Richard October 29, 1980, Brisbane, Australia
RHB, RFM: 4 ODIs, 53 runs at 26.50, HS 36*; 6 wickets at 9.16, BB 3-15.
Man of the Match on ODI debut v South Africa at Belfast in June 2007.

FOURIE, Marthinus Jacobus ("Thinus") July 23, 1979, Cape Town, South Africa
RHB, RFM: 5 ODIs, 23 runs at 11.50, HS 14*; 0 wickets.
Opening bowler from Dublin's Merrion club: took 3-31 v Canada in 2007 Intercontinental Cup final.

JOHNSTON, David Trent April 29, 1974, Wollongong, NSW, Australia
RHB, RFM: 20 ODIs, 320 runs at 22.85, HS 45*; 10 wickets at 61.50, BB 2-40.
Inspirational captain (and innovative chicken dancer) during Ireland's World Cup run.

JOYCE, Dominick Ignatius June 14, 1981, Dublin
RHB: 3 ODIs, 29 runs at 9.66, HS 18.
Younger brother of England's Ed; another brother and two sisters have also played for Ireland.

LANGFORD-SMITH, David December 7, 1976, Sydney, Australia
RHB, RFM: 19 ODIs, 122 runs at 15.25, HS 31*; 18 wickets at 36.22, BB 3-32.
Irish by marriage (like Bray and Johnston), he took three wickets in each of his first three ODIs.

McCALLAN, William Kyle August 27, 1975, Carrickfergus, Co. Antrim
RHB, OB: 22 ODIs, 223 runs at 17.15, HS 50*; 22 wickets at 29.59, BB 4-36.
Tidy offspinner from Ulster club Waringstown: took 10 wickets at 23.30 in the World Cup.

MORGAN, Eoin Joseph Gerard September 10, 1986, Dublin
LHB: 18 ODIs, 549 runs at 32.29, HS 115, 1×100.
On Middlesex's books: hit 209 (Ireland's first double-century) v UAE in Abu Dhabi in Feb 2007.*

O'BRIEN, Kevin Joseph March 4, 1984, Dublin
RHB, RFM: 20 ODIs, 573 runs at 30.15, HS 142, 1×100; 10 wickets at 42.40, BB 2-38.
Allrounder with Dublin's Railway Union club: hit 142 (11 fours, six sixes) v Kenya in Feb 2007.

O'BRIEN, Niall John November 8, 1981, Dublin
LHB, WK: 21 ODIs, 503 runs at 23.95, HS 72; 16 ct, 3 st.
Feisty keeper who has played for Kent and Northants: made 72 in World Cup win over Pakistan.

PORTERFIELD, William Thomas Stuart September 6, 1984, Londonderry
RHB: 20 ODIs, 614 runs at 34.11, HS 112*, 2×100.
Solid opener: made two ODI hundreds (v Bermuda and Kenya) in three days early in 2007.

RANKIN, William Boyd July 5, 1984, Derry
LHB, RFM: 10 ODIs, 15 runs at 15.00, HS 7*; 12 wickets at 29.08, BB 3-32.
Tall (6ft 8ins) fast bowler who impressed at the World Cup and then joined Derbyshire.

WHITE, Andrew Roland July 3, 1980, Newtownards, Co. Down
RHB, OB: 18 ODIs, 217 runs at 15.50, HS 40; 7 wickets at 43.85, BB 2-31.
Offspinner, formerly with Northants, who hit 152 on first-class debut, for Ireland v Holland in 2004.*

KENYA

Steve Tikolo:
best of the rest

Tanmay Mishra:
youthful promise

Thomas Odoyo:
over 100 ODI wickets

The British Empire spread cricket to Kenya: the first notable match was played there in 1899, and English-style country clubs still flourish in Nairobi, which can claim one cricket record – six different grounds there have staged official one-day internationals, more than any other city. Strong MCC teams have made several visits to East Africa – one of them, in the early 1960s, unearthed Basharat Hassan, who went on to enjoy a long career with Nottinghamshire. Kenyan players formed the backbone of the East African side in the first World Cup, in 1975, but soon after that they struck out on their own, joining the ICC in their own right in 1981. Kenyan cricket continued to improve quietly until they qualified for the World Cup in 1995-96, where they amazed everyone by upsetting West Indies in a group match. Players reared on hard pitches struggled in early-season England at the 1999 Cup, but the 2003 version was different: it was held in Africa, and some of the matches were played in Kenya. Helped by outside events (England refused to travel to Zimbabwe, while New Zealand boycotted Kenya for security reasons), the Kenyans progressed to the semi-finals. It seemed like the start of a golden era: instead it ushered in a depressing time, marked by player strikes and arguments about administration. Peace broke out in time for the 2007 World Cup, but with several players approaching the veteran stage – many of them come from the same Luo tribe, which is why so many of their surnames begin with O – the results were poor. Still, Kenya boast arguably the best batsman outside the Test arena, in their captain Steve Tikolo, while the solidly built allrounder Thomas Odoyo (who played in the 1996 World Cup at 17) is the only bowler from a non-Test nation to reach 100 one-day wickets.

Kenya's ODI records

Highest total	347-3	v Bangladesh at Nairobi 1997-98
Lowest total	84	v Australia at Nairobi 2002-03
Most runs	2564	SO Tikolo (avge. 31.26)
Highest score	144	KO Otieno v Bangladesh at Nairobi 1997-98
Most wickets	98	TM Odoyo (avge. 31.46)
Best bowling	5-24	CO Obuya v Sri Lanka at Nairobi 2002-03
Most matches	92	SO Tikolo (1996-2007)
World Cup record	Semi-finalists in 2002-03; first phase 1995-96, 1999, 2006-07	
Overall ODI record	Played 94: Won 27, Lost 65, No result 2	

KAMANDE, James Kabatha   December 12, 1978, Muranga
RHB, OB: 42 ODIs, 381 runs at 14.11, HS 68; 19 wickets at 48.15, BB 3-32.
Former medium-pacer who now bowls offspin, after his action was reported to the ICC.

MISHRA, Tanmay   December 22, 1986, Mumbai, India
RHB: 28 ODIs, 698 runs at 31.72, HS 66.
Talented young Indian-born batsman who scored consistently after making his debut in 2006.

MODI, Hitesh Subhash   October 13, 1971, Kisumu
LHB, occasional OB: 63 ODIs, 1109 runs at 23.59, HS 78*; 0 wickets.
Adhesive batsman whose father is an international umpire (and has twice given his son out in ODIs).

OBUYA, Collins Omondi   July 27, 1981, Nairobi
RHB, LB: 52 ODIs, 598 runs at 17.08, HS 68*; 26 wickets at 46.57, BB 5-24.
Tall legspinner who played a few matches for Warwickshire after impressing at the 2003 World Cup.

OBUYA, David Oluoch   August 14, 1979, Nairobi
RHB, WK: 43 ODIs, 782 runs at 19.55, HS 93; 26 ct, 4 st.
Opener, wicketkeeper, and brother of Collins (and of former Kenya opener Kennedy Otieno).

ODHIAMBO, Nehemiah Ngoche   August 7, 1983, Nairobi, Kenya
RHB, RFM: 17 ODIs, 142 runs at 15.77, HS 66; 10 wickets at 52.40, BB 3-25.
Fast bowler who took 5-54 on first-class debut, v Canada in 2006: brother of Lameck Onyango.

ODOYO, Thomas Migai   May 12, 1978, Nairobi
RHB, RFM: ODIs 95 (5 for Africa), 1774 runs (24.63), HS 84; 102 wkts (31.77), BB 4-25.
Hard-hitting allrounder: the first bowler from a non-Test nation to take 100 wickets in ODIs.

ONGONDO, Peter Jimmy Carter   February 10, 1977, Nairobi
RHB, RFM: 51 ODIs (1 for Africa), 301 runs at 10.37, HS 36; 57 wkts at 26.26, BB 5-51.
Handy seamer and useful tailender who once top-scored v West Indies with 36 from No. 11.

ONYANGO, Lameck Ngoche   September 22, 1973, Nairobi
RHB, RM: 11 ODIs, 60 runs at 10.00, HS 23; 10 wickets at 30.50, BB 3-37.
Seamer and late-order blocker who once went in last in an ODI and didn't bowl.

OUMA, Maurice Akumu   November 8, 1982, Kiambli
RHB, WK: 26 ODIs, 459 runs at 18.36, HS 58; 12 ct, 2 st.
Handy striker who often opens with David Obuya, with whom he vies for the keepers' gloves.

SHAH, Ravindu Dhirajilal   August 28, 1972, Nairobi
RHB, occasional RM: 56 ODIs, 1506 runs at 27.88, HS 113, 1×100; 0 wickets.
Stylish batsman who hit 247 v Pakistan A in 2004: returned after three years for the 2007 World Cup.

SUJI, Otieno Ondik ("Tony")   February 5, 1976, Nairobi
RHB, RM: 54 ODIs, 486 runs at 13.50, HS 67; 19 wickets at 59.42, BB 2-16.
Combative allrounder, brother of Martin, with whom he once opened the bowling in an ODI.

SUJI, Martin Armon   June 2, 1971, Nairobi
RHB, RFM: 64 ODIs, 247 runs at 8.23, HS 16*; 43 wickets at 50.93, BB 4-24.
Graceful opening bowler, recently hit by knee trouble: part of the team that beat West Indies in 1996.

TIKOLO, Stephen Ogonji   June 25, 1971, Nairobi
RHB, OB: 96 ODIs (4 for Africa), 2623 runs at 30.50, HS 111, 2×100; 69 wkts at 32.69, BB 4-41.
Probably the best batsman outside the Test arena: 22 hundreds for Kenya, including two doubles.

VARAIYA, Hiren Ashok   April 9, 1984, Nairobi
RHB, SLA: 18 ODIs, 26 runs at 26.00, HS 10*; 25 wickets at 21.32, BB 4-25.
Young spinner who flights the ball well: took a wicket with first ball in ODIs, v Canada in 2006.

THE NETHERLANDS

Jeroen Smits:
new captain

Alexei Kervezee:
youthful promise

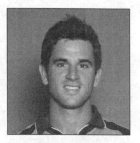

Ryan ten Doeschate:
Holland and Essex

Cricket was brought to The Netherlands by British soldiers during the Napoleonic War: by 1881 there was a Dutch team, and two years later a national board, comprising 18 clubs, four of which are still around. A league system has long flourished, and there has been a tradition of foreign players coming over to coach. Dutch cricket received a boost in 1964 when Australia visited after an Ashes tour and lost by three wickets, and more noses were tweaked in 1989, with a win over England A, captained by Peter Roebuck, which dented his hopes of skippering the full Test side. West Indies (1991) and South Africa (1994) also succumbed – it's safe to say they were more relaxed than they might have been for an official international – and another strongish England side was beaten in 1993. The Netherlands qualified for their first World Cup three years later, and weren't disgraced, and they were there again in 2003, when they beat Namibia. They just scraped in to the 2007 tournament, winning a playoff against the UAE, but again managed a consolation win, this time over Scotland, which made up for being pummelled by South Africa (for whom Herschelle Gibbs hit six sixes in one Daan van Bunge over) and Australia. Standout performers in recent years have included Roland Lefebvre, who played for Somerset and Glamorgan, and Bas Zuiderent, who had a spell with Sussex. A South African-born newcomer took the eye in 2006: Essex's Ryan ten Doeschate hammered four centuries in three ICC Intercontinental Cup games, and soon shot to the top of the national one-day runscoring and wicket-taking lists. The local players are very keen, but there are not that many of them, fans are thin on the ground, and there's no chance of a proper first-class competition. The future might not be too bright, but it's certainly orange.

The Netherlands' ODI records

Highest total	315-8	v Bermuda at Rotterdam 2007
Lowest total	80	v West Indies at Dublin 2007
Most runs	615	RN ten Doeschate (avge. 55.90)
Highest score	134*	KJJ van Noortwijk v Namibia at Bloemfontein 2002-03
Most wickets	30	RN ten Doeschate (avge. 21.80)
Best bowling	4-31	RN ten Doeschate v Canada at Nairobi 2006-07
Most matches	34	B Zuiderent (1996-2007)
World Cup record	Eliminated in first round 1995-96, 2002-03 and 2006-07	
Overall ODI record	Played 35: Won 11, Lost 22, No result 2	

THE NETHERLANDS

ADEEL RAJA, Mohammad Khalid August 15, 1980, Lahore, Pakistan
RHB, OB: 9 ODIs, 19 runs at 4.75, HS 8*; 9 wickets at 38.55, BB 4-42.
Big spinner who took 4-42 in the World Cup win over Namibia in 2003.

BORREN, Peter William August 21, 1983, Christchurch, New Zealand
RHB, RM: 18 ODIs, 256 runs at 18.28, HS 96; 15 wickets at 43.20, BB 3-54.
Combative allrounder who played for NZ Under-19s: made 105 and 96 v Canada in 2006.

BUKHARI, Mudassar December 26, 1983, Gujrat, Pakistan
RHB, RFM: 6 ODIs, 145 runs at 48.33, HS 71; 8 wickets at 18.62, BB 3-24.
Primarily a bowler, he scored 71 (after opening) and took 3-24 against Ireland in July 2007.

de GROOTH, Tom Nico May 14, 1979, The Hague
RHB, OB: 8 ODIs, 203 runs at 29.00, HS 97; 1 wicket at 2.00, BB 1-2.
Maturing batsman who hit 98 (v Scotland), 196 and 97 (v Bermuda) in successive matches in Aug 2007.

de LEEDE, Timotheus Bernardus Maria January 25, 1968, Leidschendam
RHB, RM: 29 ODIs, 400 runs at 16.66, HS 58*; 29 wickets at 34.44, BB 4-35.
Long-serving allrounder who played in all Holland's 14 World Cup matches: MoM v India in 2003.

KERVEZEE, Alexei Nicolaas September 11, 1989, Walvis Bay, Namibia
RHB, occasional RM: 18 ODIs, 341 runs at 26.23, HS 62; 0 wickets.
Precocious talent: World Cup debut at 17, and later made 98 v Canada. Joined Worcestershire for 2007.

MOHAMMAD KASHIF December 3, 1984, Khanewal, Pakistan
RHB, SLA: 7 ODIs, 1 run at 0.50, HS 1; 8 wickets at 31.62, BB 3-42.
Nicknamed "Bollywood", he practises hard and fields well, and is trying to develop a "doosra".

REEKERS, Darron John May 26, 1973, Christchurch, New Zealand
RHB, RFM: 13 ODIs, 387 runs at 29.76, HS 104, 1x100; 13 wickets at 29.92, BB 3-54.
Has opened the batting and bowling in ODIs, and hit 104 against Ireland in Feb 2007.

SCHIFERLI, Edgar May 17, 1976, The Hague
RHB, RFM: 17 ODIs, 96 runs at 9.60, HS 22; 13 wickets at 43.46, BB 3-18.
Holland's most experienced fast bowler: was unable to play in the 2007 World Cup because of a leg injury.

SMITS, Jeroen June 21, 1972, The Hague
RHB, WK: 28 ODIs, 116 runs at 16.57, HS 26; 27 ct, 4 st.
Steady keeper (and Jamiroquai fan): named captain when Luuk van Troost retired after 2007 World Cup.

STELLING, William Frederick June 30, 1969, Johannesburg, South Africa
RHB, RFM: 15 ODIs, 181 runs at 30.16, HS 45; 22 wickets at 25.77, BB 3-12.
Much-travelled allrounder, also played for Leicestershire: MoM for 3-12 v Scotland in 2007 World Cup.

SZWARCZYNSKI, Eric Stefan February 13, 1983, Vanderbijlpark, South Africa
RHB: 10 ODIs, 207 runs at 25.87, HS 56*.
Student whose favourite player is Allan Donald: made a century for Netherlands A v MCC in 2006.

ten DOESCHATE, Ryan Neil June 30, 1980, Port Elizabeth, South Africa
RHB, RFM: 17 ODIs, 615 runs at 55.90, HS 109*, 1x100; 30 wickets at 21.80, BB 4-31.
Allrounder who also plays for Essex: took 6-20 (and 3-92) then scored 259 v Canada in 2006.*

van BUNGE, Daan Lodewijk Samuel October 19, 1982, Voorburg
RHB, LB: 24 ODIs, 392 runs at 20.63, HS 62; 10 wickets at 25.90, BB 3-16.
Talented batsman ... but his legspin was hit for six sixes by Herschelle Gibbs at the 2007 World Cup.

ZUIDERENT, Bastiaan March 3, 1977, Utrecht
RHB: 34 ODIs, 612 runs at 21.10, HS 77*.
Orthodox opener who had a spell with Sussex: has played in all 14 of Holland's World Cup matches.

SCOTLAND

Ryan Watson:
new captain

Gavin Hamilton:
one England cap

Neil McCallum:
in form in 2007

Cricket crept over the border from England in the mid-18th century: soldiers played it near Perth in 1750, although the first recorded match in Scotland was not till 1785. More recently there has long been a strong amateur league system in the country, although – just as in Ireland – international aspirations have always been handicapped by the absence of a proper professional set-up, which has meant that the better players have always migrated south to England. One of them, the Ayr-born Mike Denness, captained England, while one of the few bowlers to trouble Don Bradman in 1930 was the Scottish legspinner Ian Peebles. More recently, offspinner Peter Such (born in Helensburgh) played for England, while Gavin Hamilton also won an England Test cap after impressing for Scotland at the 1999 World Cup. Unfortunately, Hamilton bagged a pair, and was soon back playing for Scotland – at the 2007 World Cup, alongside another former England player in Dougie Brown, the combative Stirling-born allrounder who had a long career with Warwickshire and played nine ODIs in 1997-98. Those have been the only appearances on the highest stage for Scotland, who left the auspices of the English board and joined the ICC in 1994, and they failed to win a match – or reach 200 – in any of their World Cup games in 1999 or 2007. They also competed in the English counties' limited-overs league for many years, without managing more than the occasional upset. The main problem lying in the way of Scotland's advancement – apart from the weather – is still the lack of a sound domestic structure which might support first-class cricket: local support is also questionable (there were very few spectators when India played a one-day international in Edinburgh in August 2007). Until this is addressed – if it ever can be – Scotland will continue to suffer from a player drain to English counties.

Scotland's ODI records

Highest total	293-8	v Canada at Mombasa 2006-07
Lowest total	68	v West Indies at Leicester 1999
Most runs	697	RR Watson (avge. 34.85)
Highest score	123*	RR Watson v Canada at Mombasa 2006-07
Most wickets	27	JAR Blain (avge. 33.77)
Best bowling	4-28	RM Haq v West Indies at Dublin 2007
Most matches	25	JAR Blain (1999-2007)
World Cup record	Eliminated in first round 1999 and 2006-07	
Overall ODI record	Played 27: Won 7, Lost 19, No result 1	

SCOTLAND

BLAIN, John Angus Rae January 4, 1979, Edinburgh
RHB, RFM: 25 ODIs, 209 runs at 14.92, HS 30*; 27 wickets at 33.77, BB 4-37.
Reliable seamer who had spells with Northants and Yorkshire.

BROWN, Douglas Robert October 29, 1969, Stirling
RHB, RFM: 25 ODIs (16 for Scotland), 319 runs at 17.72, HS 50*; 22 wickets at 41.77, BB 3-37.
Long-serving Warwickshire allrounder who played nine ODIs for England in 1997-98.

HAMILTON, Gavin Mark September 16, 1974, Broxburn, West Lothian
LHB, RFM: 22 ODIs, 649 runs at 34.15, HS 79; 3 wickets at 53.33, BB 2-36.
Played for Yorks & Durham – and once for England, after doing well for Scotland in 1999 World Cup.

HAQ Khan, Rana Majid February 11, 1983, Paisley
LHB, OB: 17 ODIs, 376 runs at 22.11, HS 71; 24 wickets at 27.79, BB 4-28.
Hard-hitting allrounder, who plays for Ferguslie with his cousin Omer Hussain (see below).

HOFFMANN, Paul Jacob Christopher January 14, 1970, Rockhampton, Australia
RHB, RFM: 18 ODIs, 85 runs at 7.72, HS 31; 16 wickets at 34.62, BB 3-22.
Fast bowler who dismissed Desmond Haynes for Australian Country XI v West Indies in 1992-93.

HUSSAIN, Rana Omer December 3, 1984, Paisley
LHB, occasional WK: 6 ODIs, 44 runs at 8.80, HS 16; 4 ct.
Useful batsman who has scored two hundreds for Scotland A, against Lancashire and Yorkshire.

LYONS, Ross Thomas December 8, 1984, Greenock
LHB, SLA: 13 ODIs, 77 runs at 38.50, HS 28; 10 wickets at 56.20, BB 2-28.
Promising spinner who dismissed Shahid Afridi in his first ODI.

McCALLUM, Neil Francis Ian November 22, 1977, Edinburgh
RHB: 20 ODIs, 465 runs at 23.25, HS 100, 1x100.
PE teacher who was Scotland's in-form batsman in 2007, making 181 v Holland and 100 v Ireland.

NEL, Johann Dewald June 6, 1980, Klerksdorp, South Africa
RHB, RFM: 8 ODIs, 5 runs, no average; 3 wickets at 93.33, BB 1-34.
Fast bowler who dismissed Inzamam-ul-Haq on his ODI debut, and played for Worcs in 2007.

POONIA, Naveed Singh May 11, 1986, Govan, Glasgow
RHB: 14 ODIs, 184 runs at 13.14, HS 67.
Stylish batsman on the Warwickshire staff: he has made seven centuries for their 2nd XI.

ROGERS, Glenn Alan April 12, 1977, Sydney, New South Wales
RHB, SLA: 10 ODIs, 81 runs at 20.25, HS 26; 6 wickets at 56.00, BB 2-22.
Promising spinner who caught typhoid just before the 2007 World Cup, but recovered in time to play.

SMITH, Colin John Ogilvie September 27, 1972, Aberdeen
RHB, WK: 18 ODIs, 245 runs at 17.50, HS 51; 13 ct, 9 st.
Policeman and dependable wicketkeeper who has played for Scotland since 1997.

WATSON, Ryan Robert November 12, 1976, Salisbury (now Harare), Zimbabwe
RHB, RM: 21 ODIs, 697 runs at 34.85, HS 123*, 1x100; 6 wickets at 42.00, BB 3-18.
Chunky batsman, at school with SA's Graeme Smith: named captain after 2007 World Cup.

WATTS, David Fraser June 5, 1979, King's Lynn, Norfolk
RHB: 18 ODIs, 430 runs at 23.88, HS 70.
Banker-turned-batsman who scored 171 not out in a one-day game against Denmark in 2006.

WRIGHT, Craig McIntyre April 28, 1974, Paisley, Renfrewshire
RHB, RFM: 16 ODIs, 204 runs at 17.00, HS 37; 24 wickets at 23.95, BB 4-29.
Scotland's leading wicket-taker in all matches, he stepped down as captain after the 2007 World Cup.

ZIMBABWE

Prosper Utseya:
tight offspinner and captain

Tatenda Taibu:
returned to the fold

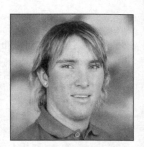

Brendan Taylor:
occasionally brilliant

The decline of cricket in Zimbabwe is one of the game's saddest tales – outranked, of course, by the decline of the country itself from prosperous to dangerous, a nation where corruption and inflation are rife. Cricket was first played in what was then Rhodesia in 1891, and for years the national side took part in South Africa's inter-provincial competition. Several Rhodesians played Tests for South Africa, notably Colin Bland ... and offspinner John Traicos, in 1970: he was still around 22 years later when Zimbabwe were given Test status themselves. That came after years of consistent performances, including a famous World Cup victory over Australia in 1983, inspired by Duncan Fletcher, later England's Ashes-winning coach. Zimbabwe were always hampered by a small player-base, but punched above their weight in internationals thanks to a nucleus of fine players including Dave Houghton, the Flower brothers and Heath Streak. Probably their strongest side was assembled for the 1999 World Cup, following the return of Neil Johnson (previously based in South Africa) and the consistent Murray Goodwin (Australia). Zimbabwe qualified for the second phase of the 1999 World Cup, and six of their eight Test wins came between October 1998 and November 2001. And then it all started to go wrong. Zimbabwe qualified for the Super Sixes again in 2003, but only because England refused to visit Harare. With the domestic political situation worsening, Andy Flower and the black fast bowler Henry Olonga sported black armbands bemoaning the "death of democracy" in Zimbabwe: their reward was to be hounded out of the country. A divisive dispute over payments and selection then tore the rest of the side apart: Goodwin and Johnson returned whence they came, Streak and Andy Blignaut have rarely played since, and even Tatenda Taibu, their first black captain, fell out with the board for a while. Zimbabwe pulled out of Test cricket in 2005, just ahead of official ICC action: two years later ICC's chief executive Malcolm Speed admitted he didn't know whether Zimbabwe "would ever be able to come back to Test cricket". There was a chink of light later in 2007, though: after some encouraging performances against South Africa (although the one-day series was still lost 3-0), helped by the return of Taibu, the ICC's new president Ray Mali claimed that the young Zimbabwe side could top the world rankings in three years. Sadly, few believe this is really possible in such a poisonous climate.

Test and **ODI records** for Zimbabwe can be found on pages 268-271

ZIMBABWE

BRENT, Gary Bazil January 13, 1976, Sinoia (now Chinhoyi)
RHB, RFM: 4 Tests, 35 runs (5.83); 7 wkts (44.85). 62 ODIs, 334 runs (11.51), 72 wkts (33.93).
Steady seamer who made ODI debut at 20 in 1996-97: recalled in 2006-07 after three years.

CHIBHABHA, Chamunorwa Justice September 6, 1986, Masvingo
RHB, RM: 0 Tests. 25 ODIs, 636 runs (25.44); 4 wkts (75.00).
Good-looking off-driver, and fine fielder: his sister Julia captains Zimbabwe's women's team.

CHIGUMBURA, Elton March 14, 1986, Kwekwe
RHB, RFM: 6 Tests, 187 runs (15.58), 9 wkts (55.33). 62 ODIs, 1247 runs (24.94), 30 wkts (43.36).
Big-hitting allrounder, and good outfielder, who made his first-class debut before he was 16.

DABENGWA, Keith Mbusi August 17, 1980, Bulawayo
LHB, SLA: 3 Tests, 90 runs (15.00), 5 wkts (49.80). 13 ODIs, 147 runs (24.50, 7 wkts (43.57).
Fitfully brilliant allrounder who scored 161 in 2005 and took 7-1 in a first-class match in 2007.

DUFFIN, Terrence March 20, 1982, Kwekwe
LHB: 2 Tests, 80 runs (20.00). 23 ODIs, 546 runs (23.73).
Adhesive opener who captained Zimbabwe in his first 13 ODIs.

MASAKADZA, Hamilton August 9, 1983, Harare
RHB, LB: 15 Tests, 785 runs (27.06), 2 wkts (19.50). 42 ODIs, 797 runs (19.92), 12 wkts (31.50).
Early-flowering batsman who made 119 on Test debut against West Indies in 2001, aged 17.

MATSIKENYERI, Stuart May 3, 1983, Harare
RHB, OB: 8 Tests, 351 runs (23.40), 2 wkts (172.50). 66 ODIs, 1223 runs (20.72), 13 wkts (50.84).
Cheerful, diminutive allrounder who made 150 for Zimbabwe v Bangladesh Board XI in 2005.

MPOFU, Christopher Bobby November 27, 1985, Plumtree
RHB, RFM: 6 Tests, 17 runs (2.83), 8 wkts (69.50). 23 ODIs, 19 runs (2.37), 26 wkts (36.73).
Tall seam bowler, and entertainingly clueless batsman: took 6-8 for Matabeleland in 2006.

MUPARIWA, Tawanda April 16, 1985, Bulawayo
RHB, RFM: 1 Test, 15 runs (15.00), 0 wkts. 22 ODIs, 149 runs (12.41), 36 wkts (27.97).
Fast bowler with a good inswinger, who impressed with the new ball in the West Indies in 2006.

RAINSFORD, Edward Charles December 14, 1984, Kadoma
RHB, RFM: 0 Tests. 24 ODIs, 38 runs (4.75), 24 wkts (38.45).
Promising fast bowler, with a good outswinger and yorker: took 6-67 v South Africa A in 2004.

SIBANDA, Vusimuzi October 10, 1983, Highfields, Harare
RHB, RM: 3 Tests, 48 runs (8.00). 54 ODIs, 1218 runs (23.88), 2 wkts (74.00).
Stylish opener who often gets out when set: made 116 in tri-series final v Bermuda in 2006.

TAIBU, Tatenda May 14, 1983, Harare
RHB, WK: 24 Tests, 1273 runs (29.60), 1 wkt (27.00). 87 ODIs, 1582 runs (27.27), 2 wkts (30.50).
Tiny keeper, big-hearted batter: the youngest Test captain at 20, he later fell out with the Board.

TAYLOR, Brendan Ross Murray February 6, 1986, Harare
RHB, OB, WK: 10 Tests, 422 runs (21.10), 0 wkts 66 ODIs, 1706 runs (28.43), 8 wkts (28.00).
Occasionally brilliant batsman, with a booming cover-drive: has had disciplinary problems.

UTSEYA, Prosper March 26, 1985, Harare
RHB, OB: 1 Test, 45 runs (22.50), 0 wkts. 65 ODIs, 340 runs (10.00), 40 wkts (56.70).
Short offspinner who keeps the runs down: took over as captain in July 2006, when he was 21.

WILLIAMS, Sean Colin September 26, 1986, Bulawayo
LHB, SLA: 0 Tests. 19 ODIs, 414 runs (25.87), 8 wkts (52.37).
Former national Under-19 captain: scored 70 not out v West Indies in the 2007 World Cup.

UMPIRES AND REFEREES

ALEEM DAR

UMPIRE

Full name	**Aleem Sarwar Dar**	*Tests*	**39 since 2003-04**
Born	**June 6, 1968, Jhang, Punjab**	*ODIs*	**97 since 1999-2000**
Country	**Pakistan**		

Aleem Dar played 17 first-class matches as an offspinning allrounder, but never surpassed the 39 he scored in his first innings, for Railways in February 1987. He took up umpiring in 1998-99, and stood in his first ODI the following season. He officiated at the 2003 World Cup, and a year later was the first Pakistani to join the ICC's elite panel. Calm and unobtrusive, he soon established a good reputation, and it was no surprise when he was chosen to stand in the 2007 World Cup final. What was a surprise was his part in the chaos in the dark at the end, for which all the officials were excluded from the World Twenty20 championships later in the year. Unlike most of his colleagues, he continues to play, and made 82 in a club game the day after umpiring a Test in Mumbai in November 2004.

ASAD RAUF

UMPIRE

Full name	**Asad Rauf**	*Tests*	**13 since 2004-05**
Born	**May 12, 1956, Lahore, Punjab**	*ODIs*	**45 since 1999-2000**
Country	**Pakistan**		

Asad Rauf was a right-hand batsman who enjoyed a solid if unspectacular first-class career in Pakistan in the 1980s, four times making more than 600 runs in a season and scoring three centuries, the highest 130 for Railways against National Bank in November 1981. He umpired his first first-class match in 1998-99, and stood in his first ODI early in 2000. It took a bit longer to crack the Test scene, but he impressed once he did, joining the ICC's elite panel in April 2006. A former offspinner himself, he is more prepared than some to give spinners lbws when batsmen prop forward hiding bat behind pads.

MARK **BENSON**

UMPIRE

Full name	**Mark Richard Benson**	*Tests*	**15 since 2004-05**
Born	**July 6, 1958, Shoreham-by-Sea, Sussex**	*ODIs*	**55 since 2004**
Country	**England**		

Mark Benson is the only elite umpire who also played international cricket. A gritty left-hander, he won his only Test cap against India in June 1986, and played his solitary ODI a week later. He played on for almost a decade without catching the selectors' eyes again, making 18,387 runs, with 48 hundreds, the highest 257 against Hampshire on his first day as Kent's captain in 1991. He became a fulltime umpire in 2000, and soon impressed: he was the TV official for an ODI the following season. He stood in an ODI for the first time in 2004, and joined the elite panel in April 2006. Later that year he had to have minor heart surgery after a turn during a Test in South Africa, but returned in time for the 2007 World Cup, in which six of his eight matches involved the South Africans.

UMPIRES AND REFEREES

BILLY **BOWDEN**

Full name **Brent Fraser Bowden**
Born **April 11, 1963, Henderson, Auckland**
Country **New Zealand**

Tests **41 since 1999-2000**
ODIs **117 since 1994-95**

Some eccentrics are born. Others thrust eccentricity upon themselves. Brent "Billy" Bowden shot to fame with a zany array of embellished signals and a preposterous eye for showmanship. Bowden turned to umpiring after the onset of arthritis in his early twenties, and earned a reputation for giving batsmen out with a curiously bent finger. The most celebrated of his antics is the hop-on-one-leg-and-reach-for-Jesus signal for six. For all the embellishments, his decision-making is usually spot-on, although in 2007 he was suspended from standing in the inaugural World Twenty20 championships following his role (as fourth umpire) in the farcical conclusion of the World Cup final in Barbados.

CHRIS **BROAD**

Full name **Brian Christopher Broad**
Born **Sept 29, 1957, Knowle, Somerset**
Country **England**

Tests **23 since 2003-04**
ODIs **100 since 2003-04**

It was a classic case of poacher turned gamekeeper when Chris Broad became a match referee: he had several jousts with authority during a largely successful 25-Test career in the 1980s, refusing to walk after being given out in a Test in Pakistan, and smashing down the stumps after being bowled for 139 in the Bicentennial Test at Sydney in 1987-88. A tall, angular left-hander, Broad did well in Australia, scoring three more Test hundreds there in the 1986-87 Ashes series. After a back injury hastened his retirement, he tried his hand at TV commentary, then in 2003 became a match referee keen on enforcing the Code of Conduct. His son, Stuart, made his England debut in 2006.

STEVE **BUCKNOR**

Full name **Stephen Anthony Bucknor**
Born **May 31, 1946, Montego Bay, Jamaica**
Country **West Indies**

Tests **119 since 1988-89**
ODIs **163 since 1988-89**

Steve Bucknor, whose trademark is nodding gently before raising the dreaded finger, was the first man to umpire 100 Tests. He also stood in five successive World Cup finals. He is not due to retire until 2011, although recently a few errors have crept in – not least his part in the farcical finish of the 2007 World Cup final, which led to his suspension for the World Twenty20 championships that September. Bucknor originally started umpiring after repeated duff decisions in his Jamaican club games. His rise to star status was rapid: he stood in the 1992 World Cup final after just four Tests and a handful of ODIs. He is a man of routine, going through a morning ritual – exercises, a verse from the Bible, and the morning papers – before arriving at the ground. He is also a qualified football referee, who once handled a World Cup qualifier.

UMPIRES AND REFEREES

JEFF **CROWE**

Full name	**Jeffrey John Crowe**	*Tests*	**20 since 2004-05**
Born	**September 14, 1958, Auckland**	*ODIs*	**79 since 2003-04**
Country	**New Zealand**		

Jeff Crowe might have played for Australia – he had several successful Sheffield Shield seasons in Adelaide – but he eventually returned to New Zealand, winning 39 Test caps, six as captain. Although he was often overshadowed by his younger brother Martin, Jeff managed three Test centuries of his own. After retirement he had a spell as New Zealand's manager, before becoming a referee in 2003. He was in charge for the 2007 World Cup final, where he presided over the embarrassing finale, which led to him and the umpires being suspended from the inaugural World Twenty20 championships later in the year.

BILLY **DOCTROVE**

Full name	**Billy Raymond Doctrove**	*Tests*	**13 since 1999-2000**
Born	**July 3, 1955, Marigot, Dominica**	*ODIs*	**71 since 1997-98**
Country	**West Indies**		

Billy Doctrove played club cricket in Dominica for a number of years, but his first love was football, particularly Liverpool, which explains his odd nickname "Toshack". In 1995 he became Dominica's first FIFA referee, and officiated in a number of internationals in the Caribbean, including a World Cup qualifier between Guyana and Grenada. In 1997 he quit football to concentrate on umpiring, and stood in his first Test in 2000. He joined the international panel in 2004 and the elite one in 2006, but his first forays at the highest level were uninspiring, and he found himself embroiled in the Pakistan ball-tampering furore at The Oval in 2006, as the "other umpire" to Darrell Hair.

DARYL **HARPER**

Full name	**Daryl John Harper**	*Tests*	**65 since 1998-99**
Born	**October 23, 1951, Adelaide**	*ODIs*	**141 since 1993-94**
Country	**Australia**		

Daryl Harper played club cricket in Adelaide for many years before turning to umpiring. He stood in his first first-class match in 1987-88, and joined Australia's international panel six years later. Quiet and undemonstrative, he was Australia's first representative on the ICC's international panel when it was set up in 2002, being chosen ahead of Darrell Hair and Simon Taufel, and is one of only three survivors (with Steve Bucknor and Rudi Koertzen) from that original intake. He likes most sports, particularly Aussie Rules football and basketball, and writes an entertaining online blog about his travels at www.cricketump.com.

UMPIRES AND REFEREES

ALAN **HURST**

Full name	**Alan George Hurst**	*Tests*	**15 since 2004-05**
Born	**July 15, 1950, Altona, Melbourne**	*ODIs*	**42 since 2004-05**
Country	**Australia**		

A strapping fast bowler, Alan Hurst won all but one of his dozen Test caps during the World Series Cricket era, after Australia's leading players had been poached by Kerry Packer. He nonetheless took 25 wickets in the 1978-79 Ashes series, which Australia lost 5-1, before the return of Lillee and Co., and a serious back injury, put paid to his future prospects. He was also a notably bad batsman, collecting ducks in exactly half his 20 Test innings. After a spell as a teacher he joined the ICC's panel of referees in 2004.

RUDI **KOERTZEN**

Full name	**Rudolf Eric Koertzen**	*Tests*	**84 since 1992-93**
Born	**March 26, 1949, Knysna, Cape Province**	*ODIs*	**177 since 1992-93**
Country	**South Africa**		

Rudi Koertzen is a modern umpire in the traditional mould, a curious blend of old and new – his flat white cap is usually offset by a pair of wraparound shades, while his trademark is a dalek-like super-slo-mo raise of the fatal finger to exterminate a batsman's innings. A lifelong cricket fan, he played league cricket while working as a railway clerk, but turned to umpiring in 1981. He first stood in a Test in 1992-93, in South Africa's first home series after readmission, and has been a fixture ever since: he has now umpired more ODIs than anyone else. An original member of the elite panel, he leaves little to chance, putting in regular sessions in the gym as well as long hours in front of the TV studying the techniques – and previous dismissals – of the batsmen at his mercy. He was one of the support officials for the 2007 World Cup final, but his lead role in the farcical finale cost him a place at the inaugural World Twenty20 championships later in the year.

RANJAN **MADUGALLE**

Full name	**Ranjan Serenath Madugalle**	*Tests*	**97 since 1993-94**
Born	**April 22, 1959, Kandy**	*ODIs*	**209 since 1993-94**
Country	**Sri Lanka**		

A stylish right-hander, Ranjan Madugalle won 21 Test caps, the first of them in Sri Lanka's inaugural Test, against England in 1981-82, when he top-scored with 65 in the first innings. He also made 103 against India in Colombo in 1985, and captained Sri Lanka twice. Not long after retiring, and trying his hand at marketing, he became one of the first match refs, and was appointed the ICC's chief referee in 2001. His easy-going exterior and charming personality are a mask for someone who has a reputation as a strict disciplinarian.

UMPIRES AND REFEREES

REFEREE

ROSHAN **MAHANAMA**

Full name **Roshan Siriwardene Mahanama**
Born **May 31, 1966, Colombo**
Country **Sri Lanka**

Tests **15 since 2003-04**
ODIs **75 since 2003-04**

Roshan Mahanama's playing career had two major highlights: he was part of the winning team in the 1996 World Cup, and the following year made 225 (the highest score in his 52 Tests) as he and Sanath Jayasuriya put on 576, then a record Test partnership, as Sri Lanka ran up 952 for 6 (another record) against India in Colombo. An attacking right-hander who made four Test centuries in all (three in nine months in 1992-93), he was also a fine fielder. He was jettisoned after the 1999 World Cup and quit not long afterwards, blaming the selectors for their shabby treatment of him in a book he called *Retired Hurt*. He joined the ICC's referees panel in 2003.

REFEREE

MIKE **PROCTER**

Full name **Michael John Procter**
Born **September 15, 1946, Durban, Natal**
Country **South Africa**

Tests **41 since 2001-02**
ODIs **137 since 2001-02**

The world's greatest allrounder for a while in the 1970s, Mike Procter did marvels with the bat (once scoring six successive first-class hundreds) and ball (hurtling in and bowling furiously quick using a peculiar wrong-footed action) for a variety of teams, especially Gloucestershire where he was a folk hero. He was restricted to seven Tests as a player, as he peaked just as South Africa were being ostracised from world sport: he still took 41 wickets at just 15.02. When South Africa were readmitted he was their first coach, then went upstairs to the referee's room. There, he exudes calm - although many thought he should have made more noise at The Oval in 2006, when he oversaw what became the first forfeited Test match after Pakistan were penalised for ball-tampering.

REFEREE

JAVAGAL **SRINATH**

Full name **Javagal Srinath**
Born **August 31, 1969, Mysore, Karnataka**
Country **India**

Tests **4 since 2006**
ODIs **19 since 2006-07**

Arguably the fastest bowler India has ever produced, Javagal Srinath took 236 wickets in Tests, and 315 more in ODIs. He was tall, and usually slanted the ball in. Unusually for a quick bowler, he did better in India than overseas, his bowling average of 26 at home being four runs lower than his overall one. He went out at the top: his last international match was the 2003 World Cup final. Sadly, there was no fairytale farewell – Srinath was caned (0 for 87) as Australia ran out easy winners. He was not long away from the international arena, though: after a spell as a commentator he joined the referees' panel in 2006. "I'll have to concentrate more than I did during my playing days," he observed.

UMPIRES AND REFEREES

SIMON **TAUFEL**

Full name **Simon James Arnold Taufel**
Born **Jan 21, 1971, St Leonards, Sydney**
Country **Australia**

Tests **43 since 2000-01**
ODIs **116 since 1999-2000**

Simon Taufel came young to umpiring: he was only 24 when he stood in his first Sheffield Shield match, and still under 30 – and younger than some of the players – when he made his Test debut on Boxing Day 2000. He took up umpiring after being forced to retire from Sydney club cricket with a back injury. Calm and collected on the field, he leaves little to chance, regularly running laps of the ground to keep fit and often standing in the practice nets to familiarise himself with players' techniques. And it has paid off: he joined the ICC's elite panel in 2003, and won the award as the world's leading umpire (voted on by the Test captains and referees) three times running from 2004.

As well as its "elite" panel of umpires, the ICC also has an "international" panel, who fill in when gaps arise in the rota. This reserve list includes:

Barbour, Kevan Christopher (Zimbabwe), b. October 23, 1949, Bulawayo

Baxter, Gary Arthur (New Zealand), b. March 5, 1953, Christchurch

Davis, Stephen James (Australia), b. April 9, 1952, London, England

de Silva, Ellawalakankanamge <u>Asoka</u> Ranjit (Sri Lanka; played 10 Tests and 28 ODIs), b. March 28, 1956, Kalutara

Duncan, Clyde R. (West Indies), b. January 7, 1954, Vreed-En-Hoop, Guyana

Enamul Haque (Bangladesh; played 10 Tests and 29 ODIs), b. February 27, 1966, Comilla, Chittagong

Gould, Ian James (England; played 18 ODIs), b. August 19, 1957, Taplow, Bucks

Hill, Anthony Lloyd (New Zealand), b. June 26, 1951, Auckland

Howell, Ian Lester (South Africa), b. May 20, 1958, Port Elizabeth, Cape Province

Jerling, Brian George (South Africa), b. August 13, 1958, Port Elizabeth, Cape Province

Llong, Nigel James (England), b. February 11, 1969, Ashford, Kent

Malcolm, Norman Alexander (West Indies), b. March 19, 1955, Manchester, Jamaica

Nadeem Ghauri, Mohammad (Pakistan; played 1 Test and 6 ODIs), b. October 12, 1962, Lahore, Punjab

Nadir Shah (Bangladesh), b. February 7, 1964, Dacca (now Dhaka)

Parker, Peter Douglas (Australia), b. July 20, 1959, Herston, Brisbane, Queensland

Saheba, Amiesh Maheshbhai (India), b. November 15, 1959, Ahmedabad, Gujarat

Shastri, Suresh Lalchand (India), b. September 15, 1955, Jodhpur, Rajasthan

Tiffin, Russell Blair (Zimbabwe), b. June 4, 1959, Salisbury (now Harare)

Wijewardene, Tyron Hirantha (Sri Lanka), b. August 29, 1961, Maradana

Zameer Haider (Pakistan), b. September 30, 1962, Lahore

OVERALL RECORDS
Test Matches

Most appearances

168	SR Waugh	A
156	AR Border	A
145	SK Warne	A
140	SR Tendulkar	I
133	AJ Stewart	E
132	CA Walsh	WI
131	Kapil Dev	I
131	BC Lara	WI*
128	ME Waugh	A
125	SM Gavaskar	I

Lara's record includes one Test for the World XI

Most runs

			Avge
11953	BC Lara	WI*	52.88
11174	AR Border	A	50.56
11150	SR Tendulkar	I	54.92
10927	SR Waugh	A	51.06
10122	SM Gavaskar	I	51.12
9492	R Dravid	I*	56.50
9368	RT Ponting	A	59.29
8900	GA Gooch	E	42.58
8832	Javed Miandad	P	52.57
8813	Inzamam-ul-Haq	WI	50.07

The records for Lara, Dravid and Inzamam include one Test for the World XI

Most wickets

			Avge
708	SK Warne	A	25.41
700	M Muralitharan	SL*	21.33
566	A Kumble	I	28.73
563	GD McGrath	A	21.64
519	CA Walsh	WI	24.44
434	Kapil Dev	I	29.64
431	RJ Hadlee	NZ	22.29
416	SM Pollock	SA	23.19
414	Wasim Akram	P	23.62
405	CEL Ambrose	WI	20.99

Muralitharan's record includes one Test for the World XI

Highest scores

400*	BC Lara	WI v Eng at St John's	2003-04
380	ML Hayden	Aust v Zim at Perth	2003-04
375	BC Lara	WI v Eng at St John's	1993-94
374	DPMD Jayawardene	SL v SA at Colombo	2006
365*	GS Sobers	WI v Pak at Kingston	1957-58
364	L Hutton	Eng v Aust at The Oval	1938
340	ST Jayasuriya	SL v India at Colombo	1997-98
337	Hanif Mohammad	Pak v WI at Bridgetown	1957-58
336*	WR Hammond	Eng v NZ at Auckland	1932-33
334*	MA Taylor	Aust v Pak at Peshawar	1998-99
334	DG Bradman	Aust v Eng at Leeds	1930

In all 21 scores of 300 or more have been made in Tests

Best innings bowling

10-53	JC Laker	Eng v Aust at Manchester	1956
10-74	A Kumble	India v Pak at Delhi	1998-99
9-28	GA Lohmann	Eng v SA at Jo'burg	1895-96
9-37	JC Laker	Eng v Aust at Manchester	1956
9-51	M Muralitharan	SL v Zim at Kandy	2001-02
9-52	RJ Hadlee	NZ v Aust at Brisbane	1985-86
9-56	Abdul Qadir	Pak v Eng at Lahore	1987-88
9-57	DE Malcolm	Eng v SA at The Oval	1994
9-65	M Muralitharan	SL v Eng at The Oval	1998
9-69	JM Patel	India v Aust at Kanpur	1959-60

There have been seven further instances of a bowler taking nine wickets in an innings

Record wicket partnerships

1st	413	MH Mankad (231) and P Roy (173)	India v New Zealand at Madras	1955-56
2nd	576	ST Jayasuriya (340) and RS Mahanama (225)	Sri Lanka v India at Colombo	1997-98
3rd	624	KC Sangakkara (287) and DPMD Jayawardene (374)	Sri Lanka v South Africa at Colombo	2006
4th	411	PBH May (285*) and MC Cowdrey (154)	England v West Indies at Birmingham	1957
5th	405	SG Barnes (234) and DG Bradman (234)	Australia v England at Sydney	1946-47
6th	346	JHW Fingleton (136) and DG Bradman (270)	Australia v England at Melbourne	1936-37
7th	347	DS Atkinson (219) and CC Depeiaza (122)	West Indies v Australia at Bridgetown	1954-55
8th	313	Wasim Akram (257*) and Saqlain Mushtaq (79)	Pakistan v Zimbabwe at Sheikhupura	1996-97
9th	195	MV Boucher (78) and PL Symcox (108)	South Africa v Pakistan at Johannesburg	1997-98
10th	151	BF Hastings (110) and RO Collinge (68*)	New Zealand v Pakistan at Auckland	1972-73
	151	Azhar Mahmood (128*) and Mushtaq Ahmed (59)	Pakistan v South Africa at Rawalpindi	1997-98

Updated records can be found at **www.cricinfo.com/db/STATS**

Test Matches — **OVERALL RECORDS**

Most catches

Fielders

181	**ME Waugh** *A*	
164	**BC Lara** *WI/World*	
159	**SP Fleming** *NZ*	
157	**MA Taylor** *A*	
156	**AR Border** *A*	

Most dismissals

Wicketkeepers		*Ct/St*
395	**IA Healy** *A*	366/29
392	**MV Boucher**	
	SA/World	376/16
381	**AC Gilchrist** *A*	344/37
355	**RW Marsh** *A*	343/12
270	**PJL Dujon** *WI*	265/5

Highest team totals

952-6d	**Sri Lanka** v India at Colombo 1997-98
903-7d	**Eng** v Australia at The Oval 1938
849	**Eng** v WI at Kingston 1929-30
790-3d	**WI** v Pakistan at Kingston 1957-58
758-8d	**Aust** v WI at Kingston 1954-55
756-5d	**Sri Lanka** v SA at Colombo 2006
751-5d	**WI** v England at St John's 2003-04
747	**WI** v SA at St John's 2004-05
735-6d	**Aust** v Zimbabwe at Perth 2003-04
729-6d	**Aust** v England at Lord's 1930

There have been four further totals of more than 700, one each day by Australia, India, Pakistan and Sri Lanka

Lowest team totals

Completed innings

26	**NZ** v Eng at Auckland 1954-55
30	**SA** v Eng at Pt Elizabeth 1895-96
30	**SA** v Eng at Birmingham 1924
35	**SA** v Eng at Cape Town 1898-99
36	**Aust** v Eng at B'ham 1902
36	**SA** v Aust at M'bourne 1931-32
42	**Aust** v Eng at Sydney 1887-88
42	**NZ** v Aust at W'ton 1945-46
42*	**India** v England at Lord's 1974
43	**SA** v Eng at Cape Town 1888-89

* One batsmen absent hurt. There have been seven further totals of less than 50, the most recent West Indies' 47 v England at Kingston in 2003-04

Best match bowling

19-90	**JC Laker**	Eng v Aust at Manchester	1956
17-159	**SF Barnes**	Eng v SA at Jo'burg	1913-14
16-136	**ND Hirwani**	India v WI at Madras	1987-88
16-137	**RAL Massie**	Aust v England at Lord's	1972
16-220	**M Muralitharan**	SL v England at The Oval	1998
15-28	**J Briggs**	Eng v SA at Cape Town	1888-89
15-45	**GA Lohmann**	Eng v SA at Pt Elizabeth	1895-96
15-99	**C Blythe**	Eng v SA at Leeds	1907
15-104	**H Verity**	England v Aust at Lord's	1934
15-123	**RJ Hadlee**	NZ v Aust at Brisbane	1985-86

Hirwani and Massie were making their Test debuts. W Rhodes (15-124) and Harbhajan Singh (15-217) also took 15 wickets in a match

Most centuries

		Tests
37	**SR Tendulkar** *India*	132
34	**SM Gavaskar** *India*	125
34	**BC Lara** *West Indies/World XI*	128
33	**RT Ponting** *Australia*	105
32	**SR Waugh** *Australia*	168
29	**DG Bradman** *Australia*	52
27	**AR Border** *Australia*	156
27	**ML Hayden** *Australia*	84
26	**GS Sobers** *West Indies*	93
25	**Inzamam-ul-Haq** *Pakistan/World XI*	113

Bradman (12) hit the most double-centuries, ahead of Lara (9) and WR Hammond (7)

Test match results

	Played	Won	Lost	Drawn	Tied	% win
Australia	687	320	178	187	2	46.71
Bangladesh	49	1	43	5	0	2.04
England	864	301	251	312	0	34.83
India	408	91	131	185	1	22.35
New Zealand	332	62	131	139	0	18.67
Pakistan	330	103	87	140	0	31.21
South Africa	320	105	115	100	0	32.81
Sri Lanka	170	50	63	57	0	29.41
West Indies	440	149	141	149	1	33.86
Zimbabwe	83	8	49	26	0	9.63
World XI	1	0	1	0	0	0.00
TOTAL	1842	1190	1190	650	2	

OVERALL RECORDS *One-day Internationals*

Most appearances

398	ST Jayasuriya	*SL/Asia*
395	SR Tendulkar	*I*
378	Inzamam-ul-Haq	*P/Asia*
356	Wasim Akram	*P*
334	M Azharuddin	*I*
327	R Dravid	*I/Asia/World*
325	SR Waugh	*A*
308	PA de Silva	*SL*
302	SC Ganguly	*I/Asia*
300	WPUJC Vaas	*SL/Asia*

A further 18 men have played in 250 or more ODIs

Most runs

			Avge
15425	SR Tendulkar	*I*	44.32
12116	ST Jayasuriya	*SL/Asia*	32.83
11739	Inzamam-ul-Haq	*P/Asia*	39.52
11147	SC Ganguly	*I/Asia*	41.43
10534	R Dravid	*I/Asia/World*	40.05
10405	BC Lara	*WI/World*	40.48
10395	RT Ponting	*A/World*	43.31
9378	M Azharuddin	*I*	36.92
9284	PA de Silva	*SL*	34.90
9144	JH Kallis	*SA/Af/World*	45.49

Six other batsmen have passed 8000 runs in ODIs, and six more have reached 7000

Most wickets

			Avge
502	Wasim Akram	*P*	23.52
455	M Muralitharan	*SL/World*	22.68
416	Waqar Younis	*P*	23.84
383	SM Pollock	*SA/Af/World*	24.15
383	WPUJC Vaas	*SL/Asia*	26.78
381	GD McGrath	*A/World*	22.02
337	A Kumble	*I/Asia*	30.89
315	J Srinath	*I*	28.08
304	ST Jayasuriya	*SL/Asia*	36.48
293	SK Warne	*A/World*	25.73

Five other bowlers have passed 250 wickets in ODIs, and 13 more have reached 200

Highest scores

194	Saeed Anwar	Pakistan v India at Chennai	1996-97
189*	IVA Richards	W Indies v England at Manchester	1984
189	ST Jayasuriya	Sri Lanka v India at Sharjah	2000-01
188*	G Kirsten	SA v UAE at Rawalpindi	1995-96
186*	SR Tendulkar	India v NZ at Hyderabad	1999-2000
183	MS Dhoni	India v Sri Lanka at Jaipur	2005-06
183	SC Ganguly	India v Sri Lanka at Taunton	1999
181*	ML Hayden	Aust v N Zealand at Hamilton	2006-07
181	IVA Richards	WI v Sri Lanka at Karachi	1987-88
175*	Kapil Dev	India v Zim at Tunbridge Wells	1983
175	HH Gibbs	SA v Aust at Johannesburg	2005-06

SR Tendulkar has scored 41 ODI centuries, ST Jayasuriya 25, RT Ponting 23, SC Ganguly 22 and Saeed Anwar 20

Best innings bowling

8-19	WPUJC Vaas	SL v Zimbabwe at Colombo	2001-02
7-15	GD McGrath	Aust v Namibia at P'stroom	2002-03
7-20	AJ Bichel	Aust v Eng at Port Elizabeth	2002-03
7-30	M Muralitharan	Sri Lanka v India at Sharjah	2000-01
7-36	Waqar Younis	Pakistan v England at Leeds	2001
7-37	Aqib Javed	Pakistan v India at Sharjah	1991-92
7-51	WW Davis	West Indies v Australia at Leeds	1983
6-12	A Kumble	India v West Indies at Calcutta	1993-94
6-14	GJ Gilmour	Australia v England at Leeds	1975
6-14	Imran Khan	Pakistan v India at Sharjah	1984-85
6-14	MF Maharoof	Sri Lanka v W Indies at Mumbai	2006-07

Waqar Younis took five in an innings 13 times, Muralitharan 8, GD McGrath 7, L Klusener, B Lee, Saqlain Mushtaq and Wasim Akram 6

Record wicket partnerships

1st	286	WU Tharanga (109) and ST Jayasuriya (152)	Sri Lanka v England at Leeds	2006
2nd	331	SR Tendulkar (186*) and R Dravid (153)	India v New Zealand at Hyderabad	1999-2000
3rd	237*	R Dravid (104*) and SR Tendulkar (140*)	India v Kenya at Bristol	1999
4th	275*	M Azharuddin (153*) and A Jadeja (116*)	India v Zimbabwe at Cuttack	1997-98
5th	223	M Azharuddin (111*) and A Jadeja (119)	India v Sri Lanka at Colombo	1997-98
6th	218	DPMD Jayawardene (107) and MS Dhoni (139*)	Asia XI v Africa XI at Chennai	2007
7th	130	A Flower (142*) and HH Streak (56)	Zimbabwe v England at Harare	2001-02
8th	138*	JM Kemp (110*) and AJ Hall (56*)	South Africa v India at Cape Town	2006-07
9th	126*	Kapil Dev (175*) and SMH Kirmani (24*)	India v Zimbabwe at Tunbridge Wells	1983
10th	106*	IVA Richards (189*) and MA Holding (12*)	West Indies v England at Manchester	1984

Updated records can be found at **www.cricinfo.com/db/STATS**

One-day Internationals **OVERALL RECORDS**

Most catches

Fielders

156	M Azharuddin *I*	
133	SP Fleming *NZ/World*	
128	DPMD Jayawardene *SL/Asia*	
127	AR Border *A*	
124	RT Ponting *A/World*	

Most dismissals

Wicketkeepers   *Ct/St*

439	AC Gilchrist *A/World*	388/51
369	MV Boucher *SA/Africa*	351/18
287	Moin Khan *P*	214/73
233	IA Healy *A*	194/39
220	Rashid Latif *P*	182/38

Highest team totals

443-9	SL v N'lands at Amstelveen	2006
438-9	SA v Aust at Johannesburg	2005-06
434-4	Australia v SA at Jo'burg	2005-06
418-5	SA v Zim at P'stroom	2006-07
413-5	Ind v Bermuda at P-o-Spain	2006-07
398-5	SL v Kenya at Kandy	1995-96
397-5	NZ v Zimbabwe at Bulawayo	2005-06
392-6	SA v Pakistan at Centurion	2006-07
391-4	Eng v B'desh at Nottingham	2005
377-6	Australia v SA at Basseterre	2006-07

NZ's 397-5 was made in 44 overs, all the other totals in 50 except SA's 438-9, when the winning run came off the fifth ball of the 50th over

Lowest team totals

Completed innings

35	Zim v SL at Harare	2003-04
36	Canada v SL at Paarl	2002-03
38	Zim v SL at Colombo	2001-02
43	Pak v WI at Cape Town	1992-93
45	Can v Eng at Manchester	1979
45	Nam v Aust at P'stroom	2002-03
54	India v SL at Sharjah	2000-01
54	WI v SA at Cape Town	2003-04
55	SL v WI at Sharjah	1986-87
63	India v Aust at Sydney	1980-81

The lowest total successfully defended in a non-rain-affected ODI is 125, by India v Pakistan (87) at Sharjah in 1984-85

Most sixes

242	ST Jayasuriya *SL/Asia*	
229	Shahid Afridi *Pak/Asia/World*	
186	SC Ganguly *I/Asia*	
163	SR Tendulkar *I*	
153	CL Cairns *NZ/World*	
144	Inzamam-ul-Haq *P/Asia*	
136	AC Gilchrist *A/World*	
133	BC Lara *WI/World*	
132	RT Ponting *A/World*	
126	IVA Richards *WI*	

Five other men have hit 100 sixes

Best strike rate

Runs per 100 balls   *Runs*

109.38	Shahid Afridi *P/Asia/World*	5072
99.43	IDS Smith *NZ*	1055
97.11	V Sehwag *I/Asia/World*	5153
96.66	RL Powell *WI*	2085
96.65	AC Gilchrist *A/World*	9038
92.26	MS Dhoni *I*	2477
95.07	Kapil Dev *I*	3783
92.31	A Symonds *A*	4226
90.50	ST Jayasuriya *SL/Asia*	12116
90.39	MEK Hussey *A*	1826

Qualification: 1000 runs

Most economical bowlers

Runs per over   *Wkts*

3.09	J Garner *WI*	146
3.28	RGD Willis *E*	80
3.30	RJ Hadlee *NZ*	158
3.32	MA Holding *WI*	142
3.37	SP Davis *A*	44
3.40	AME Roberts *WI*	87
3.48	CEL Ambrose *WI*	225
3.53	MD Marshall *WI*	157
3.54	ARC Fraser *E*	47
3.55	MR Whitney *A*	46

Qualification: 2000 balls bowled

One-day international results

	Played	Won	Lost	Tied	No result	% win
Australia	659	406	227	8	18	64.13
Bangladesh	163	36	125	0	2	22.36
England	477	231	227	4	15	50.43
India	660	313	317	3	27	49.68
Kenya	94	27	65	0	2	29.34
New Zealand	527	226	273	4	24	45.29
Pakistan	659	352	286	6	15	55.17
South Africa	388	239	133	5	11	64.24
Sri Lanka	534	245	266	3	20	47.94
West Indies	575	317	235	5	18	57.42
Zimbabwe	324	79	231	5	9	25.48
Others (see below)	180	43	129	1	7	25.00
TOTAL	**2620**	**2514**	**2514**	**22**	**84**	

Other teams: Africa XI (P6, W1, L4, NR1), Asia XI (P7, W4, L2, NR1), Bermuda (P24, W5, L19), Canada (P33, W7, L26), East Africa (P3, L3), Hong Kong (P2, L2), Ireland (P22, W6, T1, L13, NR2), Namibia (P6, L6), Netherlands (P35, W11, L22, NR2), Scotland (P27, W7, L19, NR1), United Arab Emirates (P9, W1, L8), USA (P2, L2), World XI (P4, W1, L3).

AUSTRALIA *Test Match Records*

Most appearances

168	SR Waugh
156	AR Border
145	SK Warne
128	ME Waugh
124	GD McGrath
119	IA Healy
110	RT Ponting
107	DC Boon
105	JL Langer
104	MA Taylor

10 of the 43 players with 100 or more Test caps are Australian

Most runs

		Avge
11174	AR Border	50.56
10927	SR Waugh	51.06
9368	RT Ponting	59.29
8029	ME Waugh	41.81
7739	ML Hayden	53.00
7696	JL Langer	45.27
7525	MA Taylor	43.49
7422	DC Boon	43.65
7110	GS Chappell	53.86
6996	DG Bradman	99.94

RN Harvey (6149) also reached 6000 Test runs

Most wickets

		Avge
708	SK Warne	25.41
563	GD McGrath	21.64
355	DK Lillee	23.92
291	CJ McDermott	28.63
259	JN Gillespie	26.13
248	R Benaud	27.03
246	GD McKenzie	29.78
231	B Lee	31.60
228	RR Lindwall	23.03
216	CV Grimmett	24.21

MG Hughes (212) and JR Thomson (200) also reached 200 Test wickets

Highest scores

380	ML Hayden	v Zimbabwe at Perth	2003-04
334*	MA Taylor	v Pakistan at Peshawar	1998-99
334	DG Bradman	v England at Leeds	1930
311	RB Simpson	v England at Manchester	1964
307	RM Cowper	v England at Melbourne	1965-66
304	DG Bradman	v England at Leeds	1934
299*	DG Bradman	v South Africa at Adelaide	1931-32
270	DG Bradman	v England at Melbourne	1936-37
268	GN Yallop	v Pakistan at Melbourne	1983-84
266	WH Ponsford	v England at The Oval	1934

At the time of his retirement in 1948 DG Bradman had made eight of Australia's highest ten Test scores

Best innings bowling

9-121	AA Mailey	v England at Melbourne	1920-21
8-24	GD McGrath	v Pakistan at Perth	2004-05
8-31	FJ Laver	v England at Manchester	1909
8-38	GD McGrath	v England at Lord's	1997
8-43	AE Trott	v England at Adelaide	1894-95
8-53	RAL Massie	v England at Lord's	1972
8-59	AA Mallett	v Pakistan at Adelaide	1972-73
8-65	H Trumble	v England at The Oval	1902
8-71	GD McKenzie	v West Indies at Melbourne	1968-69
8-71	SK Warne	v England at Brisbane	1994-95

Trott and Massie were making their Test debuts. Massie took 8-84 – Australia's 11th-best analysis – in the first innings of the same match

Record wicket partnerships

1st	382	WM Lawry (210) and RB Simpson (205)	v West Indies at Bridgetown	1964-65
2nd	451	WH Ponsford (266) and DG Bradman (244)	v England at The Oval	1934
3rd	315	RT Ponting (206) and DS Lehmann (160)	v West Indies at Port-of-Spain	2002-03
4th	388	WH Ponsford (181) and DG Bradman (304)	v England at Leeds	1934
5th	405	SG Barnes (234) and DG Bradman (234)	v England at Sydney	1946-47
6th	346	JHW Fingleton (136) and DG Bradman (270)	v England at Melbourne	1936-37
7th	217	KD Walters (250) and GJ Gilmour (101)	v New Zealand at Christchurch	1976-77
8th	243	MJ Hartigan (116) and C Hill (160)	v England at Adelaide	1907-08
9th	154	SE Gregory (201) and JM Blackham (74)	v England at Sydney	1894-95
10th	127	JM Taylor (108) and AA Mailey (46*)	v England at Sydney	1924-25

Updated records can be found at www.cricinfo.com/db/STATS

Test Match Records
AUSTRALIA

Most catches

Fielders

181	ME Waugh	
157	MA Taylor	
156	AR Border	
125	SK Warne	
124	RT Ponting	

Most dismissals

Wicketkeepers		*Ct/St*
395	IA Healy	366/29
381	AC Gilchrist	344/37
355	RW Marsh	343/12
187	ATW Grout	163/24
130	WAS Oldfield	78/52

Highest team totals

758-8d	v West Indies at Kingston	1954-55
735-6d	v Zimbabwe at Perth	2003-04
729-6d	v England at Lord's	1930
701	v England at The Oval	1934
695	v England at The Oval	1930
674	v India at Adelaide	1947-48
668	v West Indies at Bridgetown	1954-55
659-8d	v England at Sydney	1946-47
656-8d	v England at Manchester	1964
653-4d	v England at Leeds	1993

Australia have reached 600 on 28 occasions, 15 of them against England

Lowest team totals

Completed innings

36	v England at Birmingham	1902
42	v England at Sydney	1887-88
44	v England at The Oval	1896
53	v England at Lord's	1896
58*	v England at Brisbane	1936-37
60	v England at Lord's	1888
63	v England at The Oval	1882
65	v England at The Oval	1912
66*	v England at Brisbane	1928-29
68	v England at The Oval	1886

*One or more batsmen absent.
Australia's lowest total against anyone other than England is 75, v South Africa at Durban in 1949-50

Best match bowling

16-137	RAL Massie	v England at Lord's	1972
14-90	FR Spofforth	v England at The Oval	1882
14-199	CV Grimmett	v South Africa at Adelaide	1931-32
13-77	MA Noble	v England at Melbourne	1901-02
13-110	FR Spofforth	v England at Melbourne	1878-79
13-148	BA Reid	v England at Melbourne	1990-91
13-173	CV Grimmett	v South Africa at Durban	1935-36
13-217	MG Hughes	v West Indies at Perth	1988-89
13-236	AA Mailey	v England at Melbourne	1920-21
12-87	CTB Turner	v England at Sydney	1887-88

Massie was playing in his first Test, Grimmett (1935-36) in his last – he took 10 or more wickets in each of his last three

Hat-tricks

FR Spofforth	v England at Melbourne	1878-79
H Trumble	v England at Melbourne	1901-02
H Trumble	v England at Melbourne	1903-04
TJ Matthews	v South Africa at Manchester	1912
TJ Matthews	v South Africa at Manchester	1912
LF Kline	v South Africa at Cape Town	1957-58
MG Hughes	v West Indies at Perth	1988-89
DW Fleming	v Pakistan at Rawalpindi	1994-95
SK Warne	v England at Melbourne	1994-95
GD McGrath	v West Indies at Perth	2000-01

Fleming was playing in his first Test, Trumble (1903-04) in his last. Matthews, a legspinner, uniquely took a hat-trick in both innings of the same Test

Australia's Test match results

	Played	Won	Lost	Drawn	Tied	% win
v Bangladesh	4	4	0	0	0	100.00
v England	316	131	97	88	0	41.45
v India	68	32	15	20	1	47.05
v New Zealand	46	22	7	17	0	47.82
v Pakistan	52	24	11	17	0	46.15
v South Africa	77	44	15	18	0	57.14
v Sri Lanka	18	11	1	6	0	61.11
v West Indies	102	48	32	21	1	47.05
v Zimbabwe	3	3	0	0	0	100.00
v World XI	1	1	0	0	0	100.00
TOTAL	**687**	**320**	**178**	**187**	**2**	**46.57**

Updated records can be found at **www.cricinfo.com/db/STATS**

AUSTRALIA *One-day International Records*

Most appearances

325	SR Waugh	
279	RT Ponting	
273	AR Border	
267	AC Gilchrist	
249	GD McGrath	
244	ME Waugh	
232	MG Bevan	
208	DR Martyn	
193	SK Warne	
181	DC Boon	

A total of 21 Australians have played in more than 100 ODIs

Most runs

		Avge
10280	RT Ponting	43.01
9014	AC Gilchrist	36.05
8500	ME Waugh	39.35
7569	SR Waugh	32.90
6912	MG Bevan	53.58
6524	AR Border	30.62
6068	DM Jones	44.61
5964	DC Boon	37.04
5497	ML Hayden	44.33
5346	DR Martyn	40.80

GR Marsh (4357) and A Symonds (4226) also reached 4000 runs

Most wickets

		Avge
380	GD McGrath	21.98
291	SK Warne	25.82
267	B Lee	22.65
203	CJ McDermott	24.71
195	SR Waugh	34.67
142	JN Gillespie	25.42
134	DW Fleming	25.38
133	GB Hogg	27.10
124	A Symonds	37.57
112	NW Bracken	21.36

SP O'Donnell (108), PR Reiffel (106) and DK Lillee (103) also reached 100 wickets

Highest scores

181*	ML Hayden	v New Zealand at Hamilton	2006-07
173	ME Waugh	v West Indies at Melbourne	2000-01
172	AC Gilchrist	v Zimbabwe at Hobart	2003-04
164	RT Ponting	v South Africa at Johannesburg	2005-06
158	ML Hayden	v West Indies at North Sound	2006-07
156	A Symonds	v New Zealand at Wellington	2005-06
154	AC Gilchrist	v Sri Lanka at Melbourne	1998-99
151	A Symonds	v Sri Lanka at Sydney	2005-06
149	AC Gilchrist	v Sri Lanka at Bridgetown	2006-07
146	ML Hayden	v Pakistan at Nairobi	2002-03

Gilchrist's 149 against Sri Lanka is the highest score in the World Cup final

Best innings bowling

7-15	GD McGrath	v Namibia at Potchefstroom	2002-03
7-20	AJ Bichel	v England at Port Elizabeth	2002-03
6-14	GJ Gilmour	v England at Leeds	1975
6-39	KH MacLeay	v India at Nottingham	1983
5-13	SP O'Donnell	v New Zealand at Christchurch	1989-90
5-14	GD McGrath	v West Indies at Manchester	1999
5-15	GS Chappell	v India at Sydney	1980-81
5-16	CG Rackemann	v Pakistan at Adelaide	1983-84
5-17	TM Alderman	v New Zealand at Wellington	1981-82
5-18	GJ Cosier	v England at Birmingham	1977
5-18	A Symonds	v Bangladesh at Manchester	2005

DK Lillee took 5-34 against Pakistan at Leeds in the 1975 World Cup, the first five-wicket haul in ODIs

Record wicket partnerships

1st	212	GR Marsh (104) and DC Boon (111)	v India at Jaipur	1986-87
2nd	225	AC Gilchrist (124) and RT Ponting (119)	v England at Melbourne	2002-03
3rd	234*	RT Ponting (140*) and DR Martyn (88*)	v India at Johannesburg	2002-03
4th	237	RT Ponting (124) and A Symonds (151)	v Sri Lanka at Sydney	2005-06
5th	220	A Symonds (156) and MJ Clarke (82*)	v New Zealand at Wellington	2005-06
6th	165	MEK Hussey (109*) and BJ Haddin (70)	v West Indies at Kuala Lumpur	2006-07
7th	123	MEK Hussey (73) and B Lee (57)	v South Africa at Brisbane	2005-06
8th	119	PR Reiffel (58) and SK Warne (55)	v South Africa at Port Elizabeth	1993-94
9th	77	MG Bevan (59*) and SK Warne (29)	v West Indies at Port-of-Spain	1998-99
10th	63	SR Watson (35*) and AJ Bichel (28)	v Sri Lanka at Sydney	2002-03

Updated records can be found at www.cricinfo.com/db/STATS

AUSTRALIA

Most catches

Fielders

127	AR Border
123	RT Ponting
111	SR Waugh
108	ME Waugh
80	SK Warne

Most dismissals

Wicketkeepers		*Ct/St*
437	AC Gilchrist	387/50
233	IA Healy	194/39
124	RW Marsh	120/4
49	WB Phillips	42/7
32	BJ Haddin	28/4

Highest team totals

434-4	v South Africa at Johannesburg	2005-06
377-6	v South Africa at Basseterre	2006-07
368-5	v Sri Lanka at Sydney	2005-06
359-2†	v India at Johannesburg	2002-03
359-5	v India at Sydney	2003-04
349-6	v New Zealand at St George's	2006-07
348-6	v New Zealand at C'church	1999-2000
347-2	v India at Bangalore	2003-04
347-5	v New Zealand at Napier	2004-05
346-5	v New Zealand at Hamilton	2006-07

† *In World Cup final. All scores made in 50 overs*

Lowest team totals

Completed innings

70	v England at Birmingham	1977
70	v New Zealand at Adelaide	1985-86
91	v West Indies at Perth	1986-87
93	v S Africa at Cape Town	2005-06
101	v England at Melbourne	1978-79
101	v India at Perth	1991-92
107	v W Indies at Melbourne	1981-82
109	v England at Sydney	1982-83
120	v Pakistan at Hobart	1996-97
124	v New Zealand at Sydney	1982-83

Australia scored 101-9 in a 30-overs match against West Indies at Sydney in 1992-93 – and won

Most sixes

135	AC Gilchrist
129	RT Ponting
84	A Symonds
79	ML Hayden
68	SR Waugh
64	DM Jones
57	ME Waugh
43	AR Border
37	MEK Hussey
28	SP O'Donnell

Gilchrist (1) and Ponting (3) also hit sixes for the World XI

Best strike rate

Runs per 100 balls		*Runs*
96.60	AC Gilchrist	9014
93.98	BJ Hodge	516
92.31	A Symonds	4226
90.39	MEK Hussey	1826
88.16	IJ Harvey	715
85.71	WB Phillips	852
83.84	IA Healy	1764
82.85	MJ Clarke	3329
82.26	RW Marsh	1225
82.01	B Lee	739

Qualification: 500 runs

Most economical bowlers

Runs per over		*Wkts*
3.37	SP Davis	44
3.55	MR Whitney	46
3.58	DK Lillee	103
3.65	GF Lawson	88
3.65	TM Alderman	88
3.87	GD McGrath	380
3.92	PR Reiffel	106
3.94	CG Rackemann	82
3.94	RM Hogg	85
4.03	CJ McDermott	203

Qualification: 2000 balls bowled

Australia's one-day international results

	Played	Won	Lost	Tied	No Result	% win
v Bangladesh	13	12	1	0	0	92.30
v England	93	52	37	2	2	58.42
v India	83	51	27	0	5	65.38
v New Zealand	109	76	30	0	3	71.69
v Pakistan	74	43	27	1	3	61.42
v South Africa	67	36	28	3	0	56.25
v Sri Lanka	64	43	19	0	2	69.35
v West Indies	114	53	57	2	2	48.18
v Zimbabwe	27	25	1	0	1	96.15
v others *(see below)*	15	15	0	0	0	100.00
TOTAL	**659**	**406**	**227**	**8**	**18**	**64.13**

Other teams: Canada (P1, W1), Ireland (P1, W1), Kenya (P4, W4), Namibia (P1, W1), Netherlands (P2, W2), Scotland (P2, W2), USA (P1, W1), World XI (P3, W3).

BANGLADESH *Test Match Records*

Most appearances

47	Habibul Bashar
44	Khaled Mashud
40	Javed Omar
38	Mohammad Ashraful
31	Mohammad Rafique
25	Mashrafe Mortaza
22	Rajin Saleh
21	Tapash Baisya
17	Alok Kapali
17	Hannan Sarkar
17	Manjural Islam

Habibul Bashar has missed only two of Bangladesh's 49 Tests

Most runs

		Avge
2953	Habibul Bashar	32.09
1801	Mohammad Ashraful	25.72
1720	Javed Omar	22.05
1409	Khaled Mashud	19.04
1115	Rajin Saleh	27.19
1035	Mohammad Rafique	19.52
683	Al Sahariar	22.76
662	Hannan Sarkar	20.06
607	Shahriar Nafees	27.59
584	Alok Kapali	17.69

Habibul Bashar reached 2000 runs for Bangladesh before anyone else had made 1000

Most wickets

		Avge
94	Mohammad Rafique	40.79
59	Mashrafe Mortaza	40.30
36	Tapash Baisya	59.36
32	Enamul Haque jnr	39.46
28	Manjural Islam	57.32
25	Shahadat Hossain	46.12
18	Enamul Haque snr	57.05
14	Mohammad Sharif	79.00
14	Talha Jubair	55.07
13	Khaled Mahmud	64.00
13	Mushfiqur Rahman	63.30

Naimur Rahman (12) and Syed Rasel (12) also passed 10 wickets

Highest scores

158*	Moh'd Ashraful	v India at Chittagong	2004-05
145†	Aminul Islam	v India at Dhaka	2000-01
138	Shahriar Nafees	v Australia at Fatullah	2005-06
136	Moh'd Ashraful	v Sri Lanka at Chittagong	2005-06
129*	Moh'd Ashraful	v Sri Lanka at Colombo	2007
121	Nafees Iqbal	v Zimbabwe at Dhaka	2004-05
119	Javed Omar	v Pakistan at Peshawar	2003-04
114†	Moh'd Ashraful	v Sri Lanka at Colombo	2001-02
113	Habibul Bashar	v West Indies at Gros Islet	2004
111	Moh'd Rafique	v West Indies at Gros Islet	2004

† On debut. There have only been 3 other centuries for Bangladesh, 2 by Habibul Bashar and 1 by Khaled Mashud

Best innings bowling

7-95	Enamul Haque jnr	v Zimbabwe at Dhaka	2004-05
6-45	Enamul Haque jnr	v Zim at Chittagong	2004-05
6-77	Moh'd Rafique	v South Africa at Dhaka	2002-03
6-81	Manjural Islam	v Zim at Bulawayo	2000-01
6-122	Moh'd Rafique	v New Zealand at Dhaka	2004-05
6-132	Naimur Rahman	v India at Dhaka	2000-01
5-36	Moh'd Rafique	v Pakistan at Multan	2003-04
5-62	Moh'd Rafique	v Australia at Fatulla	2005-06
5-65	Moh'd Rafique	v Zim at Chittagong	2004-05
5-86	Shahadat Hossain	v Sri Lanka at Bogra	2005-06

Other five-wicket hauls have been recorded by Mohammad Rafique (2) and Enamul Haque jnr

Record wicket partnerships

1st	133	Javed Omar (43) and Nafees Iqbal (121)	v Zimbabwe at Dhaka	2004-05
2nd	187	Shahriar Nafees (138) and Habibul Bashar (76)	v Australia at Fatullah	2005-06
3rd	130	Javed Omar (119) and Mohammad Ashraful (77)	v Pakistan at Peshawar	2003-04
4th	120	Habibul Bashar (77) and Manjural Islam Rana (35)	v West Indies at Kingston	2004
5th	126	Aminul Islam (56) and Mohammad Ashraful (114)	v Sri Lanka at Colombo	2001-02
6th	191	Mohammad Ashraful (129*) and Mushfiqur Rahim (80)	v Sri Lanka at Colombo	2007
7th	93	Aminul Islam (145) and Khaled Mashud (32)	v India at Dhaka	2001-02
8th	87	Mohammad Ashraful (81) and Mohammad Rafique (111)	v West Indies at Gros Islet	2004
9th	77	Mashrafe Mortaza (79) and Shahadat Hossain (31)	v India at Chittagong	2006-07
10th	69	Mohammad Rafique (65) and Shahadat Hossain (3*)	v Australia at Chittagong	2005-06

Test Match Records **BANGLADESH**

Most catches

Fielders

21	Habibul Bashar
13	Mohammad Ashraful
12	Rajin Saleh
11	Shahriar Nafees
10	Al Sahariar
10	Javed Omar

Most dismissals

Wicketkeepers   *Ct/St*

87	Khaled Mashud	78/9
4	Mohammad Salim	3/1
2	Mehrab Hossain	2/0

Khaled Mashud has missed only five of Bangladesh's 49 Tests

Highest team totals

488	v Zimbabwe at Chittagong	2004-05
427	v Australia at Fatullah	2005-06
416	v West Indies at Gros Islet	2004
400	v India at Dhaka	2000-01
361	v Pakistan at Peshawar	2003-04
333	v India at Chittagong	2004-05
331	v Zimbabwe at Harare	2003-04
328	v Sri Lanka at Colombo	2001-02
319	v Sri Lanka at Chittagong	2005-06
316	v England at Chester-le-Street	2005

The 400 against India came in Bangladesh's inaugural Test

Lowest team totals

Completed innings

62	v Sri Lanka at Colombo	2007
86	v Sri Lanka at Colombo	2005-06
87	v West Indies at Dhaka	2002-03
89	v Sri Lanka at Colombo	2007
90	v Sri Lanka at Colombo	2001-02
91	v India at Dhaka	2000-01
96	v Pakistan at Peshawar	2003-04
97	v Australia at Darwin	2003
102	v S Africa at Dhaka	2002-03
104	v Eng at Chester-le-Street	2005

The lowest all-out total by the opposition is 154, by Zimbabwe at Chittagong in 2004-05 (Bangladesh's only Test victory)

Best match bowling

12-200	Enamul Haque jr	v Zimbabwe at Dhaka	2004-05
9-160	Moh'd Rafique	v Australia at Fatullah	2005-06
7-105	Khaled Mahmud	v Pakistan at Multan	2003-04
7-116	Moh'd Rafique	v Pakistan at Multan	2003-04
6-77	Moh'd Rafique	v South Africa at Dhaka	2002-03
6-81	Manjural Islam	v Zim at Bulawayo	2000-01
6-100	Enamul Haque jr	v Zim at Chittagong	2004-05
6-117	Tapash Baisya	v W Indies at Chittagong	2002-03
6-122	Moh'd Rafique	v New Zealand at Dhaka	2004-05
6-154	Naimur Rahman	v India at Dhaka	2000-01

Khaled Mahmud took only six other wickets in 11 more Tests

Hat-tricks

Alok Kapali   v Pakistan at Peshawar   2003-04

Alok Kapali's figures were 2.1-1-3-3; he ended Pakistan's innings by dismissing Shabbir Ahmed, Danish Kaneria and Umar Gul. He has taken only three other Test wickets.

Two bowlers have taken hat-tricks against Bangladesh: AM Blignaut for Zimbabwe at Harare in 2003-04, and JEC Franklin for New Zealand at Dhaka in 2004-05.

Shahadat Hossain took an ODI hat-trick for Bangladesh against Zimbabwe at Harawe in 2006

Bangladesh's Test match results

	Played	Won	Lost	Drawn	Tied	% win
v Australia	4	0	4	0	0	0.00
v England	4	0	4	0	0	0.00
v India	5	0	4	1	0	0.00
v New Zealand	4	0	4	0	0	0.00
v Pakistan	6	0	6	0	0	0.00
v South Africa	4	0	4	0	0	0.00
v Sri Lanka	10	0	10	0	0	0.00
v West Indies	4	0	3	1	0	0.00
v Zimbabwe	8	1	4	3	0	12.50
TOTAL	**49**	**1**	**43**	**5**	**0**	**2.04**

BANGLADESH *One-day International Records*

Most appearances

126	Khaled Mashud
123	Mohammad Rafique
111	Habibul Bashar
102	Mohammad Ashraful
77	Khaled Mahmud
69	Aftab Ahmed
67	Mashrafe Mortaza
59	Javed Omar
56	Tapash Baisya
55	Alok Kapali

Habibul Bashar captained in 69 ODIs, Khaled Mashud in 30

Most runs

		Avge
2168	Habibul Bashar	21.68
1918	Moh'd Ashraful	22.04
1818	Khaled Mashud	21.90
1664	Aftab Ahmed	26.41
1565	Shahriar Nafees	34.77
1312	Javed Omar	23.85
1190	Moh'd Rafique	13.52
1005	Rajin Saleh	23.92
991	Khaled Mahmud	14.36
976	Akram Khan	23.23

Alok Kapali (964) and Shakib Al Hasan (937) have also passed 800 runs

Most wickets

		Avge
119	Mohammad Rafique	38.75
91	Mashrafe Mortaza	28.84
80	Abdur Razzak	22.85
67	Khaled Mahmud	42.76
59	Tapash Baisya	41.55
44	Syed Rasel	25.88
32	Shakib Al Hasan	33.18
29	Hasibul Hossain	46.13
27	Shahadat Hossain	32.70
24	Manjural Islam	53.50

Mohammad Rafique has completed the 1000-run/100-wicket double in ODIs. He is close to it in Test cricket too

Highest scores

134*	Shakib Al Hasan	v Canada at St John's	2006-07
123*	Shahriar Nafees	v Zimbabwe at Jaipur	2006
118*	Shahriar Nafees	v Zimbabwe at Harare	2006-07
108*	Rajin Saleh	v Kenya at Fatullah	2005-06
105*	Shahriar Nafees	v Zimbabwe at Khulna	2006-07
104*	Shahriar Nafees	v Bermuda at St John's	2006-07
101	Mehrab Hossain	v Zimbabwe at Dhaka	1998-99
100	Moh'd Ashraful	v Australia at Cardiff	2005
95	Shahriar Hossain	v Kenya at Dhaka	1998-99
94	Moh'd Ashraful	v England at Nottingham	2005

Bangladesh's highest score in the World Cup is 87, by Mohammad Ashraful against South Africa at Providence in 2006-07

Best bowling figures

6-26	Mashrafe Mortaza	v Kenya at Nairobi	2006
5-31	Aftab Ahmed	v NZ at Dhaka	2004-05
5-33	Abdur Razzak	v Zimbabwe at Bogra	2006-07
5-47	Moh'd Rafique	v Kenya at Fatullah	2005-06
4-16	Tapash Baisya	v West Indies at Kingstown	2004
4-16	Rajin Saleh	v Zimbabwe at Harare	2006
4-19	Khaled Mahmud	v Zimbabwe at Harare	2003-04
4-22	Syed Rasel	v Kenya at Nairobi	2006
4-23	Abdur Razzak	v Scotland at Dhaka	2006-07
4-31	Mashrafe Mortaza	v Zimbabwe at Harare	2006-07

Aftab Ahmed has taken only seven more wickets in 68 other matches

Record wicket partnerships

1st	170	Shahriar Hossain (68) and Mehrab Hossain (101)	v Zimbabwe at Dhaka	1998-99
2nd	150	Mohammad Rafique (72) and Aftab Ahmed (81*)	v Zimbabwe at Dhaka	2004-05
3rd	134*	Shahriar Nafees (104*) and Shakib Al Hasan (42*)	v Bermuda at St John's	2006-07
4th	175*	Rajin Saleh (108*) and Habibul Bashar (64*)	v Kenya at Fatullah	2005-06
5th	116	Shakib Al Hasan (134*) and Mohammad Ashraful (60)	v Canada at St John's	2006-07
6th	123*	Al Sahariar (62*) and Khaled Mashud (53*)	v West Indies at Dhaka	1999-2000
7th	89	Alok Kapali (55) and Khaled Mashud (39)	v Kenya at Fatullah	2005-06
8th	70*	Khaled Mashud (35*) and Mohammad Rafique (41*)	v New Zealand at Kimberley	2002-03
9th	62*	Khaled Mashud (30*) and Mohammad Rafique (32*)	v West Indies at Kingstown	2004
10th	54*	Khaled Mashud (39*) and Tapash Baisya (22*)	v Sri Lanka at Colombo	2005-06

Updated records can be found at **www.cricinfo.com/db/STATS**

One-day International Records **BANGLADESH**

Most catches

Fielders

28	Mohammad Rafique	
26	Habibul Bashar	
23	Aftab Ahmed	
21	Alok Kapali	
21	Mashrafe Mortaza	

Most dismissals

Wicketkeepers		*Ct/St*
126	Khaled Mashud	91/35
24	Mushfiqur Rahim	18/6
2	Hafizur Rahman	2/0
2	Hannan Sarkar	2/0
2	Nasir Ahmed	1/1

Highest team totals

301-7	v Kenya at Bogra	2005-06
278-5	v Canada at St John's	2006-07
278-6	v Scotland at Dhaka	2006-07
272-8	v Zimbabwe at Bulawayo	2000-01
267-9	v Zimbabwe at Dhaka	2001-02
265-9	v Sri Lanka at Mohali	2006-07
267-9	v Zimbabwe at Dhaka	2001-02
260-9	v Zimbabwe at Harare	2006-07
257-9	v India at Dhaka	2004-05
257	v Zimbabwe at Nairobi	1997-98

Bangladesh passed 300 for the first time in their 119th one-day international

Lowest team totals

Completed innings

76	v Sri Lanka at Colombo	2002
76	v India at Dhaka	2002-03
77	v NZ at Colombo	2002-03
86	v NZ at Chittagong	2004-05
87*	v Pakistan at Dhaka	1999-2000
92	v Zimbabwe at Nairobi	1997-98
93	v S Africa at Birmingham	2004
94	v Pakistan at Moratuwa	1985-86
100	v Kenya at Nairobi	1997-98
103	v Zimbabwe at Harare	2000-01

* *One batsman absent hurt*

Most sixes

46	Aftab Ahmed	
29	Mashrafe Mortaza	
29	Mohammad Rafique	
20	Mohammad Ashraful	
10	Habibul Bashar	
7	Farhad Reza	
7	Khaled Mahmud	
7	Shahriar Nafees	
6	Abdur Razzak	
5	(five players)	

Almost a quarter (24.4%) of Mashrafe Mortaza's runs have come in sixes

Best strike rate

Runs per 100 balls		*Runs*
96.35	Mashrafe Mortaza	713
85.07	Aftab Ahmed	1664
72.29	Mohammad Ashraful	1918
71.81	Mohammad Rafique	1190
69.64	Shahriar Nafees	1565
67.83	Khaled Mahmud	991
67.45	Shakib Al Hasan	937
65.66	Alok Kapali	964
60.45	Habibul Bashar	2168
59.63	Tushar Imran	547

Qualification: 500 runs

Most economical bowlers

Runs per over		*Wkts*
3.98	Abdur Razzak	80
4.09	Shakib Al Hasan	19
4.14	Syed Rasel	44
4.39	Mohammad Rafique	119
4.42	Mushfiqur Rahman	19
4.54	Mashrafe Mortaza	54
4.84	Manjural Islam	24
4.95	Naimur Rahman	10
4.96	Shahadat Hossain	27
5.01	Alok Kapali	15

Qualification: 1000 balls bowled

Bangladesh's one-day international results

	Played	Won	Lost	Tied	No Result	% win
v Australia	13	1	12	0	0	7.69
v England	8	0	8	0	0	0.00
v India	17	2	15	0	0	11.76
v New Zealand	8	0	8	0	0	0.00
v Pakistan	18	1	17	0	0	5.55
v South Africa	8	1	7	0	0	12.50
v Sri Lanka	22	1	21	0	0	4.54
v West Indies	13	0	11	0	2	0.00
v Zimbabwe	33	15	18	0	0	45.45
v others (see below)	21	13	8	0	0	61.90
TOTAL	**161**	**34**	**125**	**0**	**2**	**21.38**

Other teams: Bermuda (P2, W2), Canada (P2, W1, L1), Hong Kong (P1, W1), Ireland (P1, L1), Kenya (P14, W8, L6), Scotland (P1, W1)

Updated records can be found at www.cricinfo.com/db/STATS

ENGLAND
Test Match Records

Most appearances

133	AJ Stewart
118	GA Gooch
117	DI Gower
115	MA Atherton
114	MC Cowdrey
108	G Boycott
102	IT Botham
100	GP Thorpe
96	N Hussain
95	APE Knott

Cowdrey was the first man to reach 100 Tests, in 1968

Most runs

		Avge
8900	GA Gooch	42.58
8463	AJ Stewart	39.54
8231	DI Gower	44.25
8114	G Boycott	47.72
7728	MA Atherton	37.69
7624	MC Cowdrey	44.06
7249	WR Hammond	58.45
6971	L Hutton	56.67
6806	KF Barrington	58.67
6744	GP Thorpe	44.66

ME Trescothick (5825), DCS Compton (5807) and N Hussain (5764) also passed 5500 runs

Most wickets

		Avge
383	IT Botham	28.40
325	RGD Willis	25.20
307	FS Trueman	21.57
297	DL Underwood	25.83
252	JB Statham	24.84
240	MJ Hoggard	29.76
236	AV Bedser	24.89
234	AR Caddick	29.91
229	D Gough	28.39
202	JA Snow	26.66

SJ Harmison (201) has also taken more than 200 wickets

Highest scores

364	L Hutton	v Australia at The Oval	1938
336*	WR Hammond	v New Zealand at Auckland	1932-33
333	GA Gooch	v India at Lord's	1990
325	A Sandham	v West Indies at Kingston	1929-30
310*	JH Edrich	v New Zealand at Leeds	1965
287	RE Foster	v Australia at Sydney	1903-04
285*	PBH May	v West Indies at Birmingham	1957
278	DCS Compton	v Pakistan at Nottingham	1954
262*	DL Amiss	v West Indies at Kingston	1973-74
258	TW Graveney	v West Indies at Nottingham	1957

Foster was playing in his first Test, Sandham in his last

Best innings bowling

10-53	JC Laker	v Australia at Manchester	1956
9-28	GA Lohmann	v South Africa at Johannesburg	1895-96
9-37	JC Laker	v Australia at Manchester	1956
9-57	DE Malcolm	v South Africa at The Oval	1994
9-103	SF Barnes	v S Africa at Johannesburg	1913-14
8-7	GA Lohmann	v S Africa at Port Elizabeth	1895-96
8-11	J Briggs	v South Africa at Cape Town	1888-89
8-29	SF Barnes	v South Africa at The Oval	1912
8-31	FS Trueman	v India at Manchester	1952
8-34	IT Botham	v Pakistan at Lord's	1978

Botham also scored 108 in England's innings victory

Record wicket partnerships

1st	359	L Hutton (158) and C Washbrook (195)	v South Africa at Johannesburg	1948-49
2nd	382	L Hutton (364) and M Leyland (187)	v Australia at The Oval	1938
3rd	370	WJ Edrich (189) and DCS Compton (208)	v South Africa at Lord's	1947
4th	411	PBH May (285*) and MC Cowdrey (154)	v West Indies at Birmingham	1957
5th	254	KWR Fletcher (113) and AW Greig (148)	v India at Bombay	1972-73
6th	281	GP Thorpe (200*) and A Flintoff (137)	v New Zealand at Christchurch	2001-02
7th	197	MJK Smith (96) and JM Parks (101*)	v West Indies at Port-of-Spain	1959-60
8th	246	LEG Ames (137) and GOB Allen (122)	v New Zealand at Lord's	1931
9th	163*	MC Cowdrey (128*) and AC Smith (69*)	v New Zealand at Wellington	1962-63
10th	130	RE Foster (287) and W Rhodes (40*)	v Australia at Sydney	1903-04

Updated records can be found at www.cricinfo.com/db/STATS

Test Match Records

ENGLAND

Most catches

Fielders

120	IT Botham	
120	MC Cowdrey	
110	WR Hammond	
105	GP Thorpe	
103	GA Gooch	

Most dismissals

Wicketkeepers		*Ct/St*
269	APE Knott	250/19
241	AJ Stewart	227/14
219	TG Evans	173/46
174	RW Taylor	167/7
165	RC Russell	153/12

Highest team totals

903-7d	v Australia at The Oval	1938
849	v West Indies at Kingston	1929-30
658-8d	v Australia at Nottingham	1938
654-5	v South Africa at Durban	1938-39
653-4d	v India at Lord's	1990
652-7d	v India at Madras	1984-85
636	v Australia at Sydney	1928-29
633-5d	v India at Birmingham	1979
629	v India at Lord's	1974
627-9d	v Australia at Manchester	1934

England have made five other totals of more than 600

Lowest team totals

Completed innings

45	v Australia at Sydney	1886-87
46	v WI at Port-of-Spain	1993-94
52	v Australia at The Oval	1948
53	v Australia at Lord's	1888
61	v Aust at Melbourne	1901-02
61	v Aust at Melbourne	1903-04
62	v Australia at Lord's	1888
64	v NZ at Wellington	1977-78
65*	v Australia at Sydney	1894-95
71	v W Indies at Manchester	1976

One batsman absent

Best match bowling

19-90	JC Laker	v Australia at Manchester	1956
17-159	SF Barnes	v S Africa at Johannesburg	1913-14
15-28	J Briggs	v S Africa at Cape Town	1888-89
15-45	GA Lohmann	v S Africa at Port Elizabeth	1895-96
15-99	C Blythe	v South Africa at Leeds	1907
15-104	H Verity	v Australia at Lord's	1934
15-124	W Rhodes	v Australia at Melbourne	1903-04
14-99	AV Bedser	v Australia at Nottingham	1953
14-102	W Bates	v Australia at Melbourne	1882-83
14-144	SF Barnes	v South Africa at Durban	1913-14

Barnes took ten or more wickets in a match a record seven times for England

Hat-tricks

W Bates	v Australia at Melbourne	1882-83
J Briggs	v Australia at Sydney	1891-92
GA Lohmann	v S Africa at Port Elizabeth	1895-96
JT Hearne	v Australia at Leeds	1899
MJC Allom	v New Zealand at Christchurch	1929-30
TWJ Goddard	v S Africa at Johannesburg	1938-39
PJ Loader	v West Indies at Leeds	1957
DG Cork	v West Indies at Manchester	1995
D Gough	v Australia at Sydney	1998-99
MJ Hoggard	v West Indies at Bridgetown	2003-04

Allom was playing in his first match, and went on to take four wickets in five balls

England's Test match results

	Played	Won	Lost	Drawn	Tied	% win
v Australia	316	97	131	88	0	30.69
v Bangladesh	4	4	0	0	0	100.00
v India	97	34	18	45	0	35.05
v New Zealand	88	41	7	40	0	46.59
v Pakistan	67	19	12	36	0	28.35
v South Africa	130	54	26	50	0	41.53
v Sri Lanka	18	8	5	5	0	44.44
v West Indies	138	41	52	45	0	29.71
v Zimbabwe	6	3	0	3	0	50.00
TOTAL	**864**	**301**	**251**	**312**	**0**	**34.83**

Updated records can be found at **www.cricinfo.com/db/STATS**

ENGLAND
One-day International Records

Most appearances

170	AJ Stewart
158	D Gough
131	PD Collingwood
125	GA Gooch
124	A Flintoff
123	ME Trescothick
122	AJ Lamb
120	GA Hick
116	IT Botham
114	DI Gower

PAJ DeFreitas (103) and NV Knight (100) also played 100 ODIs

Most runs

		Avge
4677	AJ Stewart	31.60
4335	ME Trescothick	37.37
4290	GA Gooch	36.98
4010	AJ Lamb	39.31
3846	GA Hick	37.33
3637	NV Knight	40.41
3290	PD Collingwood	35.76
3170	DI Gower	30.77
2989	A Flintoff	31.46
2419	RA Smith	39.01

Seven other batsmen have scored 2000 runs in ODIs for England

Most wickets

		Avge
234	D Gough	26.29
145	IT Botham	28.54
145	A Flintoff	24.22
115	PAJ DeFreitas	32.82
113	JM Anderson	27.23
80	RGD Willis	24.60
76	JE Emburey	30.86
69	AR Caddick	28.47
67	PD Collingwood	41.04
67	MA Ealham	32.79
67	SJ Harmison	30.70

Six further bowlers have taken 50 wickets ODIs for England

Highest scores

167*	RA Smith	v Australia at Birmingham	1993
158	DI Gower	v New Zealand at Brisbane	1982-83
152	AJ Strauss	v Bangladesh at Nottingham	2005
142*	CWJ Athey	v New Zealand at Manchester	1986
142	GA Gooch	v Pakistan at Karachi	1987-88
137	DL Amiss	v India at Lord's	1975
137	ME Trescothick	v Pakistan at Lord's	2001
136	GA Gooch	v Australia at Lord's	1989
131	KWR Fletcher	v New Zealand at Nottingham	1975
130	DI Gower	v Sri Lanka at Taunton	1983
130	ME Trescothick	v West Indies at Gros Islet	2003-04

Trescothick has scored 12 centuries in ODIs, Gooch 8, Gower 7, GA Hick, NV Knight and KP Pietersen 5

Best innings bowling

6-31	PD Collingwood	v B'desh at Nottingham	2005
5-15	MA Ealham	v Zim at Kimberley	1999-2000
5-20	VJ Marks	v NZ at Wellington	1983-84
5-21	C White	v Zim at Bulawayo	1999-2000
5-26	RC Irani	v India at The Oval	2002
5-31	M Hendrick	v Australia at The Oval	1980
5-32	MA Ealham	v Sri Lanka at Perth	1998-99
5-33	GA Hick	v Zim at Harare	1999-2000
5-33	SJ Harmison	v Australia at Bristol	2005
5-35	PW Jarvis	v India at Bangalore	1992-93

Collingwood also scored 112 in the same match.*
All Ealham's 5 wickets at Kimberley were lbw, an ODI record

Record wicket partnerships

1st	200	ME Trescothick (114*) and VS Solanki (106)	v South Africa at The Oval	2003
2nd	202	GA Gooch (117*) and DI Gower (102)	v Australia at Lord's	1985
3rd	213	GA Hick (86*) and NH Fairbrother (113)	v West Indies at Lord's	1991
4th	226	AJ Strauss (100) and A Flintoff (123)	v West Indies at Lord's	2004
5th	174	A Flintoff (99) and PD Collingwood (79*)	v India at The Oval	2004
6th	150	MP Vaughan (90*) and GO Jones (80)	v Zimbabwe at Bulawayo	2004-05
7th	110	PD Collingwood (100) and C White (48)	v Sri Lanka at Perth	2002-03
8th	99*	RS Bopara (43*) and SCJ Broad (45*)	v India at Manchester	2007
9th	100	LE Plunkett (56) and VS Solanki (39*)	v Pakistan at Lahore	2005-06
10th	50*	D Gough (46*) and SJ Harmison (11*)	v Australia at Chester-le-Street	2005

Updated records can be found at www.cricinfo.com/db/STATS

One-day International Records — **ENGLAND**

Most catches

Fielders

79	PD Collingwood
64	GA Hick
45	GA Gooch
45	ME Trescothick
44	DI Gower/NV Knight

Most dismissals

Wicketkeepers		*Ct/St*
163	AJ Stewart	148/15
72	GO Jones	68/4
47	RC Russell	41/6
43	CMW Read	41/2
32	RW Taylor	26/6

Highest team totals

391-4	v Bangladesh at Nottingham	2005
363-7	v Pakistan at Nottingham	1992
334-4	v India at Lord's	1975
333-9	v Sri Lanka at Taunton	1983
327-4	v Pakistan at Lahore	2005-06
325-5	v India at Lord's	2002
322-6	v New Zealand at The Oval	1983
321-7	v Sri Lanka at Leeds	2006
320-8	v Australia at Birmingham	1980
320-8	v India at Bristol	2007

England have reached 300 on nine other occasions

Lowest team totals

Completed innings

86	v Australia at Manchester	2001
88	v SL at Dambulla	2003-04
89	v NZ at Wellington	2001-02
93	v Australia at Leeds	1975
94	v Aust at Melbourne	1978-79
101	v NZ at Chester-le-Street	2004
103	v SA at The Oval	1999
107	v Zim at Cape Town	1999-2000
110	v Aust at Melbourne	1998-99
110	v Aust at Adelaide	2006-07

The lowest totals against England are 45 by Canada at Manchester in 1979, and 70 by Australia at Birmingham in 1977

Most sixes

86	A Flintoff*
44	IT Botham
43	KP Pietersen*
41	GA Hick
41	ME Trescothick
35	PD Collingwood
30	AJ Lamb
26	AJ Stewart
22	DI Gower
22	RA Smith

*Also hit one six for the World XI

Best strike rate

Runs per 100 balls		*Runs*
89.60	KP Pietersen	2259
87.75	A Flintoff	2989
85.21	ME Trescothick	4335
83.83	PAJ DeFreitas	690
79.10	IT Botham	2113
78.21	GO Jones	815
75.82	AJ Strauss	2239
75.54	AJ Lamb	4010
75.45	JE Emburey	501
75.44	PD Collingwood	3290

Qualification: 500 runs

Most economical bowlers

Runs per over		*Wkts*
3.28	RGD Willis	80
3.54	ARC Fraser	47
3.79	GR Dilley	48
3.84	AD Mullally	63
3.96	IT Botham	145
3.96	PAJ DeFreitas	115
4.01	AR Caddick	69
4.08	MA Ealham	67
4.10	JE Emburey	76
4.17	GC Small	58

Qualification: 2000 balls bowled

England's one-day international results

	Played	Won	Lost	Tied	No result	% win
v Australia	93	37	52	2	2	41.57
v Bangladesh	8	8	0	0	0	100.00
v India	65	30	33	0	2	47.61
v New Zealand	59	27	28	1	3	49.09
v Pakistan	63	35	26	0	2	57.37
v South Africa	35	11	22	1	1	33.33
v Sri Lanka	38	19	19	0	0	50.00
v West Indies	75	32	39	0	4	45.07
v Zimbabwe	30	21	8	0	1	72.41
v others (see below)	11	11	0	0	0	100.00
TOTAL	477	231	227	4	15	50.43

Other teams: Canada (P2, W2), East Africa (P2, W2), Ireland (P2, W2), Kenya (P2, W2), Namibia (P1, W1), Netherlands (P2, W2), United Arab Emirates (P1, W1).

Test Match Records

Most appearances

140	SR Tendulkar
131	Kapil Dev
125	SM Gavaskar
118	A Kumble
116	DB Vengsarkar
111	R Dravid
99	M Azharuddin
96	SC Ganguly
91	GR Viswanath
88	SMH Kirmani

Gavaskar played 106 consecutive matches between 1974-75 and 1986-87

Most runs

		Avge
11150	SR Tendulkar	54.92
10122	SM Gavaskar	51.12
9469	R Dravid	57.04
6868	DB Vengsarkar	42.13
6215	M Azharuddin	45.03
6080	GR Viswanath	41.93
5812	SC Ganguly	41.21
5248	Kapil Dev	31.05
5083	VVS Laxman	42.71
4378	M Amarnath	42.50

Tendulkar has scored 37 centuries, Gavaskar 34, Dravid 24, Azharuddin 22

Most wickets

		Avge
566	A Kumble	28.73
434	Kapil Dev	29.64
266	BS Bedi	29.74
242	BS Chandrasekhar	29.74
238	Harbhajan Singh	29.86
236	J Srinath	30.49
189	EAS Prasanna	30.38
162	MH Mankad	32.32
160	Z Khan	33.33
156	S Venkataraghavan	36.11

In all 15 Indians have reached 100 wickets

Highest scores

309	V Sehwag	v Pakistan at Multan	2003-04
281	VVS Laxman	v Australia at Kolkata	2000-01
270	R Dravid	v Pakistan at Rawalpindi	2003-04
254	V Sehwag	v Pakistan at Lahore	2005-06
248*	SR Tendulkar	v Bangladesh at Dhaka	2004-05
241*	SR Tendulkar	v Australia at Sydney	2003-04
236*	SM Gavaskar	v West Indies at Madras	1983-84
233	R Dravid	v Australia at Adelaide	2003-04
231	MH Mankad	v New Zealand at Madras	1955-56
227	VG Kambli	v Zimbabwe at Delhi	1992-93

Dravid has scored five double-centuries, Gavaskar and Tendulkar four

Best innings bowling

10-74	A Kumble	v Pakistan at Delhi	1998-99
9-69	JM Patel	v Australia at Kanpur	1959-60
9-83	Kapil Dev	v WI at Ahmedabad	1983-84
9-102	SP Gupte	v W Indies at Kanpur	1958-59
8-52	MH Mankad	v Pakistan at Delhi	1952-53
8-55	MH Mankad	v England at Madras	1951-52
8-61	ND Hirwani	v W Indies at Madras	1987-88
8-72	S Venkataraghavan	v N Zealand at Delhi	1964-65
8-75	ND Hirwani	v W Indies at Madras	1987-88
8-76	EAS Prasanna	v NZ at Auckland	1975-76

Hirwani's two performances were in the same match, his Test debut

Record wicket partnerships

1st	413	MH Mankad (231) and P Roy (173)	v New Zealand at Madras	1955-56
2nd	344*	SM Gavaskar (182*) and DB Vengsarkar (157*)	v West Indies at Calcutta	1978-79
3rd	336	V Sehwag (309) and SR Tendulkar (194*)	v Pakistan at Multan	2003-04
4th	353	SR Tendulkar (241*) and VVS Laxman (178)	v Australia at Sydney	2003-04
5th	376	VVS Laxman (281) and R Dravid (180)	v Australia at Calcutta	2000-01
6th	298*	DB Vengsarkar (164*) and RJ Shastri (121*)	v Australia at Bombay	1986-87
7th	235	RJ Shastri (142) and SMH Kirmani (102)	v England at Bombay	1984-85
8th	161	M Azharuddin (109) and A Kumble (88)	v South Africa at Calcutta	1996-97
9th	149	PG Joshi (52*) and RB Desai (85)	v Pakistan at Bombay	1960-61
10th	133	SR Tendulkar (248*) and Z Khan (75)	v Bangladesh at Dhaka	2004-05

*Updated records can be found at **www.cricinfo.com/db/STATS***

Test Match Records

Most catches

Fielders

152	R Dravid	
108	SM Gavaskar	
105	M Azharuddin	
93	SR Tendulkar	
90	VVS Laxman	

Most dismissals

Wicketkeepers — Ct/St

198	SMH Kirmani	160/38
130	KS More	110/20
107	NR Mongia	99/8
82	FM Engineer	66/16
63	MS Dhoni	53/10

Highest team totals

705-7d	v Australia at Sydney	2003-04
676-7	v Sri Lanka at Kanpur	1986-87
675-5d	v Pakistan at Multan	2003-04
664	v England at The Oval	2007
657-7d	v Australia at Kolkata	2000-01
644-7d	v West Indies at Kanpur	1978-79
633-5d	v Australia at Kolkata	1997-98
628-8d	v England at Leeds	2002
610-3d	v Bangladesh at Dhaka	2006-07
609-6d	v Zimbabwe at Nagpur	2000-01

India have reached 600 on four other occasions

Lowest team totals

Completed innings

42*	v England at Lord's	1974
58	v Australia at Brisbane	1947-48
58	v England at Manchester	1952
66	v S Africa at Durban	1996-97
67	v Aust at Melbourne	1947-48
75	v West Indies at Delhi	1987-88
81*	v NZ at Wellington	1975-76
81	v W Indies at Bridgetown	1996-97
82	v England at Manchester	1952
83*	v England at Madras	1976-77
83	v N Zealand at Mohali	1999-2000

One or more batsmen absent

Best match bowling

16-136	ND Hirwani	v West Indies at Madras	1987-88
15-217	Harbhajan Singh	v Australia at Chennai	2000-01
14-124	JM Patel	v Australia at Kanpur	1959-60
14-149	A Kumble	v Pakistan at Delhi	1998-99
13-131	MH Mankad	v Pakistan at Delhi	1952-53
13-132	J Srinath	v Pakistan at Calcutta	1998-99
13-181	A Kumble	v Australia at Chennai	2004-05
13-196	Harbhajan Singh	v Australia at Kolkata	2000-01
12-104	BS Chandrasekhar	v Australia at Melbourne	1977-78
12-108	MH Mankad	v England at Madras	1951-52

Hirwani's feat was on his Test debut

Hat-tricks

Harbhajan Singh   v Australia at Kolkata   2000-01

The wickets of RT Ponting, AC Gilchrist and SK Warne, as India fought back to win after following on.

IK Pathan   v Pakistan at Karachi   2005-06

Salman Butt, Younis Khan and Mohammad Yousuf with the fourth, fifth and sixth balls of the match – Pakistan still won the match by 341 runs.

India have never conceded a hat-trick in a Test match

India's Test match results

	Played	Won	Lost	Drawn	Tied	% win
v Australia	68	15	32	20	1	22.38
v Bangladesh	5	4	0	1	0	80.00
v England	97	18	34	45	0	18.55
v New Zealand	44	14	9	21	0	31.81
v Pakistan	56	8	12	36	0	14.28
v South Africa	19	4	9	6	0	21.05
v Sri Lanka	26	10	3	13	0	38.46
v West Indies	82	11	30	41	0	13.41
v Zimbabwe	11	7	2	2	0	63.63
TOTAL	**408**	**91**	**131**	**185**	**1**	**22.35**

Updated records can be found at **www.cricinfo.com/db/STATS**

INDIA
One-day International Records

Most appearances

395	SR Tendulkar
334	M Azharuddin
323	R Dravid
299	SC Ganguly
269	A Kumble
229	J Srinath
225	Kapil Dev
196	A Jadeja
191	AB Agarkar
180	Yuvraj Singh

Robin Singh played 136 ODIs for India – but only one Test match

Most runs

		Avge
15425	SR Tendulkar	44.32
11005	SC Ganguly	41.37
10413	R Dravid	40.05
9378	M Azharuddin	36.92
5359	A Jadeja	37.47
5017	Yuvraj Singh	36.09
4875	V Sehwag	31.86
4413	NS Sidhu	37.08
4091	K Srikkanth	29.01
3783	Kapil Dev	23.79

DB Vengsarkar (3508), RJ Shastri (3108) and SM Gavaskar (3092) also reached 3000 runs

Most wickets

		Avge
334	A Kumble	30.83
315	J Srinath	28.08
288	AB Agarkar	27.85
253	Kapil Dev	27.45
196	BKV Prasad	32.30
175	Z Khan	29.54
170	Harbhajan Singh	32.45
157	M Prabhakar	28.87
152	SR Tendulkar	43.71
129	RJ Shastri	36.04

IK Pathan (115) has also reached 100 wickets

Highest scores

186*	SR Tendulkar	v N Zealand at Hyderabad	1999-2000
183*	MS Dhoni	v Sri Lanka at Jaipur	2005-06
183	SC Ganguly	v Sri Lanka at Taunton	1999
175*	Kapil Dev	v Zimbabwe at Tunbridge Wells	1983
159*	D Mongia	v Zimbabwe at Guwahati	2001-02
153*	M Azharuddin	v Zimbabwe at Cuttack	1997-98
153*	SC Ganguly	v New Zealand at Gwalior	1999-2000
153	R Dravid	v N Zealand at Hyderabad	1999-2000
152	SR Tendulkar	v Nam at Pietermaritzburg	2002-03
148	MS Dhoni	v Pakistan at Visakhapatnam	2004-05

Tendulkar has scored 41 centuries (the ODI record), Ganguly 22, Dravid 12 and V Sehwag 8

Best bowling figures

6-12	A Kumble	v West Indies at Calcutta	1993-94
6-23	A Nehra	v England at Durban	2002-03
6-42	AB Agarkar	v Australia at Melbourne	2003-04
6-55	S Sreesanth	v England at Indore	2005-06
6-59	A Nehra	v Sri Lanka at Colombo	2005
5-6	SB Joshi	v South Africa at Nairobi	1999-2000
5-15	RJ Shastri	v Australia at Perth	1991-92
5-16	SC Ganguly	v Pakistan at Toronto	1997-98
5-21	Arshad Ayub	v Pakistan at Dhaka	1988-89
5-21	N Chopra	v West Indies at Toronto	1999-2000

Agarkar has taken four wickets in an ODI innings 12 times, Kumble and J Srinath 10

Record wicket partnerships

1st	258	SC Ganguly (111) and SR Tendulkar (146)	v Kenya at Paarl	2001-02
2nd	331	SR Tendulkar (186*) and R Dravid (153)	v New Zealand at Hyderabad	1999-2000
3rd	237*	R Dravid (104*) and SR Tendulkar (140*)	v Kenya at Bristol	1999
4th	275*	M Azharuddin (153*) and A Jadeja (116*)	v Zimbabwe at Cuttack	1997-98
5th	223	M Azharuddin (111*) and A Jadeja (119)	v Sri Lanka at Colombo	1997-98
6th	158	Yuvraj Singh (120) and MS Dhoni (67*)	v Zimbabwe at Harare	2005-06
7th	102	HK Badani (60*) and AB Agarkar (53)	v Australia at Melbourne	2003-04
8th	82*	Kapil Dev (72*) and KS More (42*)	v New Zealand at Bangalore	1987-88
9th	126*	Kapil Dev (175*) and SMH Kirmani (24*)	v Zimbabwe at Tunbridge Wells	1983
10th	64	Harbhajan Singh (41*) and L Balaji (18)	v England at The Oval	2004

Updated records can be found at www.cricinfo.com/db/STATS

One-day International Records

INDIA

Most catches

Fielders

156	M Azharuddin	
116	R Dravid	
116	SR Tendulkar	
99	SC Ganguly	
85	A Kumble	

Most dismissals

Wicketkeepers		*Ct/St*
154	NR Mongia	110/44
97	MS Dhoni	79/18
90	KS More	63/27
86	R Dravid	72/14

Highest team totals

413-5	v Bermuda at Port-of-Spain	2006-07
376-2	v N Zealand at Hyderabad	1999-2000
373-6	v Sri Lanka at Taunton	1999
356-9	v Pakistan at Visakhapatnam	2004-05
353-5	v New Zealand at Hyderabad	2003-04
351-3	v Kenya at Paarl	2001-02
350-6	v Sri Lanka at Nagpur	2005-06
349-7	v Pakistan at Karachi	2003-04
348-5	v Bangladesh at Dhaka	2004-05
341-3	v West Indies at Vadodara	2006-07

All scored in 50 overs

Lowest team totals

Completed innings

54	v Sri Lanka at Sharjah	2000-01
63	v Australia at Sydney	1980-81
78	v Sri Lanka at Kanpur	1986-87
79	v Pakistan at Sialkot	1978-79
91	v S Africa at Durban	2006-07
100	v WI at Ahmedabad	1993-94
100	v Australia at Sydney	1999-2000
108	v N Zealand at Auckland	2002-03
108	v NZ at Christchurch	2002-03
112	v Pakistan at Lahore	1989-90

The lowest score against India is Zimbabwe's 65 at Harare in 2005-06

Most sixes

185	SC Ganguly	
163	SR Tendulkar	
85	A Jadeja	
77	M Azharuddin	
69	Yuvraj Singh	
68	V Sehwag	
67	Kapil Dev	
64	MS Dhoni	
44	NS Sidhu	
41	Robin Singh	
41	K Srikkanth	

Best strike rate

Runs per 100 balls		*Runs*
96.87	V Sehwag	4875
95.07	Kapil Dev	3783
94.61	MS Dhoni	2303
89.43	SB Joshi	584
86.31	Yuvraj Singh	5017
85.63	SR Tendulkar	15425
83.54	SM Patil	1005
82.67	Z Khan	544
80.62	AB Agarkar	1269
80.09	IK Pathan	1006

Qualification: 500 runs

Most economical bowlers

Runs per over		*Wkts*
3.71	Kapil Dev	253
3.95	Maninder Singh	66
4.05	Madan Lal	73
4.13	Harbhajan Singh	170
4.21	RJ Shastri	129
4.27	M Prabhakar	157
4.29	A Kumble	334
4.33	M Amarnath	46
4.36	SLV Raju	63
4.44	SB Joshi	69
4.44	J Srinath	315

Qualification: 2000 balls bowled

India's one-day international results

	Played	Won	Lost	Tied	No result	% win
v Australia	83	27	51	0	5	34.61
v Bangladesh	17	15	2	0	0	88.23
v England	65	33	30	0	2	52.38
v New Zealand	75	36	35	0	4	50.70
v Pakistan	108	40	64	0	4	38.46
v South Africa	57	20	35	0	2	36.36
v Sri Lanka	95	49	37	0	9	56.97
v West Indies	90	35	53	1	1	39.77
v Zimbabwe	49	39	8	2	0	82.97
v others (see below)	21	19	2	0	0	90.47
TOTAL	**660**	**313**	**317**	**3**	**27**	**49.68**

Other teams: Bermuda (P1, W1), East Africa (P1, W1), Ireland (P1, W1), Kenya (P13, W11, L2), Namibia (P1, W1), Netherlands (P1, W1), Scotland (P1, W1), United Arab Emirates (P2, W2).

NEW ZEALAND *Test Match Records*

Most appearances

104	SP Fleming
86	RJ Hadlee
82	JG Wright
81	NJ Astle
78	AC Parore
77	MD Crowe
72	DL Vettori
63	IDS Smith
62	CL Cairns
61	BE Congdon

Vettori also played one Test for the World XI against Australia in October 2005

Most runs

		Avge
6620	SP Fleming	39.64
5444	MD Crowe	45.36
5334	JG Wright	37.82
4702	NJ Astle	37.02
3448	BE Congdon	32.22
3428	JR Reid	33.28
3320	CL Cairns	33.53
3124	RJ Hadlee	27.16
3116	CD McMillan	38.46
2991	GM Turner	44.64

Fleming has reached 50 on 50 occasions, but has gone on to 100 only nine times: Crowe holds the NZ record with 17 Test centuries

Most wickets

		Avge
431	RJ Hadlee	22.29
228	DL Vettori	33.94
218	CL Cairns	29.40
160	DK Morrison	34.68
130	BL Cairns	32.92
123	EJ Chatfield	32.17
116	RO Collinge	29.25
111	BR Taylor	26.60
106	CS Martin	34.30
102	JG Bracewell	35.81

RC Motz (100) also took 100 Test wickets. Vettori also took one wicket for the World XI

Highest scores

299	MD Crowe	v Sri Lanka at Wellington	1990-91
274*	SP Fleming	v Sri Lanka at Colombo	2002-03
267*	BA Young	v Sri Lanka at Dunedin	1996-97
262	SP Fleming	v South Africa at Cape Town	2005-06
259	GM Turner	v West Indies at Georgetown	1971-72
239	GT Dowling	v India at Christchurch	1967-68
230*	B Sutcliffe	v India at Delhi	1955-56
224	L Vincent	v Sri Lanka at Wellington	2004-05
223*	GM Turner	v West Indies at Kingston	1971-72
222	NJ Astle	v England at Christchurch	2001-02

There have been four other double-centuries, two by MS Sinclair and one each by MP Donnelly and SP Fleming

Best innings bowling

9-52	RJ Hadlee	v Australia at Brisbane	1985-86
7-23	RJ Hadlee	v India at Wellington	1975-76
7-27	CL Cairns	v West Indies at Hamilton	1999-2000
7-52	C Pringle	v Pakistan at Faisalabad	1990-91
7-53	CL Cairns	v Bangladesh at Hamilton	2001-02
7-65	SB Doull	v India at Wellington	1998-99
7-74	BR Taylor	v West Indies at Bridgetown	1971-72
7-74	BL Cairns	v England at Leeds	1983
7-87	SL Boock	v Pakistan at Hyderabad	1984-85
7-87	DL Vettori	v Australia at Auckland	1999-2000

Hadlee took five or more wickets in an innings 36 times: the next-best for NZ is 13, by CL Cairns and DL Vettori

Record wicket partnerships

1st	387	GM Turner (259) and TW Jarvis (182)	v West Indies at Georgetown	1971-72
2nd	241	JG Wright (116) and AH Jones (143)	v England at Wellington	1991-92
3rd	467	AH Jones (186) and MD Crowe (299)	v Sri Lanka at Wellington	1990-91
4th	243	MJ Horne (157) and NJ Astle (114)	v Zimbabwe at Auckland	1997-98
5th	222	NJ Astle (141) and CD McMillan (142)	v Zimbabwe at Wellington	2000-01
6th	246*	JJ Crowe (120*) and RJ Hadlee (151*)	v Sri Lanka at Colombo	1986-87
7th	225	CL Cairns (158) and JDP Oram (90)	v South Africa at Auckland	2003-04
8th	256	SP Fleming (262) and JEC Franklin (122*)	v South Africa at Cape Town	2005-06
9th	136	IDS Smith (173) and MC Snedden (22)	v India at Auckland	1989-90
10th	151	BF Hastings (110) and RO Collinge (68*)	v Pakistan at Auckland	1972-73

Updated records can be found at www.cricinfo.com/db/STATS

Most catches

Fielders

159	SP Fleming
71	MD Crowe
70	NJ Astle
64	JV Coney
54	BA Young

Most dismissals

Wicketkeepers		*Ct/St*
201	AC Parore	194/7
176	IDS Smith	168/8
96	KJ Wadsworth	92/4
70	BB McCullum	64/6
59	WK Lees	52/7

Highest team totals

671-4	v Sri Lanka at Wellington	1990-91
630-6d	v India at Chandigarh	2003-04
595	v South Africa at Auckland	2003-04
593-8d	v South Africa at Cape Town	2005-06
586-7d	v Sri Lanka at Dunedin	1996-97
563	v Pakistan at Hamilton	2003-04
561	v Sri Lanka at Napier	2004-05
553-7d	v Australia at Brisbane	1985-86
551-9d	v England at Lord's	1973
545-6d	v Bangladesh at Chittagong	2004-05

671-4 is the record score in any team's second innings in a Test match

Lowest team totals

Completed innings

26	v England at Auckland	1954-55
42	v Australia at Wellington	1945-46
47	v England at Lord's	1958
54	v Australia at Wellington	1945-46
65	v England at Christchurch	1970-71
67	v England at Leeds	1958
67	v England at Lord's	1978
70	v Pakistan at Dacca	1955-56
73	v Pakistan at Lahore	2001-02
74	v W Indies at Dunedin	1955-56
74	v England at Lord's	1958

26 is the lowest total by any team in a Test match

Best match bowling

15-123	RJ Hadlee	v Australia at Brisbane	1985-86
12-149	DL Vettori	v Australia at Auckland	1999-2000
12-170	DL Vettori	v Bangladesh at Chittagong	2004-05
11-58	RJ Hadlee	v India at Wellington	1975-76
11-102	RJ Hadlee	v West Indies at Dunedin	1979-80
11-152	C Pringle	v Pakistan at Faisalabad	1990-91
11-155	RJ Hadlee	v Australia at Perth	1985-86
11-169	DJ Nash	v England at Lord's	1994
11-180	CS Martin	v South Africa at Auckland	2003-04
10-88	RJ Hadlee	v India at Bombay	1988-89

Hadlee took 33 wickets at 12.15 in the three-Test series in Australia in 1985-86

Hat-tricks

PJ Petherick	v Pakistan at Lahore	1976-77
JEC Franklin	v Bangladesh at Dhaka	2004-05

*Petherick's hat-trick was on Test debut: he dismissed Javed Miandad (who had made 163 on **his** debut), Wasim Raja and Intikhab Alam. Petherick won only five more Test caps.*

Franklin is one of only four men to have scored a century and taken a hat-trick in Tests: the others are J Briggs of England, and Abdul Razzaq and Wasim Akram of Pakistan.

*The only man to take a Test hat-trick **against** New Zealand is MJC Allom of England at Christchurch in 1929-30: it was his Test debut, and he took four wickets in five balls in all*

New Zealand's Test match results

	Played	Won	Lost	Drawn	Tied	% win
v Australia	46	7	22	17	0	15.21
v Bangladesh	4	4	0	0	0	100.00
v England	88	7	41	40	0	7.95
v India	44	9	14	21	0	20.45
v Pakistan	45	6	21	18	0	13.33
v South Africa	33	4	18	11	0	12.12
v Sri Lanka	24	9	5	10	0	37.50
v West Indies	35	9	10	16	0	25.71
v Zimbabwe	13	7	0	6	0	53.84
TOTAL	**332**	**62**	**131**	**139**	**0**	**18.67**

NEW ZEALAND *One-day International Records*

Most appearances

279	SP Fleming
250	CZ Harris
223	NJ Astle
214	CL Cairns
197	CD McMillan
197	DL Vettori
179	AC Parore
149	JG Wright
143	MD Crowe
133	SB Styris

Fleming (1), Cairns (1) and Vettori (4) have also played in official ODIs for the World XI

Most runs

		Avge
8007	SP Fleming	32.41
7090	NJ Astle	34.92
4881	CL Cairns	29.22
4704	MD Crowe	38.55
4379	CZ Harris	29.00
4707	CD McMillan	28.18
3891	JG Wright	26.46
3314	AC Parore	25.68
3143	KR Rutherford	29.65
2784	AH Jones	35.69

Astle has scored 16 centuries: Fleming is next with six. Fleming also scored 30 runs and Cairns 69 for the World XI

Most wickets

		Avge
203	CZ Harris	37.50
200	CL Cairns	32.78
195	DL Vettori	33.38
158	RJ Hadlee	21.56
140	EJ Chatfield	25.84
126	DK Morrison	27.53
125	SE Bond	19.32
116	SB Styris	32.62
114	MC Snedden	28.39
113	GR Larsen	35.39

JDP Oram (110) and C Pringle (103) also took 100 wickets. Vettori also took 8 wickets, and Cairns 1, for the World XI

Highest scores

172	L Vincent	v Zimbabwe at Bulawayo	2005-06
171*	GM Turner	v East Africa at Birmingham	1975
145*	NJ Astle	v USA at The Oval	2004
141	SB Styris	v Sri Lanka at Bloemfontein	2002-03
140	GM Turner	v Sri Lanka at Auckland	1982-83
134*	SP Fleming	v SA at Johannesburg	2002-03
130	CZ Harris	v Australia at Madras	1995-96
128*	RL Taylor	v Sri Lanka at Napier	2006-07
122*	NJ Astle	v England at Dunedin	2001-02
120	NJ Astle	v Zimbabwe at Auckland	1995-96
120	NJ Astle	v India at Rajkot	1999-2000

Turner's 171 was the highest score in the first World Cup*

Best bowling figures

6-19	SE Bond	v India at Bulawayo	2005-06
6-23	SE Bond	v Australia at Port Elizabeth	2002-03
6-25	SB Styris	v West Indies at Port-of-Spain	2001-02
5-22	MN Hart	v West Indies at Margao	1994-95
5-22	AR Adams	v India at Queenstown	2002-03
5-23	RO Collinge	v India at Christchurch	1975-76
5-23	SE Bond	v Australia at Wellington	2006-07
5-25	RJ Hadlee	v Sri Lanka at Bristol	1983
5-25	SE Bond	v Australia at Adelaide	2001-02
5-26	RJ Hadlee	v Australia at Sydney	1980-81
5-26	JDP Oram	v India at Auckland	2002-03

In all Hadlee took five wickets in an ODI on five occasions

Record wicket partnerships

1st	204	L Vincent (172) and SP Fleming (93)	v Zimbabwe at Bulawayo	2005-06
2nd	156	L Vincent (102) and NJ Astle (81)	v West Indies at Napier	2005-06
3rd	181	AC Parore (96) and KR Rutherford (108)	v India at Baroda	1994-95
4th	168	LK Germon (89) and CZ Harris (130)	v Australia at Chennai	1995-96
5th	148	RG Twose (80*) and CL Cairns (60)	v Australia at Cardiff	1999
6th	165	CD McMillan (117) and BB McCullum (86*)	v Australia at Hamilton	2006-07
7th	115	AC Parore (78) and LK Germon (52)	v Pakistan at Sharjah	1996-97
8th	79	SB Styris (63) and DL Vettori (47)	v Zimbabwe at Harare	2005-06
9th	74*	BB McCullum (50*) and DL Vettori (23*)	v Australia at Christchurch	2005-06
10th	65	MC Snedden (40) and EJ Chatfield (19*)	v Sri Lanka at Derby	1983

Updated records can be found at www.cricinfo.com/db/STATS

Most catches

Fielders

132	SP Fleming	
96	CZ Harris	
83	NJ Astle	
66	CL Cairns	
66	MD Crowe	

Most dismissals

Wicketkeepers		*Ct/St*
143	BB McCullum	132/11
136	AC Parore	111/25
85	IDS Smith	80/5
38	TE Blain	37/1
30	LK Germon	21/9
30	WK Lees	28/2

Highest team totals

397-5	v Zimbabwe at Bulawayo	2005-06
363-5	v Canada at St Lucia	2006-07
350-9	v Australia at Hamilton	2006-07
349-9	v India at Rajkot	1999-2000
348-8	v India at Nagpur	1995-96
347-4	v USA at The Oval	2004
340-5	v Australia at Auckland	2006-07
338-4	v Bangladesh at Sharjah	1989-90
335-5	v Australia at Perth	2006-07
332-8	v Australia at Christchurch	2005-06

The 397-5 came from 44 overs; all the others were from 50, except 350-9 (49.3), 340-5 (48.4) and 332-8/(49)

Lowest team totals

Completed innings

64	v Pakistan at Sharjah	1985-86
73	v Sri Lanka at Auckland	2006-07
74	v Aust at Wellington	1981-82
74	v Pakistan at Sharjah	1989-90
94	v Aust at Christchurch	1989-90
97	v Aust at Faridabad	2003-04
105	v Aust at Auckland	2005-06
108	v Pakistan at Wellington	1992-93
110	v Pakistan at Auckland	1993-94
112	v Aust at Port Elizabeth	2002-03

The lowest score against New Zealand is 70, by Australia at Adelaide in 1985-86

Most sixes

151	CL Cairns	
86	NJ Astle	
84	CD McMillan	
63	SP Fleming	
51	SB Styris	
46	JDP Oram	
43	CZ Harris	
41	BL Cairns	
40	BB McCullum	
37	MJ Greatbatch	

CL Cairns also hit 2 for the World XI

Best strike rate

Runs per 100 balls		*Runs*
104.88	BL Cairns	987
99.43	IDS Smith	1055
83.76	CL Cairns	4881
82.70	BB McCullum	1636
81.05	RL Taylor	706
79.37	JDP Oram	1547
78.65	SB Styris	3158
78.42	DL Vettori	1232
77.87	CM Spearman	936
75.94	CD McMillan	4707

Qualification: 500 runs

Most economical bowlers

Runs per over		*Wkts*
3.30	RJ Hadlee	158
3.57	EJ Chatfield	140
3.76	GR Larsen	113
4.06	BL Cairns	89
4.14	W Watson	74
4.17	DN Patel	45
4.17	JV Coney	54
4.20	SE Bond	125
4.22	DL Vettori	195
4.28	CZ Harris	203

Qualification: 2000 balls bowled

New Zealand's one-day international results

	Played	Won	Lost	Tied	No result	% win
v Australia	109	30	76	0	3	28.30
v Bangladesh	8	8	0	0	0	100.00
v England	59	28	27	1	3	50.90
v India	75	35	36	0	4	49.29
v Pakistan	78	29	47	1	1	38.15
v South Africa	47	16	27	0	4	37.20
v Sri Lanka	68	34	30	1	3	53.12
v West Indies	46	18	23	0	5	43.90
v Zimbabwe	28	19	7	1	1	73.07
v others (see below)	9	9	0	0	0	100.00
TOTAL	**527**	**226**	**273**	**4**	**24**	**45.29**

Other teams: Canada (P2, W2), East Africa (P1, W1), Ireland (P1, W1), Kenya (P1, W1), Netherlands (P1, W1), Scotland (P1, W1), United Arab Emirates (P1, W1), United States of America (P1, W1).

PAKISTAN
Test Match Records

Most appearances

124	Javed Miandad
118	Inzamam-ul-Haq
104	Wasim Akram
103	Salim Malik
88	Imran Khan
87	Waqar Younis
81	Wasim Bari
78	Zaheer Abbas
76	Mudassar Nazar
75	Mohammad Yousuf

Inzamam-ul-Haq also played one Test for the World XI

Most runs

		Avge
8832	Javed Miandad	52.57
8872	Inzamam-ul-Haq	50.64
6553	Mohammad Yousuf	56.00
5768	Salim Malik	43.69
5062	Zaheer Abbas	44.79
4291	Younis Khan	48.21
4114	Mudassar Nazar	38.09
4052	Saeed Anwar	45.52
3931	Majid Khan	38.92
3915	Hanif Mohammad	43.98

Mohammad Yousuf was known as Yousuf Youhana until September 2005

Most wickets

		Avge
414	Wasim Akram	23.62
373	Waqar Younis	23.56
362	Imran Khan	22.81
236	Abdul Qadir	32.80
208	Saqlain Mushtaq	29.83
198	Danish Kaneria	32.36
185	Mushtaq Ahmed	32.97
177	Sarfraz Nawaz	32.75
171	Iqbal Qasim	28.11
169	Shoaib Akhtar	25.30

Fazal Mahmood (139), Intikhab Alam (125) and Abdul Razzaq (100) also took 100 wkts

Highest scores

337	Hanif Mohammad	v WI at Bridgetown	1957-58
329	Inzamam-ul-Haq	v NZ at Lahore	2001-02
280*	Javed Miandad	v India at Hyderabad	1982-83
274	Zaheer Abbas	v Eng at Birmingham	1971
271	Javed Miandad	v NZ at Auckland	1988-89
267	Younis Khan	v India at Bangalore	2004-05
260	Javed Miandad	v England at The Oval	1987
257*	Wasim Akram	v Zim at Sheikhupura	1996-97
240	Zaheer Abbas	v England at The Oval	1974
237	Salim Malik	v Aust at Rawalpindi	1994-95

Wasim Akram's innings included 12 sixes, a record for a Test innings

Best innings bowling

9-56	Abdul Qadir	v England at Lahore	1987-88
9-86	Sarfraz Nawaz	v Australia at Melbourne	1978-79
8-58	Imran Khan	v Sri Lanka at Lahore	1981-82
8-60	Imran Khan	v India at Karachi	1982-83
8-69	Sikander Bakht	v India at Delhi	1979-80
8-164	Saqlain Mushtaq	v England at Lahore	2000-01
7-40	Imran Khan	v England at Leeds	1987
7-42	Fazal Mahmood	v India at Lucknow	1952-53
7-49	Iqbal Qasim	v Australia at Karachi	1979-80
7-52	Intikhab Alam	v NZ at Dunedin	1972-73
7-52	Imran Khan	v Eng at Birmingham	1982

Wasim Akram took five or more wickets in a Test innings on 25 occasions, Imran Khan 23

Record wicket partnerships

1st	298	Aamer Sohail (160) and Ijaz Ahmed (151)	v West Indies at Karachi	1997-98
2nd	291	Zaheer Abbas (274) and Mushtaq Mohammad (100)	v England at Birmingham	1971
3rd	451	Mudassar Nazar (231) and Javed Miandad (280*)	v India at Hyderabad	1982-83
4th	350	Mushtaq Mohammad (201) and Asif Iqbal (175)	v New Zealand at Dunedin	1972-73
5th	281	Javed Miandad (163) and Asif Iqbal (166)	v New Zealand at Lahore	1976-77
6th	269	Mohammad Yousuf (223) and Kamran Akmal (154)	v England at Lahore	2005-06
7th	308	Waqar Hasan (189) and Imtiaz Ahmed (209)	v New Zealand at Lahore	1955-56
8th	313	Wasim Akram (257*) and Saqlain Mushtaq (79)	v Zimbabwe at Sheikhupura	1996-97
9th	190	Asif Iqbal (146) and Intikhab Alam (51)	v England at The Oval	1967
10th	151	Azhar Mahmood (128*) and Mushtaq Ahmed (59)	v South Africa at Rawalpindi	1997-98

Updated records can be found at **www.cricinfo.com/db/STATS**

Test Match Records

PAKISTAN

Most catches

Fielders

93	Javed Miandad	
81	Inzamam-ul-Haq	
66	Majid Khan	
65	Salim Malik	
64	Younis Khan	

Most dismissals

	Wicketkeepers	*Ct/St*
228	Wasim Bari	201/27
147	Moin Khan	127/20
130	Rashid Latif	119/11
126	Kamran Akmal	108/18
104	Salim Yousuf	91/13

Highest team totals

708	v England at The Oval	1987
699-5	v India at Lahore	1989-90
679-7d	v India at Lahore	2005-06
674-6	v India at Faisalabad	1984-85
657-8d	v West Indies at Bridgetown	1957-58
652	v India at Faisalabad	1982-83
643	v New Zealand at Lahore	2001-02
636-8d	v England at Lahore	2005-06
624	v Australia at Adelaide	1983-84
616-5d	v New Zealand at Auckland	1988-89

Pakistan have made three other scores of 600 or more

Lowest team totals

Completed innings

53*	v Australia at Sharjah	2002-03
59	v Australia at Sharjah	2002-03
62	v Australia at Perth	1981-82
72	v Australia at Perth	2004-05
77*	v West Indies at Lahore	1986-87
87	v England at Lord's	1954
90	v England at Manchester	1954
92	v SA at Faisalabad	1997-98
97*	v Australia at Brisbane	1995-96
100	v England at Lord's	1962

* One batsman retired hurt or absent hurt. The lowest two totals came in the same game

Best match bowling

14-116	Imran Khan	v Sri Lanka at Lahore	1981-82
13-101	Abdul Qadir	v England at Lahore	1987-88
13-114	Fazal Mahmood	v Australia at Karachi	1956-57
13-135	Waqar Younis	v Zimbabwe at Karachi	1993-94
12-94	Fazal Mahmood	v India at Lucknow	1952-53
12-94	Danish Kaneria	v Bangladesh at Multan	2001-02
12-99	Fazal Mahmood	v England at The Oval	1954
12-100	Fazal Mahmood	v West Indies at Dacca	1958-59
12-130	Waqar Younis	v NZ at Faisalabad	1990-91
12-165	Imran Khan	v Australia at Sydney	1976-77

Imran Khan took ten or more wickets in a match six times, Abdul Qadir, Waqar Younis and Wasim Akram five each.

Hat-tricks

Wasim Akram	v Sri Lanka at Lahore	1998-99
Wasim Akram	v Sri Lanka at Dhaka	1998-99
Abdul Razzaq	v Sri Lanka at Galle	1999-2000
Mohammad Sami	v Sri Lanka at Lahore	2001-02

Wasim Akram's hat-tricks came in successive matches: he also took Pakistan's first two hat-tricks in one-day internationals.

RS Kaluwitharana was the first victim in both Wasim Akram's first hat-trick and in Abdul Razzaq's

Pakistan's Test match results

	Played	Won	Lost	Drawn	Tied	% win
v Australia	52	11	24	17	0	21.15
v Bangladesh	6	6	0	0	0	100.00
v England	67	12	19	36	0	17.91
v India	56	12	8	36	0	21.42
v New Zealand	45	21	6	18	0	46.66
v South Africa	14	3	7	4	0	21.42
v Sri Lanka	32	15	7	10	0	46.87
v West Indies	44	15	14	15	0	34.09
v Zimbabwe	14	8	2	4	0	57.14
TOTAL	**330**	**103**	**87**	**140**	**0**	**31.21**

Updated records can be found at www.cricinfo.com/db/STATS

PAKISTAN
One-day International Records

Most appearances

375	Inzamam-ul-Haq
356	Wasim Akram
283	Salim Malik
262	Waqar Younis
250	Ijaz Ahmed
247	Saeed Anwar
235	Mohammad Yousuf
235	Shahid Afridi
233	Javed Miandad
227	Abdul Razzaq

Moin Khan (219) also played in more than 200 ODIs

Most runs

		Avge
11701	Inzamam-ul-Haq	39.53
8823	Saeed Anwar	39.21
7915	Mohammad Yousuf	41.43
7381	Javed Miandad	41.70
7170	Salim Malik	32.88
6564	Ijaz Ahmed	32.33
5841	Rameez Raja	32.09
5035	Shahid Afridi	23.75
4780	Aamer Sohail	31.86
4416	Abdul Razzaq	30.24

Younis Khan (3988), Wasim Akram (3717), Imran Khan (3709), Shoaib Malik (3641) and Moin Khan (3266) also passed 3000 runs

Most wickets

		Avge
502	Wasim Akram	23.52
416	Waqar Younis	23.84
288	Saqlain Mushtaq	21.78
245	Abdul Razzaq	30.80
202	Shahid Afridi	35.31
202	Shoaib Akhtar	22.96
182	Aqib Javed	31.43
182	Imran Khan	26.61
161	Mushtaq Ahmed	33.29
132	Abdul Qadir	26.16

Azhar Mahmood (123), Mohammad Sami (118), Mudassar Nazar (111) and Shoaib Malik (105) also took 100 wickets

Highest scores

194	Saeed Anwar	v India at Chennai	1996-97
160	Imran Nazir	v Zimbabwe at Kingston	2006–07
144	Younis Khan	v Hong Kong at Colombo	2004
143	Shoaib Malik	v India at Colombo	2004
141*	Mohammad Yousuf	v Zim at Bulawayo	2002-03
140	Saeed Anwar	v India at Dhaka	1997-98
139*	Ijaz Ahmed	v India at Lahore	1997-98
137*	Inzamam-ul-Haq	v NZ at Sharjah	1993-94
137	Ijaz Ahmed	v England at Sharjah	1998-99
135	Salim Elahi	v SA at Port Elizabeth	2002-03

Saeed Anwar scored 20 centuries, Mohammad Yousuf 11, Ijaz Ahmed and Inzamam-ul-Haq 10.

Best innings bowling

7-36	Waqar Younis	v England at Leeds	2001
7-37	Aqib Javed	v India at Sharjah	1991-92
6-14	Imran Khan	v India at Sharjah	1984-85
6-16	Shoaib Akhtar	v NZ at Karachi	2001-02
6-18	Azhar Mahmood	v WI at Sharjah	1999-2000
6-26	Waqar Younis	v Sri Lanka at Sharjah	1989-90
6-27	Naved-ul-Hasan	v India at Jamshedpur	2004-05
6-30	Waqar Younis	v NZ at Auckland	1993-94
6-35	Abdul Razzaq	v Bangladesh at Dhaka	2001-02
6-44	Waqar Younis	v NZ at Sharjah	1996-97

Waqar Younis took five or more wickets in an innings 13 times (the ODI record), Saqlain Mushtaq and Wasim Akram 6

Record wicket partnerships

1st	204	Saeed Anwar (110) and Rameez Raja (109*)	v Sri Lanka at Sharjah	1992-93
2nd	263	Aamer Sohail (134) and Inzamam-ul-Haq (137*)	v New Zealand at Sharjah	1993-94
3rd	230	Saeed Anwar (140) and Ijaz Ahmed (117)	v India at Dhaka	1997-98
4th	172	Salim Malik (84) and Basit Ali (127*)	v West Indies at Sharjah	1993-94
5th	162	Inzamam-ul-Haq (72) and Mohammad Yousuf (88)	v Australia at Lord's	2004
6th	144	Imran Khan (102*) and Shahid Mahboob (77)	v Sri Lanka at Leeds	1983
7th	124	Mohammad Yousuf (91*) and Rashid Latif (66)	v Australia at Cardiff	2001
8th	92	Mohammad Yousuf (92) and Shoaib Akhtar (36)	v Australia at Karachi	1998-99
9th	73	Shoaib Malik (52*) and Mohammad Sami (46)	v South Africa at Centurion	2006-07
10th	72	Abdul Razzaq (46*) and Waqar Younis (33)	v South Africa at Durban	1997-98

Updated records can be found at www.cricinfo.com/db/STATS

One-day International Records

PAKISTAN

Most catches

Fielders

113	Inzamam-ul-Haq	
90	Ijaz Ahmed	
88	Wasim Akram	
83	Shahid Afridi	
81	Salim Malik	

Most dismissals

Wicketkeepers		*Ct/St*
287	Moin Khan	214/73
220	Rashid Latif	182/38
103	Salim Yousuf	81/22
71	Kamran Akmal	60/11
62	Wasim Bari	52/10

Highest team totals

371-9	v Sri Lanka at Nairobi	1996-97
353-6	v England at Karachi	2005-06
351-4	v South Africa at Durban	2006-07
349	v Zimbabwe at Kingston	2006-07
344-5	v Zimbabwe at Bulawayo	2002-03
344-8	v India at Karachi	2003-04
343-5	v Hong Kong at Colombo	2004
338-5	v Sri Lanka at Swansea	1983
335-6	v South Africa at Port Elizabeth	2002-03
330-6	v Sri Lanka at Nottingham	1975

Pakistan have reached 300 on 31 further occasions

Lowest team totals

Completed innings

43	v W Indies at Cape Town	1992-93
71	v W Indies at Brisbane	1992-93
74	v England at Adelaide	1991-92
81	v West Indies at Sydney	1992-93
85	v England at Manchester	1978
87	v India at Sharjah	1984-85
89	v S Africa at Mohali	2006-07
107	v S Africa at Cape Town	2006-07
108	v Australia at Nairobi	2002-03
109	v SA at Johannesburg	1994-95

Against India in 1984-85 Pakistan were chasing only 126 to win

Most sixes

227	Shahid Afridi	
143	Inzamam-ul-Haq	
121	Wasim Akram	
103	Abdul Razzaq	
97	Saeed Anwar	
87	Ijaz Ahmed	
79	Mohammad Yousuf	
61	Moin Khan	
45	Imran Khan	
44	Javed Miandad	
44	Shoaib Malik	

Afridi hit 2 other sixes in official ODIs

Best strike rate

Runs per 100 balls		*Runs*
109.24	Shahid Afridi	5035
89.60	Manzoor Elahi	741
88.33	Wasim Akram	3717
84.80	Zaheer Abbas	2572
82.48	Kamran Akmal	1253
81.30	Moin Khan	3266
80.66	Saeed Anwar	8823
80.53	Imran Nazir	1729
80.40	Abdul Razzaq	4416
80.30	Ijaz Ahmed	6564

Qualification: 500 runs

Most economical bowlers

Runs per over		*Wkts*
3.63	Sarfraz Nawaz	63
3.71	Akram Raza	38
3.89	Imran Khan	182
3.89	Wasim Akram	502
4.06	Abdul Qadir	132
4.14	Arshad Khan	56
4.14	Tauseef Ahmed	55
4.24	Mudassar Nazar	111
4.26	Mushtaq Ahmed	161
4.28	Aqib Javed	182

Qualification: 2000 balls bowled

Pakistan's one-day international results

	Played	Won	Lost	Tied	No result	% win
v Australia	74	27	43	1	3	38.57
v Bangladesh	18	17	1	0	0	94.44
v England	63	26	35	0	2	42.62
v India	108	64	40	0	4	61.53
v New Zealand	78	47	29	1	1	61.84
v South Africa	47	14	32	0	1	30.43
v Sri Lanka	110	67	39	1	3	63.20
v West Indies	110	44	64	2	0	40.74
v Zimbabwe	35	31	2	1	1	93.93
v others (see below)	16	15	1	0	0	93.75
TOTAL	659	352	286	6	15	55.17

Other teams: Canada (P1, W1), Hong Kong (P1, W1), Ireland (P1, L1), Kenya (P5, W5), Namibia (P1, W1), Netherlands (P3, W3), Scotland (P2, W2), United Arab Emirates (P2, W2).

SOUTH AFRICA *Test Match Records*

Most appearances

107	SM Pollock
106	JH Kallis
101	MV Boucher
101	G Kirsten
84	HH Gibbs
75	M Ntini
72	AA Donald
70	DJ Cullinan
68	WJ Cronje
53	GC Smith

Kallis, Boucher and Smith all also played one Test for the World XI against Australia

Most runs

		Avge
8347	JH Kallis	54.91
7289	G Kirsten	45.27
5943	HH Gibbs	43.37
4554	DJ Cullinan	44.21
4273	GC Smith	48.01
3827	MV Boucher	30.61
3781	SM Pollock	32.31
3714	WJ Cronje	36.41
3471	B Mitchell	48.88
2960	AD Nourse	53.81

Kallis (83 runs), Smith (12) and Boucher (17) also played one Test for the World XI against Australia

Most wickets

		Avge
416	SM Pollock	23.19
330	AA Donald	22.25
308	M Ntini	27.48
212	JH Kallis	31.68
170	HJ Tayfield	25.91
134	PR Adams	32.87
123	TL Goddard	26.22
116	PM Pollock	24.18
104	NAT Adcock	21.10
100	N Boje	42.65

Kallis also took one wicket for the World XI against Australia

Highest scores

277	GC Smith	v England at Birmingham	2003
275*	DJ Cullinan	v New Zealand at Auckland	1998-99
275	G Kirsten	v England at Durban	1999-2000
274	RG Pollock	v Australia at Durban	1969-70
259	GC Smith	v England at Lord's	2003
255*	DJ McGlew	v New Zealand at Wellington	1952-53
236	EAB Rowan	v England at Leeds	1951
231	AD Nourse	v Australia at Johannesburg	1935-36
228	HH Gibbs	v Pakistan at Cape Town	2002-03
222*	JA Rudolph	v Bangladesh at Chittagong	2002-03

Smith's innings were in consecutive matches. Rudolph's was on Test debut

Best innings bowling

9-113	HJ Tayfield	v England at Johannesburg	1956-57
8-53	GB Lawrence	v N Zealand at Johannesburg	1961-62
8-64	L Klusener	v India at Calcutta	1996-97
8-69	HJ Tayfield	v England at Durban	1956-57
8-70	SJ Snooke	v England at Johannesburg	1905-06
8-71	AA Donald	v Zimbabwe at Harare	1995-96
7-23	HJ Tayfield	v Australia at Durban	1949-50
7-29	GF Bissett	v England at Durban	1927-28
7-37	M Ntini	v W Indies at Port-of-Spain	2004-05
7-63	AE Hall	v England at Cape Town	1922-23

Klusener and Hall were making their Test debuts

Record wicket partnerships

1st	368	GC Smith (151) and HH Gibbs (228)	v Pakistan at Cape Town	2002-03
2nd	315*	HH Gibbs (211*) and JH Kallis (148*)	v New Zealand at Christchurch	1998-99
3rd	429*	JA Rudolph (222*) and HH Dippenaar (177*)	v Bangladesh at Chittagong	2002-03
4th	249	JH Kallis (177) and G Kirsten (137)	v West Indies at Durban	2003-04
5th	267	JH Kallis (147) and AG Prince (131)	v West Indies at St John's	2004-05
6th	200	RG Pollock (274) and HR Lance (61)	v Australia at Durban	1969-70
7th	246	DJ McGlew (255*) and ARA Murray (109)	v New Zealand at Wellington	1952-53
8th	150	ND McKenzie (103) and SM Pollock (111)	v Sri Lanka at Centurion	2000-01
	150	G Kirsten (130) and M Zondeki (59)	v England at Leeds	2003
9th	195	MV Boucher (78) and PL Symcox (108)	v Pakistan at Johannesburg	1997-98
10th	103	HG Owen-Smith (129) and AJ Bell (26*)	v England at Leeds	1929

Updated records can be found at **www.cricinfo.com/db/STATS**

Test Match Records **SOUTH AFRICA**

Most catches

Fielders

101	JH Kallis
85	HH Gibbs
83	G Kirsten
72	SM Pollock
67	DJ Cullinan

Most dismissals

Wicketkeepers		*Ct/St*
390	MV Boucher	374/16
152	DJ Richardson	150/2
141	JHB Waite	124/17
56	DT Lindsay	54/2
51	HB Cameron	39/12

Highest team totals

682-6d	v England at Lord's	2003
658-9d	v West Indies at Durban	2003-04
622-9d	v Australia at Durban	1969-70
621-5d	v New Zealand at Auckland	1998-99
620-7d	v Pakistan at Cape Town	2002-03
620	v Australia at Johannesburg	1966-67
604-6d	v West Indies at Centurion	2003-04
600-3d	v Zimbabwe at Harare	2001-02
595	v Australia at Adelaide	1963-64
594-5d	v England at Birmingham	2003

The 620 was scored in the second innings

Lowest team totals

Completed innings

30	v Eng at Port Elizabeth	1895-96
30	v Eng at Birmingham	1924
35	v Eng at Cape Town	1898-99
36	v Aust at Melbourne	1931-32
43	v Eng at Cape Town	1888-89
45	v Aust at Melbourne	1931-32
47	v Eng at Cape Town	1888-89
58	v England at Lord's	1912
72	v Eng at Johannesburg	1956-57
72	v Eng at Cape Town	1956-57

South Africa's lowest total since their return to Test cricket in 1991-92 is 84 against India at Johannesburg in 2006-07

Best match bowling

13-132	M Ntini	v W Indies at Port-of-Spain	2004-05
13-165	HJ Tayfield	v Australia at Melbourne	1952-53
13-192	HJ Tayfield	v England at Johannesburg	1956-57
12-127	SJ Snooke	v England at Johannesburg	1905-06
12-139	AA Donald	v India at Port Elizabeth	1992-93
12-181	AEE Vogler	v England at Johannesburg	1909-10
11-112	AE Hall	v England at Cape Town	1922-23
11-113	AA Donald	v Zimbabwe at Harare	1995-96
11-127	AA Donald	v England at Jo'burg	1999-2000
11-150	EP Nupen	v England at Jo'burg	1930-31

Hall was making his Test debut. His performance, and Vogler's, were at the old Wanderers ground in Johannesburg

Hat-tricks

GM Griffin	v England at Lord's	1960

Griffin achieved the feat in his second and final Test (he was no-balled for throwing in the same match).

GA Lohmann (for England at Port Elizabeth in 1895-96), TJ Matthews (twice in the same match for Australia at Manchester in 1912) and TWJ Goddard (for England at Johannesburg in 1938-39) have taken Test hat-tricks against South Africa

South Africa's Test match results

	Played	Won	Lost	Drawn	Tied	% win
v Australia	77	15	44	18	0	19.48
v Bangladesh	4	4	0	0	0	100.00
v England	130	26	54	50	0	20.00
v India	19	9	4	6	0	47.36
v New Zealand	33	18	4	11	0	54.54
v Pakistan	14	7	3	4	0	50.00
v Sri Lanka	17	8	4	5	0	47.05
v West Indies	19	12	2	5	0	63.15
v Zimbabwe	7	6	0	1	0	85.71
TOTAL	**320**	**105**	**115**	**100**	**0**	**32.81**

Updated records can be found at **www.cricinfo.com/db/STATS**

SOUTH AFRICA *One-day International Records*

Most appearances

281	SM Pollock
256	JH Kallis
245	MV Boucher
245	JN Rhodes
213	HH Gibbs
188	WJ Cronje
185	G Kirsten
171	L Klusener
164	AA Donald
157	M Ntini

Pollock (9), Kallis (5), Boucher (5) and Ntini (1) also appeared in official ODIs for composite teams

Most runs

		Avge
9115	JH Kallis	46.50
6889	HH Gibbs	36.25
6798	G Kirsten	40.95
5935	JN Rhodes	35.11
5565	WJ Cronje	38.64
4296	GC Smith	40.14
3860	DJ Cullinan	32.99
3817	MV Boucher	28.48
3576	L Klusener	41.10
3300	HH Dippenaar	44.00

Kallis (29 runs), Smith (0), Boucher (163) and Dippenaar (91) also appeared in official ODIs for composite teams

Most wickets

		Avge
377	SM Pollock	23.94
272	AA Donald	21.78
241	M Ntini	23.87
229	JH Kallis	31.54
192	L Klusener	29.95
114	WJ Cronje	34.78
95	N Boje	35.27
95	PS de Villiers	27.74
95	AJ Hall	26.47
89	A Nel	27.62

Pollock (6 wickets), Ntini (1), Kallis (4) and Boje (1) also appeared in official ODIs for composite teams

Highest scores

188*	G Kirsten	v UAE at Rawalpindi	1995-96
175	HH Gibbs	v Australia at Johannesburg	2005-06
169*	DJ Callaghan	v N Zealand at Verwoerdburg	1994-95
161	AC Hudson	v Netherlands at Rawalpindi	1995-96
153	HH Gibbs	v B'desh at Potchefstroom	2002-03
147*	MV Boucher	v Zimbabwe at Potchefstroom	2006-07
146	AB de Villiers	v West Indies at St George's	2006-07
143	HH Gibbs	v N Zealand at Johannesburg	2002-03
139	JH Kallis	v W Indies at Johannesburg	2003-04
134*	GC Smith	v India at Kolkata	2005-06

Gibbs has scored 17 one-day hundreds, Kallis 15 and Kirsten 13

Best bowling figures

6-22	M Ntini	v Australia at Cape Town	2005-06
6-23	AA Donald	v Kenya at Nairobi	1996-97
6-35	SM Pollock	v W Indies at East London	1998-99
6-49	L Klusener	v Sri Lanka at Lahore	1997-98
5-18	AJ Hall	v England at Bridgetown	2006-07
5-20	SM Pollock	v Eng at Johannesburg	1999-2000
5-21	L Klusener	v Kenya at Amstelveen	1999
5-21	N Boje	v Australia at Cape Town	2001-02
5-21	M Ntini	v Pakistan at Mohali	2006-07
5-23	SM Pollock	v Pakistan at Johannesburg	2006-07

Klusener has taken five wickets in an ODI innings six times, Pollock five and Ntini four

Record wicket partnerships

1st	235	G Kirsten (115) and HH Gibbs (111)	v India at Kochi	1999-2000
2nd	209	G Kirsten (124) and ND McKenzie (131*)	v Kenya at Cape Town	2001-02
3rd	186	JA Morkel (97) and AB de Villiers (107)	v Zimbabwe at Harare	2007
4th	232	DJ Cullinan (124) and JN Rhodes (121)	v Pakistan at Nairobi	1996-97
5th	183*	JH Kallis (109*) and JN Rhodes (94*)	v Pakistan at Durban	1997-98
6th	137	WJ Cronje (70*) and SM Pollock (75)	v Zimbabwe at Johannesburg	1996-97
7th	114	MV Boucher (68) and L Klusener (75*)	v India at Nagpur	1999-2000
8th	138*	JM Kemp (100*) and AJ Hall (56*)	v India at Cape Town	2006-07
9th	61	SM Pollock (46) and J Botha (15*)	v Australia at Melbourne	2005-06
10th	67*	JA Morkel (23*) and M Ntini (42*)	v New Zealand at Napier	2003-04

Updated records can be found at **www.cricinfo.com/db/STATS**

Most catches

Fielders

105	JN Rhodes	
103	SM Pollock	
100	JH Kallis	
90	HH Gibbs	
73	WJ Cronje	

Most dismissals

Wicketkeepers		*Ct/St*
360	MV Boucher	343/17
165	DJ Richardson	148/17
9	SJ Palframan	9/0
6	AB de Villiers	6/0

Highest team totals

438-9	v Australia at Johannesburg 2005-06
418-5	v Zimbabwe at Potchefstroom 2006-07
392-6	v Pakistan at Centurion 2006-07
363-3	v Zimbabwe at Bulawayo 2001-02
356-4	v West Indies at St George's 2006-07
354-3	v Kenya at Cape Town 2001-02
353-3	v Netherland at Basseterre 2006-07
329-6	v Zimbabwe at Durban 2004-05
328-3	v Netherlands at Rawalpindi 1995-96
326-3	v Australia at Port Elizabeth 2001-02

438-9 was the highest total in all ODIs, and came from 49.5 overs; all the others above were scored in 50 overs, apart from 353-3 (40)

Lowest team totals

Completed innings

69	v Australia at Sydney 1993-94
101*	v Pakistan at Sharjah 1999-2000
106	v Australia at Sydney 2001-02
107	v England at Lord's 2003
107	v England at Lord's 2003
108	v New Z at Mumbai 2006-07
123	v Aust at Wellington 1994-95
129	v Eng at East London 1995-96
149	v Pakistan at Jo'burg 1999-2000
152	v WI at Port-of-Spain 1991-92

* One batsman retired hurt. SA also had 50-overs totals of 140-9 (v WI , 1992-93), 144-9 (v Aust, 1999-2000) and 147-7 (v NZ, 1993-94)

Most sixes

112	JH Kallis	
107	HH Gibbs	
94	WJ Cronje	
76	L Klusener	
70	MV Boucher	
53	SM Pollock	
50	JM Kemp	
47	JN Rhodes	
33	DJ Cullinan	
30	AB de Villiers	

Boucher (2), Pollock (3), Kemp (1) and de Villiers (4) also hit sixes for the Africa XI

Best strike rate

Runs per 100 balls		*Runs*
89.91	L Klusener	3576
89.29	N Boje	1410
86.77	AB de Villiers	1476
85.39	SM Pollock	2953
84.72	JM Kemp	1320
83.61	PL Symcox	694
82.69	GC Smith	4296
82.64	HH Gibbs	6889
81.42	AP Kuiper	539
84.67	MV Boucher	3817

Qualification: 500 runs

Most economical bowlers

Runs per over		*Wkts*
3.57	PS de Villiers	95
3.68	SM Pollock	377
3.94	CR Matthews	79
4.15	AA Donald	272
4.15	PL Symcox	72
4.28	BM McMillan	70
4.37	M Ntini	241
4.44	WJ Cronje	114
4.50	RP Snell	44
4.51	N Boje	95
4.51	AJ Hall	95

Qualification: 2000 balls bowled

South Africa's one-day international results

	Played	Won	Lost	Tied	No result	% win
v Australia	67	28	36	3	0	43.75
v Bangladesh	8	7	1	0	0	87.50
v England	35	22	11	1	1	66.66
v India	57	35	20	0	2	63.63
v New Zealand	47	27	16	0	4	62.79
v Pakistan	47	32	14	0	1	69.56
v Sri Lanka	45	22	21	1	1	51.16
v West Indies	40	27	12	0	1	69.23
v Zimbabwe	27	24	2	0	1	92.30
v others (see below)	15	15	0	0	0	100.00
TOTAL	388	239	133	5	11	64.24

Other teams: Canada (P1, W1), Ireland (P2, W2), Kenya (P8, W8), Netherlands (P2, W2), Scotland (P1, W1), United Arab Emirates (P1, W1).

SRI LANKA
Test Match Records

Most appearances

112	M Muralitharan
107	ST Jayasuriya
98	WPUJC Vaas
93	PA de Silva
93	A Ranatunga
88	MS Atapattu
88	DPMD Jayawardene
83	HP Tillakaratne
67	KC Sangakkara
52	RS Mahanama

Ranatunga uniquely played in his country's first Test, and their 100th

Most runs

		Avge
6791	ST Jayasuriya	40.42
6630	DPMD Jayawardene	49.84
6361	PA de Silva	42.97
5492	KC Sangakkara	54.37
5330	MS Atapattu	38.90
5105	A Ranatunga	35.69
4545	HP Tillakaratne	42.87
2684	WPUJC Vaas	23.54
2576	RS Mahanama	29.27
2452	AP Gurusinha	38.92

TM Dilshan (2152) and TT Samaraweera (2089) also reached 2000 runs

Most wickets

		Avge
695	M Muralitharan	21.25
319	WPUJC Vaas	29.21
96	ST Jayasuriya	34.17
85	GP Wickremasinghe	41.87
83	SL Malinga	30.73
77	CRD Fernando	30.36
73	RJ Ratnayake	35.10
69	HDPK Dharmasena	42.31
64	DNT Zoysa	33.70
59	ALF de Mel	36.94

Muralitharan also took 5 wickets for the World XI

Highest scores

374	DPMD Jayawardene	v SA at Colombo	2006
340	ST Jayasuriya	v India at Colombo	1997-98
287	KC Sangakkara	v SA at Colombo	2006
270	KC Sangakkara	v Zim at Bulawayo	2003-04
267	PA de Silva	v NZ at Wellington	1990-91
253	ST Jayasuriya	v Paki at Faisalabad	2004-05
249	MS Atapattu	v Zim at Bulawayo	2003-04
242	DPMD Jayawardene	v India at Colombo	1998-99
237	DPMD Jayawardene	v SA at Galle	2004-05
232	KC Sangakkara	v SA at Colombo	2004-05

de Silva made 20 Test centuries, Jayawardene 18, and Atapattu 16. Atapattu and Sangakkara both have 6 double-centuries

Best innings bowling

9-51	M Muralitharan	v Zimbabwe at Kandy	2001-02
9-65	M Muralitharan	v England at The Oval	1998
8-46	M Muralitharan	v West Indies at Kandy	2005
8-70	M Muralitharan	v England at Nottingham	2006
8-83	JR Ratnayeke	v Pakistan at Sialkot	1985-86
8-87	M Muralitharan	v India at Colombo	2001-02
7-46	M Muralitharan	v England at Galle	2003-04
7-71	WPUJC Vaas	v West Indies at Colombo	2001-02
7-84	M Muralitharan	v South Africa at Galle	2000-01
7-94	M Muralitharan	v Zimbabwe at Kandy	1997-98

Muralitharan has taken five or more wickets in an innings a record 60 times

Record wicket partnerships

1st	335	MS Atapattu (207*) and ST Jayasuriya (188)	v Pakistan at Kandy	2000
2nd	576	ST Jayasuriya (340) and RS Mahanama (225)	v India at Colombo	1997-98
3rd	624	KC Sangakkara (287) and DPMD Jayawardene (374)	v South Africa at Colombo	2006
4th	240*	AP Gurusinha (116*) and A Ranatunga (135*)	v Pakistan at Colombo	1985-86
5th	280	TT Samaraweera (138) and TM Dilshan (168)	v Bangladesh at Colombo	2005-06
6th	189*	PA de Silva (143*) and A Ranatunga (87*)	v Zimbabwe at Colombo	1997-98
7th	223*	HAPW Jayawardene (120*) and WPUJC Vaas (100*)	v Bangladesh at Colombo	2007
8th	170	DPMD Jayawardene (237) and WPUJC Vaas (69)	v South Africa at Galle	2004-05
9th	105	WPUJC Vaas (50*) and KMDN Kulasekera (64)	v England at Lord's	2006
10th	79	WPUJC Vaas (68*) and M Muralitharan (43)	v Australia at Kandy	2003-04

Updated records can be found at **www.cricinfo.com/db/STATS**

Most catches

Fielders

123	DPMD Jayawardene	
89	HP Tillakaratne	
78	ST Jayasuriya	
62	M Muralitharan	
57	MS Atapattu	

Most dismissals

Wicketkeepers		*Ct/St*
147	KC Sangakkara	127/20
119	RS Kaluwitharana	93/26
35	HP Tillakaratne	33/2
34	SAR Silva	33/1
32	HAPW Jayawardene	26/6

Highest team totals

952-6d	v India at Colombo	1997-98
756-5d	v South Africa at Colombo	2006
713-3d	v Zimbabwe at Bulawayo	2003-04
628-8d	v England at Colombo	2003-04
627-9d	v West Indies at Colombo	2001-02
610-6d	v India at Colombo	2001-02
591	v England at The Oval	1998
590-9d	v West Indies at Galle	2001-02
577-6d	v Bangladesh at Colombo	2007
555-5d	v Bangladesh at Colombo	2001-02

952-6d is the highest total in all Tests.
Sri Lanka have reached 500 on 20 occasions

Lowest team totals

Completed innings

71	v Pakistan at Kandy	1994-95
73*	v Pakistan at Kandy	2005-06
81	v England at Colombo	2000-01
82	v India at Chandigarh	1990-91
93	v NZ at Wellington	1982-83
95	v S Africa at Cape Town	2000-01
97	v N Zealand at Kandy	1983-84
97	v Australia at Darwin	2004
101	v Pakistan at Kandy	1985-86
109	v Pakistan at Kandy	1985-86

* One batsman absent hurt

Best match bowling

16-220	M Muralitharan	v England at The Oval	1998
14-191	WPUJC Vaas	v West Indies at Colombo	2001-02
13-115	M Muralitharan	v Zimbabwe at Kandy	2001-02
13-171	M Muralitharan	v South Africa at Galle	2000
12-82	M Muralitharan	v Bangladesh at Kandy	2007
12-117	M Muralitharan	v Zimbabwe at Kandy	1997-98
12-225	M Muralitharan	v South Africa at Colombo	2006
11-93	M Muralitharan	v England at Galle	2003-04
11-132	M Muralitharan	v England at Nottingham	2006
11-161	M Muralitharan	v South Africa at Durban	2000-01

Muralitharan has taken ten or more wickets in a match a
record 20 times; the only others to do it for Sri Lanka are Vaas
(twice) and UDU Chandana (once)

Hat-tricks

DNT Zoysa	v Zimbabwe at Harare	1999-2000

He dismissed TR Gripper, MW Goodwin and NC
Johnson with the first three balls of his first over, the
second of the match.

Four hat-tricks have been taken against Sri Lanka in
Tests, all of them for Pakistan: two by Wasim Akram (in
successive Tests in the Asian Test Championship at
Lahore and Dhaka in 1998-99), Abdul Razzaq (at Galle
in 2000-01) and Mohammad Sami (at Lahore in
2001-02)

Sri Lanka's Test match results

	Played	Won	Lost	Drawn	Tied	% win
v Australia	18	1	11	6	0	5.55
v Bangladesh	10	10	0	0	0	100.00
v England	18	5	8	5	0	27.77
v India	26	3	10	13	0	11.53
v New Zealand	24	5	9	10	0	20.83
v Pakistan	32	7	15	10	0	21.87
v South Africa	17	4	8	5	0	23.52
v West Indies	10	5	2	3	0	50.00
v Zimbabwe	15	10	0	5	0	66.66
TOTAL	**170**	**50**	**63**	**57**	**0**	**29.41**

SRI LANKA
One-day International Records

Most appearances

394	ST Jayasuriya	
308	PA de Silva	
299	WPUJC Vaas	
290	M Muralitharan	
269	A Ranatunga	
268	MS Atapattu	
251	DPMD Jayawardene	
213	RS Mahanama	
200	HP Tillakaratne	
196	KC Sangakkara	

In all 18 Sri Lankans have played more than 100 ODIs

Most runs

		Avge
12050	ST Jayasuriya	33.01
9284	PA de Silva	34.90
8529	MS Atapattu	37.57
7456	A Ranatunga	35.84
6872	DPMD Jayawardene	32.88
5607	KC Sangakkara	35.48
5162	RS Mahanama	29.49
3950	RP Arnold	35.26
3902	AP Gurusinha	28.27
3789	HP Tillakaratne	29.60

RS Kaluwitharana (3711) also reached 3000 runs

Most wickets

		Avge
444	M Muralitharan	22.65
382	WPUJC Vaas	26.70
301	ST Jayasuriya	36.40
151	UDU Chandana	31.72
142	CRD Fernando	30.78
138	HDPK Dharmasena	36.21
109	GP Wickremasinghe	39.64
108	DNT Zoysa	29.75
106	PA de Silva	39.40
90	MF Maharoof	25.47

During 2005 Muralitharan became the first bowler to take 1000 international wickets (Tests + ODIs)

Highest scores

189	ST Jayasuriya	v India at Sharjah	2000-01
157	ST Jayasuriya	v Netherlands at Amstelveen	2006
152	ST Jayasuriya	v England at Leeds	2006
151*	ST Jayasuriya	v India at Mumbai	1996-97
145	PA de Silva	v Kenya at Kandy	1995-96
140	ST Jayasuriya	v N Zealand at Bloemfontein	1994-95
138*	KC Sangakkara	v India at Jaipur	2005-06
134*	ST Jayasuriya	v Pakistan at Lahore	1997-98
134	PA de Silva	v Pakistan at Sharjah	1996-97
134	ST Jayasuriya	v Pakistan at Singapore	1995-96

ST Jayasuriya has scored 25 ODI centuries, MS Atapattu and PA de Silva 11

Best bowling figures

8-19	WPUJC Vaas	v Zimbabwe at Colombo	2001-02
7-30	M Muralitharan	v India at Sharjah	2000-01
6-14	MF Maharoof	v West Indies at Mumbai	2006-07
6-25	WPUJC Vaas	v B'desh at P'maritzburg	2002-03
6-29	ST Jayasuriya	v England at Moratuwa	1992-93
5-9	M Muralitharan	v New Zealand at Sharjah	2001-02
5-14	WPUJC Vaas	v India at Sharjah	2000-01
5-17	ST Jayasuriya	v Pakistan at Lahore	2004-05
5-23	M Muralitharan	v Pakistan at Benoni	1997-98
5-23	M Muralitharan	v Pakistan at Dambulla	2002-03
5-23	M Muralitharan	v Zimbabwe at Harare	2003-04

Vaas's 8-19 are the best bowling figures in all ODIs

Record wicket partnerships

1st	286	WU Tharanga (109) and ST Jayasuriya (152)	v England at Leeds	2006
2nd	170	S Wettimuny (74) and RL Dias (102)	v India at Delhi	1982-83
	170	ST Jayasuriya (120) and HP Tillakaratne (81*)	v New Zealand at Bloemfontein	2002-03
3rd	226	MS Atapattu (102*) and DPMD Jayawardene (128)	v India at Sharjah	2000-01
4th	171*	RS Mahanama (94*) and A Ranatunga (87*)	v West Indies at Lahore	1997-98
5th	166	ST Jayasuriya (189) and RP Arnold (52*)	v India at Sharjah	2000-01
6th	133	MS Atapattu (59) and RP Arnold (68)	v India at Vadodara	2005-06
7th	126*	DPMD Jayawardene (94*) and UDU Chandana (44*)	v India at Dambulla	2005-06
8th	91	HDPK Dharmasena (51*) and DK Liyanage (43)	v West Indies at Port-of-Spain	1996-97
9th	76	RS Kalpage (44*) and WPUJC Vaas (33)	v Pakistan at Colombo	1994-95
10th	51	RP Arnold (103) and KSC de Silva (2*)	v Zimbabwe at Bulawayo	1999-2000

SRI LANKA

Most catches

Fielders

122	DPMD Jayawardene	
115	M Muralitharan	
114	ST Jayasuriya	
109	RS Mahanama	
95	PA de Silva	

Most dismissals

Wicketkeepers		*Ct/St*
207	KC Sangakkara	158/49
206	RS Kaluwitharana	131/75
45	HP Tillakaratne	39/6
34	DSBP Kuruppu	26/8
30	RG de Alwis	27/3

Highest team totals

443-9	v Netherlands at Amstelveen	2006
398-5	v Kenya at Kandy	1995-96
349-9	v Pakistan at Singapore	1995-96
343-5	v Australia at Sydney	2002-03
339-4	v Pakistan at Mohali	1996-97
329	v West Indies at Sharjah	1995-96
324-2	v England at Leeds	2006
321-6	v Bermuda at Port-of-Spain	2006-07
319-8	v England at The Oval	2006
318-4	v B'desh at Port-of-Spain	2006-07
318-7	v England at Manchester	2006

The 324-2 was scored in 37.3 overs

Lowest team totals

Completed innings

55	v W Indies at Sharjah	1986-87
78*	v Pakistan at Sharjah	2001-02
86	v W Indies at Manchester	1975
91	v Australia at Adelaide	1984-85
96	v India at Sharjah	1983-84
98	v S Africa at Colombo	1993-94
98	v India at Sharjah	1998-99
99	v England at Perth	1998-99
102	v W Indies at Brisbane	1995-96
105	v SA at Bloemfontein	1997-98

* One batsman absent hurt

Most sixes

240	ST Jayasuriya
102	PA de Silva
64	A Ranatunga
42	AP Gurusinha
37	DPMD Jayawardene
25	KC Sangakkara
22	UDU Chandana
22	WPUJC Vaas
21	RP Arnold
18	MF Maharoof
18	RJ Ratnayake

Best strike rate

Runs per 100 balls		*Runs*
90.56	ST Jayasuriya	12050
87.42	MF Maharoof	716
86.80	RJ Ratnayake	612
81.13	PA de Silva	9284
79.06	TM Dilshan	2444
77.91	A Ranatunga	7456
77.70	RS Kaluwitharana	3711
76.37	DPMD Jayawardene	6872
75.07	LRD Mendis	1527
74.27	KC Sangakkara	5607

Qualification: 500 runs

Most economical bowlers

Runs per over		*Wkts*
3.84	M Muralitharan	444
4.17	WPUJC Vaas	382
4.18	SD Anurasiri	32
4.27	HDPK Dharmasena	138
4.29	CPH Ramanayake	68
4.29	VB John	34
4.50	DS de Silva	32
4.50	RS Kalpage	73
4.52	DNT Zoysa	108
4.53	GP Wickremasinghe	109

Qualification: 2000 balls bowled

Sri Lanka's one-day international results

	Played	Won	Lost	Tied	No result	% win
v Australia	64	19	43	0	2	30.64
v Bangladesh	22	21	1	0	0	95.45
v England	38	19	19	0	0	50.00
v India	95	37	49	0	9	43.02
v New Zealand	68	30	34	1	3	46.87
v Pakistan	110	39	67	1	3	36.79
v South Africa	45	21	22	1	1	48.83
v West Indies	43	18	24	0	1	42.85
v Zimbabwe	37	30	6	0	1	83.33
v others (see below)	12	11	1	0	0	91.66
TOTAL	**534**	**245**	**266**	**3**	**20**	**47.94**

Other teams: Bermuda (P1, W1), Canada (P1, W1), Ireland (P1, W1), Kenya (P5, W4, L1), Netherlands (P3, W3), United Arab Emirates (P1, W1).

WEST INDIES
Test Match Records

Most appearances

132	CA Walsh
130	BC Lara
121	IVA Richards
116	DL Haynes
110	CH Lloyd
108	CG Greenidge
104	S Chanderpaul
102	CL Hooper
98	CEL Ambrose
93	GS Sobers

Sobers played 85 successive Tests between 1954-55 and 1971-72

Most runs

		Avge
11912	BC Lara	53.17
8540	IVA Richards	50.23
8032	GS Sobers	57.78
7558	CG Greenidge	44.72
7515	CH Lloyd	46.67
7487	DL Haynes	42.29
7182	S Chanderpaul	46.63
6227	RB Kanhai	47.53
5949	RB Richardson	44.39
5762	CL Hooper	36.46

Greenidge and Haynes put on 6482 runs together, the Test record by any pair of batsmen

Most wickets

		Avge
519	CA Walsh	24.44
405	CEL Ambrose	20.99
376	MD Marshall	20.94
309	LR Gibbs	29.09
259	J Garner	20.97
249	MA Holding	23.68
235	GS Sobers	34.03
202	AME Roberts	25.61
192	WW Hall	26.38
161	IR Bishop	24.27

In all 17 West Indians have reached 100 Test wickets

Highest scores

400*	BC Lara	v England at St John's	2003-04
375	BC Lara	v England at St John's	1993-94
365*	GS Sobers	v Pakistan at Kingston	1957-58
317	CH Gayle	v South Africa at St John's	2004-05
302	LG Rowe	v England at Bridgetown	1973-74
291	IVA Richards	v England at The Oval	1976
277	BC Lara	v Australia at Sydney	1992-93
270*	GA Headley	v England at Kingston	1934-35
261*	RR Sarwan	v Bangladesh at Kingston	2003-04
261	FMM Worrell	v England at Nottingham	1950

Lara scored 34 Test centuries, Sobers 26, Richards 24

Best innings bowling

9-95	JM Noreiga	v India at Port-of-Spain	1970-71
8-29	CEH Croft	v Pakistan at Port-of-Spain	1976-77
8-38	LR Gibbs	v India at Bridgetown	1961-62
8-45	CEL Ambrose	v England at Bridgetown	1989-90
8-92	MA Holding	v England at The Oval	1976
8-104	AL Valentine	v England at Manchester	1950
7-22	MD Marshall	v England at Manchester	1988
7-25	CEL Ambrose	v Australia at Perth	1992-93
7-37	CA Walsh	v New Zealand at Wellington	1994-95
7-49	S Ramadhin	v England at Birmingham	1957

Valentine was playing in his first Test, Croft and Noreiga in their second

Record wicket partnerships

1st	298	CG Greenidge (149) and DL Haynes (167)	v England at St John's	1989-90
2nd	446	CC Hunte (260) and GS Sobers (365*)	v Pakistan at Kingston	1957-58
3rd	338	ED Weekes (206) and FMM Worrell (167)	v England at Port-of-Spain	1953-54
4th	399	GS Sobers (226) and FMM Worrell (197*)	v England at Bridgetown	1959-60
5th	322	BC Lara (213) and JC Adams (94)	v Australia at Kingston	1998-99
6th	282*	BC Lara (400*) and RD Jacobs (107*)	v England at St John's	2003-04
7th	347	DS Atkinson (219) and CC Depeiaza (122)	v Australia at Bridgetown	1954-55
8th	148	JC Adams (101*) and FA Rose (69)	v Zimbabwe at Kingston	1999-2000
9th	161	CH Lloyd (161*) and AME Roberts (68)	v India at Calcutta	1983-84
10th	106	CL Hooper (178*) and CA Walsh (30)	v Pakistan at St John's	1992-93

Updated records can be found at **www.cricinfo.com/db/STATS**

Test Match Records — **WEST INDIES**

Most catches

Fielders

164	BC Lara	
122	IVA Richards	
115	CL Hooper	
109	GS Sobers	
96	CG Greenidge	

Most dismissals

Wicketkeepers		*Ct/St*
270	PJL Dujon	265/5
219	RD Jacobs	207/12
189	DL Murray	181/8
101	JR Murray	98/3
90	FCM Alexander	85/5

Highest team totals

790-3d	v Pakistan at Kingston	1957-58
751-5d	v England at St John's	2003-04
747	v South Africa at St John's	2004-05
692-8d	v England at The Oval	1995
687-8d	v England at The Oval	1976
681-8d	v England at Port-of-Spain	1953-54
660-5d	v New Zealand at Wellington	1994-95
652-8d	v England at Lord's	1973
644-8d	v India at Delhi	1958-59
631-8d	v India at Kingston	1961-62
631	v India at Delhi	1948-49

West Indies have passed 600 in Tests on seven further occasions

Lowest team totals

Completed innings

47	v England at Kingston	2003-04
51	v Aust at Port-of-Spain	1998-99
53	v Pakistan at Faisalabad	1986-87
54	v England at Lord's	2000
61	v England at Leeds	2000
76	v Pakistan at Dacca	1958-59
77	v NZ at Auckland	1955-56
78	v Australia at Sydney	1951-52
82	v Australia at Brisbane	2000-01
86*	v England at The Oval	1957

*One batsman absent hurt

Best match bowling

14-149	MA Holding	v England at The Oval	1976
13-55	CA Walsh	v N Zealand at Wellington	1994-95
12-121	AME Roberts	v India at Madras	1974-75
11-84	CEL Ambrose	v England at Port-of-Spain	1993-94
11-89	MD Marshall	v India at Port-of-Spain	1988-89
11-107	MA Holding	v Australia at Melbourne	1981-82
11-120	MD Marshall	v N Zealand at Bridgetown	1984-85
11-126	WW Hall	v India at Kanpur	1958-59
11-134	CD Collymore	v Pakistan at Kingston	2004-05
11-147	KD Boyce	v England at The Oval	1973

Marshall took ten or more wickets in a Test four times, Ambrose and Walsh three

Hat-tricks

WW Hall	v Pakistan at Lahore	1958-59

The first Test hat-trick not for England or Australia.

LR Gibbs	v Australia at Adelaide	1960-61

Gibbs had taken three wickets in four balls in the previous Test, at Sydney.

CA Walsh	v Australia at Brisbane	1988-89

The first Test hat-trick to be split over two innings.

JJC Lawson	v Australia at Bridgetown	2002-03

Also split over two innings

West Indies' Test match results

	Played	Won	Lost	Drawn	Tied	% win
v Australia	102	32	48	21	1	31.68
v Bangladesh	4	3	0	1	0	75.00
v England	138	52	41	45	0	37.68
v India	82	30	11	41	0	36.58
v New Zealand	35	10	9	16	0	28.57
v Pakistan	44	14	15	15	0	31.81
v South Africa	19	2	12	5	0	10.52
v Sri Lanka	10	2	5	3	0	20.00
v Zimbabwe	6	4	0	2	0	66.66
TOTAL	**440**	**149**	**141**	**149**	**1**	**33.94**

Updated records can be found at www.cricinfo.com/db/STATS

WEST INDIES *One-day International Records*

Most appearances

295	BC Lara
238	DL Haynes
227	CL Hooper
224	RB Richardson
222	S Chanderpaul
205	CA Walsh
187	IVA Richards
176	CEL Ambrose
169	PJL Dujon
158	AL Logie

In all 23 West Indians have played more than 100 ODIs

Most runs

		Avge
10348	BC Lara	40.90
8648	DL Haynes	41.37
6975	S Chanderpaul	38.96
6721	IVA Richards	47.00
6248	RB Richardson	33.41
6129	CH Gayle	39.28
5761	CL Hooper	35.34
5134	CG Greenidge	45.03
4099	RR Sarwan	44.55
3675	PV Simmons	28.93

Lara scored 19 ODI centuries, Haynes 17, Gayle 15, Greenidge and Richards 11

Most wickets

		Avge
227	CA Walsh	30.47
225	CEL Ambrose	24.12
193	CL Hooper	36.05
157	MD Marshall	26.96
146	J Garner	18.84
142	MA Holding	21.36
140	CH Gayle	32.32
130	M Dillon	32.44
118	IR Bishop	26.50
118	IVA Richards	35.83

WKM Benjamin (100) and RA Harper (100) also reached 100 wickets

Highest scores

189*	IVA Richards	v England at Manchester	1984
181	IVA Richards	v Sri Lanka at Karachi	1987-88
169	BC Lara	v Sri Lanka at Sharjah	1995-96
156	BC Lara	v Pakistan at Adelaide	2004-05
153*	IVA Richards	v Australia at Melbourne	1979-80
153*	CH Gayle	v Zimbabwe at Bulawayo	2003-04
153	BC Lara	v Pakistan at Sharjah	1993-94
152*	DL Haynes	v India at Georgetown	1988-89
152*	CH Gayle	v S Africa at Johannesburg	2003-04
152	CH Gayle	v Kenya at Nairobi	2001-02

S Chanderpaul scored 150 against South Africa at East London in 1998-99

Best bowling figures

7-51	WW Davis	v Australia at Leeds	1983
6-15	CEH Croft	v England at Kingstown	1980-81
6-22	FH Edwards	v Zimbabwe at Harare	2003-04
6-29	BP Patterson	v India at Nagpur	1987-88
6-41	IVA Richards	v India at Delhi	1989-90
6-50	AH Gray	v Aust at Port-of-Spain	1990-91
5-1	CA Walsh	v Sri Lanka at Sharjah	1986-87
5-17	CEL Ambrose	v Australia at Melbourne	1988-89
5-22	AME Roberts	v England at Adelaide	1979-80
5-22	WKM Benjamin	v Sri Lanka at Bombay	1993-94

Edwards's feat was in his first ODI; he had earlier taken 5-36 on his Test debut

Record wicket partnerships

1st	200*	SC Williams (78*) and S Chanderpaul (109*)	v India at Bridgetown	1996-97
2nd	221	CG Greenidge (115) and IVA Richards (149)	v India at Jamshedpur	1983-84
3rd	195*	CG Greenidge (105*) and HA Gomes (75*)	v Zimbabwe at Worcester	1983
4th	226	S Chanderpaul (150) and CL Hooper (108)	v South Africa at East London	1998-99
5th	154	CL Hooper (112*) and S Chanderpaul (67)	v Pakistan at Sharjah	2001-02
6th	154	RB Richardson (122) and PJL Dujon (53)	v Pakistan at Sharjah	1991-92
7th	115	PJL Dujon (57*) and MD Marshall (66)	v Pakistan at Gujranwala	1986-87
8th	84	RL Powell (76) and CD Collymore (3)	v India at Toronto	1999-2000
9th	77	RR Sarwan (65) and IDR Bradshaw (37)	v New Zealand at Christchurch	2005-06
10th	106*	IVA Richards (189*) and MA Holding (12*)	v England at Manchester	1984

Updated records can be found at **www.cricinfo.com/db/STATS**

Most catches

Fielders

120	CL Hooper	
117	BC Lara	
100	IVA Richards	
80	CH Gayle	
75	RB Richardson	

Most dismissals

Wicketkeepers   *Ct/St*

204	PJL Dujon	183/21
189	RD Jacobs	160/29
68	CO Browne	59/9
53	D Ramdin	51/2
51	JR Murray	44/7

Highest team totals

360-4	v Sri Lanka at Karachi	1987-88
347-6	v Zimbabwe at Bulawayo	2003-04
339-4	v Pakistan at Adelaide	2004-05
333-6	v Zimbabwe at Georgetown	2005-06
333-7	v Sri Lanka at Sharjah	1995-96
333-8	v India at Jamshedpur	1983-84
324-4	v India at Ahmedabad	2002-03
324-8	v India at Nagpur	2006-07
315-4	v Pakistan at Port-of-Spain	1987-88
315-6	v India at Vijayawada	2002-03

All these totals came from 50 overs except 333-8 (45) and 315-4 (47)

Lowest team totals

Completed innings

54	v S Africa at Cape Town	2003-04
80	v Sri Lanka at Mumbai	2006-07
87	v Australia at Sydney	1992-93
91	v Zimbabwe at Sydney	2000-01
93	v Kenya at Pune	1995-96
103	v Pak at Melbourne	1996-97
110	v Australia at Manchester	1999
111	v Pak at Melbourne	1983-84
113	v Aust at Kuala Lumpur	2006-07
114	v Pak at Pt-of-Spain	1999-2000

The 87 was in a match reduced to 30 overs: Australia made 101-9

Most sixes

133	BC Lara
126	IVA Richards
95	CH Gayle
81	CG Greenidge
75	RL Powell
69	S Chanderpaul
65	CL Hooper
54	RB Richardson
53	DL Haynes
49	WW Hinds

Greenidge and Powell share the West Indian record with 8 sixes in one innings

Best strike rate

Runs per 100 balls   *Runs*

101.54	DR Smith	791
96.66	RL Powell	2085
90.20	IVA Richards	6721
81.22	CH Lloyd	1977
80.29	CH Gayle	6129
79.62	BC Lara	10348
79.10	DJ Bravo	992
76.90	RR Sarwan	4099
76.64	MD Marshall	955
76.63	CL Hooper	5761

Qualification: 500 runs

Most economical bowlers

Runs per over   *Wkts*

3.09	J Garner	146
3.32	MA Holding	142
3.40	AME Roberts	87
3.48	CEL Ambrose	225
3.53	MD Marshall	157
3.83	CA Walsh	227
3.97	RA Harper	100
4.00	CE Cuffy	41
4.09	EAE Baptiste	36
4.15	WKM Benjamin	100

Qualification: 2000 balls bowled

West Indies' one-day international results

	Played	Won	Lost	Tied	No result	% win
v Australia	114	57	53	2	2	51.81
v Bangladesh	13	11	0	0	2	100.00
v England	75	39	32	0	4	54.92
v India	90	53	35	1	1	60.22
v New Zealand	46	23	18	0	5	56.09
v Pakistan	110	64	44	2	0	59.25
v South Africa	40	12	27	0	1	30.76
v Sri Lanka	43	24	18	0	1	57.14
v Zimbabwe	32	24	7	0	1	77.41
v others (see below)	12	10	1	0	1	90.90
TOTAL	**575**	**317**	**235**	**5**	**18**	**57.42**

Other teams: Canada (P1, W1), Ireland (P2, W1, NR1), Kenya (P6, W5, L1), Netherlands (P1, W1), Scotland (P2, W2).

ZIMBABWE

Test Match Records

Most appearances

67	GW Flower
65	HH Streak
63	A Flower
60	ADR Campbell
46	GJ Whittall
37	SV Carlisle
30	HK Olonga
29	DD Ebrahim
27	CB Wishart
26	BC Strang

Zimbabwe's most recent Test match was against India in September 2005

Most runs

		Avge
4794	A Flower	51.54
3457	GW Flower	29.54
2858	ADR Campbell	27.21
2207	GJ Whittall	29.42
1990	HH Streak	22.35
1615	SV Carlisle	26.91
1464	DL Houghton	43.05
1414	MW Goodwin	42.84
1273	T Taibu	29.60
1225	DD Ebrahim	22.68

CB Wishart (1098) and GJ Rennie (1023) also reached 1000 runs

Most wickets

		Avge
216	HH Streak	28.14
70	PA Strang	36.02
69	RW Price	35.86
68	HK Olonga	38.52
56	BC Strang	39.33
53	AM Blignaut	37.05
51	GJ Whittall	40.94
32	M Mbangwa	31.43
30	DH Brain	30.50
26	EA Brandes	36.57

GW Flower, TJ Friend and AG Huckle all took 25 wickets

Highest scores

266	DL Houghton	v Sri Lanka at Bulawayo	1994-95
232*	A Flower	v India at Nagpur	2000-01
203*	GJ Whittall	v New Zealand at Bulawayo	1997-98
201*	GW Flower	v Pakistan at Harare	1994-95
199*	A Flower	v South Africa at Harare	2001-02
188*	GJ Whittall	v New Zealand at Harare	2000-01
183*	A Flower	v India at Delhi	2000-01
166*	MW Goodwin	v Pakistan at Bulawayo	1997-98
156*	GW Flower	v Pakistan at Bulawayo	1997-98
156	A Flower	v Pakistan at Harare	1994-95

Of Zimbabwe's 42 Test centuries, 18 came from the Flower family – 12 by Andy and 6 by Grant

Best innings bowling

8-109	PA Strang	v New Zealand at Bulawayo	2000-01
6-59	DT Hondo	v Bangladesh at Dhaka	2004-05
6-73	RW Price	v West Indies at Harare	2003-04
6-73	HH Streak	v India at Harare	2005-06
6-87	HH Streak	v England at Lord's	2000
6-90	HH Streak	v Pakistan at Harare	1994-95
6-109	AG Huckle	v New Zealand at Bulawayo	1997-98
6-121	RW Price	v Australia at Sydney	2003-04
5-27	HH Streak	v WI at Port-of-Spain	1999-2000
5-31	TJ Friend	v Bangladesh at Dhaka	2001-02

AJ Traicos took 5-86 in Zimbabwe's inaugural Test, against India in 1992-93: he was 45, and had played three Tests for South Africa 22 years previously

Record wicket partnerships

1st	164	DD Ebrahim (71) and ADR Campbell (103)	v West Indies at Bulawayo	2001
2nd	135	MH Dekker (68*) and ADR Campbell (75)	v Pakistan at Rawalpindi	1993-94
3rd	194	ADR Campbell (99) and DL Houghton (142)	v Sri Lanka at Harare	1994-95
4th	269	GW Flower (201*) and A Flower (156)	v Pakistan at Harare	1994-95
5th	277*	MW Goodwin (166*) and A Flower (100*)	v Pakistan at Bulawayo	1997-98
6th	165	DL Houghton (121) and A Flower (59)	v India at Harare	1992-93
7th	154	HH Streak (83*) and AM Blignaut (92)	v West Indies at Harare	2001
8th	168	HH Streak (127*) and AM Blignaut (91)	v West Indies at Harare	2003-04
9th	87	PA Strang (106*) and BC Strang (42)	v Pakistan at Sheikhupura	1996-97
10th	97*	A Flower (183*) and HK Olonga (11*)	v India at Delhi	2000-01

Test Match Records
ZIMBABWE

Most catches

Fielders

60	ADR Campbell
43	GW Flower
34	SV Carlisle
19	GJ Whittall
17	DL Houghton/HH Streak

Most dismissals

Wicketkeepers		Ct/St
151	A Flower	142/9
51	T Taibu	47/4
16	WR James	16/0

Flower (9) and Taibu (1) also took catches in the field

Highest team totals

563-9d	v West Indies at Harare	2001
544-4d	v Pakistan at Harare	1994-95
542-7d	v Bangladesh at Chittagong	2001-02
507-9d	v West Indies at Harare	2003-04
503-6	v India at Nagpur	2000-01
462-9d	v Sri Lanka at Bulawayo	1994-95
461	v New Zealand at Bulawayo	1997-98
457	v Bangladesh at Bulawayo	2000-01
456	v India at Harare	1992-93
441	v Bangladesh at Harare	2003-04

Zimbabwe's 456 in 1992-93 is the highest by any country in their first Test match

Lowest team totals

Completed innings

54	v S Africa at Cape Town	2004-05
59	v N Zealand at Harare	2005-06
63	v WI at Port-of-Spain	1999-2000
79	v Sri Lanka at Galle	2001-02
83	v England at Lord's	2000
94	v Eng at Chester-le-Street	2003
99	v N Zealand at Harare	2005-06
102	v S Africa at Harare	1999-2000
102	v WI at Kingston	1999-2000
102	v Sri Lanka at Harare	2003-04

Zimbabwe were bowled out twice in a day by New Zealand at Harare in 2005-06, only the second such instance in Test cricket

Best match bowling

11-255	AG Huckle	v New Zealand at Bulawayo	1997-98
10-158	PA Strang	v New Zealand at Bulawayo	2000-01
10-161	RW Price	v West Indies at Harare	2003-04
9-72	HH Streak	v WI at Port-of-Spain	1999-2000
9-105	HH Streak	v Pakistan at Harare	1994-95
9-235	RW Price	v West Indies at Bulawayo	2003-04
8-104	GW Flower	v Pakistan at Chittagong	2001-02
8-105	HH Streak	v Pakistan at Harare	1994-95
8-110	AM Blignaut	v Bangladesh at Bulawayo	2000-01
8-114	HH Streak	v Pakistan at Rawalpindi	1993-94

Blignaut was playing in his first Test, Huckle in his second

Hat-tricks

AM Blignaut	v Bangladesh at Harare	2003-04

Blignaut dismissed Hannan Sarkar, Mohammad Ashraful and Mushfiqur Rahman to reduce Bangladesh to 14-5.

The only Test hat-trick against Zimbabwe was taken by DNT Zoysa for Sri Lanka at Harare in 1999-2000, when he removed TR Gripper, MW Goodwin and NC Johnson with the first three balls he bowled, in the second over of the match

Zimbabwe's Test match results

	Played	Won	Lost	Drawn	Tied	% win
v Australia	3	0	3	0	0	0.00
v Bangladesh	8	4	1	3	0	50.00
v England	6	0	3	3	0	0.00
v India	11	2	7	2	0	18.18
v New Zealand	13	0	7	6	0	0.00
v Pakistan	14	2	8	4	0	14.28
v South Africa	7	0	6	1	0	0.00
v Sri Lanka	15	0	10	5	0	0.00
v West Indies	6	0	4	2	0	0.00
TOTAL	83	8	49	26	0	9.63

Updated records can be found at www.cricinfo.com/db/STATS

ZIMBABWE
One-day International Records

Most appearances

219	GW Flower
213	A Flower
188	ADR Campbell
187	HH Streak
147	GJ Whittall
111	SV Carlisle
95	PA Strang
90	CB Wishart
86	T Taibu
82	DD Ebrahim

A Flower missed only 5 matches between his debut in 1991-92 and his enforced retirement after the 2002-03 World Cup

Most runs

		Avge
6786	A Flower	35.34
6536	GW Flower	33.69
5185	ADR Campbell	30.50
2901	HH Streak	28.44
2740	SV Carlisle	27.67
2705	GJ Whittall	22.54
1818	MW Goodwin	27.13
1719	CB Wishart	23.32
1706	BRM Taylor	28.43
1679	NC Johnson	36.50

T Taibu (1572), DL Houghton (1530), DD Ebrahim (1443), S Matsikenyeri (1223), E Chigumbura (1196), V Sibanda (1138) and PA Strang (1090) also reached 1000 runs

Most wickets

		Avge
237	HH Streak	29.81
104	GW Flower	40.25
96	PA Strang	33.05
88	GJ Whittall	39.55
72	GB Brent	33.93
70	EA Brandes	32.37
61	DT Hondo	35.59
58	HK Olonga	34.08
49	AM Blignaut	41.24
46	BC Strang	37.34

Brandes took Zimbabwe's only ODI hat-trick, against England at Harare in 1996-97

Highest scores

172*	CB Wishart	v Namibia at Harare	2002-03
145	A Flower	v India at Colombo	2002-03
142*	GW Flower	v Bangladesh at Bulawayo	2000-01
142*	A Flower	v England at Harare	2001-02
142	DL Houghton	v New Zealand at Hyderabad	1987-88
140	GW Flower	v Kenya at Dhaka	1998-99
132*	NC Johnson	v Australia at Lord's	1999
131*	ADR Campbell	v Sri Lanka at Harare	1994-95
124	ADR Campbell	v Australia at Hobart	2000-01
121*	SV Carlisle	v Sri Lanka at Harare	1999-2000
121	DD Ebrahim	v Bangladesh at Dhaka	2001-02

Campbell made a record seven ODI centuries for Zimbabwe

Best bowling figures

6-19	HK Olonga	v England at Cape Town	1999-2000
6-20	BC Strang	v Bangladesh at Nairobi	1997-98
6-28	HK Olonga	v Kenya at Bulawayo	2002-03
5-21	PA Strang	v Kenya at Patna	1995-96
5-22	PA Strang	v Kenya at Dhaka	1998-99
5-28	EA Brandes	v England at Harare	1996-97
5-32	HH Streak	v India at Bulawayo	1996-97
5-41	EA Brandes	v India at Paarl	1996-97
5-44	ACI Lock	v New Zealand at Napier	1995-96
4-8	HH Streak	v West Indies at Sydney	2000-01

Lock's feat came in the second of his eight ODIs, six of which were in the World Cup

Record wicket partnerships

1st	161	GW Flower (79) and A Flower (81)	v Bangladesh at Nairobi	1997-98
2nd	150	GW Flower (78) and GJ Rennie (76)	v Kenya at Nairobi	1997-98
3rd	166*	CB Wishart (172*) and GW Flower (78*)	v Namibia at Harare	2002-03
4th	202	SV Carlisle (109) and SM Ervine (100)	v India at Adelaide	2003-04
5th	186*	MW Goodwin (112*) and GW Flower (96*)	v West Indies at Chester-le-Street	2000
6th	114	S Matsikenyeri (89) and E Chigumbura (70*)	v Bangladesh at Harare	2006
7th	130	A Flower (142*) and HH Streak (56)	v England at Harare	2001-02
8th	117	DL Houghton (142) and IP Butchart (54)	v New Zealand at Hyderabad	1987-88
9th	55	KM Curran (62) and PWE Rawson (19)	v West Indies at Birmingham	1983
10th	47	HK Olonga (31) and DT Hondo (15*)	v Pakistan at Harare	2002-03

Updated records can be found at **www.cricinfo.com/db/STATS**

One-day International Records — ZIMBABWE

Most catches

Fielders

86	GW Flower	
74	ADR Campbell	
45	HH Streak	
39	SV Carlisle	
36	GJ Whittall	

Most dismissals

Wicketkeepers — Ct/St

165	A Flower	133/32
86	T Taibu	78/8
45	BRM Taylor	33/12
12	DL Houghton	10/2

Highest team totals

340-2	v Namibia at Harare	2002-03
338-7	v Bermuda at Port-of-Spain	2005-06
325-6	v Kenya at Dhaka	1998-99
312-4	v Sri Lanka at New Plymouth	1991-92
310-6	v Bangladesh at Dhaka	1998-99
309-6	v Bangladesh at Dhaka	2001-02
308-4	v Bangladesh at Bulawayo	2000-01
305-4	v Bangladesh at Nairobi	1997-98
301-6	v Australia at Perth	2000-01
301-8	v Netherlands at Bulawayo	2002-03

Zimbabwe also scored 300-7 against New Zealand at Taupo in 2000-01

Lowest team totals

Completed innings

35	v Sri Lanka at Harare	2003-04
38	v Sri Lanka at Colombo	2001-02
65	v India at Harare	2005-06
69	v Kenya at Harare	2005-06
85	v WI at Ahmedabad	2006-07
92	v England at Bristol	2003
94	v Pakistan at Sharjah	1996-97
99*	v WI at Hyderabad	1993-94
99	v Pakistan at Kingston	2006-07
102	v England at Harare	2004-05

* One batsman absent or retired hurt

Most sixes

48	HH Streak
44	ADR Campbell
37	E Chigumbura
37	GW Flower
28	SV Carlisle
26	A Flower
26	GJ Whittall
24	BRM Taylor
21	DL Houghton
21	CB Wishart

Best strike rate

Runs per 100 balls — Runs

106.65	AM Blignaut	625
85.53	SM Ervine	698
80.75	E Chigumbura	1196
75.94	CN Evans	764
75.69	TJ Friend	548
74.59	A Flower	6786
73.61	HH Streak	2901
70.99	DL Houghton	1530
70.81	DA Marillier	672
70.57	CB Wishart	1719

Qualification: 500 runs

Most economical bowlers

Runs per over — Wkts

3.88	AJ Traicos	19
4.04	P Utseya	40
4.13	BC Strang	46
4.14	RW Price	15
4.37	PA Strang	96
4.37	AR Whittall	45
4.50	HH Streak	237
4.52	AH Shah	18
4.54	EC Rainsford	24
4.63	GW Flower	104

Qualification: 1000 balls bowled

Zimbabwe's one-day international results

	Played	Won	Lost	Tied	No result	% win
v Australia	27	1	25	0	1	3.84
v Bangladesh	33	18	15	0	0	54.54
v England	30	8	21	0	1	27.58
v India	49	8	39	2	0	17.02
v New Zealand	28	7	19	1	1	26.92
v Pakistan	35	2	31	1	1	6.06
v South Africa	27	2	24	0	1	7.69
v Sri Lanka	37	6	30	0	1	16.66
v West Indies	32	7	24	0	1	22.58
v others (see below)	26	20	3	1	2	80.00
TOTAL	324	79	231	5	9	25.48

Other teams: Bermuda (P2, W2), Canada (P1, W1), Ireland (P1, T1), Kenya (P20, W15, L3, NR 2), Namibia (P1, W1), Netherlands (P1, W1).

Updated records can be found at www.cricinfo.com/db/STATS

INTERNATIONAL SCHEDULE 2007–08

	Tests	ODIs		Tests	ODIs
October 2007			**May 2008**		
India v Australia	0	7	England v New Zealand	3	5
Pakistan v South Africa	2	5	Zimbabwe v India	2*	3*
			S Africa v Kenya v Scotland	0	7*
November 2007					
Sri Lanka v England	3	5	**June 2008**		
Australia v Sri Lanka	2	0	Scotland v England	0	1
India v Pakistan	3	5	Scotland v New Zealand	0	2
South Africa v New Zealand	2	5	Afro-Asia Cup in Kenya	0	3
Zimbabwe v West Indies	2*	3*			
			July 2008		
			England v South Africa	4	5
December 2007			Australia v Bangladesh	2	3
Australia v New Zealand	0	3	Sri Lanka v India	3	5
Australia v India	4	0			
South Africa v West Indies	4	5	**August 2008**		
			W Indies v Bermuda v Canada	0	7*
January 2008					
Australia v India v Sri Lanka	0	14/15	**September 2008**		
Pakistan v Zimbabwe	0	3	Champions Trophy in Pakistan	0	21*
February 2008			**October 2008**		
New Zealand v England	3	5	India v Australia	4	0
Pakistan v Australia	3	5			
Bangladesh v South Africa	2	0	**November 2008**		
Bangladesh v India v S Africa	0	7*	India v England	3	7
			Australia v New Zealand	2	0
March 2008			South Africa v Bangladesh	2	3
Bangladesh v India	0	3	Sri Lanka v Zimbabwe	2*	3*
India v South Africa	3	0			
West Indies v Sri Lanka	3	5	**December 2008**		
			Australia v South Africa	3	5
April 2008			Pakistan v India	3	5
West Indies v Australia	4	5	New Zealand v West Indies	3	5
Asia Cup in Pakistan	0	7*	Bangladesh v Sri Lanka	2	3

Details subject to change. Home side shown first. Some tours may continue into the month after the one shown above. An asterisk signifies that the number of matches is unconfirmed